Shapers of Religious Traditions in Germany, Switzerland, and Poland, 1560–1600

Shapers of Religious Traditions in Germany, Switzerland, and Poland, 1560 - 1600

Edited, with an Introduction, by
JILL RAITT

Foreword by ROBERT M. KINGDON

New Haven and London
Yale University Press

Designed by: James J. Johnson
and set in Garamond No. 3 type.
Printed in the United States of America by
Vail-Ballou Press, Binghampton, N.Y.

274.303X
Sh22

81120832

Library of Congress Cataloging in Publication Data
Main entry under title:

Shapers of religious traditions in Germany, Switzerland, and
    Poland, 1560–1600.

    Includes bibliographical references and index.
    1. Reformation—Germany—Addresses, essays, lectures.
2. Counter-Reformation—Germany—Addresses, essays,
lectures.   3. Reformation—Switzerland—Addresses, essays,
lectures.   4. Counter-Reformation—Switzerland—Addresses,
essays, lectures.   5. Reformation—Poland—Addresses,
essays, lectures.   6. Counter-Reformation—Poland—
Addresses, essays, lectures.   7. Creeds—History and criticism—
Addresses, essays, lectures.   8. Switzerland—Church history—
Addresses, essays, lectures.   9. Poland—Church history—
Addresses, essays, lectures.
I. Raitt, Jill.
BR855.S53   274.3'06   80–23287
ISBN 0–300–02457–6

10   9   8   7   6   5   4   3   2   1

CONTENTS

Foreword by Robert M. Kingdon   vii

Introduction   xi

1. MATTHIAS FLACIUS ILLYRICUS   1
    OLIVER K. OLSON

2. JOHANN WIGAND   19
    RONALD E. DIENER

3. MARTIN CHEMNITZ   39
    FRED KRAMER

4. JAKOB ANDREAE   53
    ROBERT KOLB

5. HEINRICH BULLINGER   69
    ROBERT C. WALTON

6. THEODORE BEZA   89
    JILL RAITT

7. LAMBERT DANEAU   105
    OLIVIER FATIO (Translated by Jill Raitt)

8. ZACHARIAS URSINUS   121
    DERK VISSER

9. PETER CANISIUS   141
    JOHN PATRICK DONNELLY

10. STANISLAS HOSIUS   157
    GEORGE HUNTSTON WILLIAMS

11. PETER SKARGA   175
    GEORGE HUNTSTON WILLIAMS

12. FAUSTUS SOCINUS   195
    ZBIGNIEW OGONOWSKI (Translated by Zofia Grzybowska)

Contributors   211

Index   213

FOREWORD

Reformation studies have been distorted for a long time by excessive concentration on the movement's founders, Luther and Calvin. Their charismatic personalities, their dramatic careers, their mastery of vernacular prose, the availability of their works in full editions and translations—all tempt the scholar to dwell upon them and go no further. But we must go further if we are ever to have a full and balanced study of the movements they launched. We must also consider the dozens of lieutenants who developed, modified, and applied their ideas. We must consider the thousands of leaders, both lay and clerical, who passed the new message on to the laity. We must consider the millions whose ideas and behavior were influenced so profoundly by the sixteenth-century reforms of religion, whether contained within the traditional structure of the Roman Catholic Church or within the new structures of Evangelical, Reformed, and Radical churches.

This volume distills the work of a number of scholars who seek to enrich our understanding of the Reformation by going beyond its founders. They have been examining the careers and ideas of several ecclesiastical leaders who, lacking the originality and independent reputation of their predecessors, nevertheless attained great prominence in their own right. They explore for this volume twelve theologians who helped in the drafting or promulgating of confessions, the definitive statements of religious belief created by this age, far more important historically and legally than the theological writings of any one man, no matter how prominent. The confessions defined religious groups for their own members and separated them with precision from other religious groups. They are of the essence of the religious traditions that many of the modern descendants of sixteenth-century Christian groups value so highly and wish to preserve. They are also the principal obstacles to the reunion of all Christianity, to which the modern ecumenical movement is so ardently committed. And they are an essential part of the defining characteristics of religious groups, and therefore of interest to modern social scientists. They are thus worthy of attention from several different points of view.

Chronologically the work of creating confessions of significance enduring down to the present began early in the Reformation, most notably in the Augsburg Confession of 1530, drafted primarily by Philip Melanchthon in consultation with Luther and assisted by a number of others including, significantly, some laymen. Continuing well into the seventeenth century, the work led, for example, to the decrees of the Council of Dort of 1618–19 and to the Westminster Confession of 1646. But the great age of confession building was the later part of the sixteenth century. Geographically the work of creating these confessions began and developed furthest in Germany, the cradle of the Reformation and the area in which the controversies it provoked became most significant and most dangerous, and then spread throughout Europe. This book accordingly focuses upon Germany, along with adjacent countries influenced by its religious development, in the period between 1560 and 1600.

The confessions of the late sixteenth century can be grouped into three primary categories: Evangelical, Reformed, and Catholic. The Evangelical (Lutheran) confessions assumed a definitive shape in the Formula of Concord of 1577, put together by Martin Chemnitz and Jakob Andreae. This collection defined Evangelical faith to exclude a number of Reformed options at the insistence of a Gnesio-Lutheran party led by the brilliant Matthias Flacius Illyricus. It also excluded an expanded number of Catholic options attacked by Flacius, Johann Wigand, and Chemnitz. While others participated, these four men were involved in particularly significant if differing ways in the history of the Formula. Chapters of this book are devoted to each of them.

One cannot point to any single confession of faith which is as definitive an expression of the Reformed faith, largely because the Reformed were more international than the Evangelicals and tended to epitomize their beliefs in a variety of national confessions not reduced to a single formula. Thus the Reformed in Scotland produced a confession in 1560; the Reformed in France another confession in 1559, further developed and refined in 1571; the Reformed in the Netherlands yet another confession in 1561. Consequently the Reformed active within German-speaking lands also developed independent confessions of their own. Their two most important statements of faith were the Second Helvetic Confession, drafted by Heinrich Bullinger of Zürich upon a base established and accepted by Theodore Beza of Geneva and other Reformed leaders in 1566, and the Heidelberg Catechism of 1563, drafted by Zacharias Ursinus, who, with Olevianus, led in establishing a Reformed church in the Palatinate. Chapters of this book are accordingly devoted to Bullinger, Beza, and Ursinus. Another chapter is devoted to Lambert Daneau, who assisted Beza for a time in Geneva and taught for a time in the Netherlands, but who served most of his life as a pastor or as a teacher in France. His systematic writings, above all his *Isagoge*, gave the position of the Reformed confessions one of its most authoritative explanations and thus both illuminate this age of confessionalism and link it to the succeeding age of Reformed scholasticism.

The definitive Catholic confession, of course, was embodied in the dogmatic decrees of the Council of Trent, which began meeting in 1545, but which did not conclude until 1563, and whose decisions were being promulgated and explained step by step throughout Catholic Europe until 1600 and beyond. The drafting of these decrees may have involved less theological originality than the Evangelical and Reformed confessions, since they grew more naturally out of late medieval traditions and required less self-conscious reexamination of the biblical and patristic sources of all Christian thought. But they nevertheless drew upon a wide variety of intellectual talents, coordinated by leaders of the Roman Catholic hierarchy. One of these Tridentine leaders, Cardinal Stanislas Hosius, who helped preside over the council's climactic closing sessions, is thus an appropriate subject for yet another chapter. The dogmatic message of Trent was then passed on and explained to the general Catholic population by many gifted spokesmen, most from religious orders and above all from the new Society of Jesus. Probably the single most influential Catholic catechist produced in this period and certainly the one with the greatest impact in Germany was the Dutch Jesuit Peter Canisius, treated in chapter 9. Chapter 11 is devoted to a catechist with a similar influence in Poland, the Jesuit Peter Skarga.

Not all Christians remained within these three main categories. A few spilled over into smaller, more radical, and generally rather ephemeral groups. One radical group that proved to have an enduring, if indirect, influence on later generations of liberal Christians was the Polish Brethren, which drafted its most important confessional statements at Raków in 1574 and 1605. Its intellectual inspiration came from Italian immigrants of whom the most distinguished was Faustus Socinus (chapter 12). Although not a member of the Brethren, he nevertheless inspired its members and remained on good terms with them.

Each chapter consists of three parts: a biographical sketch, an analysis of the subject's theology, and a concluding assessment of his ecclesiastical role. The combination is necessary for a full appreciation of the age of confessionalism. Each confession was a carefully drafted theological statement and must be set within its theological context to be fully understood. But each confession of importance was also a political act, not the product of a scholar's study but rather the work of ecclesiastical statesmen who were at once religious leaders and agents of governments. The original reason for the drafting of most confessions was to demonstrate to a hostile government the orthodoxy and the reasonableness of the beliefs of a group accused of heresy and sedition. But confessions also came to be platforms for the building or maintaining of military alliances. Thus the Schmalkaldic League was united by the Augsburg Confession and similarly the Reformed cities of Zürich and Geneva and their allies were held together by the Helvetic Confessions. Inexperienced theologians who ignored the political need to maintain an alliance ran the risk of severe censure, as young Beza and Andreae discovered when they attempted to draft an Evangelical-Reformed agreement at Göppingen in 1557 without consulting their superiors or home governments. On the Reformed side, Bullinger was furious and Calvin moved quickly to mollify him, forcing Beza to back away. The alliance with Bullinger's Zürich was essential to the security of Calvin's Geneva, and theological compromises could not be permitted to obscure that fact. On the Evangelical side, Andreae faced similar criticism.

Confessions could even serve as manifestos for parties attempting to organize armed resistance to a superior government. Thus the Augsburg Confession provided an ideological platform for a coalition of German cities and princes determined to resist the attempts of the imperial government to enforce religious uniformity. And the Gallican Confession served as a platform to rally French noblemen behind the Bourbon princes of the blood royal in a rebellion against the French crown. Religion and politics were so intimately connected during the Reformation that one cannot untangle them without distorting our understanding of the period. Our authors have illustrated this point neatly by including in each biography an account of the subject's political career.

This book is by no means a definitive exploration of the age of confessionalism in Europe. Each chapter could be expanded into a book of its own. There were other clerical shapers of tradition of considerable influence in the period who also deserve study and whose political and intellectual biographies would complement those presented here. There were, in addition, a number of influential lay shapers of these traditions, whose influence was great but who are only peripherally visible here. It is a mistake to view the Augsburg Confession of 1530, for example, as solely the work of its principal author, the theologian Philip Melanchthon. Chancellor Brück of Saxony drafted the preamble to it and officially presented it to the imperial diet. Both kinds of leaders, lay and clerical, furthermore operated within a political context whose dynamics need further exploration.

But these biographies do represent an important step forward in our knowledge of this period. They incorporate the research and thinking of some of the ablest scholars now working on confessionalism in several different countries ranging from distinguished elder historians to brilliant younger scholars. Their work has been assembled and sensitively coordinated by Jill Raitt of the Duke University Divinity School. May their collective contribution to our knowledge of the age of confessionalism stimulate further work on this important period in religious history.

University of Wisconsin   Robert M. Kingdon
Madison

INTRODUCTION

It is a cold wintery day in Worms on December 1, 1557. Philip Melanchthon sat in his room writing letters. He had already written and delivered his Declaration in the names of the Lutheran collocutors who remain in Worms and delivered his set of documents affirming Lutheran unity to the president of the colloquy, Julius Pflug. Ferdinand I had wanted the colloquy to continue, dreaming, as had his brother Charles V, that Roman Catholics and Lutherans could be reconciled. Then a united empire could turn back the Turks pressing at its eastern borders. [1] If only that Jesuit, Peter Canisius, had not used the Lutherans' internal strife to break up the colloquy: "But the adversaries have artfully sought a distraction so that they might have a pretext for disrupting the colloquy," Melanchthon had written in his Declaration. [2]

Melanchthon turned to his letters. He signed the one to Heinrich Bullinger, [3] hoping that the *antistes* of Zurich would understand how dangerous it was for him to write anything specific. He told Bullinger that their correspondence had been intercepted by his enemies. How pleased they would be to condemn Melanchthon as a "Zwinglian!" This time, the correspondence had been carried by Laelius Socinus to Melanchthon from Bullinger and from John Lasky (Jan Lasky), Poland's Reformed leader. [4] Poor Poland, so hard beset by strife within and Turks without. "How sad," wrote Melanchthon, "that the same problems burn in Poland that rage in miserable Germany." He addressed his next letter to Sigismund Augustus, king of Poland. [5] He congratulated him and grieved with him over the hard task of keeping the Turks from the rest of Europe. To Sigismund, Melanchthon also recommended Laelius Socinus, [6] who was "learned and pious and free from fan-

1. Gustav Wolf, *Zur Geschichte der deutschen Protestanten, 1555–1559* (Berlin: Oswald Seehagen, 1888), pp. 16–17.

2. C. G. Bretschneider, ed. *Corpus Reformatorum, Philippi Melanthonis Opera quae supersunt omnia* (Halle: C. A. Schwetschke and Son, 1842), 9: 386 (hereafter cited as *C.R.* plus volume and column number).

3. *C.R.* 9: 379.

4. John Lasky died in 1560. No single individual, to my knowledge, replaced him as a leader among the Protestants in Poland.

5. *C.R.* 9: 380.

6. Laelius Socinus (d. 1562) was the uncle of Faustus Socinus. On the Socini see Antonio Rotondo, *Calvin and the Italian Antitrinitarians*, trans. J. and A. Tedeschi (St. Louis, Mo.: Foundation for Reformation Research, 1968); Delio Cantimori, *Italienische Haeretiker der Spätrenaissance* (Basel: Benno Schwabe and Co., 1949).

aticism."[7] Laelius would need more protection on his journey, so Melanchthon addressed similar letters for him to King Maximilian[8] and to a learned Evangelical in Vienna.[9] Melanchthon was glad to perform such services for traveling scholars. Only two months earlier, he had written a similar letter for a deserving student, Zacharius Ursinus, who was traveling about to "hear good and learned men."[10]

But today was a day for writing to royalty, it seemed. Melanchthon, and other sympathetic Lutherans at the colloquy—Brenz, Marbach, Diller, Pistorius, Andreae, and Karg—had written a joint letter to Henry II of France on behalf of the Protestants imprisoned in Paris.[11] Earlier, the same German theologians had written to their princes asking them to intercede with Henry II on behalf of the French Protestants.[12] The Lutherans were persuaded to take these actions by a delegation of exiled Frenchmen who had come to Worms and met them at nearby Göppingen the previous October. The principal speakers were William Farel, the tough old reformer of Geneva and Montbéliard, and an engaging young man, Theodore Beza, now teaching at the academy in Lausanne. They had been asked, of course, to provide a confession of faith. After some negotiation over the article dealing with the Lord's Supper, the Lutherans found them orthodox and agreed to intercede for their compatriots.[13]

From the work he had done that day with his colleagues, Melanchthon's mind moved to a subject of bitterness and anger, the Flacianists from Weimar. Why had they been invited to Worms at all? Thank God Flacius Illyricus himself had been prevented from coming, but nothing had prevented him from stirring up trouble with his letters.[14] His henchmen, Schnepf and Mörlin, had wanted to condemn everyone but themselves, and the whole contingent had walked out when it was suggested that perhaps Flacius's doctrine was itself sectarian and ought to be condemned! If only the Weimar theologians could understand that they must put aside their differences in order to gain ground against the Roman Catholics. And what a shame, mused Melanchthon, that the intelligent Martin Chemnitz, whom he had personally recruited for Wittenberg, was under Mörlin's influence. Chemnitz had lectured brilliantly on Melanchthon's own *Loci communes* only a few years ago. Where would all this division end?

---

7. It is ironic that apparently neither Bullinger nor Melanchthon suspected the sort of letter that Laelius was writing to Faustus, which revealed his Antitrinitarianism and other unorthodox beliefs.

8. *C.R.* 9: 381.

9. *C.R.* 9: 382–83.

10. *C.R.* 9: 318. The letter is dated October 1, 1557.

11. *C.R.* 9: 383–85.

12. *C.R.* 9: 334–36. The letter is dated October 8, 1557.

13. *C.R.* 9: 332–34. See also cols. 329–31.

14. *C.R.* 9: 199–213, 232–36. On the Weimer Delegation and its correspondence see Wolf, *Zur Geschichte*, pp. 300–75.

Philip Melanchthon, preceptor of Germany and still the most influential Lutheran in the empire in spite of his accommodation to the Interim,[15] wearily put down his pen. He was less than three years from his death. The stage was set for the age of confessionalism.

The period 1560–1600 has been called, for want of a better label, the late Reformation, although those who apply this name generally have reservations about its appropriateness.[16] I prefer the term *age of confessionalism*,[17] because the answers to many of the period's problems were worked out through the writing and application of confessions. Not only were confessions written, gathered, and published, but once established, they tended to become the means of testing or proving the correct understanding of Scripture. Confessions were often accompanied by catechisms, especially after Luther's catechisms had made this means of education so much more effective than it had been previously. The age was also a period of continued controversy,[18] so the shapers of traditions who appear in these pages were engaged in writing not only confessions and catechisms but also polemical pieces that frustrated attempts to reunite western Christendom and drove further apart the increasingly self-conscious Protestant churches. The twelve churchmen represented here were concerned, therefore, with two major doctrinal tasks, education and defense, which had two far-reaching results, the clarification of theological *loci* and the grounding of denominational orthodoxy.

Intimately involved with these tasks was the establishment of ecclesiastical polity and the working out of church-state relations. Churchmen not only had to preach, pastor their churches, and teach and write in defense of their beliefs, they also had to deal with princes and magistrates. The colloquy at Worms in 1557 is a good example of the interweaving of political and religious concerns that grew more marked in the next four decades. In fact, the authors of the chapters on the four Lutherans cannot discuss any aspect of their lives and work without making evident the powerful role of the prince in the Lutheran churches of Germany. Jakob Andreae's life in particular exem-

15. For a grudging account of Melanchthon's popularity in Worms as the colloquy opened, see Monnerus's letter to Flacius, *C.R.* 9: 245–47, especially col. 246.

16. Peter F. Barton, *Um Luthers Erbe: Studien und Texte zur Spätreformation: Tilemann Heshusius, 1527–1559* (Witten: Luther Verlag, 1972), introduction.

17. See Hans Baron, *Calvins Staatsanschauung und das Konfessionelle Zietalter* (Berlin: Verlag R. Oldenbourg, 1924). Baron sets the beginning of the age of confessionalism in 1530 (p. 3). Of its importance he writes that the age of confessionalism is the moment of birth of the "Volkscharacktere" of modern Europe (p. 5). I am pleased to find so fine a treatment of the period and I contest only the early date. For Baron, the Reformation ended in 1530. While any vital movement is difficult to confine within specific dates and while confessions were certainly written prior to 1560, nevertheless I argue that the forty years between 1560 and 1600 were particularly active ones in this regard.

18. See Kurt Dietrich Schmidt, *Die Kirche in Ihrer Deschichte: Die Katholische Reform und die Gegenreformation* (posthumous), ed. Manfred Jacobs (Göttingen: Vandenhoeck and Ruprecht, 1975), introduction, with notes for a discussion of this period as "Counter-Reformation," the age of "Glaubenskämpfe," and their relation to the writing of confessions, especially in the work of Hubert Jedin and E. W. Zeeden. I am indebted to James Bullard for this note and for n. 17.

plifies the capitulation of a Lutheran churchman who at first favored greater
ecclesiastical independence from the state, but who yielded to strong control of the Württemberg church by Duke Christoph and his ecclesiastical
officials. Indeed, E. William Monter has characterized the late sixteenth and
early seventeenth centuries as the "age of Erastus."[19]

Erastus's doctrine of magisterial control of church discipline, especially
excommunication, came to be called Erastianism, although the policy was not
new with Erastus. Zwingli had inaugurated such a state-church relationship
in Zürich and Bullinger defended Erastus against Beza's efforts to refute the
doctrine. Geneva, and those churches that looked to Geneva for guidance, believed that the right to excommunicate belonged to the ministers of the
church, not to the civil magistrates.[20] Daneau, firmly grounded in Genevan
polity, failed to win this ecclesiastical battle for the Leyden church. In Geneva
itself, Beza barely maintained the freedom of the ministers to preach and
reprimand magistrates from the pulpit. He had also to defend the Consistory from the encroachments of the magistrates upon their right to excommunicate.

On the theological side, the divisions among the Lutherans that Melanchthon had so deplored and refused to admit in formal debate led directly
to the Formula (1577) and the *Book of Concord* (1580). The demand of Flacius
Illyricus, through Schnepf and Mörlin at Worms, to condemn the Adiaphorists, Osiandrians, Majorists, Zwinglians, Anabaptists, and Schwenckfelders was finally satisfied, but Flacius's doctrine concerning the nature of
original sin was also condemned. Andreae and Martin Chemnitz were the
chief architects of the *Formula of Concord*, which must have have appeared as an
almost miraculous event to the badly divided Lutherans. For his part, Flacius
and his friend Johann Wigand contributed to the arsenal of Protestant
educational material through the powerful thirteen volumes known as the
Magdeburg Centuries.

At Worms, as at most of the colloquies between Protestants and Roman
Catholics (Regensburg 1541) or between Lutherans and Reformed (Marburg
1529, Maulbronn 1564, Montbéliard 1586), the central dispute was the
manner of Christ's presence in the Lord's Supper. Roman Catholics held to the
doctrine of transubstantiation and the sacrifice of the Mass, a doctrine denied
by all Protestants. Lutherans taught the real bodily presence of Christ, which
was considered to be consumed orally by all who received communion
including the impious and the infidel, who ate to their damnation. To defend
the real bodily presence, the Württemberg theologians, Brenz and after him
Andreae, argued that the *ubiquity* of the divine nature was communicated
to the human nature of Christ. This doctrine was slightly modified by Chem-

19. "Pew and Pulpit in Geneva," a paper delivered before a joint session of the American Society of
Church History and the American Society for Reformation Research in San Francisco, Dec. 1978.

20. Tadataka Maruyama, *The Ecclesiology of Theodore Beza: The Reform of the True Church* (Geneva,
Librairie Droz, 1978), pp. 112–22.

nitz, who preferred not to speak of ubiquity, but rather of the *genus majes-taticum*. According to this teaching, the divine attributes were communicated to the human nature of Christ at the moment of the Incarnation so that Christ could be, even bodily, wherever he willed to be. Christ lived as an ordinary man, with the exception of his miracles, because he had accepted the state of humiliation, the *kenosis* Paul wrote of in Philippians 2:5–11. At his glorification, the true power of the God-man became apparent.

The first champions of the basic scriptural interpretation of the Lord's Supper according to the Reformed tradition were Oecolampadius of Basel and Zwingli of Zurich, who opposed Luther and Melanchthon at Marburg in 1529. Bullinger was Zwingli's successor in Zurich, while Calvin and then Beza taught a slightly less radical Reformed sacramental theology in Geneva. Apparently influenced by his friendship for many of the Reformed, Melanchthon modified his eucharistic doctrine until it was not too far from the Genevan position. For all the Reformed, Christ and the faithful communicant were truly united through the power of the Holy Spirit. But the body of Christ, according to the doctrine of the Ascension, was in heaven and could be nowhere else until the Second Coming. To ascribe ubiquity to the human nature of Christ was to deny the reality of Christ's humanity, which requires that his human body be locally circumscribed. The Reformed agreed, however, that communion with the whole Christ was genuine and would occur through the power of the Holy Spirit, using the instrument of the divine gift of faith. Hence the Reformed called their communion true and spiritual. Those who lacked true faith would receive only bread and wine since they would have no capacity to receive Christ, who nevertheless offers himself to all in the Supper.

The bitterness of this controversy is difficult to imagine. The Lutherans called the Reformed "sacramentarians" and "fanatics." The Reformed called the Lutherans "ubiquitarians" and "Capernaites." But the controversies were not limited to theological name-calling. The populations of large areas within the empire were affected, some suffering exile for their convictions.

While the Lutherans preferred to call themselves "Evangelicals," in other words, followers of the Gospel, there were other churches that laid special claim to that name, which then also meant 'followers of the Augsburg Confession." Their reasons were both theological and political, since only Roman Catholics and those who professed the Augsburg Confession were legitimate in the empire after 1555. These "Evangelicals" professed a Lutheran doctrine of predestination and a Reformed sacramental doctrine. They lived in the French-speaking lands around Basel that were within the empire but were reformed under the influence of Basel's Oecolampadius[21] and in the German Palatinate where, as followers of Melanchthon, they were called

21. Jill Raitt, "The French Theological Response," in *Discord, Dialogue, and Concord: Studies in the Lutheran Reformation's Formula of Concord,* ed. Lewis W. Spitz and Wenzel Lohff (Philadelphia: Fortress Press, 1977), pp. 178–190.

"Philippists" or "crypto-Calvinists" by the Gnesio, or "genuine," Luther-ans. Because of their Eucharistic doctrine, their place within the empire was called in question in 1564 at the Maulbronn Colloquy where Ursinus, who had just completed the Heidelberg Catechism, was opposed by Andreae. The Palatinate was again endangered in the Augsburg Reichstag of 1566, in which Emperor Maximillian came close to condemning the Reformed doc-trine as outside the Augsburg Confession and to exiling those pastors who refused to confess a sufficiently Lutheran doctrine. Only the efforts of multinational Reformed churches saved their coreligionists in Germany from imperial judgment.[22]

In France, the Reformed were in even greater difficulty. The concern of the Swiss Reformed was manifested in the correspondence between Melanch-thon and Bullinger and by the delegation sent to Worms from Geneva. That the discussion almost broke down over the doctrine of the Lord's Supper is not surprising; it is more interesting that they agreed sufficiently to join forces on behalf of the beleagured French Protestants. The French churches looked primarily to Geneva for doctrinal and pastoral guidance. French refugees crowded Geneva and the Genevan Academy sent pastors into France as rapidly as they could be suitably trained. For this reason, the title of this book includes neither France nor the Netherlands. For although Beza and Daneau, like Calvin, were born and raised in France, Geneva was the city-state which became the model and the source of strength for the French Reformed churches and the school in which pastor-professors like Daneau were trained. Daneau's *Isagoge* was written out of his experience as a teacher and is one of the works which mark the transition from the age of confes-sionalism to the period of Protestant scholasticism in the seventeenth cen-tury.

In German-speaking Switzerland, Heinrich Bullinger was the leader to whom all looked and whose strong, somewhat bearish support helped Geneva to maintain its precarious independence by interceding with the militarily strong city of Bern. Bullinger was also far less optimistic than the Genevans about the outcome of the colloquies. He was not surprised when the accord struck by Farel and Beza with the Lutherans broke down. In fact Bullinger protested vigorously the Genevans' use of the word *substance* in that agree-ment. Bullinger refused the notion that the substance of Christ could be present in the Supper; for him it meant capitulation to the Lutherans. Never-theless it was Bullinger who supplied the Second Helvetic Confession in 1566, which was received by the international Reformed community, there-by demonstrating its unity to Emperor Maximilian.

---

22. See Walter Holweg, *Der Augsburger Reichstag von 1566 und seine Bedeutung für die Entstehung der Reformierten Kirche und Ihres Bekenntnisses* (Neukirch: Neukirchener Verlag des Erziehungsvereins Ltd., 1964).

Zacharias Ursinus was caught in the same dilemma as the other "Evangelicals." But from the peace-seeking professor at Heidelberg came the foundation stones of the German Reformed Church, the Heidelberg Catechism (1563), its Defense (1564), and the Heidelberg Confession (1574). Also active on behalf of the Palatinate Reformed was Theodore Beza, who set aside his own composition, recognizing in Bullinger's confession the instrument needed to gain international support. Beza also presided at the Synod of La Rochelle in 1571, which established the Gallican Confession, and then he supervised the work of Jean François Salvard in gathering the Reformed confessions included in the *Harmonia confessionum fidei* (1581), which served as a Reformed answer to the Lutheran Book of Concord. Thirty years after their meeting near Worms, Beza and Andreae faced one another again, principally over the related problems of Christology and the Lord's Supper. But this time, there would be no reconciliation. In fact, by then the Lutherans were saying that it was better to deal with Jesuits than with Calvinists![23]

Lutherans were not of that mind in Worms in 1557, when they blamed the failure of the colloquy on the Jesuit, Peter Canisius. Canisius defended tradition by pointing out the serious differences among those who claimed to be ruled by Scripture alone. Even with the Augsburg Confession as a guide, the split in the Lutheran camp was profound and dealt with doctrines that were at the heart of the Reformation itself: justification, good works, the sacraments. It was clear, Canisius argued, that before the colloquy could make progress, criteria should be established for interpreting such difficult passages as *Hoc est corpus meum*. Those criteria, he suggested, were the creeds, councils, and the writings of the Fathers.

It was not Canisius, however, but Michael Helding, bishop of Merseberg, who "asked the Protestants to state whether they regarded the Zwinglians, Calvinists, and the followers of Osiander and Flacius Illyricus as true adherents of the *Confession of Augsburg*."[24] This was a perfectly legitimate question. The Diet of Regensburg had allowed for a colloquy only between the two religions recognized in the empire by the Peace of Augsburg: the Roman Catholics and the followers of the Augsburg Confession of 1530. The Roman Catholics had to know which Lutheran party was the true interpreter of the Augsburg Confession.[25] However legitimate, this request set the Lutherans upon each other and the colloquy broke up after the departure of the Gnesio-Lutherans. In his account, however, Melanchthon blamed Canisius

23. Beza, *Correspondance*, vol. 8 (1567), (Geneva: Librairie Droz, 1975), p. 101. The current saying was "melior papista quam calvinista" or even, with relation to Andreae, "melior jesuita quam calvinista."

24. James Brodrick, *Saint Peter Canisius, S.J., 1521–1597* (Baltimore, Md.: The Carroll Press, 1950), p. 408.

25. Wolf, *Zur Geschichte*, p. 103.

for the failure of the colloquy.[26] But historians, both Catholic and Protestant, agree that the colloquy failed because the Lutherans did not reconcile their differences before it began.[27]

Among Canisius's primary works are his catechisms, although like the other religious leaders in this book, he was also an educator par excellence, and bore his share of the burden in colloquies and councils, serving as theologian at the third session of the Council of Trent (1562–63). There he again aided his friend Cardinal Hosius, who presided over Trent's final session. Hosius himself produced a *Confessio Catholicae fidei Christiana* and influenced both the Tridentine Confession of Faith and the Roman Catechism, which he used to regain Poland for Roman Catholicism. He was aided in this task by another Jesuit, Peter Skarga, who worked in Poland as Canisius had worked in Germany, establishing schools and writing and preaching for the court and the academy with powerful effect.

Both Hosius and Skarga fought against the policy of tolerance in Poland, which allowed various sects, including the Antitrinitarians and the Anabaptists, to find a refuge there. Such a one was the Antitrinitarian Faustus Socinus, nephew of the Laelius Socinus recommended by Melanchthon at Worms. Faustus Socinus applied *sola scriptura* according to norms established by a humanist understanding of the gospels that excluded the creeds and councils, no matter how early. And yet only one year after his death, Faustus Socinus's work led to the formulation of the Racovian Catechism (1605), which was, in effect, the confession of faith of the Polish Brethren, the forerunners of Unitarianism.

By 1600, the work of these shapers of traditions was completed. The various churches had built solid ramparts and could now defend their positions against one another's polemics. Out of the confessions and their defense grew the handbooks that characterize the seventeenth century, the period of Protestant scholasticism. The Council of Trent and its decrees, anathemas, and teaching materials, its far-reaching reforms and its seminaries, built an ecclesiastical citadel that proved nearly impervious to all challenges for four hundred years.

The forty years upon which this volume concentrates are therefore important years in Christendom. Too little is known about them. Few texts or courses extend into this period except to trace developments in Elizabethan England. If Continental developments beyond 1560 do receive attention, it is either scanty or motivated by narrow denominational concerns. Roman Catholics study the Counter-Reformation, Lutherans are concerned about the shapers of their tradition, and the various Reformed schools attend to their antecedents in France and the Lowlands, or in Scotland and England.

---

26. *C.R.* 9: 394–395. Melanchthon wrote his own account of the Worms Colloquy, which is entitled *Historia Conventus Theologorum Wormaciae 1557.*

27. See Brodrick, *Canisius,* p. 418, for the judgment of Ranke and others.

General studies of the period 1560–1600 are few in number and tend to reflect either a denominational bias,[28] or a preestablished, and usually derogatory, thesis about the relation of these years to the period of the Reformation.[29] According to this thesis, the rich insights of Luther and Calvin, their powerful use of the vernacular, their impatience with scholasticism, all are seen to fall into the pit of Protestant scholasticism because of the lack of first-rate minds in the latter half of the sixteenth century. Latin again prevails, scholastic forms of debate govern style, and the fresh wind of the Gospel promise dies away in a desert of propositions.

Recently, a number of scholars have challenged this facile set of generalizations. From their detailed studies of the theologians of the late sixteenth century have come new insights which lead to questions such as that asked by Olivier Fatio about the most scholastic of the shapers of traditions in this volume, Lambert Daneau: "Why consider the rational framework to which he resorted as a corruption of the existential discoveries of the Reform? It would be better to recognize it as a pedagogical support favoring the presentation of ideas easily put to use and corresponding to the process of scholarly transmission and the establishment of the Reform."[30]

An appropriate evaluation of the age of confessionalism requires much better knowledge of the period. Studies of particular individuals and their works need to be integrated with political, social, and economic history in order to provide a true picture of this important era. It is the hope of the editor and the contributors that scholars will continue to enter this long-neglected field in increasing numbers to join in the study of these and of other shapers of traditions.

A word needs to be said with regard to the different perspectives of the authors of the chapters of this volume. Flacius Illyricus has found a rare advocate, and an able one, in Oliver Olson, whose studies have given him an insight into this difficult character that has often been lacking in the past. On the other hand, Flacius has usually been given full credit for the *Magdeburg Centuries*. Ronald Diener rightly points out that although Flacius conceived and began this work that changed the way ecclesiastical history would henceforward be written, it was Johann Wigand who carried the project through its thirteen volumes.

Andreae and Chemnitz were both major contributors to the *Formula of Concord*. Robert Kolb traces the history of the development of the *Formula* and Andreae's preliminary work. But the revision and final form, Kolb contends,

---

28. An excellent study of this period is Émile G. Léonard, *Histoire Générale du Protestantisme II: L'Établissement (1564–1700)* (Paris: Presses Universitaires de France, 1961). Excellent though it is, it reveals its primary concern with Calvinism and, within Calvinism, with its development in France.

29. This position is particularly evident in the work of Ernst Bizer and his students. They are not alone, however, for the attitude was fairly general as late as ten years ago.

30. See below, chapter 7, p. 111.

were due to the more peaceable and theologically gifted Martin Chemnitz. Thereafter, Andreae became the *Formula's* most untiring propagator.

Robert Walton underscores Heinrich Bullinger's steadying influence on the whole Reformed movement and challenges the priority generally given Calvin and Geneva. Certainly Bullinger's friendship was critical to both Calvin and Beza and deeply appreciated by both. Bullinger's influence on England and the Netherlands was particularly profound, while in Geneva Calvin's and Beza's academy provided pastors and professors for France, Scotland, the Netherlands, and middle Europe.

Both John Donnelly and George Williams note that the Catholic shapers of this period were dependent upon Tridentine doctrine. The contributions of Canisius, Hosius, and Skarga were primarily in the area of education and defense of the Roman Catholic church. The two Poles were also continually involved in church-state negotiations within ecclesiastically pluralist Poland.

Socinus stands apart. In the latter half of the sixteenth century, the law cooperated with the churches of republics, of nations, and of the empire to outlaw anyone so unorthodox as an Antitrinitarian. Only in Poland could Socinus and the Polish Brethren develop the 1574 catechism into the definitive Racovian Catechism of 1605.

I wish to acknowledge here the encouragement and advice of many colleagues. Lewis Spitz and Ken Hagen first read and commented on the manuscript suggesting changes for its improvement. James Bullard pointed out bibliographical omissions, such as the Hans Baron monograph in relation to the age of confessionalism, and also assisted with corrections in style. Paul Nelson read the whole manuscript and offered helpful criticisms throughout. It is a pleasure to thank the Yale University Press, especially Edward Tripp, who encouraged me in this endeavor from the beginning, and Sally Serafim, whose judicious editing is equaled only by her equanimity and cordiality.

Many typists have assisted in various stages of this work: Norma Tate, Sarah Freedman, Anne Daniels, and Jacqueline Norris deserve special thanks.

Finally, I thank each of the contributors for their work and their patience, especially Robert Kolb, who helped to integrate the Lutheran essays, and Robert Kingdon, who offered critical comments in addition to writing the foreword.

The Divinity School   Jill Raitt
Duke University
Durham, North Carolina

*Shapers of Religious Traditions in
Germany, Switzerland, and Poland,
1560–1600*

1

MATThIAS FLACIUS ILLYRICUS
1520–1575
OLIVER K. OLSON

LIFE   Matija Vlačić, or—to use the family's other name, Franco-
vić—was born March 3, 1520, near the Mediterranean at
Albona, Istria. His lifelong affection for his homeland was
reflected by his adopting the cognomen, "Illyricus," from the Roman name
for the province, *Illyria*. Modern Yugoslavia gives evidence that the regard is
mutual—a street named for him in the old Venetian port of Pula, a recent
Serbo-Croat edition of his Protestant martyrology, the *Catalogus testium
veritatis*,[1] and especially his biography by the Zagreb historian, Mijo Mirković.[2] Vlačić's father, Andreas Vlačić, was a small landholder; his mother,
Jacoba, was a member of the patrician Luciana family. Albona, now a small
town called Labin (relocated recently to avoid collapse into the Tito mine),
then belonged to Venice.[3] The boy's elementary education was Italian. After
the early death of his father, he was supervised by a Milanese tutor, Franciscus
Ascerius. Later, he studied with the city rhetorician of Venice, Giambattista
Cipelli (Baptista Egnatius), who was a friend of Erasmus of Rotterdam.

The time for the young Croat to choose a career came at the high point of
Lutheran influence in Venice. In the Istrian province, that influence was so
strong it appeared probable that the remarkable bishop of Capo d'Istria, Peter
Paul Vergerio, would be able to bring about a complete reform.[4] Another
highly placed churchman caught up in the movement was Fra Baldo Lup-
etino, Franciscan provincial and Vlačić's uncle.[5] When Vlačić considered

---

1. *Katalog svjedoka istine* (Zagreb: Yugoslavian Academy of Sciences and Arts, 1960).
2. *Matija Vlačić Ilirik* (Zagreb: Yugoslavian Academy of Sciences and Arts, 1960) (hereafter cited
as *Vlačić*). Mirković emphasizes Vlačić's relationship to Croatia and his nontheological achievements.
3. Cf. Vladimir Vratović, "The Basic Characteristics of Croatian Latinity" in *Humanistica Lovan-
iensia* 20 (1971): 40.
4. Jules Bonnet, "La Réforme à Venise," *Bulletin historique et littéraire de la Société de l'Histoire du
Protestantisme Français* 19–20 (1870/71): 156. Cf. Anne Jacobson Schutte, *Pier Paolo Vergerio: The Making of
an Italian Reformer* (Geneva: Droz, 1977).
5. Cf. Emilio Comba, *I Nostri Protestanti* (Florence: Libreria Claudiana, 1897), 2: 325–327.

entering one of the famous convents of his uncle's order at Padua or Bologna, Fra Baldo advised him to study instead at Luther's university. After stays at Augsburg, Basel, and Tübingen, Vlačić, on whom the southern sun had shone for most of his twenty-one years, arrived in gray Wittenberg in 1541.

Psychic wounds from the early death of his father, one feels sure, and "culture shock" must have been partly responsible for the depression and the struggle with the problem of evil he experienced during his early years in Germany. Because of the importance of the theme of evil in his later works, we might like to know more about his late adolescent crisis, but we have not much more than a reticent report:

> Toward the end of my third year in Wittenberg, when I was living at the home of Dr. Friedrich Backofen, at that time deacon, the evil became so bad that I was sure I was going to die, and he [Backofen] noticed that because of inner confusion I could not work. He pressed me so long that I admitted what was wrong. He buoyed me up with promise and with prayer and arranged that Dr. Pomeranus [John Bugenhagen] bring me to Martin Luther. As he [Luther] comforted me with his own example and that of others and from God's Word, and the congregation included me in its prayer, the evil decreased from day to day and at year's end I was well.[6]

In the Berlin lecture credited with stimulating modern Flacian research,[7] August Twesten, follower and successor of Friedrich Schleiermacher, called this experience the key to understanding Vlačić's life.[8]

We may be able to understand Vlačić's inner development better if we imagine his reactions to visiting soon afterward the Venetian prison cell of his uncle, Fra Baldo, who had been denounced to the Inquisition. For more than twenty years to come, the years of Vlačić's greatest historical influence, Fra Baldo would refuse conditional release in order to practice what he preached: "non recantare, anzi cantare" ("Don't recant, sing!").[9]

The young immigrant, whose name we must now use in its latinized, academic form, Matthias Flacius, made his mark quickly. An impecunious foreigner at twenty-one, he was a university professor of Hebrew at twenty-four. With Luther in attendance, he was married in 1545. At the same time his first major work, De vocabulo fidei, was finished and supplied with a

6. *Apologia M. Fl. Ill. ad Scholam Vitebergensem in Adiaphororum causa*, in *Omnia Latina Scripta . . .* (Magdeburg, 1550), sig. K5.

7. Cf. Wilhelm Preger in the standard biography, *Matthias Flacius Illyricus und seine Zeit*, 2 vols. (Erlangen: 1859–61) (reprinted 1964, Hildesheim: Georg Olms Verlag, and Nieuwkoop: B. de Graaf), I, iif. More than a century old, Preger's work needs updating. There are, for instance, more than fifty Flacian publications to be found that are not included in his extensive bibliography. A new biography has been undertaken by Oliver K. Olson.

8. *Matthias Flacius Illyricus, eine Vorlesung* (Berlin: G. Bethge, 1844).

9. Mirković, *Vlačić*, p. 589.

dedication by Philip Melanchthon to Thomas Cranmer, archbishop of Canterbury. [10] The prospects for placid academic life, however, were cut off by the military defeat of the Evangelical princes at Mühlberg in April 1547. Faculty and students scattered. Melanchthon and Flacius found employment in Braunschweig in a short-lived school, the *Paedagogicum*, made up of the senior classes of St. Catherine's and St. Martin's schools, combined to foster advanced work. [11] By the time internal difficulties forced the school's closing, the university had reopened and Melanchthon and Flacius were once again in Wittenberg.

The future of the Wittenberg university now depended on the favor of the victorious emperor, Charles V, determined to restore religious unity. Flacius suspected that the new laws regulating religion *medio tempore*, [12] "in the meanwhile," (hence the usual term for the arrangements, *Interim*), were a mere stay of execution. As soon as the church council already meeting at Trent had finished its work, he reasoned, its decisions would be imposed by the emperor everywhere in an effort to cancel out the Reformation. [13] The threat to the church from the emperor's usurpation of ecclesiastical jurisdiction, he warned, dwarfed all other considerations. The hour demanded massive resistance—an "act of confession." He urged that all specifically religious directives from the emperor's government had to be resisted since making distinctions between various regulations served only to strengthen the status quo. That is what he meant by his famous statement, *"in casu confessionis et scandali nihil est adiaphoron"* ("When provocations demand an act of confession there is no such thing as an indifferent practice"). [14] His efforts as a junior faculty member to persuade his colleagues to present a common front were not successful, and he turned to a more promising medium, publicity. In his lifetime he published more than three hundred books and pamphlets. For the moment using cautious pseudonyms (Johannes Waremund, Theodor Henetus, and Christian Lauterwar), he was already drafting works that were, in Mirković's words, "totally passion and flame."

Decisions about policy at the university were up to Philip Melanchthon, the famed *praeceptor Germaniae*, who saw things differently from Flacius.

---

10. Wittenberg, 1549. Among his shorter works at the time was his *Carmina Vetusta* (Wittenberg: 1548); 2nd ed., *Pia quaedam vetustissima poemata* (Magdeburg: 1552), consisting of medieval hymn texts. A complete collection of Flacius's hymnological works was undertaken by Gustav Milchsak, who published only one volume, *Hymni et Sequentiae . . . post M. Flacii Illyrici curas congessit, . . .* (Halle: Niemeyer, 1886).

11. *Gymnasium Martino-Katheraneum Braunschweig. Festschrift zur 200-Jahr-Feier am 17. und 18. März 1926*, ed. Richard Elster (Braunschweig: Friedrich Vieweg und Sohn, 1926), p. 13.

12. Joachim Mehlhausen, ed., *Das Augsburger Interim von 1548* (Neukirchen-Vluyn: Neukirchener Verlag, 1970), p. 31.

13. The plans of Charles V are still debated. Cf. Robert Kolb. *Nikolaus von Amsdorf (1483–1565)* (Nieuwkoop: B. de Graaf, 1978), p. 114.

14. The slogan is a quotation from *Quod hoc tempore nulla penitus mutatio in religione sit in gratiam impiorum facienda* (Magdeburg?: 1549?), sig. vi.

Luther, Melanchthon observed, had had no serious objection to some of the practices the emperor wanted to reintroduce. They were, in fact, *adiaphora*— Melanchthon used a Stoic term for matters of less than primary importance. What was crucial for him was the future of the university; to save it, he was ready to compromise.[15] Since Flacius saw that he could carry on an effective resistance only if he broke with Melanchthon, he fled Wittenberg at Easter, 1549.

After visits to Lüneburg and Hamburg where the pastors expressed their warm approval of his stand, Flacius arrived in Magdeburg, a last pocket of military resistance. He cast his lot there with other young men, drawn to the city by their impatience with compromise. The tense situation, in which it seemed that Luther's movement was about to be crushed, helped form an ecclesiastical party that in one guise or other has persisted within the Lutheran tradition ever since, a party claiming to have preserved Luther's true intent. Thus Melanchthon's observation that "these absurd persons consider themselves the only *gnesio* [true] Lutherans" had a kernel of truth.[16] Their convictions were expressed by the soldiers of the city's garrison. Outnumbered six to one, they defended Magdeburg as the Saxon elector, in a mopping-up operation after the Schmalkaldic War, mounted a siege against the city on the emperor's behalf. Under constant fire, they sang about themselves as the last, faithful remnant of Luther's cause—modern Maccabees.

That Luther had approved such armed resistance was the argument of the 1550 *Confession, Instruction and Warning*. This Confession of Magdeburg made the claim that it was not original, but rather only a rehearsal of Luther's own thought, now stripped of his cautious, pastoral, pre-war ambiguity.[17] Although the signatories of the document were approximately the same men who have been called the "Flacian circle," it is not clear what influence Flacius had on its preparation. The evidence points to his associate, Nicolaus Gallus, pastor of St. Ulrich's Church, as the primary author. As the main justification for Magdeburg's resistance movement, however, which was the central event of Flacius's career, the confession is important as context for his early work.

Agreeing with the contention of the Saxon court lawyers that German dukes were no mere delegates of the emperor, but that their authority derived directly from God, in the sense of St. Paul's Epistle to the Romans 13, the signatories made the same claim for the Magdeburg city council. They also

---

15. Clyde L. Manschreck. "A Critical Examination and Appraisal of the Adiaphoristic Controversy in the Life of Philip Melanchthon," (Ph.D. diss., Yale University, 1948), pp. 35ff.

16. *Corpus Reformatorum* 3:453. Cf. Otto Ritschl, *Dogmengeschichte des Protestantismus* (Leipzig: J. C. Hinrichs'sche Buchhandlung, 1908) 2:326.

17. *Bekentnis Unterricht und Vermanung der Pfarrhern und Prediger der Christlichen Kirchen zu Magdeburg* (Magdeburg: 1550). See Cynthia Grant Shoenberger, "The Confession of Magdeburg and the Lutheran Doctrine of Resistance" (Ph.D. diss., Columbia University, 1972). An English edition of the Magdeburg Confession is in preparation. Cf. Oliver K. Olson, "Theology of Revolution: Magdeburg, 1550–1551," *Sixteenth Century Journal* 3, no. 1 (April 1972): 56–72.

assumed Luther's distinction between the rule of God "on the left hand," through human government, and his rule "on the right hand," through the divine Word. Combining the two ideas, they developed a justification for armed resistance that was not seditious. If one level of secular government should tamper seriously with religion, the Magdeburg pastors argued, another level must resist it "according to its [legitimate] office," that is, by force of arms. Thus the Flacian circle summarized the discussion of the Schmalkaldic period in a classic and readily exportable form.[18]

Flacius's own publications rolled from the Magdeburg presses in torrents.[19] He demonstrated his ability to transform an abstract issue into a concrete one first by distinguishing between essential and nonessential church practices in his *Liber de veris et falsis adiaphoris* (Magdeburg, 1549), and then by demanding that pastors refuse to practice ceremonies without biblical warrant if those ceremonies had already been abandoned. In that case, their only authority was an unacceptable government fiat. He did not hesitate to demand sacrifices. In one case, although it would mean automatic loss of position and exile, he defined a specific point of resistance for a group of clergymen at Meissen as the refusal to wear the white linen surplice.[20] That Flacius's influence extended to Britain is apparent from the quotation of a key section of his *Liber de . . . adiaphoris* in the Puritan manifesto, *The Fortresse of Fathers.*[21]

As it would be later in England, the immediate goal of both sides in the Continental struggle was the control of the liturgy. The suffragan bishop of Mainz, Michael Helding, at the "armored diet" of Augsburg insisted that the Latin order must be used unchanged, since it had been written in Latin by the apostles themselves.[22] Flacius turned his historical skills to account in challenging the bishop's claim. In many ways his conclusions anticipate the

---

18. W. D. J. Cargill Thompson, "Luther and the Right of Resistance to the Emperor," in *Church, Society and Politics* (Oxford: Blackwell, 1975), pp. 200 and 202: "There can be little doubt that Calvin, Beza, and the English Marian exiles were drawing on a well-established Lutheran tradition when they propounded the theory of the right of inferior magistrates to resist their superiors." Sources from the discussion within the Schmalkaldic League are in Heinz Scheible, ed., *Das Widerstandsrecht als Problem der deutschen Protestanten 1523 bis 1546* (Gütersloh: Gütersloh Verlagshaus G. Mohn, 1969).

19. Bibliography in Friedrich Hülsse, "Beiträge zur Geschichte der Buchdruckerkunst in Magdeburg," repr. in *Bibliographiae Reconditae I*, (Amsterdam: P. Schippers, 1966), pp. 346ff.

20. *Responsio M. N. Galli et M. Fl. Ill. ad quorundam Misensium Concionatorum literas de questione, An Potius Cedere, Quam Lineam Vestem Induere Debeant* (Magdeburg: Christian Rhodius, n.d).

21. *The Fortresse of Fathers, ernestlie defending the puritie of Religion and Ceremonies, by the trew exposition of certain places of Scripture: against such as wold bring in an Abuse of idol Stouff, and of thinges indifferent and do appoinct th'aucthority of Princes and Prelates larger than the trueth is: Translated out of the Latine into English for there sakes that understand no Latine by I.B.* (1566). Cf. Leonard J. Trinterud, *Elizabethan Puritanism* (New York: Oxford University Press, 1970), pp. 101–106.

22. Sermon for the First Sunday in Advent, 1547, *Von der Hailigsten Messe* (Ingolstadt: Alexander Weissenhorn, 1548).

results of modern liturgical scholarship.[23] Among other things, he argued that the Mass was not one solid prayer to be prayed by the celebrant, but that "each part of the Mass had a special function. . . . Some parts were common prayers, some praise and thank God, some are instruction, some the communion of the people, etc."—very unusual comments in his period.[24] He argued that the use of plural forms (*communicantes, sumentibus,* etc.), assumed the presence of a community. To refute the claim that the Latin rite had been uniform since the time of the apostles (a claim that, by implication, made liturgical reform unthinkable), Flacius published a series of documents illustrating that the ritual had developed gradually, and not necessarily in the best possible fashion, with great diversity in different areas of the world. The most important of Flacius's publications on the liturgy is the order of worship now known by his name, the Missa Illyrica.[25] Subsequent scholarship by the Jesuit, Joseph Braun, has shown that Flacius was three centuries early in dating it around 700 A.D.,[26] and the Premonstratensian Boniface Luykx has shown that the Missa Illyrica is part of the lush liturgical synthesis of Roman and Germanic elements that took place in the ninth-century Rhineland.[27] Therefore neither Flacius, who claimed it was pre-Roman, nor his opponents who, with Cardinal Giovanni Bona, insisted that it was "a true and pure Roman mass interpolated with diverse prayers,"[28] were quite correct. Since the Missa Illyrica is "from any point of view . . . a liturgical monstrosity,"[29] it could serve as a persuasive piece of evidence for the point Flacius wanted to make: the order of the Mass had changed through history. Hence it could be used to make a historical-critical challenge to his opponent Helding's liturgical fundamentalism.

The success of Flacian polemics in wresting theological leadership from Melanchthon still lay in the future. But already at the end of the Magdeburg resistance the remarkable effectiveness of the Illyrian's writing had become plain. If we should accept the judgment of those historians who think that by influencing public opinion he induced the elector Moritz to join the Protestant bloc, it must follow that Flacius, before his twenty-seventh birthday,

23. His summary of the history of the offertory in "Some Observations on the Antiquity of the Mass," *Missa latina, quae olim ante romanam circa 700. Domini annum in usu fuit bona fide ex vetusto authenticoque codice descripta* (commonly called the "Missa Illyrica") (Strassburg: Christian Mylius, 1557), pp. 88f. English translation in Oliver K. Olson, "The 'Missa Illyrica' and the Liturgical Thought of Flacius Illyricus" (Th.D. diss., Hamburg, 1966), p. 162, is essentially the same as Josef Jungmann's in *Missarum Solemnia* (Vienna: Herder, 1962), p. 5. Flacius anticipates Jungmann's genetic method.

24. *Rufutatio Missae* (n.p., 1555), sig. D. iii.

25. See n. 23 above. The manuscript he transcribed is the Wolfenbüttel Codex Helmstedt (1151).

26. "Alter und Herkunft der sog. 'Missa Illyrica,' " *Stimmen aus Maria Laach* 69 (1905): 143–155.

27. "Essai sur les Sources de l'Ordo Missa Premontré," *Analecta Praemonstratensia* 22/23 (1945–46): 35–90. Cf. Oliver K. Olson, "Flacius Illyricus als Liturgiker," *Jahrbuch für Hymnologie und Liturgie* 12 (1967): 45–69.

28. *Rerum liturgicarum libri duo* (Rome, 1671), col. 1303.

29. Edmund Bishop, "The Litany of Saints in the Stowe Missal," *Journal of Theological Studies* 7 (1906): 123, n. 2.

had defeated the emperor himself. Whatever the case, the dynamics of his literary wars are worth investigation. Such a study has been attempted by Christina Hasslinger, who draws attention to Flacius's appeals to select audiences, his tireless repetition of arguments, and his instinct for the rhythm of a controversy.[30]

As the opportunistic Moritz was about to change sides and join the Protestants, Magdeburg, with its resources running low, came to terms with the elector and the siege was lifted. The speculations that Flacius might be hanged for his part in the resistance proved groundless. On the contrary, he now enjoyed a new prestige, which he promptly turned to account by demanding censure of the Wittenbergers. In simplified terms, Flacius made two charges against his Lutheran opponents, both concerning tactics they had allegedly adopted in coming to terms with the Interim: First, his opponents held that the human will somehow cooperates in salvation, that one has a certain native ability to make "a decision for Christ," and second, they contended that the government (the prince) has a right to rule in church matters. Both these positions, Flacius asserted, were departures from the axioms of the Reformation. Inevitably, Flacius's demands for censure were understood as personal attacks on Melanchthon.[31] Efforts were made to smooth over the differences between the two leaders by personal reconciliation. The duke of Württemberg suggested "mutual amnesty." But the differences were substantive ones, and the contest between "Philippists" and "Flacians" would continue to torment Protestant Germany for a third of a century.[32]

A center for the Flacian circle was soon forthcoming. Deprived of the city of Wittenberg and of its university by the war, Duke Johann Friedrich II established a substitute university at Jena. Among the earliest faculty members was Matthias Flacius, called at a handsome salary, with concomitant responsibility as superintendent of all churches in Ernestine Saxon lands. The Lutheran movement had survived near obliteration, and now the maritime cities of Lübeck, Lüneburg, and Hamburg adopted religious confessions of

30. "Die Religiöse Propaganda des Matthias Flacius Illyricus und seiner Epigonen: Ein Beitrag zur Flugschriftenliteratur der Reformationszeit" (Ph.D. diss., University of Vienna, 1970).

31. As late as the eighteenth century G. J. Planck, the historian of doctrine, could write that Flacius "had no other motivation than personal enmity against Melanchthon." *Geschichte der Entstehung, der Veränderung und der Bildung unseres protestantischen Lehrbegriffs* (Leipzig: 1796), 4: 184.

32. The presupposition for Flacius's attacks on Melanchthon and his associates was the consensus that Luther's teaching should be maintained. That Adolf Sperl could call Ernst Troeltsch's nineteenth-century discovery of Melanchthon's deep roots in humanism pioneering work (Sperl, *Melanchthon zwischen Humanismus und Reformation* [Munich: Christian Kaiser Verlag, 1959], p. 9) suggests why for so long Flacius's concerns seemed baffling. The gulf between Luther's biblical fideism and Melanchthon's philosophical humanism was simply not perceived by theologians and historians. How profoundly Flacius himself understood Luther is, of course, a further question. However, the growing scholarly consensus on Melanchthon's departure from Luther on basic points suggests at least a new look at his contemporary challenger.

the rigorous sort Flacius advocated. The prospects of bringing the Reformation to the whole church from a North German base seemed favorable.

Flacius's rigorism had been reinforced by research on the Hussite movement in Bohemia, which convinced him that the basic mistake which made possible the betrayal of the Taborite party and the subsequent collapse of the whole Hussite cause was the naiveté in consenting even to begin formal conversations with the Roman curia.[33] Consequently, he advised the Saxon duke to safeguard the German movement from a similar fate by refusing to participate in the proposed religious consultations.

Under imperial sponsorship, however, the Religious Colloquy of Worms in 1557 could not very well be avoided. As the delegates from Ernestine Saxony very well knew, it was politically wise to present a united Protestant front. Since in granting civil rights to those who held to the Confession of Augsburg the 1555 Peace of Augsburg recognized only one sort of Protestant, disunity in Protestant ranks was not only embarrassing but dangerous as well. Yet the delegates decided that religious concerns were more urgent than political ones and chose to view the occasion as a "time of confession." When Bishop Helding pointedly asked them whether, among other heresies, they accepted Flacius's view on the bondage of the will, they took it as a challenge to a fundamental position of Luther. Rather than being outvoted in a conciliatory Protestant caucus, they left the meeting, breaking up the last attempt by the imperial government to reconcile the religious schism and making the Protestants' internal division clear for all Europe to see.

The political advantages of pan-Protestantism were still so obvious to the princes concerned that when they gathered for the coronation of Ferdinand I they attempted yet again to achieve another formula for unity—this time without the inconvenient theologians. Flacius's reaction to this "Frankfurt Recess" of 1558 was a *Book of Confutation*, published by authority of the Ernestine duke, who generally agreed with his firm adviser Flacius. The document pronounced clear judgment on every current rival of Luther's doctrine.[34] Still another attempt at a comprehensive agreement was made by Protestant princes at Naumburg in 1561 by rallying around the Augsburg Confession—with alterations, notably the section on Holy Communion, so as not to exclude the Swiss. This time Duke Johann Friedrich himself decided that too much of substance might be bargained away and left the conference in protest. The political aftermath of his demonstration was unexpected: Most of

33. Mirković, Vlačić, p. 501. His research resulted in an edition of *Ioannis Hus et Hieronymi Pragensis Confessorum Christi Historia et Monumenta*, 2 vols., (Nürnberg: 1558), and the Taborite *Confessio Waldensium* (Basel: 1568).

34. The work is discussed in the context of the perennial attempt to distinguish the Christian tradition from its social and cultural context by the Heidelberg professor Hans-Werner Gensichen, *We Condemn: How Luther and Sixteenth Century Lutheranism Condemned False Doctrine* (St. Louis: Concordia Publishing House, 1967), pp. 123–152.

the Protestant princes eventually fell in behind the Saxon duke, and by so doing, settled the contest. The latitudinarian Philippists had lost; the strict Flacians had won. The eventual religious settlement chose doctrinal continuity with Luther over politically expedient Protestant solidarity.

Although as subsequent history shows, Flacius's success in challenging Melanchthon's leadership can hardly be overestimated, nevertheless he is remembered more for his personal defeat. Deprived of his professorship, he was forced to spend the remainder of his life as a fugitive and exile. Since he was correctly held responsible for the sabotage of the negotiations at Worms in 1557, it was understandable that he was unpopular at the imperial court. More serious for him, however, was his fall from favor in his own duchy. It began with a formal disputation in the Weimar palace in August 1560, a classic episode in the long Western debate on the freedom of the will. Flacius's Philippist opponent, Viktorin Strigel, argued that the effect of sin on natural freedom was described adequately by the Aristotelian term *accident*. Opposed to what he considered a shallow view, Flacius used the opposite term. Sin, he said, was man's *substance*.[35] His statement would be seized on later as evidence of heresy. What mattered at the moment, however, was that during the inconclusive proceedings, Johann Friedrich II's attitude toward Strigel improved. His attitude toward Flacius, on the other hand, turned hostile. The events in Weimar and Jena in 1561 that led to Flacius's exile have not yet been fully studied. It is clear, however, that Flacius and his supporters engaged in a vigorous and significant resistance to the introduction of direct state government of the church.[36] Although the inspiring example of Johann Friedrich II's father, the elector Johann Friedrich I, who chose prison rather than renounce Luther, influenced him to favor Flacius's firmness, that example in no way suggested to him that he permit self-determination to the church. The vigorous efforts of Flacius and his supporters to arrange for the convocation of a church synod with authority to determine doctrinal matters struck the elector as a direct challenge to his own authority.[37] Following an incident involving the church's authority to reject baptismal sponsors, the duke announced the organization of a six-man consistorial government for the church, responsible to him. And as a cautionary measure, he decreed censorship of the press.[38] It was not difficult for Flacius's enemies in court circles, led by Chancellor Christian Brück, to orchestrate the events which led to a court hearing on the

35. An analysis of the debate is found in Hans Kropatschek, "Das Problem theologischer Anthropologie auf dem Weimarer Gespräch 1560 zwischen Matthias Flacius Illyricus und Viktorin Strigel" (Th.D. thesis, University of Göttingen, 1943).

36. Cf. the study of the bishop of Berlin, Martin Kruse, *Spener's Kritik am Landesherrlichen Kirchenregiment und ihre Vorgeschichte* (Witten: Luther Verlag, 1970), pp. 57–63.

37. Preger, *Matthias Flacius Illyricus*, p. 137. Cf. *Supplicatio quorundum Theologorum, qui post obitum Lutheri Sectis contradixerunt, pro legitima Synodo ad Joannem Fridericum II. Ducem Saxoniae* (n.p., 1560).

38. Although his arguments are not the usual modern ones, interest attaches to Flacius's protest, *De Praelorum Libertate* [On the Freedom of the Press], Wolfenbüttel Codex 11.7 Aug. Fol. Bl. 209–301.

charge of insubordination and the dismissal of Flacius and Professor Johann Wigand (see chapter 2 below) on December 10, 1561.

With his wife and seven or eight children, Flacius found temporary refuge in a neighboring town and then, in February 1562, in Regensburg. The church superintendent there, Flacius's Magdeburg colleague, Nicolaus Gallus, assisted the family, but difficulties mounted. The city council was warned against Flacius not only by Duke Johann Friedrich, whose charges were printed and sent in all directions, but also by the emperor, who at one time sent his imperial secretary and at another the captain of the imperial cavalry with messages. From Venice, moreover, came the news that his uncle, Fra Baldo, had been drowned by official order in a canal. Lastly, his wife and several of his children died.

Not fluent enough in German to serve as a clergyman, Flacius spent his time primarily in writing, living on capital. He could now devote himself to the second of the Reform's basic needs, a Bible-study guide. The result was his *Clavis Scripturae*, "Key to the Scripture" (Basel, 1567), which some admirers have called the "golden key." Of extraordinary importance for students of German literature was his publication of the preface to the Old Saxon epic, the *Heliand* ("Savior"), as appendix to the second edition of the *Catalogus* in 1562. Since the manuscript of the rare ninth-century writing has been lost, the only record is Flacius's.[39]

His spectacular appeal to the emperor to convoke an evangelical synod—at which he could be vindicated—misfired and served merely to increase the princes' resentment. Since it was now politically impossible for the Regensburg council to extend his residence permit, he accepted a call to go to Antwerp to write a confession and a church order for the Lutheran congregation there. But the opposition of the Archduchess Margaret cut his stay short, and Flacius, now remarried, spent the next five years in Strassburg. Especially important from the Strassburg period was his edition of the ninth-century *Evangelienbuch* of Otfrid of Weissenberg, which one scholar enthusiastically called "the most valuable publication of the sixteenth century."[40] Although his 1,400-page *Glossa compendaria* on the New Testament was published (Basel, 1570), at his death, Flacius left behind thousands of manuscript pages of biblical commentary, along with the largest private

---

39. Outstanding among the more than one thousand books and articles on the *Heliand* and its preface is Kurt Hannemann's literary coup, "Die Lösung des Rätsels der Herkunft der Heliandpraefatio," *Forschung und Fortschritte* 15 (1939): 327–329, in which the suggestion that Flacius may have forged the preface was finally proven false.

40. Hermann Paul, *Grundriss der Germanischen Philologie* (Strassburg: Karl J. Truebner, 1891), 1:15. Noting the failure of the humanist scholar, Beatus Rhenanus, to act on a similar opportunity to publish the Otfrid manuscript, Kurt Hannemann observes that the Protestant challenge to traditional interpretations of church history had a positive side effect in rescuing medieval literature—in contrast to the humanists, whose attempts to restore antiquity made them indifferent to the Middle Ages. "Der Humanist Georg Fabricius in Meissen, etc.," *Filologia Germanica* 17 (1974):74.

library of the sixteenth century, most of which are now held by the Herzog-August Library at Wolfenbüttel.

Banished from Strassburg in 1573 as too controversial by a city council intimidated by Flacius's foe, Elector August of Saxony, he found a last refuge for himself and his family in the cloister of St. Mary Magdalene in Frankfurt am Main. Without a residence permit, he was still tolerated temporarily since most of his time was spent in conferences and disputations outside the city. Returning exhausted and ill, he was cared for in his final illness by the Evangelical prioress, Catherine von Meerfeld. Just in time to avoid being banished yet once more, on March 10, 1575, he died.

THEOLOGY   Flacius did not try to be original; his efforts were exerted instead to establishing Luther's legacy. To that end he worked toward a biblical, as opposed to a philosophical, theology. It was already clear that Luther's concerns could not be adequately expressed in the normal medieval thought patterns. Luther had criticized the traditional distinction between the *letter* and the *spirit*; a more satisfactory distinction in biblical studies for him was between two voices: *Law*, by which judgment is pronounced and which, in Christian conversion, brings about a personal crisis, and *Gospel*, the direct and effectual pronouncement of forgiveness. Flacius took his task to be to protect this sort of theological understanding from being transformed in the universities into mere ideas.[41]

As a sometime professor of Hebrew and a scholar of Aristotle,[42] Flacius was highly aware of the subtle threat to biblical categories posed by the philosophical tradition. In *On the Materials and Limits of the Sciences and the Errors of Philosophy in Divine Matters* (Basel, 1561) he proposed that philosophy's role within the discipline of theology be restricted to conceptual clarification. Against the reintroduction of Aristotle into Lutheran theology, apparent in the successively more philosophical editions of Melanchthon's *Loci communes*, he offered as challenge his *Clavis Scripturae*, a work with a theological lexicon whose articles were written specifically to exclude Aristotelian concepts.[43]

Negatively, Flacius's program can be called *de-hellenization*. A positive term for it, which was meant to imply the distinction of biblical philosophy

41. Günther Moldaenke thinks he succeeded. *Schriftverständnis und Schriftdeutung im Zeitalter der Reformation, Teil I: Matthias Flacius Illyricus* (Stuttgart: Verlag von W. Kohlhammer, 1936). Moldaenke's conclusion is criticized by Lauri Haikola in *Gesetz und Evangelium bei Matthias Flacius Illyricus* (Lund: Gleerup, 1952).

42. Flacius's scholarly contribution to the preparation of the third Basel edition of Aristotle's complete works is praised in the editor's introduction to *Aristotelis Opera . . cum notis et emendationis J. Velsii, M. Flacii . . .* (Basel: Jo. Bebelium et Mich. Isingrenium, 1550).

43. Karl Adolf von Schwarz, "Die Theologische Hermeneutik des Matthias Flacius Illyricus," *Lutherjahrbuch* (1933): 145.

not only from hellenistic philosophy but also from other influences, is the sixteenth-century expression, *pure doctrine*. Accurate use of the latter term, of course, depends upon remembering that the word *doctrine* then had not yet acquired its later rationalist overtones, but could still imply preaching or confession of one's faith. To forge a stable consensus in the religious confusion of the period after Luther's death, Flacius worked tirelessly and systematically in a long series of controversies against what he considered nonbiblical influence on church teaching, for example, against the mysticism of Kaspar Schwenckfeld, against what seemed to him a sub-Christian legalism in the writings of Georg Major, and against the novel teaching on justification of Nürnberg's reformer, Andreas Osiander.[44]

An independent spirit who had known Luther in the early days, Osiander was not so overawed by the great reformer's reputation that he was hindered from reading and being influenced by the speculations of Pico della Mirandola and, through Johann Reuchlin, by the medieval Cabbala. Justification, he explained, came about through the indwelling of the *inner word*, for him a metaphysical quantity, to be distinguished from the mere *outer word* of preaching. Flacius was easily able to demolish Osiander's exegesis and to show that from first to last the word *justify* in biblical use means "to pronounce just."[45] Osiander was wrong, he said, in holding that justification was accomplished by the divine nature only. Christ also satisfied the ethical demands of the law, and the merit he won as a man can be imputed to the believer.

Osiander's tart observation about the storm of opposition to his teaching was accurate: "If sixty thousand wrote against me, it is still nothing but the one song of Philip."[46] Flacius's strong emphasis on justification-as-pronouncement, known technically as "forensic" justification, was characteristic of the teaching of Philip Melanchthon. By making common cause with his teacher, Flacius lent his support to the Philippists' intense campaign to determine the exact way in which the central issue of the Reformation would be transformed from the complex subtleties of Luther's treatises into simple and memorable instruction formulae. His siding with Melanchthon has been praised on the one hand as proof that he was concerned more for the theological enterprise itself than for establishing himself as an independent authority. On the other hand, he was criticized for strengthening the unfortunate impression that the theological categories of *justification* and *regeneration* were not only to be distinguished but separated.[47]

44. Flacius's theological controversies are described extensively, and in a somewhat hagiographical fashion, by Frederick Bente, *Historical Introduction to the Book of Concord* (St. Louis: Concordia Publishing House, 1966).

45. *Clavis Scripturae* (Frankfurt, 1719) 1:308ff.

46. Quoted by Emanuel Hirsch, *Die Theologie des Andreas Osiander und ihre geschichtliche Voraussetzungen* (Göttingen: Vandenhoek und Ruprecht, 1919), p. 234.

47. Hirsch, *Die Theologie*, p. 267.

Unpleasant and often bitter, the controversies of the thirty years be-tween 1547 and the religious settlement of 1577, the Formula of Concord, can be understood—from the calm distance of four centuries—as a necessary presupposition for the stability of the subsequent Lutheran theological tradition. Although no small credit for that stability belongs to Flacius, in the end he was the first theologian to be rejected and is now remembered chiefly as a heretic.[48]

The "Flacian controversy" was hard-fought and complex.[49] We can limit ourselves here to considering Flacius's motivation. Aware that his claim, "sin is man's substance," would meet resistance, he tried to strain out stray, unwanted Aristotelian overtones by careful definition of terms, and offered even to abandon the statement entirely if what he considered to be biblical teaching on the issue could be preserved by using other terms. What mattered to him was combating his opponent Strigel's optimistic distinction between man's sinful life and some deeper, purely personal core, a distinction he considered platonic. What a man is, he insisted, cannot be distinguished from the moral quality of his life. Man is not composed of two parts, but constitutes a unity. As a unity, he is submissive either to God or to Satan. Like Luther, who in *On the Bondage of the Will* had used the illustration of a horse who could have only one rider, Flacius did not shrink from drawing the consistent conclusions that would subject him to the charge of "new Manichaeism."[50] A serious judgment on Flacius's anthropology must include the question whether his alternatives for men—as reflections either of the *imago Dei*, the image of God, or the *imago diaboli*, the image of Satan—are actually more radical than Luther's.[51]

Ranging above his other publications in importance are two projects he undertook to meet major needs of the Reformation's second generation. One was a church history; the other a guide to Bible study. In the peaceful lull after the lifting of the Magdeburg siege, he addressed himself to the former. It was important, he thought, that the Reform be perceived not as something novel and sectarian, but as having come from the central, catholic tradition of the church, and that this interpretation of church history be bolstered by scholarly

48. His position on original sin is rejected in the first article of the *Formula of Concord*, 1577.

49. The standard account is Eduard Schmidt, "Des Flacius Erbsünde-Streit," *Zeitschrift für die historische Theologie* 19 (1849) pp. 3–78 and 218–79. The discussion after 1577 has been described by Walter Sparn, "Substanz oder Subjekt," *Widerspruch, Dialog und Einigung: Studien zur Konkordienformel der Lutherischen Reformation*, ed. Wenzel Lohff and Lewis W. Spitz (Stuttgart: Calwer Verlag, 1977), pp. 107–235.

50. So called for the heresiarch Manes (c. 216–270), who taught a cosmic struggle between equally balanced powers of good and evil.

51. Jörg Baur considers Flacius strongest precisely at the point at which he was most sharply attacked: the doctrine of man. Noting the similarity of Flacius's thought to that of Ricoeur, he suggests a continued relevance. "Flacius—Radikale Theologie," in *Matthias Flacius Illyricus 1575–1975* (Regens-burg: Verlag Lassleben, 1975) p. 47. The article is reprinted in *Zeitschrift für Theologie und Kirche* 72, no. 4 (December 1975), cf. p. 376.

evidence. Flacius therefore organized a team of scholars versed in the most advanced humanist techniques for a thorough search of all available source material to vindicate the historical rightness of the Lutheran reform. The result was the thirteen-volume *Ecclesiastica historia*, published between 1559 and 1574, and known popularly as the *Magdeburg Centuries*.[52] The decision to organize the volumes for easy reference in divisions of one hundred years each—an arbitrary decision, but an advance over the typical medieval organization of history according to the four monarchies of Daniel 2—was responsible not only for its popular name, but also eventually for the modern word "century" as a basic division of time.[53]

Serving as a kind of preliminary study for the *Centuries* was Flacius's martyrology, the *Catalogus testium veritatis*. With the same theme as the larger work, the catholicity of the Reformation, it presents short biographies of more than four hundred "witnesses" through the centuries whose faith Flacius thought similar to Luther's. Beyond its effect on continental Protestants, the *Catalog*, as the main source of John Foxe's *Book of Martyrs*, was partly responsible for the robust Protestant self-assurance of Elizabethan England.[54]

Flacius's vast plan to make the Reformation seem legitimate worked well. For the success of the *Magdeburg Centuries* project we have no less eminent a witness than Pope John XXIII, from his book on Caesar Baronius, the Roman cardinal whose *Annales ecclesiastici* (twelve folio volumes, 1588–1607) would later to a large extent counteract the effect of the *Centuries*: "The manner in which the *Centuries* series was prepared, published and distributed," wrote the future pope, "the considerable moral and financial influence of the princes and kings and the spiritual ferment of those years, all conspired to give this undertaking an extraordinary weight. Thus it came about that while the Protestants felt their scruples of conscience disappearing and comforted themselves with the *ipse dixit* of the centuriators, the genuine Catholics felt defeated, humiliated and despondent on the very territory of tradition and history on which defending their right of possession had seemed so simple and certain."[55]

For Flacius, catholicity was the *cursus verbi*, the "course of the Word" in its constant struggle against the *mysterium iniquitatis*, "the mystery of evil,"

52. Flacius's contribution to the *Centuries* undertaking was the basic conception, the organization of the *collegium* and its working methods, and in collecting material for the enterprise. That the actual writing was done not by Flacius but by the staff writers has been emphasized by Heinz Scheible in "Der Plan der Magdeburger Zenturien und ihre ungedruckte Reformationsgeschichte" (Th.D. diss. Heidelberg, 1960), p. 39, and by Ronald Diener. See below, chapter 2, pp. 22–23 and 33–35.

53. Johannes Burkhardt, *Die Entstehung der modernen Jahrhundertrechnung: Ursprung und Ausbildung einer historiographischen Technik von Flacius bis Francke* (Göppingen: Verlag Alfred Kümmerle, 1971).

54. An example of a lengthy quotation of Flacius by Foxe (without credit) is given by Frances A. Yates, "Queen Elizabeth as Astraea," *Journal of the Warburg and Courtauld Institutes* 10 (1947): 43–44.

55. Angelo Roncalli, *Baronius* (Einsiedeln: Johannes Verlag, 1963), pp. 49ff.

or, put in another way, the proclamation of *Christonomy*.[56] To make Christonomy, "the rule of Christ," a historiographical structure is a distinctly theological undertaking and, as critics have often commented, leaves little room either for the medieval addiction to biographies or for causation *within* history, or to use the nineteenth-century organic metaphor, for "unfolding." On the other hand, it attempts to come to terms with what relativist historiography has increasingly come to abandon: the problem of good and evil.

Flacius achieved distinction also as editor of church-historical documents, including first editions of Sulpicius Severus and Firmicus Maternus as well as the Coburg letters of Luther. A survey of his professional work as historian is furnished by Pontien Polman.[57] The legend of the famous *culter flacianus*, "Flacius's knife," which he is supposed to have hidden under a flowing cloak and used to cut out useful portions of precious books on journeys to sixteenth-century libraries,[58] and the doubts about Flacius's trustworthiness as editor[59] have no apparent basis in fact.

Flacius's other main project, the guide to Bible study, was singled out for praise by the nineteenth-century philosopher, Wilhelm Dilthey. Noting that in the *Clavis Scripturae* Flacius delivers a summary of the complete hermeneutical discussion of antiquity as well as the rhetorical tradition he had learned from Melanchthon, Dilthey credits Flacius with "the kernel of a modern theory on the procedure of interpretation," which has been "of the greatest importance in providing a secure basis of philological-historical knowledge."[60] Since Dilthey, Flacius has been regularly accorded a place as a forerunner of both theological[61] and philosophical hermeneutics.[62]

---

56. S. L. Verheus, *Zeugnis und Gericht: Kirchengeschichtliche Betrachtungen bei Sebastian Franck und Matthias Flacius* (Nieuwkoop: B. de Graaf, 1971), p. 69. Verheus makes the serious mistake of assuming Flacius's participation in the writing of the actual text (above, n. 52). Since what he says here has to do with the basic conception of the work, which was to a great extent Flacius's own, we can accept the basic tendency Verheus describes as Flacian.

57. "Flacius Illyricus, Historien de l'Eglise," *Revue d'Histoire Ecclesiastique* 27 (1931): 27–73.

58. Oliver K. Olson, "Rufmord an Matthias Flacius," *Wolfenbüttler Beiträge* 4 (1980).

59. He is defended, e.g., by Ernst Perels, "Ein erhaltener Brief aus der verschollenen Fuldaer Briefsammlung," *Neues Archiv der Gesellschaft für ältere Geschichtskunde* 30 (1905): 145ff.

60. *Weltanschauung und Analyse des Menshen seit Renaissance und Reformation* (vol. 2 of *Gesammelte Schriften*), 8th ed. (Stuttgart: B. J. Tübner Verlagsgesellschaft, 1957; reprint ed., 1969), p. 123. Cf. the estimate of J. Wach: "The *Clavis* of the famous Illyrian (1567) dominated the hermeneutic of the seventeeth century. The great church historian and biblical expert surpasses his predecessors and most of his successors in originality and systematic power." *Das Verstehen: Grundzüge einer Geschichte der hermeneutischen Theorie im 19. Jahrhundert* (Tübingen: 1926; reprint ed., Hildesheim: 1966), 1:14, n. 2.

61. Karl Holl, pioneer of the Luther Renaissance, in a section on Flacius's hermeneutics, corrects Dilthey by emphasizing Flacius's greater dependence on Luther than on Melanchthon. "Luthers Bedeutung für den Fortschrifft der Auslegungskunst," in *Gesammelte Aufsätze I: Luther*), 6th ed. (Tübingen: J. C. B. Mohr, 1932), pp. 578–582.

Thus modern hermeneutical thought began with Flacius's response to the acute Protestant crisis of authority. Luther had argued that the Bible was authoritative, but he had not solved the problem completely of how chaos could be avoided when everyone began to interpret the Bible for himself. A great many thoughtful people, then, were happy to leave responsibility for official scriptural interpretation in the hands of the bishops, as it had been in the Middle Ages. Without an official interpretation, it was argued, the Bible's message was obscure. One biblical manuscript, moreover, differed from another and the text of the Old Testament, for example, could not be trusted since the Hebrew consonants were written at one time, the vowels at another.

Flacius, taking up that challenge, favored individual interpretation as little as did Luther's critics; he assumed the tradition of a "teaching office." That office, however, could not be based on a mere possession of ecclesiastical rank, but had to do with responsible explication of Scripture. He shared the Reformation assumption that the basic message of the Bible was a coherent one that could be established by a disciplined hermeneutical method, involving the knowledge of the original languages, historical and geographical factors, and whatever helped to establish the specific *scopus*, or intent, of the text itself. For God the Holy Spirit worked not through facile allegories but through the basic sense of the biblical passage. Although his defense of the notion that Hebrew consonants and vowel points were written down simultaneously was not a happy one,[63] his emphasis on the varying styles of biblical books makes a distinctly modern impression.

ROLE IN THE CHURCH   It is possible to consider every one of Flacius's positive achievements as contributions to the church. Perhaps that is true especially since the Flacian theology emphasizes concrete matters of "practical theology" such as liturgics, church administration, and the relationship of church and state, which a more philosophically oriented theological tradition has often neglected.[64]

One of the most interesting questions to rise from the Flacian biography is whether he was responsible for saving the Reformation. Experienced observers in 1547 would have pronounced the Reformation movement doomed with the military victory of Charles V over the Protestants. It was only a change in the balance of power resulting from the crucial shift of the

63. In the sixth tractate of the *Clavis*. Cf. Emanuel Hirsch, *Hilfsbuch zum Studium der Dogmatik*, 4th ed. (Berlin: Walter de Gruyter & Co., 1964), p. 314.

64. That his contributions to culture in general are by-products of his labors for the church is especially clear in the case of his contributions to modern literary Serbo-Croat, contributions made in the course of his efforts to bring the Reformation to the southern Slavs. Erwin Wedel, "Matthias Flacius Illyricus, Ein Bedeutender Kroatischer Humanist," in *Matthias Flacius Illyricus, 1575–1975*, vol. 2 of *Schriftenreihe des Regensburger Osteuropainstituts* (Regensburg: Verlag Lassleben, 1975).

Elector Moritz of Saxony from the Catholic to the Protestant side that made the legal existence of Protestantism within the Holy Roman Empire possible. Our question then is, did Flacius's propaganda campaign force the hand of Moritz? Was Flacius responsible for the shift in the European power balance? Mirković is skeptical.[65] Flacius's eighteenth-century biographer, on the other hand, wrote, "Flacius did not say in so many words . . . that the people should be stirred up to revolt, but that is obviously what he had in mind—to convince the princes thaere would be a rebellion" if the old order were imposed.[66] Melanchthon complained about the same thing.[67] Gustav Kawerau says, "if Luther's work was rescued in those days it was in a special way due to Flacius."[68] And Lutz Geldsetzer says flatly, "Surely it is not saying too much to consider Flacius the rescuer of an independent Protestant movement."[69]

Flacius's gift to the church, for good or ill, is probably no less significant than the survival of the Reformation. A final judgment on his life is inextricably bound up with judgment on Luther's movement itself, to which Flacius gave himself fully, without counting the cost in personal suffering or professional disadvantage. For those who see wisdom in Karl Marx's eleventh thesis on Feuerbach, it may now be possible to see Matthias Flacius in a new light: "the philosophers have heretofore interpreted the world in various ways; the thing, however, is to change it." There is no doubt that the bravery, the dogged persistence, and the piety of the fiery Slav changed the history of the church.

65. "Whether and to what extent the Resistance of the Magdeburgers and with them also of the North German and maritime cities and Flacius's writings exerted a direct influence on the politics and strategy of Moritz of Saxony remains unclear." *Vlačić*, p. 499.

66. Johann Balthazar Ritter, *Matthiae Flacii Illyrici . . . Leben und Tod* (Frankfurt: Zeigler, 1725), p. 153.

67. *Epistola Philippi Melanthonis, in qua Respondetur Flacio Illyrico* (Wittenberg: 1549).

68. *Realencyclopädie für Protestantische Theologie und Kirche*, 3rd ed., 6:83.

69. *Realencyclopädie*, introduction, n.p.

2

JOhANN WIGAND

1523–1587

RONALD E. DIENER

LIFE   Johann Wigand, ecclesiastical historian and polemicist, was born in Mansfeld in 1523 of Hessian parentage. His father, a close friend of the ministers of the word in Mansfeld, was himself illiterate, but "destined his son from tenderest years for his studies, and often prayed over the lad's cot that the Lord God bestow His grace on his son, so that the boy might some day help in the propagation of the purified teaching which He was again illuminating by His minister, Martin Luther."[1]

---

1. The basic sources for the life of Johann Wigand are: (1) His autobiography, first published in the article "Leben D. Joh. Wigandi," *Fortgesetzte Sammlung von alten und neuen theologischen Sachen* (Leipzig, 1738), pp. 601–20, was transcribed from the manuscript of the Stadtbibliothek Königsberg (see A. Seraphim, *Handschriften-Katalog der Stadtbibliothek Königsberg i. Pr.*, Mitteilungen aus der Stadtbibliothek Königsberg i. Pr., 1 [Königsberg, 1909], pp. 2–7), ms. S3, fol. 300ff. (2) The funeral oration—not sermon—by his brother-in-law, Conrad Schlüsselburg, *Oratio funebris de vita et obitu D. Ioannis VVigandi conscripta & habita in Schola Vuismariensi* (Frankfurt: Joannes Spies, 1591), which is based on the autobiography to the extent that key sentences and phrases are word-for-word copies. (3) Surveys of Wigand's own library, now housed in the Herzog-August Bibliothek (Wolfenbüttel), by Christian August Salig, *Vollständige Historie der Augspurgischen Confession und derselben Apologie* (Halle: Renger, 1730–35) [A bicentennial history of the Augsburg Confession], passim. And (4) modern encyclopedia articles. The changing fortunes of Wigand's reputation can be seen in the three editions of the Herzog encyclopedia. Neudecker characterized Wigand, in 1864, with the words: "Ein unruhiger Kopf und Ultralutheraner, der als ein stets schlagfertiger Polemiker mit leidenschaftlicher Heftigkeit ein rühriges Glied der flacianischen Partei war" (*Real-Encyclopädie für protestantische Theologie und Kirche* [Gotha: Rudolf Besser, 1864], 18:133–36). Julius Wagenmann rewrote the biography for the second edition, in which he began his treatment with: lutherischer Streittheolog, Kirchenhistoriker und Bischof des 16. Jahrhunderts (*Real-Encyclopädie für protestantische Theologie und Kirche*, 2. Aufl. [Leipzig: Hinrichs, 1896], 17:104–10). When Gustav Kawerau revised the Wagenmann article, he shortened the prefatory characterization to: luther. Theolog (*Real-Encyclopädie für protestantische Theologie und Kirche*, 3. Aufl. [Leipzig: Hinrichs, 1908], 21:270–74).

Wigand's education at the University of Wittenberg was notable, as one might expect, for the fact that he heard Martin Luther lecture publicly. Besides the usual academic lights—Philip Melanchthon, Caspar Cruciger, Justus Jonas, Veit Winsheim—in his autobiography he recalled fondly a teacher who did much for his personal development, Johann Marcellus, an undistinguished mathematician who enjoyed excellent relations with the students.

From 1541 to 1544, Wigand taught in the famous St. Lorenz School in Nürnberg, an assignment that he took on the advice of parents and friends. He stayed for three long years, captive to the indiscretion of asking other people's counsel. What he wanted most was to return to Wittenberg to study while Luther was still alive, and he did so in 1544.

In 1545 he reached the magisterial degree. After consulting again with parents and friends, he decided upon further intensive study at Wittenberg and bent mind and body to the challenging task. But it was not to be. In February 1546 Luther died. In summer the Schmalkald League was at war with Emperor Charles V and brought the conflict south to the imperial patrimony in Austria. The following spring Charles V brought the "German War" back north to Saxony.[2] Wigand was forced to abandon his schooling, because, in the words of the old maxim, the Muses had nothing in common with Mars.

It is indicative of Wigand's extraordinary character that he was first called to his own hometown to assist the aged pastor, Martin Seligmann. In autumn of 1546, at age twenty-three, he was ordained by Johann Spangenberg, the Mansfeld superintendent, in the first ordination of an Evangelical in Mansfeld. There he preached, conducted the pastoral care of the parish, and taught dialectics and physics in the gymnasium.

The article by Adolf Brecher, in *Allgemeine Deutsche Biographie* 52 (1897): 452–54, is a cut version of the Wagenmann biography. The articles in *Evangelische Kirchen Lexicon* (Göttingen: Vandenhoeck & Ruprecht, 1959), 3:1816 (unsigned), and in *Die Religion in Geschichte und Gegenwart*, 3. Aufl. (Tübingen: Mohr [Siebeck], 1962), 6:1709 (by Reinhold Jauernig) are undistinguished. The translation of Kawerau's article in the English Schaff-Herzog encyclopedia was severely shortened and incorporated several errors of fact and translation.

The quotation is taken from "Leben D. Joh. Wigandi," pp. 601–02.

2. The term "Schmalkald War" seems to have arisen in the eighteenth century. In Karl Schottenloher's bibliography, *Bibliographie zur deutschen Geschichte im Zeitalter der Glaubensspaltung* (Leipzig: Hiersemann, 1933–), items 41672 to 41693b speak only of the "German War" but 41693c to 41709 mention the "Schmalkald War"—with but two exceptions in the latter group. The contemporary witness called it the "German War" (e.g., *De bello Germanico dialogus* [n.p., 1547]; Lambert Hortensius, *De bello Germanico libri septem* [Basel: Oporinus, 1560]). The greatest compend on the subject was written by Friedrich Hortleder (Frankfurt: Hartmann Palthenius, 1617–18; Gotha: Endter, 1645); the title spoke of the "German War of the Emperor Charles V against the leaders of the Schmalkald League." The difference is not trivial: *Schmalkald* War implies an initiative by the Schmalkald League, a culpable act of aggression; *German* War puts the onus on the emperor and his Spanish troops, an onus that was fully accepted and praised in the imperial court.

He began his writing career with the encouragement of Spangenberg. His *Refutatio* of Michael Helding's catechism was published in Magdeburg in 1550, bringing him to the attention of the Magdeburg resistance to the imperial religious settlement of 1548 (the Augsburg Interim). One of the framers of that religious settlement, Helding (otherwise known as Chorbischoff of Sidon and hence styled *Sidonius*), was the imperially appointed bishop of Merseburg—a formidable opponent indeed for a fledgling theologian.

Only through the intervention of several well placed friends was the popular Wigand allowed to leave the Mansfeld ministerium to serve in Magdeburg. Since Spangenberg's death, Wigand had served—and served well—as the Mansfeld superintendent and represented his ministerium at the Synod of Eisleben in 1552. Now with Wigand's added experience and maturity, the Ascanian prince Wolfgang von Anhalt thought him indispensable for his lands in general and for Mansfeld in particular. But, permission secured, Wigand moved to Magdeburg around Michaelmas, 1553, to become superintendent of the city ministerium of Magdeburg. He was thirty years old.

From the time of his arrival in Magdeburg, he was engaged in almost daily conflict with the cathedral chapter during his seven years' ministry there. A ruinous siege had been conducted for eighteen months, in part because of the archbishop's and chapter's claims, and had lifted shortly after Wigand arrived.[3] When the aged leader of the resistance, City Syndic Levin von Embden, died and no one could fill his shoes as diplomat-politician and lay spiritual leader, Wigand tried to carry out the ideas and programs of the von Embden party, represented by some members of the prestigious Alemann family and the physician Martin Copus (Kopf?). As a result of Wigand's efforts, several canons of the cathedral chapter "converted to the truth of the Gospel and later instituted and conducted their rites and preaching in accord with the Augsburg Confession." But, in the face of steadily weakening political support in the city council and betrayal by former allies, Wigand's position deteriorated by 1560 to the point that his departure was as much a demission from an impossible situation in Magdeburg as it was a call to teach in the University of Jena.

3. The conflict preceded the siege of 1550–51, when Nicolaus Gallus was the superintendent of Magdeburg, and continued long after it. An extended treatment of the earlier phases is in Friedrich Wilhelm Hoffmann, *Geschichte der Stadt Magdeburg*, 2 vols., revised by Gustav Hertel and Friedrich Hülse (Magdeburg: Albert Rathke, 1885), 1:475–569. The heroics of the earlier phases (standing up to the empire, asserting ancient rights and privileges against the archbishop, defying the cathedral chapter, refusing to allow the Mass inside the city) left a rich legacy in German song and story, a theme revived in the middle of the last century in the best-selling work by Wilhelm Raabe, *Unsers Herrgotts Canzlei: Eine Erzählung von Jakob Corbinus* (Braunschweig, 1862, 1st ed., published in scores of editions in the past 120 years). The later phases (1552–66) are reported in unfortunate generalities and summaries by Hoffmann (2:1–32); but the third volume of Salig, *Vollständige Historie*, is full of important detail, written as it was from Wigand's own documents and papers.

In Magdeburg, his major theological work was directed against the Adiaphorists, who believed that the conditions of the Augsburg Interim of 1548 could be met because they involved religious customs or practices that were neither forbidden nor commanded by the clear word of God: matters indifferent or "adiaphoristic" (see chapter 1, pp. 3–5). He made common cause with opponents of the Adiaphorists and their spiritual leader, Philip Melanchthon. He also wrote against the sacramentarians,[4] among whom he included those theologians who had resolved the mystery of the Eucharist with a theology of symbol.

While in Magdeburg Wigand took responsibility for the ongoing organization and writing of the *Magdeburg Centuries* (see chapter 1, pp. 13–14), the monumental ecclesiastical history planned by Matthias Flacius Illyricus and published by Johann Oporinus of Basel from 1559 to 1574. Taking over the project after the first three years of work by Flacius, Wigand, together with his friend and colleague Matthaeus Judex,[5] wrote the *Centuries*

4. The sacramentarian controversy is a complex issue, because it was defined in almost mutually exclusive terms by the two sides, and because the controversy in the north went through two distinct phases.

The controversy concerned eucharistic theology, as defined by Reformed and Lutheran theologians: the Reformed defined the controversy in terms of a doctrine of "real presence" and "sacramental use"; the Lutherans defined the controversy with three criteria (*manducatio oralis, manducatio indignorum* and *unio sacramentalis*—note the offensive term *manducatio* instead of a more refined word, *manducatio* meaning "chewing," or even better in colloquial English, "chomping"). The two sides never did agree on the terms or definitions of the controversy.

The controversy in the north is divided into two phases: the earlier phase that focused on Reformed (i.e., Swiss and Rhinish) theologians and the later phase that focused on the Philippism (i.e., Crypto-Calvinism) of the University of Wittenberg. The critical year was 1574, when there was published in two editions the work of Joachim Curaeus, *Exegesis perspicua* (n.p., 1573 [*sic*]; Leipzig: Ernst Voegelin, 1574) (see the work by Wilhelm Scheffer, [*Inauguratio*]: Inest exegesis perspicua controversiae de sacra coena a. 1574 sine nomine edita [Marburg: Bayroffer, 1853]). Wigand's own work of 1574 is important for its identification of issues raised in the anonymous *Exegesis perspicua*, namely in his *Christliche Erinnerung von der Theologen in Meissen vom Abendmal, jetzt newlich ausgangen* (Königsberg: Johan Daubmanns Erben, 1574), pp. Alv ff., on Curaeus's work, pp. A3r–B2v on the sacramentalism of Melanchthon.

The Reformed doctrine of "real presence" was meant to satisfy the refutation of Romish theology and did not meet the argument of the Lutherans on a meaningful level. The "sacramental use" distinctions were meant to allay fears of arbitrary objectiveness in eucharistic theology. The Lutherans were sublimely uncritical of the objectiveness problem: in fact, they made it as offensive as possible. The three Lutheran criteria were meant to eliminate subjectivity on three levels: the individual or psychological level ("oral chewing" of the body and blood of Christ meant to be supremely offensive); the corporate or social level ("chewing" of the sacramental elements by "the unworthy" involved the body and blood of Christ to the same extent that the "chewing" by "the worthy"—thus, eliminating any predisposition of the eucharistic community); and the lofty christological level (the "sacramental union" preserving the divine/human distinctions, in union, of the two natures of Christ on the level of the body/bread and blood/wine of the eucharist).

5. Judex was a member of Levin von Embden's household in Magdeburg, earlier trained at the gymnasium in Magdeburg and at the University of Wittenberg. His biography appeared appended to the posthumously published *Epistolarum festivalium explicatio* (Eisleben: Andreas Petri, n.d.), pp. 18r–n8v. The work was edited by the second husband of Judex's widow, Andreas Schoppe. One might assume, then, that the biography is that of Judex's beloved Anna, filled with intimate details of family life and relations. The

under the auspices of a small corporation *(collegium)* made up of members of the von Embden political circle, members of the Magdeburg ministerium, and faculty of the gymnasium.

After Easter, 1560, Wigand moved to the University of Jena, called by the dukes Johann Friedrich and Johann Wilhelm to replace Erasmus Sarcerius on the theological faculty. Wigand, accompanied by Judex, rejoined Flacius, who had been there for over two years by this time serving as theological professor and *Obersuperintendent*. The faculty at Jena was attempting to implement the "Gnesio-Lutheran program,"[6] beginning with a deliberate stripping away from Luther's theology of what they considered to be aberrations by Philip Melanchthon and his colleagues (chiefly, but not only, Georg Major), and by Kaspar Schwenckfeld, Andreas Osiander, and the sacramentarians. The Thuringian duke, Johann Friedrich, called upon the Jena theologians to be meticulous and thorough in their efforts and asked the magistracies to be thorough in carrying out any stern judgments that they might be required to render. Wigand taught and carried on church visitations, presupposing and receiving strong political support from the Thuringian courts.

In Wigand's first year at Jena, his lord decided to resolve a major problem between the leaders of the two major contending factions in Jena's theological faculty. Held in the prince's own court, the Weimar Disputation[7] saw Flacius clash with Victorin Strigel, an earlier member of the faculty, with two major results. First, Wigand and Judex as well as Flacius now came into conflict with influential members of the court who were particularly close to Strigel and to Strigel's friends and supporters in Jena, and Chancellor Christian Brück made their life impossible. Unlike Judex and Flacius, who

only modern biography of note is that of Philipp Hedwig Külb in the Ersch-Gruber *Allgemeine Encyclopädie der Wissenschaften und Künste* (Leipzig: J. F. Gleditsch, 1818–89), 2:27:347–49. The work by Thomas Crenius (i.e., Crusius), *Animadversiones philologicae et historicae* (Lugdunum Batavorum: F. Häring, 1696–97), 6:49–74, is simply a transcription of Anna's biography, not a new work.

6. The Gnesio-Lutheran program was founded on the so-called *Confutationsbuch* of 1559, which was published both in German (Jena: Christian Rödinger) and in Latin (Jena: Thomas Rebhardt). In later analyses, this work has been seen as pivotal in the development of the so-called intellectual subjectivism of orthodox Lutheranism (i.e., in Hans Emil Weber, *Reformation, Orthodoxie, und Rationalismus*, 2 vols. [Gütersloh: Gerd Mohn, 1940], 1:2:253–312, passim). The doctrinal consensus was broadly accepted in Thuringia; the most serious issues concerned the ethical and juridical implications of the *Confutationsbuch*.

A major problem in the discussion about Gnesio-Lutheranism in general is that the classic analysts of Protestant theology link Flacianism and Gnesio-Lutheranism. While there may be genetic commonalities, there was also a major distinction between the two in the 1560s, mutual repudiation in the 1570s, and mutual declaration of heresy in the 1580s. I have found no major treatment of the term Gnesio-Lutheran helpful in unraveling this major historic issue.

7. The protocol of the Weimar Disputation was composed by Wigand from the secretarial records, introduced by Simon Musaeus, and (according to unpublished correspondence between Jena and Basel) published by Johann Oporinus—or by a business associate of his. The title of the work begins, *Disputatio de originali peccato et libero arbitrio, inter Matthiam Flacium Illyricum & Victorinum Strigelium publice Vinariae per integram hebdomadam, praesentibus Illustriss. Saxoniae Principibus, Anno 1560, initio mensis Augusti habita* (n.p., 1563).

were banished from Thuringia, Wigand was asked to remain. But considering exile preferable to a bad conscience, Wigand resigned. Second, in the colloquy itself Flacius was pushed by Strigel into a dangerous admission: when applying the distinctions of substance and accidents—a scholastic methodology and an artificial distinction that he abhorred—he said that original sin is of the substance of man. Flacius's statement developed into a major issue, and in the end he was branded a heretic for that formula, which was denounced as Manichaeism or neo-Manichaeism.

From Jena Wigand returned briefly to Magdeburg. There the situation had deteriorated further in his two-year absence. The time of negotiation and debate was over. The new city syndic, Franz Pfeil, successor of Levin von Embden, desiring the lifting of imperial sanctions and access to imperial and Saxon courts, was prepared to readmit the archbishop and cathedral chapter into the city. With readmission came decades' worth of liabilities and indemnities, small cost to some, considered in long-range terms. But with readmission also came the return of the hated Mass within the city walls, a sacrilege that neither Tilemann Hesshus (superintendent and successor to Wigand) nor many of his colleagues could condone. The city syndic, with support from the majority of the city council, had the last word: resisters were banned, including Wigand, Judex, and Hesshus and his supporters.

By Michaelmas of 1562, however, Wigand again had a position, this time as superintendent of Wismar in the duchy of Mecklenburg. He came with the support of the ducal brothers, Johann Albrecht and Ulrich. His first task, he said, would be to eradicate the sacramentarians and Anabaptists of the city. Enjoying the favor of the ducal houses, he was still able to preach and speak prophetically on matters of justice. He treasured his close ties with the University of Rostock, especially with David Chytraeus, Simon Pauli, Conrad Becker, and Simon Musaeus. In 1563, he was promoted to doctor of theology by order of the princes and by acclaim of the theological faculty.

In Wismar, Wigand proved himself a competent leader, establishing Evangelical organizations and institutions, organizing work for joint or collaborative participation, teaching people of all ages at many levels of sophistication, and endearing himself to persons of authority and common people alike without compromising his principles. It was natural, then, for him to accompany the duke or dukes to important meetings as an adviser (for instance, to the Diet of Augsburg in 1566) or to confer closely on important constitutional matters (as with the several Mecklenburg *Ordnungen* of the 1560s).

In 1568 Wigand returned to Jena. He looked upon his second tenure there as completing his seven-year commitment to the university and church of Thuringia. Although he had been allowed a one-year leave of absence from Wismar by the Mecklenburg ducal houses, he was to remain in Jena for a total of five years. Wigand accepted with trepidation this return to Thuringia. The Gnesio-Lutheran program of Thuringia had failed seven years earlier. The

Saxon dukes were trying to set themselves apart from the present elector of Saxony, August (brother and successor of Moritz), and from the Electoral University of Wittenberg. In religion, the *Confutationsbuch* of 1559 had defined Thuringian theology and distinguished it from the elector's Wittenbergian Philippism. In politics, the elector's faithful, consistent pro-imperial stance was countered in Thuringia with a new sense of German federalism. Foreign policy in Thuringia had come under the virtual control of Wilhelm von Grumbach, who forged new alliances that eventually brought Thuringia into a pan-European antiimperial conspiracy. However, just as the religious experiment had failed in application, so also the antiimperial political program came to ruin both for Thuringia and for the duke, Johann Friedrich, and for Grumbach as well. Thuringia was taken by force of arms and put under the elector's garrisons in the spring of 1567. Johann Friedrich, captured on April 15, 1567, died in an Austrian prison almost thirty years later (1595). Grumbach was captured, condemned, and quartered in the public square of Gotha on April 18, 1567. Thus, by 1568, partisans of the Thuringian religious program had been forewarned that Elector August would not stand by idly when challenged and that when he acted, he would act decisively.

Wigand's first official act as superintendent of Jena and professor of theology was to represent Thuringian theology at the Colloquy of Altenburg,[8] opposing the elector's Philippist theologians. Unlike his first residence in Jena, he could now work aggressively and confidently for Gnesio-Lutheranism with the full support of the ducal court. The Altenburg meeting proved beyond a shadow of a doubt that the differences between Philippism and Gnesio-Lutheranism were real.

Thuringia was unable, however, to recover from the "Grumbach Affair." Elector August was encouraged by the emperor to take a direct hand in the government of Ducal Saxony, and in 1573, following the death of Duke Johann Wilhelm, he redivided the lands of the Wettin patrimony, newly enfeoffing many prebends of the Thuringian house and rekindling old grudges in doing so. He appointed Laurentz Lindemann to be his special legate in charge of the duke's public and familial affairs. Wigand and Hesshus were given four days to vacate their university positions and leave Thuringia. Wigand headed immediately for Braunschweig. There, he served as advisor to

---

8. This colloquy lasted from October 20, 1568, to March 9, 1569. Wigand wrote the most important protocol: *Colloquium zu Altenburgk in Meissen* (Jena, 1569). The opposition put out a counter-protocol: *Gantze vnd vnuerfelschete Acta vnd Handlung des Colloqui zwischen den churfürstlichen vnd fürstlichen zu Sachsen Theologen* (Wittenberg, 1570). In the end, the elector August became convinced that his theologians had, in fact, perverted Luther's theology, so that he cleaned house in Wittenberg in 1574, "the darkest period" in the history of the University of Wittenberg, according to Kurt Aland ("Die Leucorea während des 16. Jahrhunderts," *450 Jahre Martin-Luther Universität Halle-Wittenberg,* 3 vols. [Halle-Wittenberg, 1952], 1:180). Each side had to salve the other's sense of outrage at being victimized: the electoral side offered up Melanchthon; the Thuringian side offered up Flacius. In the eventual "peace treaty," the *Formula Concordiae,* both of these men were declared heretics.

Duke Julius of Braunschweig-Lüneburg and enjoyed the company of the renowned superintendent Martin Chemnitz (see chapter 3).

Called to the University of Königsberg in the autumn of 1573, he moved from there two years later to the village of Liebemühl in Pomezania to become bishop of Pomezania. Here, far from the centers of the theological fray, Wigand carried out the common episcopal chores: preaching, lecturing privately, writing dogmatic and polemical works, visiting churches, settling controversies, attending to episcopal financial affairs. He took a leading role in gaining acceptance for the *Book of Concord* in Prussia—in the court and in the churches. He also conducted a long series of colloquies throughout his realm to secure the signatures of clergy to the *Concordia*. And he saw to it on a day-to-day basis that the theology of the University of Königsberg remained consonant with the teachings of the *Book of Concord*.

At Liebemühl he rekindled his lifelong interests in science. He wrote a natural history of the Prussian elk, the first such modern work of its kind. He repaired and remodeled the episcopal gardens. He applied his extraordinary skills in horticulture and botanical taxonomy, providing proven seed of high quality for his people and compiling the most exhaustive systematic botany of herbs and edibles of the region.

Both Wigand and his biographer (and brother-in-law) Conrad Schlüsselburg are silent about what must be considered the sorriest chapter of his life, the controvery with and deposing of Tilemann Hesshus, bishop of Samland.[9] Wigand himself became guilty of episcopal pluralism when he assumed the two sees of Pomezania and Samland. However, though a special commission judged him worthy to be deposed himself, Wigand was supported by the magistrates and lesser officials of Pomezania and Prussia and retained his sees.

Wigand died of kidney failure in the forty-first year of his ministry, the last Lutheran bishop in the eastern German lands.

THEOLOGY   Wigand's theology took shape in three ways. First, he spoke from a confessional orientation that saw divine authority in the catholic creeds, in the Augsburg Confession, and in Luther's catechisms. These confessions were lifelong touchstones of his theology. Second, Wigand became involved in a long succession

9. The two most important studies of this controversy are the documentary history of Christopher Hartknoch, *Preussische Kirchen = Historia* (Frankfurt and Leipzig: Simon Beckenstein, 1686), pp. 463–71, and the more biographical work by Johann Georg Leuckfeld, *Historia Heshusiana* (Quedlinburg and Aschersleben: Ernst Gottlob Struntz, 1716), pp. 129–92. See also Alfred Nicolovius, *Die bischöfliche Würde in Preussens evangelischer Kirche: Ein Beitrag zur Geschichte der evangelischen Kirchenrechts* (Königsberg: August Wilhelm Unzer, 1834), pp. 83ff. Hesshus and Wigand did not go unreconciled into their graves. Toward the end of their lives, Duke Julius of Braunschweig-Lüneburg reconciled the two men, without, however, restoring them to friendship.

of controversies. They forced him to seek answers to questions that were unasked in his confessional tradition. Third, at a young age (his early thirties) he embarked upon a systematic study of the Bible, from first to last syllable, and upon an exhaustive research into all known ecclesiastical history.

The result was a very learned and well-read theologian. He resuscitated long-dormant theological argument from ancient Byzantium in his work on the two natures of Christ. His eucharistic theology was truly a sum of fifteen centuries of Christian thought on the subject. At the same time, he did not treat his topic piecemeal. Time after time, his writings presented a program: a theological program that was consistent with and supportive of life's "most serious and necessary things"—thus betraying the degree to which he was moved by the strangely untheological arguments of utility and necessity. The argument of utility or usefulness *(utilitas)* was mediated by Agricola and Melanchthon from the Ciceronian rhetorical tradition. The argument of necessity ($\dot{\alpha}\nu\dot{\alpha}\gamma\kappa\eta$) was the more metaphysical formulation by Aristotle that was revived in the mid-sixteenth century. The two lines of argumentation were employed frequently by Wigand, and one cannot help but wonder whether he did so because he found these lines of argumentation mightily persuasive—they are patently offensive in modern rhetoric—or because he was employing the expected rhetorical devices of the day. The arguments of utility and necessity were shot through the entire theological program of Wigand, not only in the methodological prolegomena, but also at the level of technical or narrow definition and development. Nevertheless, Wigand's theological program was implemented in university curricula (chiefly, the *Syntagma*), in gymnasia (the catechetical materials), and in the churches (his widely read *postilles*, or sermons and sermon outlines).

Wigand's contribution to theology was assessed in his lifetime in two parts. The first was his own self-analysis and the second, Chytraeus's evaluation of his work on theological method and historical studies upon his promotion to doctor of theology. The two parts did, in fact, land upon the distinctive and lasting contributions of Wigand to the theology of the church. While there may be points of detail that warrant further comment, the perception of the time has proved to be decidedly accurate and persuasive.

In the last section of Wigand's autobiography he listed his writings under nine headings. The first section is a chronological narrative of his life. Between the first and final section are two important paragraphs of self-evaluation (written in the third person, as was the rest of the autobiography).

We know that faithful ministers of God's word have a double charge: to be winsome as teacher and refuter. Thus in this dual role, Wigand labored with whatever strength the Lord God kindly granted him as his public contributions give evidence. He exposed and refuted the several errors of the papists, orally and in writing. Indeed, at first he wrote a booklet against the work of Michael Helding *Sidonius, item* against the catechism of the Jesuits, [i.e., by Canisius]. When the adiaphorists tried to impose their machinations and lies, he with others was opposed on the basis of the divine word, refuting them in writing. He denounced Georg Major's several monstrosities about good works necessary for salvation: he also exposed Major's fallacies, compared to others' simpler mistakes, in several booklets. Certain Antinomian doctrines, that the Law does not concern unbelief in Christ, that is to say, that the Law is not a norm for human activities, he exposed in *Liber de Antinomia* and in another about the third use of the Law. The madness of the Sacramentarians and their blasphemous dogmas he disapproved and refuted, as appear out of the contradictory arguments of the Sacramentarians themselves and from the entire context of Sacramentarianism, and in other books. He responded to the delusions of the Adiaphorists, with bases demonstrated out of God's word as can be seen in his refutations of Anabaptism. Although he experienced many malicious reactions for them, he opposed the Manichaeans, also mad people who contend that the sin of origin is substance. Finally, he exposed and very clearly refuted the Servetians' and Arians' blasphemous dogmas in several books. But concerning these and other struggles, his books are listed after this. His books witness to whatever vision and steadfastness and to how much strength he mustered against these monstrosities. For without long windings, he pointed out the scope of the matter clearly to his readers. He joined arguments with cloudy obscurities when the vice got him, as though he were directing with a pointed finger and shaping pious opinions. But the rages of the adversaries, the warnings, the censures, the rebukes, the lies, the parodies, he bore for God's honor while the Holy Spirit supported his strength. Indeed, he was mindful that God sees everything and will vindicate in his own good time: many illuminating examples of that could be pointed out right here, but they would last too long. In afflictions, he used to say, let man be broken in pieces, let God be glorified.[10]

Wigand saw his distinctive contribution "as teacher and refuter," carrying out the burdens laid upon him as a minister of God's word. While he mentioned the teaching role first, he dwelled longer on his work as a polemicist. Written when he was an aged churchman (somewhere between sixty and sixty-four years old)—perhaps in the heat of his controversy with Hesshus—this autobiographical critique can be viewed as a sad commentary on his own life.

While Wigand's view was accurate, further commentary is required to understand his role as refuter in a larger context. While he wrote his self-evaluation in the early 1580s, he had virtually abandoned the completion of the *Magdeburg Centuries*, particularly Century XVI, overwhelmed by the

---

10. "Das Leben D. Joh. Wigandi," pp. 619ff.

massive amount of material he had gathered throughout his lifetime. Instead of attempting to sum up the whole of the sixteenth century, he proceeded to collect (in the technical sense of *colligere*, that is, "systematize") documents from his immense copybooks. He wrote what we would call historical documentaries. He called all of them *libri polemici*, usually with the subtitle, *integra historia*. In the bibliography of his own works, Wigand listed only four of them: *De Osiandrismo, De Manichaeismo, De Anabaptismo,* and *De Sacramentariismo*. These are, however, fewer than half of his works of this type. In addition, one must count his hefty tomes *De Seruetianismo seu de Antitrinitarijs, De Stancarismo, De Maiorismo, De Synergismo, De Adiaphorismo,* and *De Schwenckfeldianismo*. (These works were not omitted because they were edited in collaboration with other colleagues: two of the four that Wigand listed were also done collaboratively.) They are each very extended studies including protocols of colloquies and contemporary dissertations in their entirety. These rich, full studies have never been adequately mined in modern times. Immersed as he was in the task of compiling and then handing over the results to Schlüsselburg and his colleague (and son-in-law) Andreas Corvinus, Wigand saw himself at the very center of many controversies that he documented. He saw the function of his work in existential, practical terms: documentary evidence for further refutations. He was not able to consider the function of his work in modern terms, that is, as the richest contemporary published documentation of the theological times.

The point can be made another way. One need only review Wigand's autobiobibliography. Of the several sections (*dogmatici, exegetici, polemici, historici, orationes, propositiones ad disputandum propositae, Lehr-Bücher, Leich-Bücher, Streit-Bücher*), the controversial literature was surely his most voluminous. Even the dogmatic, exegetic, and historic books had an essentially contradictory fundament. As Wigand reviews his lifework, then, small wonder that he saw his own historic significance most clearly as teacher and polemicist, but chiefly as polemicist.

The sad light in which Wigand cast his own biography was reflected saddest of all in two conflicts with two former colleagues, when Wigand entered the lists against Flacius and against Hesshus.

Wigand did not mention his disagreement with Flacius—or even Flacius's name—in the autobiography. And yet Wigand was one of the leading polemicists against Flacius among the later Gnesio-Lutherans. Wilhelm Preger, in his generally accepted definitive biography of Flacius, called it "betrayal,"[11] but that does not account for Wigand's purposes.

---

11. *Matthias Flacius Illyricus und seine Zeit* (Erlangen: Theodor Bläsing, 1859–61), 2:318ff. Flacius had asserted, at the Weimar Colloquy, that original sin was a substance, or was of the substance of man. Colleagues implored that he not use such an expression, because of the logical and methodological snares that he had laid for himself—and he did desist for several years. Unique among his peers, Flacius did *not* have the rigorous training in rhetoric and dialectics, the then-modern Melanchthonian grammar and trivial schooling. Heedless to critics, however, Flacius persisted in his strange assertions and eventually had to be

Rather, it could be argued, Wigand was caught in webs of theological method of his very own spinning, as noted below. The point is neither tendentious nor obscurantist. The standard German encyclopedias, literary handbooks, and national biographies have stressed Wigand's seemingly feckless contentiousness, without balancing that view—Wigand's own view of himself—with a more contextual examination of his contribution to the theology of the church and to the study of history. In this instance, the key to Wigand's opposition to Flacius was the fact that Flacius had recklessly tripped over a scholastic land mine. In the beginning, Flacius had intended to do no more than emphasize human, natural depravity in the strongest possible language. One might say that he wanted to *substantiate* the seriousness of original sin or that he wanted people to *realize* its gravity. But he chose terms that had technical, theological definition, so that his expressions went beyond emphasizing a serious point, to an inexcusable blunder in the technical, scholastic terminology of theology.

Nor, for that matter, did Wigand mention his role in the demission of his old colleague and battle-scarred friend, Tilemann Hesshus. Four pastors from the diocese of Samland, where Hesshus served as bishop, brought charges against their prelate for the following formulation. Hesshus had said that one can go beyond the point of saying that the man Christ *in concreto* is worthy of adoration (by virtue of the communication of attributes), to the point that the humanity of Christ *in abstracto* is likewise worthy of such adoration. While Hesshus was attempting little more than to show how radically anti-Calvinist he could be, he had left himself open to sharp criticism. The critique became part of the general palace intrigues of the Kneiphof, the court-city of Königsberg. Charges of false doctrine were brought against Hesshus, and he was cited to appear before a ducal tribunal, over which the court had persuaded Wigand to preside (January 16, 1577). Hesshus refused to submit his position in writing; still worse, he refused to submit to the authority of the tribunal and of Wigand as the presiding officer of the tribunal. For his refusal, he was unceremoniously dismissed from his position by the duke, thereby leaving vacant the bishopric of Samland. The court turned to Wigand to assume responsibility for the diocese of Samland; when Wigand did so, he became guilty of pluralism. It was assumed and

answered by his colleagues. Tilemann Hesshus, *Epistola ad M. Matthiam Flacium Illyricum de controuersia An peccatum Originis sit substantia* (Jena: Christian Rhodius, 1570), was brutal, heaping on scorn, ridicule, opprobrium, and insult. Wigand met Flacius's assertions with a string of tracts and tomes—nine of them between 1570 and 1573, plus three major, later works (the longest and most definitive of them *De Manichaeismo renovato* [Leipzig: Henning Grossius, 1587], posthumously published, as edited from Wigand's papers by Andreas Corvinus). In the most popular, earlier tracts (two of them in German), he did not mention Flacius by name, he sought to persuade rather than confront and confound, and he refrained from ridicule and the usual bombast. Flacius's most loyal defender, the brilliant poet-theologian-medievalist Cyriacus Spangenberg, painted the anti-Flacians with a rather monochrome palette in song, rhyme, tract, and tome—a portrayal that was borrowed whole by Preger.

asserted by many that Wigand had conspired with the four pastors who brought charges against Hesshus, namely, Benedict Morgenstern, Johann Weidmann (or Wedemann), Hieronymus Mörlin, and Conrad Schlüsselburg: Morgenstern, an amateur botanical taxonomist and horticulturist like Wigand, was a close personal friend of the Pomezanian bishop; Weidmann was a former student and assistant; Mörlin, the son of Wigand's colleague in Jena, was a lifelong family friend and former student; and Schlüsselburg was Wigand's brother-in-law (later also his biographer). The case was reviewed by a panel of theologians when Hesshus was being considered for the position of theological professor at the new University of Helmstedt. In that review, Wigand's participation in the so-called *Schisma Prutencia* cost him several friendships: with Jakob Andreae, Martin Chemnitz, Nicolaus Selnecker, Andreas Musculus, and Timotheus Kirchner (who became Hesshus's staunchest defender in Braunschweig-Wolfenbüttel). Although Duke Julius of Braunschweig-Lüneburg effected something of a reconciliation later on, the damage had been done and the wounds could not be healed. As Wigand reviewed the ruins of his reputation and the grief of the dioceses of Samland and Pomezania at the end of his life, he could very well have seen his chief significance as that of the reviled polemicist throughout his career—a distortion then and a distortion now.

Wigand was promoted to doctor of theology in a colorful ceremony at the University of Rostock on July 12, 1563. It was one of the few promotion ceremonies of the day for which the complete text and description were recorded and published—in this case, in connection with Chytraeus's oration on the death of Wigand's predecessor, the Wismar superintendent Johann Freder.[12]

In the ceremony itself, the theological faculty and its head, Simon Pauli, had to cite the cause: the bases for Wigand's eligibility to be a doctor of theology were his theological method and his ecclesiastical history.

As the term was used by Wigand and his contemporaries, *methodus* had a twofold meaning. Just as the word *politeia* could mean both the state in an abstract sense *and* the constitution or theory of a particular state, so also

12. The full title of this extremely rare work is: *Oratio de vita Iohannis Frederi Senioris, Superintendentis ecclesiae VVismariensis. habita a Davide Chytraeo. Cum Gradus Doctoris Theologiae, Reuerendo & cl. viro, D. Iohanni VVigando, Frederi in eiusdem ecclesiae inspectione successori, publice decerneretur: die 12. Iulij, Anno M.D. LXIII.* (Rostock: August Freber, 1591), signed A-D[8]. The complete text and rubrics are given for the entire ceremony.

A year later, as the same group of friends and colleagues gathered in Rostock to honor and to promote Matthaeus Judex, friend and companion and co-worker of Wigand, the young Judex fell ill and suddenly died. Instead of a festive promotion ceremony, the friends gathered in solemn memorial and prayer for their beloved Matthaeus. Hieronymus Mentzel, superintendent in Mansfeld, wrote a poem to comfort his predecessor in Mansfeld and longtime friend, Wigand; and Christopher Irenaeus composed verses, saying that dear Matthaeus had experienced the ultimate promotion, God's *doctorandum (Luctus et testimonia ecclesiae quae est in comitatu Mansfeldensi de obitu reuerendi viri D. Matthaei Iudicis* [Eisleben, 1565]).

methodus could mean both the technique or rationale for a structured or systematic theology *and* the specific systematic dogmatic theology itself.

Pauli's reference was doubtless to the dual *Syntagma*, which were—according to Otto Ritschl[13]—the starting point for orthodox Lutheran dogmatic theology. This Wigand-Judex *corpus doctrinae* (see above, p. 22) treated the *loci dogmatici*, the biblical dogmatic commonplaces, but with technical philological refinement and hermeneutical principles that marked their efforts as the very first in a tradition that was to last for over three centuries.

The influence of the *Syntagma* was very widespread. It was reproduced in toto frequently by the publisher, Johann Oporinus of Basel, and was reorganized into at least eight other works in complete form (that is, a complete theological system) and into over twenty other works in the form of individual articles of doctrinal theology. Wigand and Judex joined systematic theology and catechetics, to bring the entire body of theological dogma into every school, wherever they were involved with ministeria and ministry: in Magdeburg, in Jena (and hence in all of Thuringia), in Wismar (and thereby in all of Mecklenburg); later also Wigand alone in Pomezania and Samland (and thus in all of Evangelical East Prussia).

A brief exposition on the technique or rationale of theological method was published in the dedication of *Syntagma novi Testamenti*, offered to the councilors and magistrates of Lübeck, Hamburg, and Lüneburg, and is paraphrased here. Wigand and Judex taught that method is necessary for teaching and learning, specifically, that it is the best rationale for explaining, perceiving, and experiencing very serious and necessary matters according to chapters and divisions which the rationale itself, or the light of man, dictates. This organization of knowledge is not accidental: it is the boundless gift of God. As the image of God remains, the light in man shines; in the natural state, there are only dense shadows and darkness. The method is appropriate not only in philosophy, but also in theology: witness David's psalms, St. Paul's letters. The proper application of method can be seen when other artists' work is compared with the masterful technique of Dürer or Lucas [Cranach]. The many features and members—as in the human body—have determinable functions: the rationale follows the function. The difference between philosophy and theology arises because philosophy has its origins in first principles and in proofs, while theology arises from the revealed word of God.

A methodology can be developed in this [sixteenth] century, the authors wrote, more readily than previously because by God's mercy the Gospel's teaching shines more purely than earlier. The purposes for composing a method of the New Testament were: (1) that the pious may have a basic

---

13. *Dogmengeschichte der Protestantismus*, 4 vols. (incomplete) (Leipzig: Hinrichs, 1908–27), 1:133. He pointed out the essential differences between Melanchthon's and Wigand's *loci*.

systematic theology; (2) that a complete or total method be based on Christ's and the Apostles' very words; (3) that there may be a standard or norm for judging all serious matters for all times; (4) that the explanations or expositions of the fathers may be measured and judged; (5) that the argument of antiquity (à la Tertullian) could be truly tested, so that the doctrinal corruptions, profanations of the sacramentarians, idolatry, and superstitious rites "with their golden pallium of antiquity" could be rejected out of hand and refuted. The *Syntagma* had, in addition, the character and role of a confession—and it did, in fact, become Wigand's own deathbed confession of faith.

The chapters or divisions by which very serious or very necessary matters were structured were to be found in a large, logical framework. It was, then, a "commonplaces," or *loci*, methodology.[14] Wigand very rarely referred to the chapters as *loci*, perhaps because of the close association of the technique with Melanchthon and the arts faculty of the University of Wittenberg. He usually referred to them as *capita*. The commonplaces or *loci* or *capita* were a catalogue of terms, arranged scientifically—what the modern computer indexer would call a controlled vocabulary, the librarian would call subject headings, or the botanist would call taxonomical names.

The commonplaces of the *Syntagma* were none other than the very same commonplaces—and full text—of the *Ecclesiastical History*, the *Magdeburg Centuries*. That was the case because the *Syntagma novi Testamenti* was the fourth *caput* of the two halves of the first century. Wigand and Judex were fully aware of the significance of their composition when they completed the fair copy of the work, as they wrote to their publisher, Oporinus, on June 10, 1558, that he should publish *capitulo 4.* in octavo, in cursive type—which he did. To see the significance of the commonplaces applied to theology and church history, let us turn to the *Magdeburg Centuries*.

The ecclesiastical history project, proposed by Flacius to a friend and former student, the courtier of Vienna, Caspar von Nidbruck, in 1552 and 1553, resulted in two major works: the *Catalogus testium veritatis* and the *Ecclesiastica historia*, commonly known as the *Magdeburg Centuries*.[15] The *Catalogus*, originally planned and proposed by Flacius, was compiled and

14. The commonplaces methodology is the development and application of a structure of terms. It has nothing to do with the research into literary themes and genres, the key terms being *topoi* and *loci*, as debated in the fifth decade of this century at the University of Göttingen; see the work of Ernst Robert Curtius—in English in Willard R. Trask's translation, *European Literature and the Latin Middle Ages* (New York: Harper and Row, 1952), chap. 5.

15. Few compliments could surpass that of Adolf von Harnack: Die protestantische Historiographie ist durch das Interim veranlasst worden, und Flacius ist der Vater (*Lehrbuch der Dogmengeschichte* Freiburg and Leipzig: Mohr [Siebeck], 1:28, n. 2). The most reliable recent research on the *Magdeburg Centuries* is that of Heinz Scheible, *Die Entstehung* der Magdeburger Zenturien, Schriften des Vereins für Reformationsgeschichte, no. 183, Jahrgang 72 (Gütersloh: Mohn, 1966). See also the dissertation by Ronald E. Diener, "The Magdeburg Centuries: A Bibliothecal and Historiographical Analysis," Harvard University Divinity School, Th.D., 1979.

brought to fair copy by Flacius's colleague-secretary, Marx Wagner, and appeared in many editions, playing an important role in Lutheran historical catholicity. The *Magdeburg Centuries*, on the other hand, required much more organization and administration than Flacius could apply, and he turned over his initial work to a small corporation in Magdeburg to handle funds, maintain a staff, and approve a methodology. The critical meetings on methodology took place in February 1556, resulting in the rejection of the heavily biographical/anecdotal approach, as well as the essentially political or ecclesio-political approach. Gottschalk Praetorius, the original secretary of the corporation who had proposed the biographical/anecdotal historiography, resigned in high dudgeon, changing his address (from Magdeburg to Frankfurt an der Oder), his name (from Gottschalk to Abdias), and his theology (from Gnesio-Lutheran to Philippist)—he was to become later an outspoken critic of the *centuriatores*. Praetorius's place was taken—until autumn 1560— by Basilius Faber[16] and after 1560 by Judex, who assumed both the secretarial duties and the responsibility for the first draft of the history in its successive volumes.

Other approaches were rejected in favor of a commonplaces technique. Church history was divided into sixteen *capita*—slightly adjusted after the first two centuries. Each *caput* was subdivided into as many *loci* as seemed appropriate to the subject matter. All known and reliable available historical writings and documents were read and excerpted, either by paid staff of the project or by the friends and colleagues of the centuriators—as they liked to call themselves. To facilitate the collecting of the excerpts into copybooks of manageable size, a span of time was determined, arbitrary in length so as not to impose an artificial periodization: centuries. (Hence the popular name, *Magdeburg Centuries*.) The copying and recopying of citations followed the organization and structure of the sixteen *capita* with subheadings. Some errors in transcription occurred, but there was surprisingly little wholesale text corruption. (The irony of it all, of course, is that the thousands, the tens of thousands, of pages of copybooks could have been avoided if the readers had put their excerpts on slips or cards, that is, unit records.) The longest *caput* was the fourth, *De doctrina*. This fourth chapter of the first century—the biblical witness—was the *Syntagma novi Testamenti*. Later, Judex drafted, and Wigand with Judex revised the *Syntagma veteris Testamenti*—completed when they were in Wismar together. Before his death, Judex also translated into German the first four centuries and both volumes of the *Syntagma*.

Ecclesiastica historia remains incomplete: the first century was first published in 1559 (1560, reissued with corrections; 1562, again reissued

16. Faber went on to become a schoolmaster and lexicographer, producing the magnificent *Thesaurus eruditionis scholastici* (Leipzig, 1571, 1st ed.). I have tabulated eighteen editions of this work that appeared with the proper title and credits. It was frequently pirated and retitled. The citations in Faber's work went on to become the basis for the Freund Latin/German dictionary, which in turn was translated to form the basis for the Latin/English dictionary of Andrews, Lewis, and Short.

with further corrections; 1564, corrected fully in the text) and the last volume—the thirteenth century—appeared in published form in 1574. Between 1559 and 1574 the volumes were issued—usually bound in seven tomes. In terms of sheer volume, most of the published text was produced when Judex and Wigand were resident in Wismar, leading the Mecklenburg church historian Daniel Springinsguth to suggest that the work be renamed the "Wismar Centuries."

The *Magdeburg Centuries* was the first comprehensive ecclesiastical history "from Christ to the present time" since Eusebius of Caesarea (ca. 263–399?). They opened a new age, a new style, and a daring touchstone of historical scholarship. Scores of histories were written with techniques and materials borrowed from the *Magdeburg Centuries*, of which one of the last—and perhaps most important—was Gottfried Arnold's *Unparteyische Kirchen- und Ketzer-Historie* (Frankfurt, 1699–1702; Schaffhausen, 1710). The refutations by Catholics—chiefly those of Caesar Baronius and Robert Bellarmine—opened a new era in historical studies for the Catholic Church. The *Syntagma*, whether the fourth chapter of the *Magdeburg Centuries* or a separate publication, marks the beginnings of modern *Dogmengeschichte*. The University of Rostock appropriately cited Wigand for his work on method and on ecclesiastical history.

Assessing Wigand's theology and his contribution to the church's teaching ministry is rendered very difficult because of the length, breadth, and scope of his published works. A survey of his copybooks shows that his published works represent but a fraction of his complete writings, particularly those copybooks to be found today in the Herzog-August Bibliothek's *codices extravagantes*. His sense of history in general and especially his sense of his own personal historic role and responsibility combined and led him to document his life and work with amazing completeness and precision. One can mark development from month to month and year to year for long periods of his life.

His was an objectification of theology, furnished with a systematic structure, explained by a known and respected and scientific technique. It was a technique that Wigand had applied successfully to natural history, horticulture, systematic botany (i.e., taxonomy), and chronology (calendar reform). Wigand—with Judex—was the key figure in the development of Lutheran scholasticism or Lutheran orthodoxy, if that development can be said to spring from a commonplaces-biblical methodology. His life revolved around pursuing his theological inquiries and letting the results lead him wherever necessary. Rather than to assume that Wigand "used" theology to accomplish a goal or aim, perhaps one understands him best by thinking of him as "used" by the results of his methodology. That is, his personal tragedies, triumphs, and relationships were the result of his acting out his theological conclusions. The tragedies occurred, at least in part, because life is not as coherent and as systematic as scientific methodology demands.

At the same time, there is no undervaluing the quality and compass of his work. Hans Emil Weber, the renowned historian of sixteenth- and seventeenth-century theology, surveyed all the published systematic theologies he could find in a lifetime, and he attempted to summarize his lifework in *Reformation, Orthodoxie und Rationalismus* (Gütersloh, 1940), in which, next to Luther and Melanchthon, Wigand is the most frequently cited author.

ROLE IN THE CHURCH   With the promulgation of the *Book of Concord* (see also chapters 3 and 4), the direction of the Lutherans was very clear. They decided against a church that would conform to the compromises of the imperial religious settlement of 1548, the Augsburg Interim, thereby readmitting the bishops and chapters to those areas of Protestant Germany whence they had been previously displaced. On the other hand, the Peace of Augsburg of 1555 that allowed the princes the right to determine the ecclesiastical establishment in their lands also opened the door to grave abuses, especially by those princes whose policies were controlled solely or chiefly by their courts and universities. Not that there was any single solution, any simple or quick fix, to the problem of the church's institutionalization in the second half of the sixteenth century. By trial and error, churchmen tried to forge a wholesome established church. Wigand was involved in the sifting of options as superintendent, as superintendent-professor, as *Professor theologiae primarius*, and finally as bishop.

By the end of the 1580s, the German princes had succeeded almost everywhere in subjecting the princely established church to consistories, which were mixed bodies of clergy, jurists, and nobles who sat in judgment in matters of case-law (for example, marriage, broken oaths, etc.), in clergy discipline (such as drunkenness, promiscuity, false doctrine), and in appeals to clergy-imposed discipline (for example, the ban or acts of repentance). Wigand suffered much at the hand of such consistories, and he opposed them several times in his career. He was the last Evangelical bishop of that age in Gemany; on his death in 1587, the office of bishop of Pomezania and Samland was replaced by a ducal consistory. The powers of the consistory came into conflict with the prerogatives of superintendents and bishops:[17] in Thuringia

17. On one level, one might say that the difference between *superintendent* and *bishop* is simply etymological; superintendent from the Latin and bishop from the Greek—meaning approximately the same thing, "overseer." On another level, there is a historic context and a historic usage to contend with. The dioceses, episcopal ceremonies and courts, and bishop's prebends were retained in parts of Scandinavia and Prussia; the superintendent (the terms superattendent, deacon, senior, metropolitan, prior being used in some areas to mean the equivalent of superintendent) replaced the historic episcopacy in most places where the Evangelicals found the situation to be unreformable. The superintendents were generally of two types: those in free cities and those in principalities. Those in free cities came into conflict with the

Wigand's resignation was brought about in part because of the conflict of a superintendent's discipline of people favored by the court; in Rostock the city's prerogatives came into conflict with the dukes' courts and consistories over matters of appointment and enfoeffment. Wigand attempted to keep the courtiers and jurists out of church discipline, because this discipline could—and did—provide yet another means of exacting taxes and meting out punishments. Meanwhile, at a loss for acceptable canonical procedures, the law experts were concerned about legal process and about the appeal of unjust punishment, rather than about applications of the principles of equity and—what Wigand would call—the practice of true theology, which he would define as "discerning the cross."[18]

The work of the superintendent and bishop included regular visitation of parishes. The visitation procedure involved depositions of evidence in absentia and protocols of oral testimony. The work of pastors and teachers was regularly monitored and evaluated. The superintendent and the clergy responsible to him eventually worked out common sets of expectations. Within weeks of his arrival in Wismar, for example, Wigand presented his expectations and responsibilities, and he asked the clergy to subscribe. The visitation was a formal evaluation at which mutual goals could be reviewed. Time after time, in Thuringia, in Mecklenburg, and in Pomezania, Wigand was hailed as a spiritual father and as an honest, forthright visitor. Even when it was pointed out by a specially appointed commission that Wigand had treated Hesshus shabbily in the Samland affair, and when it was proposed that Wigand be forced from office, the lesser magistrates and townspeople rallied to his side and protested against the commission on Wigand's behalf. He was, to be sure, a strict disciplinarian in the spirit of his age; but he was also honest and his expectations were known, never capricious, always treating the seriousness of the offense, never respecting the person or office.

In the end, however, the extraordinary fact about Wigand's ministry and churchmanship was the man's ability to deal successfully with the church on many levels, in many roles. As professor, he brought his pastoral experience into the classroom and prepared parsons. One need only review the prop-

---

city councils—occasionally with the city ministeria, their charges. Those in principalities came into conflict with the prince's ecclesiastical consistoria. In both instances, the lifetime term of appointment and the final authority to "bind and loose" were severely compromised. Eventually the consistories overwhelmed the real authority of both superintendents and Prussian bishops (Wigand was the last Reformation-age Prussian bishop); the consistories being a mixed body of clergy, burghers, and nobles or of clergy and nobles. The Reformation inherited seriepiscopal duties and had to accommodate somehow: once the bishops were gone, new ways had to be found to adjudicate marriage law (degrees of consanguinity, dissolution of marriage, divorce, incest, sodomy, bestiality, etc.), certain classes of sumptuary law, classic forms of "church discipline" (the agreed minimal requirement of observance, such as annual confession and attendance at the three highest Eucharists of the church calendar), and clergy discipline.

18. *Syntagma veteris Testamenti* (Basel:Johann Oporinus, 1565), p. 1405.

ositions for public disputation from Jena, Rostock, and Königsberg that Wigand wrote for promotions: on penance, on the word of God, on God, on man, on creation, on good and evil angels, and so forth. At first glance, these topics might appear to be heady, ivory-tower reductionisms and abstractions. But Wigand applied such topics to the concrete situations of parish life, full of wisdom and experience. On the other hand, he brought a rigorously thorough knowledge and understanding of theology to the churches he served. His interest in gymnasia, his institution of long-term catechetical programs (some lasting into the early twentieth century), his lectures and disputations in the nonuniversity cities of Magdeburg and Wismar, all bear witness to his skill in bringing theology to the people of the church.

3
MARTIN Chemnitz
1522–1586
FRED KRAMER

LIFE

Martin Chemnitz was born November 9, 1522, in the little town of Treuenbrietzen north of Wittenberg.[1] His father, Paul, was a wool merchant. His mother was Euphemia Koldeborn of Jüterbog. At home Martin appears to have lacked the love that a child would ordinarily find in his own family. The lack was partially filled by Laurentius Barthold, the local schoolmaster, who sensed in the boy superior gifts that would one day flower into genius. When Chemnitz was eleven years old, however, his father died, and Martin's older brother Matthew determined to apprentice him in the wool business. Barthold saved the situation by persuading Martin's mother to send him to study Latin in Wittenberg. There Martin preferred to see and hear the illustrious men of Wittenberg, especially Martin Luther. When Chemnitz's mother discovered that he was not learning his grammar, he was sent home to the local school. After two years, Martin was apprenticed in the wool trade, for which he had no liking and in which he did poor work.

Martin's study at Wittenberg had not been as unfruitful as his teacher had reported. The boy was found reading with great pleasure the elegant Latin speeches of the great Italian humanist Lorenzo Valla and he even translated the book of Jesus Sirach from German into Latin. Meanwhile he prayed that his mother would send him back to school. This was finally accomplished when learned friends of his mother pleaded on behalf of the boy and promised to give him aid. Martin was then sent to school at Magdeburg, where he studied for three years. Among other things, he studied logic, astronomy, and Greek.

After completing his studies at Magdeburg, Martin wanted to attend a university, but his mother and brother were unwilling to give him any money for this purpose. With the aid of the rector of the Magdeburg school, Martin secured a position as assistant teacher at the school in Calbe. With the money he saved during his first year of teaching he entered the University of

1. The biographical data in the following chapter are based on Chemnitz's autobiography, an English translation of which, prepared by Augustus L. Graebner, is found in *Theological Quarterly* 3 (Oct. 1899): 472–87.

Frankfurt on the Oder where, after only one year, he found himself again without funds. He turned again to teaching and became schoolmaster at Writzen on the Oder. The town needed someone to collect fish taxes, and Chemnitz applied for and secured the position. With two incomes he could follow one of his heart's desires, to purchase books by famous authors. These he read diligently while taking care of two jobs.

After a year and a half, in 1545, much against the urging of his brother, Chemnitz went to Wittenberg to study under Philip Melanchthon. He studied in particular the classical Greek authors and mathematics, which at that time included astrology. More importantly, he heard Luther preach and lecture. He was not, however, at this time studying theology; Melanchthon urged him to continue in astrology. He learned to prepare calendars and set up horoscopes, a skill that later was to bring him into favor with a princely patron and provide welcome funds.

Melanchthon wanted Chemnitz to earn the degree of magister, which would enable him to teach on a higher level. But in 1546, the Schmalkald War broke out, temporarily disrupting the University of Wittenberg. With a relative, George Sabinus, Chemnitz journeyed to Königsberg, where Duke Albrecht of Prussia had recently founded a university. There he attained the coveted master's degree in 1548.

Meanwhile he had come to the favorable attention of Duke Albrecht, who needed someone to prepare calendars and horoscopes.[2] Since Chemnitz had the necessary training, he got the position, which paid well. Before long, however, the perceptive Chemnitz realized that astrology rested on weak foundations and turned to his real life's work, theology. In 1549 Chemnitz became fascinated with the study of the Church Fathers and with the theology of Martin Luther, whose writings he studied diligently. About this time Duke Albrecht needed a librarian for the excellent ducal library.[3] Because of Chemnitz's great usefulness already as astrologer for the duke's family, Chemnitz was appointed ducal librarian, a post which allowed him to increase his careful studies of theology.

Chemnitz's own plan of studies took him first to all the books of Scripture, which he read in order in all the available versions. His quotations from Scripture in later theological writings show a thorough knowledge of the Latin Vulgate and of the New Testament in Greek and a high degree of mastery of the available texts.[4] The study of Hebrew he undertook only later,

2.   For a description of the respect astrology enjoyed in the learned and the political world at that time see C. G. H. Lentz, *Martin Chemnitz* (Gotha: Friedrich Andreas Perthes, 1866), pp. 48ff.

3.   Eduard Preuss, *Vita Martini Chemnicii*, appended to the Berlin edition of Chemnitz's *Examen Concilii Tridentini* (Berlin: Gustav Schlawitz., 1861). Page 926 describes the library as "quae optimis quibusque libris instructissima erat."

4.   Chemnitz in all probability used the so-called *textus receptus*, based on Byzantine manusipts, which alone were available to Protestants at the time of the Reformation. The painstaking textual criticism, which was to give the church the excellent New Testament text which we enjoy today, was then still two hundred years in the future.

when he was thirty-four years of age. In reading the works of the Church Fathers Chemnitz also proceeded carefully and systematically, beginning with the most ancient and proceeding to the more recent, taking copious notes. After he had completed the reading of the ancient fathers, Chemnitz proceeded to the theological writings of his own time, particularly those of the reformers, who showed not only their beliefs and teachings but also the foundations for them in Scripture and the earlier Church Fathers. This concentrated reading and study occupied him for three years.

While at Königsberg, Chemnitz formed a lasting friendship with a local pastor, the fiery Joachim Mörlin, at that time preacher at the cathedral church at Königsberg. The two men were of very dissimilar temperaments. Mörlin was quick to judge and had a tendency to violence in controversy. Chemnitz was more quiet, preferring to think things through and to speak with moderation when he had reached a conclusion.

In the year 1550 at Königsberg, at the direction of Duke Albrecht, Chemnitz publicly debated with Andreas Osiander, a theologian who had taught a doctrine of justification that appeared to many Lutherans to be a departure from the teachings of Luther.[5] Osiander taught that the righteousness that justifies the sinner is the essential righteousness of Christ who dwells in the believer. Chemnitz, whose massive learning in theology was beginning to be recognized, pressed Osiander so sharply that he all but lost the affection of the duke, who thought highly of Osiander at this time. The young librarian would undoubtedly have been dismissed from his position if the Duke had not needed his services as calendar maker and astrologer.

Osiander himself then resorted to such violent language against Chemnitz's theological position that Mörlin, also inclined to intemperate language in controversy, violently attacked Osiander from the pulpit. For this Duke Albrecht dismissed Mörlin and ordered him out of the country. Chemnitz, though he was not without a sense of gratitude toward the duke, was not willing to remain after the exile of his friend Mörlin. Chemnitz's separation from the duke seems to have been amicable, for Albrecht gave him a parting gift of 200 thalers, and stipulated that Chemnitz should annually describe for him a number of movements of the stars.

Chemnitz journeyed to Wittenberg, where he attended the theological lectures of Philip Melanchthon, with whom he had maintained cordial relations. In fact Melanchthon, sensing the extensive and solid theological learning that Chemnitz had acquired during his years of study in the ducal library at Königsberg, urged him to lecture on his own (Melanchthon's) *Loci communes*. Chemnitz began his lectures at the University of Wittenberg in 1554. So great was the acclaim with which these lectures were received that it became necessary to assign him a large auditorium.

5.   A thorough review of the teaching of Osiander on justification, with pertinent quotations from Osiander's works, is found in Reinhold Seeberg, *Textbook of the History of Doctrines*, trans. H. E. Hay (Grand Rapids, Michigan: Baker Book House, 1964), vol. 2, pp. 369ff.

Meanwhile events were taking place elsewhere that were to affect the career of Chemnitz for the rest of his life. His friend Mörlin, who had become ecclesiastical superintendent[6] at Braunschweig, needed a coadjutor or assistant. His choice fell on Martin Chemnitz. Members of the theological faculty of Wittenberg, particularly Melanchthon, tried hard to keep the popular young theologian. But Chemnitz, drawn in part by the importance of the position offered to him, in part by his friendship for Mörlin, decided to follow the call to Braunschweig. Students and faculty bade him farewell with every indication of esteem, and Johann Bugenhagen ordained him without the usual previous examination.[7]

At Braunschweig Chemnitz's work included the duty to preach. Those who heard his first sermons reported that he was not an outstanding preacher. However, he quickly developed skills in this area. His sermons were short, simple, clear, instructive, and stressed essentials.

Meanwhile the sentiments of Duke Albrecht toward Mörlin and Chemnitz were undergoing a change. Some thirteen years after Mörlin had been exiled, Duke Albrecht wrote to him and asked him to return to Königsberg to help quell the disturbances that were still raging over Osiander's view of justification. Without at once accepting this invitation, Mörlin and Chemnitz journeyed to Königsberg and worked out an agreement to the effect that a new confession was not necessary, but that the churches in Prussia should abide by the Augsburg Confession, its *Apologia* and the Schmalkald Articles as these were explained in Luther's own writings. After this agreement had been made, the two men returned to Braunschweig, having promised that they would return to their former positions at Königsberg provided they could get a peaceful dismissal from the city council at Braunschweig. After considerable debate, the council agreed that Mörlin might accept the call to Königsberg provided that Chemnitz remain at Braunschweig and assume the office of superintendent.[8]

Before Chemnitz accepted the office of superintendent, he drew up in German five articles for the pastors in which he showed how unity in doctrine and brotherly harmony was to be fostered in the churches under his care. One of the stipulations was that all the pastors should assemble one day every two weeks under the leadership of the superintendent to discuss Christian doctrine and church discipline.[9] In addition to the articles for the pastors, he drew up six articles for the city council[10] in which he stipulated that the council should not interfere with the teaching and discipline that the pastors exercised by virtue of their office. However, he expressly granted the council the right, in case it believed the pastors were not performing their office in the right way,

6. The superintendent was the Lutheran counterpart of the Roman Catholic bishop.

7. So reported by Chemnitz himself, "Autobiography," p. 485.

8. Ibid., vol. 4, pp. 118–22.

9. Ibid., p. 122.

10. These articles are quoted in their entirety, ibid., pp. 126ff.

to speak to them about it. He specified further that the council should not call any pastor, nor deprive any pastor of his office, without the consent of the college of pastors and of the superintendent. Finally he stipulated that, in view of the fact that Christian schools belong to the Christian church, the engaging of teachers and the supervision of the schools should remain in the hands of the pastors and the superintendent. These articles were a masterly effort to distinguish clearly between the duties of the clergy on the one hand and the rights and duties of the civil government on the other in a situation where church and state were inseparably intertwined.

Chemnitz's strong convictions regarding the relationship of church and prince later embroiled him in a dispute with Duke Julius of Braunschweig-Wolfenbüttel, the principality in which the town of Braunschweig lay. Though the two had worked closely for some years following Julius's accession and the conversion of his duchy to Lutheranism in 1568, and though Julius had expended a great deal of energy and money in promoting Chemnitz's activities in the composition of the Formula of Concord in the mid-1570s, they broke decisively in 1578. In an effort to extend the power and holdings of his family, Julius had his son, Heinrich Julius, consecrated bishop of Halberstadt according to Roman Catholic rites. He had no intention of permitting his son to become Roman Catholic but simply wanted to insure his legal control of the diocese. Chemnitz protested so strongly against this compromise with external legal prescriptions that Julius refused, finally, to support the Formula of Concord, in which he, in part through Chemnitz, had invested so much.

In addition to the articles for the clergy and city fathers, Chemnitz also drew up brief regulations for the *cistarii*,[11] or treasurers, who collected and disbursed the monies for the church, specifying that they were to see to the temporal needs of the pastors and their families and to seek counsel from the pastors with respect to the needs of the poor who were receiving aid from the church treasury.

It would appear that Chemnitz, as superintendent of the churches at Braunschweig, would have had enough work just taking care of his administrative duties. But the labors that were to occupy him to a very large extent, to exhaust him prematurely, and for which he was to be remembered by future generations, were not in the field of church administration, but theology. In this field he labored with signal diligence and success until at sixty he became seriously ill. Two years later he resigned from office, and after an additional two years of great weakness, he died on April 8, 1586.

THEOLOGY   The studies that Chemnitz had pursued in Scripture, in the Church Fathers, in Luther's writings, and in the works of the reformers generally, as well as in the writings of

11. Ibid., p. 135.

their opponents, fitted him eminently, not only to be a knowledgeable Lutheran bishop but to be an influential theologian far beyond the boundaries of Braunschweig. Opportunity for this soon presented itself.

During his stay at Wittenberg, Chemnitz had begun to lecture to students on Melanchthon's *Loci communes*, and he continued these lectures at Braunschweig. Four times a year he gathered the pastors of his diocese together and discussed with them a portion of Christian doctrine in a systematic manner.[12] These lectures continued until near the end of his life, when ill health put an end to them. The lectures, which did not cover all topics customarily treated in Lutheran dogmatics, were published posthumously as *Loci theologici*. Chemnitz also began an exegetical work on the four gospels, which was carried forward after his death by Polycarp Leyser, finally completed by John Gerhard, and published under the title *Harmonia Evangelistarum*.

Although Chemnitz was by nature a quiet and peaceable man, and not addicted to controversy, his chief theological work grew out of the controversies that troubled the churches in his day. His theological labors had three foci: the Roman Catholic attacks against the Lutheran churches, proceeding from the newly founded Jesuit order and from the Council of Trent; the attacks against certain teachings of Luther on the part of Reformed theologians, particularly in the area of the real presence of Christ's body and blood in the Lord's Supper, which led to christological disputes; and finally certain controversies that had arisen among the adherents of the Augsburg Confession, and that were threatening to destroy the Lutheran Church.

Chemnitz himself informs us in the beginning of his *Examen Concilii Tridentini*[13] that he had three years earlier written a booklet in which he described the origin and teachings of the newly established Jesuit order. The booklet brought Chemnitz to the attention of wider circles in the church, both Roman Catholic and Protestant. When, therefore, the Council of Trent had adjourned and its canons and decrees had been published, who in Lutheran circles could be judged better able to answer them than Martin Chemnitz? The council had ended December 4, 1563. On April 29, 1565, Chemnitz presented the first volume of his *Examen* in which he analyzed what the Council had decreed concerning: (1) the sacred Scriptures; (2) traditions; (3) original sin; (4) the remnants of original sin after baptism; (5) whether the Blessed Virgin was conceived without original sin; (6) the works of unbelievers; (7) free will; (8) justification; (9) faith; and, (10) good works.[14]

In developing these topics Chemnitz always quotes the chapter or canon of the Council of Trent that he proposes to examine. Then he seeks to make sure that he understands clearly, not only the literal wording of the

---

12. E. Preuss, *Vita*, p. 928.

13. *Examination of the Council of Trent*, vol. 1. trans. Fred Kramer (St. Louis: Concordia Publishing House, 1971), p. 25.

14. Ibid., table of contents, pp. 3–7.

particular chapter or canon, but also its intent.[15] In this he was greatly aided by a book published by Jacob Payva Andrada, a Portuguese Jesuit, who had been present at the council and interpreted the council's thinking and intention. Andrada helped Chemnitz see a number of snares hidden in the wording of various chapters and canons. For this Chemnitz at times thanks Andrada in the *Examen*.[16]

Having established the meaning and intent of the particular canon or decree, he proceeds to examine it first of all according to the Scripture. One cannot but marvel at the wealth of biblical knowledge that Chemnitz exhibits time after time. There is with him little of the stereotyped use of scriptural proof texts for which later Lutheran theologians were sometimes justly censured. He makes sure that he has understood the text correctly and is using it properly. Chemnitz then proceeds to examine the particular canon or decree according to the best and most ancient fathers. These are for him above all others St. Irenaeus and St. Augustine, and, to a lesser degree, St. Jerome, St. Chrysostom, and less well known fathers. He appears to have read and excerpted them all. For church history he draws heavily on the *Historia Tripartita*.[17] While Chemnitz quotes the Church Fathers voluminously and with telling effect, he very rarely quotes Luther. Although he was a great admirer and student of Luther, he realized that one does not best defend Luther by quoting Luther, but by showing that Luther's teaching is in full accord with the teachings of the ancient teachers of the church.

On December 18, 1566, Chemnitz was able to dedicate volume 2 of the *Examen*[18] to John, elector of Brandenburg. In this second volume Chemnitz examines the teachings of Trent concerning the sacraments. He maintains that the term "sacrament" is not a biblical term, but came into the language of the western church via the Vulgate.[19] On the basis of his study of the Scripture and the Church Fathers he concludes that only two of the seven sacraments claimed by the Council of Trent have specific commands and promises from God for all time and employ a combination of both external means and the Word of God, namely baptism and the Lord's Supper. The teaching of Trent

15. Ibid., p. 30.

16. Ibid., p. 317.

17. About the middle of the sixth century, A.D., Cassiodorus, a Christian scholar, caused the works of three church historians who had written in Greek to be translated into Latin. These works were then combined into one complete narrative under the title *Historia Tripartita*. The Latin text is found in J.–P. Migne, *Patrologia Latina*, vol. 69 (1865): 879–1214.

18. The publication of the *Examen*, which was to bring Chemnitz fame, also brought him some disappointment. He complains, "I could not read the first part without anger on account of the manifold and most abominable misprints, some of which are of such a nature that they make a right understanding totally impossible." He therefore prepared a list of the chief misprints and added it to the first volume. Unfortunately, the printers continued make *errata* which persist in part even in the Preuss edition of 1861, which, while it corrects some of the old misprints, manages to leave many uncorrected and to add not a few new ones. However, contrary to Chemnitz's complaint, most of the misprints do not interfere seriously with a correct understanding of the text.

19. The Vulgate consistently translates the Greek term *mysterion* as *sacramentum*.

concerning confirmation, he maintains, not only has no foundation in Scripture, but detracts seriously from the dignity and value of baptism.

In January of 1573 the second volume of the *Examen* was followed by a somewhat shorter volume, treating virginity, the celibacy of priests, purgatory, and the invocation of saints. August of the same year saw the completion of the fourth and final volume of the *Examen*, which deals with the relics of the saints, images, indulgences, fasting, laws concerning foods, and festival days. This volume is considerably shorter than the other three.

S   The theological world quickly realized the importance of Chemnitz's *Examen*, and not only Lutherans but also not a few Calvinists welcomed and praised it. A German translation prepared by Georg Nigrinus appeared at Frankfurt am Main in 1576. In London the part of volume 1 concerning traditions was translated and published in 1582 by Thomas Purfoot and William Punsonbee under the title, *"A Discouverie and batterie of the great Fort of unwritten Traditions: otherwise an examination of the Counsell of Trent touching the decree of traditions*, Done by Martinus Chemnitz in Latine, and translated into English by R.U."

As was to be expected, many Roman Catholic theologians attacked and tried to refute the *Examen*. The Portuguese Jesuit, Andrada, who had given Chemnitz so much ammunition for his four-volume work, wrote a book against the *Examen*,[20] accusing Chemnitz of overweening pride, but was nevertheless compelled to admit that he was a man of sharp intellect, experienced in debate, and not unskilled in speech. Of all Roman Catholic antagonists against Chemnitz, the most famous was Cardinal Robert Bellarmine, who accused Chemnitz of being so full of lies that he could tell five of them in four short sentences! Chemnitz was defended against Bellarmine by many Lutherans, including the famous seventeenth-century dogmatician John Gerhard.[21] How greatly Roman Catholic theologians were worried by Chemnitz's *Examen* is evidenced by the fact that attempts to refute the book continued to appear for decades, not only in Latin, but also in German.

The polemical theological work of Chemnitz was not, however, wholly concerned with examining and refuting certain teaching of Rome; he felt compelled to deal also with certain teachings of the Reformed churches. Reformed teaching with respect to the Lord's Supper differed from Lutheran teaching in that it recognized a "spiritual but true" eating and drinking of Christ's body and blood. Into the Reformed argument against the Lutheran doctrine of the real corporal presence entered the understanding of the person of the incarnate Christ, specifically the question whether, in view of Christ's

20. The title of this work is *Defensio Tridentinae fidei catholicae et integerrimae, quinque libris comprehensa, adversus haereticorum detestabiles calumnias et praesertim M. Chemnicii Germani, autore R. D. Diego Payva d'Andrada Lusitano D. Theol. Olissipponae* (1578).

21. A list of Reformed theologians who joined the Lutherans in prase of the *Examen* is found in E. Preuss, *Vita*, p. 962.

ascension into heaven, the body and blood of Christ could be present in the sacrament.

Against this background of over three decades of intra-Protestant dispute concerning the real presence, Chemnitz wrote *De duabus naturis in Christo*.[22] The book deals with the modes, or *genera*, of the communication of attributes, the *communicatio idiomatum*, or *koinonia*, between the human and divine natures of Christ. Following Chalcedon, Chemnitz teaches that the person of the Logos assumes human nature and thereby becomes the composite person of Christ subsisting in two natures, although without change to the second person of the Trinity.[23] Because of this hypostatic union, which, following John Damascene, may be called inhypostatic, there result three genera of communication between the two natures. The first genus is not disputed and consists in the communication of the attributes of each nature to the person of Christ,[24] so that those attributes are predicated concretely *(in concreto)* of Christ and abstractly *(in abstracto)* of the natures. Thus one may say that "God died on the cross," meaning that Jesus Christ, who is God as well as man, died on the cross. But one may not say that the divinity died. *God* is taken concretely; divinity abstractly. The second genus refers to the offices of Christ so that what each nature effects is done in communion with the other. Thus Christ is savior because he is divine, but he saves in and through his human nature. Chemnitz says that "each nature in Christ performs in communion with the other that which is proper to each."[25] The third genus, the so-called *genus majestaticum*, is the one which involved the most controversy.[26] It is in this genus that Chemnitz asserts the direct communication between the two natures so that the human nature participates in the divine attributes. In arguing for this genus, Chemnitz also lays the foundation for the kenotic controversies of the seventeenth century. According to Chemnitz, the exegesis of Philippians 2:5–11 and especially of the term "form of a servant" ($\mu o \rho \phi \grave{\eta}$ $\delta o \acute{\upsilon} \lambda o \upsilon$), refers not to Christ's human nature, which is indicated by $\sigma \chi \tilde{\eta} \mu \alpha$[27] but rather to his state of humiliation. In this view, Christ's human nature enjoyed, from conception, the prerogatives of the divine nature summed up under the term "majesty." But while on earth, Christ voluntarily set aside this majesty, allowing only glimpses of it when he performed miracles and especially at the time of the transfiguration.

In the long chapters devoted to each of the three genera, Chemnitz quotes extensively from the fathers up to and including John Damascene and,

22. This work is available in English, translated by J. A. O. Preuss (St. Louis: Concordia Publishing House, 1971), under the title *The Two Natures in Christ*.
23. Ibid., pp. 70–81.
24. Ibid., p. 163.
25. Ibid., p. 164.
26. Ibid., p. 257.
27. Ibid., p. 326.

less frequently, Bernard of Clairvaux. He even credits the scholastics with correct doctrine, except with regard to the third genus.[28] Chemnitz specifically attacks those who would limit the *communicatio idiomatum* to the person of Christ.[29] There is, argues Chemnitz, a real communication of the divine attributes to the human nature, which may not be reduced to the form of either a merely verbal predication or to finite created gifts.

Toward the end of his long book, Chemnitz comes to the disputed doctrine out of which the two-natures controversy arose, namely the Lord's Supper. He summarizes the points of the controversy[30] and then sums up his own teaching:

> There is no contradiction if some body is said to be in one place according to its essential properties, in the natural way, and in many places according to its supernatural attributes through the will and power of God who works in a supernatural, heavenly, or divine manner. For there are no contradictions if contrary qualities are attributed to the same thing in different respects and in different ways.[31]

In short, Christ can be present with his body where and when he wills.[32]

These doctrines are distilled in the *Formula of Concord*, which owes most of its theological language to Chemnitz, especially on original sin, Christology, the Lord's Supper, good works, and election. With regard to the Lord's Supper, Chemnitz taught a two-fold eating, the first a spiritual eating of the flesh of Christ through faith whenever believers respond to the Gospel in preaching and sacraments.

> The other eating of the body of Christ is oral or sacramental, when all who eat and drink the blessed bread and wine in the Lord's Supper receive and partake of the true and essential body and blood of Christ orally. Believers receive it as a certain pledge and assurance that their sins are truly forgiven, that Christ dwells and is efficacious in them; unbelievers receive it orally too, but to their judgment and damnation. . . . This command can only be understood as referring precisely to oral eating and drinking—not, however, in a coarse, carnal, Capernaitic manner, but in a supernatural, incomprehensible manner.[33]

This confessional teaching remains the official doctrine of Lutheran churches.

A word remains to be said about Chemnitz's influence on Lutheran theology with regard to predestination, or, as Lutherans prefer to call it, "the

28. Ibid., pp. 263, 265.
29. Ibid., pp. 278–80.
30. Ibid., pp. 433ff.
31. Ibid., pp. 436–37.
32. Ibid., p. 444.
33. Theodore G. Tappert, *The Book of Concord*, ed. Jaroslav Pelikan et al. (St. Louis: Concordia Publishing House, 1959), p. 581.

election of grace." There had been, up to the time of the Formula of Concord, no major controversy among Lutherans about this doctrine. Chemnitz and his co-workers saw correctly that controversy on this matter might well break out among Lutherans at some time in the future. For in this doctrine a number of seemingly irreconcilable teachings meet: (1) the eternal election by God of a part of mankind to eternal life; (2) universal redemption of all mankind by Christ, and universal grace, according to which God wants all to be saved; (3) *sola gratia*, according to which the sinner is saved solely by the grace of God without any merit or worthiness in himself; (4) conversion solely by the power of God, working through the means of grace; (5) unbelief and damnation of the sinner solely through his own fault and not because of any adverse eternal decree on the part of God.

All this Luther had taught, as he was persuaded, on the basis of Scripture. He had not systematized these teachings in a dogmatics or in a confessional statement. This systematization was done by Martin Chemnitz and his co-workers in article 11 of the *Formula of Concord*. There, emphasis is placed on predestination as concerned only with the pious of whose salvation it is the cause. As such, it is a doctrine of great comfort since not even the gates of hell can prevail against it. It is to be accepted, therefore, and not investigated by an overcurious mind. The *Formula* denies that the passage, "Many are called but few are chosen," means that God does not will to save everyone. Rather, condemnation is the result of a willful hardening of one's heart and closing of one's ears to the Word of God and the action of the Holy Spirit. "The devil and man himself, and not God, are the cause of their being fitted for damnation." The doctrine is summed up:

> This must not be misconstrued as if it had never been God's gracious will that such people should come to the knowledge of the truth and be saved. God's revealed will involves both items: First, that he would receive into grace all who repent and believe in Christ; second, that he would punish those who deliberately turn away from the holy commandment and involve themselves again in the filth of this world (2 Pet. 2:20), prepare their hearts for Satan (Luke 11:24, 25), and outrage the Holy Spirit (Heb. 10:29), and that he would harden, blind, and forever damn them if they continue therein.[34]

The warning of the formulators against overcurious investigation into this difficult doctrine was not heeded in ensuing centuries.[35]

---

34. Ibid., p. 630.
35. See below, pp. 50–51.

ROLE IN THE   As a theologian Chemnitz has had a lasting impact on the
CHURCH   Christian Church. That his *Examen* of the canons and
decrees of Trent made an impact on the Roman Catholic
Church we know from the testimony of Catholics them-
selves. Chemnitz's enemies complained about the harm he had done the
Roman Catholic cause. A certain cardinal is reported to have asserted that no
one, after the death of Luther, had harmed the Roman church more than had
Chemnitz with his *Examen*.[36] On the other hand there were also Roman
Catholics who were convinced by reading the *Examen* that the teachings of
Trent were in error and came over to the Lutheran side. A certain Franciscus
Leopoldus de Reissing, a papal canon in Styria, who converted to Luther-
anism, confessed: "What shall I write concerning Martin Chemnitz, to
whom, next to God, I owe my conversion? His irrefutable *Examen* of the
Council of Trent puts to shame all libraries of the papalists." He adds that he
found the *Examen* never fully answered by the papacy.[37]

It is, however, in Lutheranism itself that the impact of Chemnitz's work
must most of all be sought. Not only by his *Examen* and other theological
writings, but most of all by his work, together with other theologians, in the
composition of the *Formula of Concord* has Chemnitz had an abiding impact on
the Lutheran Church.

Held back by the force of Luther's personality during the reformer's
lifetime, serious controversies broke out in the Lutheran ranks shortly after
Luther's death. So deep were the theological divisions, and so violent the
language of some of the parties to these controversies, that it seemed that the
church of the Augsburg Confession would destroy itself. It was at that
particular point that Martin Chemnitz was once again called into the field to
aid the church with his solid theological learning and his calm, temperate way
of dealing both with erroneous theological positions and with the persons who
advocated them. The work in which he became engaged was to lead to the
composition and acceptance by the vast majority of Lutherans in Germany of
the *Formula of Concord*, the last of the great Lutheran confessions in which the
doctrinal points that were in controversy among the Lutherans were taken up
one by one, carefully examined, the point at issue defined, the true teaching of
Scripture shown, and the doctrine set forth in clear, simple language.

Chemnitz's work here differed from his previous theological labors.
Previously he had largely labored alone. Here he worked with a number of
other prominent Lutheran theologians, notably Jacob Andreae and David
Chytraeus (1531–1600).[38]

36. E. Preuss, p. 963.
37. Ibid., p. 931.
38. See below, chapter 4, "Jacob Andreae," for an account of the development of the *Formula of
Concord*. See also *Discord, Dialogue, and Concord: Studies in the Lutheran Reformation's Formula of Concord*, eds.
Lewis W. Spitz and Wenzel Lohff, vol. 1 (Philadelphia: Fortress Press, 1977) and vol. 2 (Stuttgart: Calwer
Verlag, 1977). For a straightforward history of the disputes see F. Bente, "Historical Introductions to the
Symbolical Books of the Evangelical Lutheran Church" in *Concordia Triglotta*, ed. F. Bente (St. Louis:
Concordia Publishing House, 1921), pp. 93–256.

In one area, the attempt of the authors of the *Formula of Concord* failed to prevent future controversy. Not many years after the acceptance of the *Formula*, the famous Lutheran dogmatician, John Gerhard (1582–1637), introduced into Lutheran dogmatics a formulation that was, at a later period, to occasion prolonged and bitter controversy within Lutheranism. He taught that God had elected those whom he had elected *intuitu fidei*, that is, in view of the faith they would have.[39] This expression, which was widely adopted and used by Lutheran dogmaticians during the period of orthodoxy and beyond,[40] can be understood in a way that does not contradict the *sola gratia* of Lutheranism. John Gerhard undoubtedly so understood it. It also lends itself, however, to a synergistic understanding, and this in time led to a prolonged and bitter controversy particularly in the Lutheran church in America. The controversy was never officially settled in a council of all Lutheran synods. Rather, it gradually wore itself out, and as the leaders in the controversy passed from the scene, the teaching of the *Formula of Concord* prevailed. In this respect, also, the impact of Martin Chemnitz continues to make itself felt within Lutheranism.

Not all countries in which the Lutheran Church became dominant accepted the *Formula of Concord*, not because they rejected its teaching, but because they had not been troubled by the dissentions which rent the churches of the Augsburg Confession in Germany. A Scandinavian Lutheran has expressed the matter well: "It is possible to be a Lutheran without the *Formula*; it is not possible to be a Lutheran against the *Formula*."[41]

Martin Chemnitz was truly the conserver of Luther's teaching. All his theological work tended to that end. A seventeenth-century epigram summed it up: "If the second Martin had not come, the first Martin would scarcely have endured."

---

39. Cf. Joannis Gerhardi, *Loci Theologici*, ed. E. Preuss, (Berlin: Sumtibus Gust. Schlawitz., 1863), vol. 2, pp. 86ff.

40. Heinrich Schmid, *Doctrinal Theology of the Evangelical Lutheran Church*, translated by C. A. Hay and H. E. Jacobs (Minneapolis, Minn.: Augsburg Publishing House, 1961), p. 288ff.

41. Lief Aalen in a lecture to the faculty of Concordia Theological Seminary, Springfield, Illinois.

4

JAKOB ANDREAE

1528–1590

ROBERT KOLB

LIFE   When in 1570 Jakob Andreae published a list of fifty-four nasty names pinned on him by his antagonists, he had hardly begun to be the object of the ridicule and rancor of theologians and government counselors throughout Evangelical Germany. Yet just six years later the moot prominent of his princely patrons, Elector August of Saxony, observed "how faithfully, carefully, assiduously, and diligently Dr. Jakob has proven himself to be; . . . he commands such regard and authority among other theologians that they gladly follow him, yes, even love and revere him." While few of either his antagonists or his supporters would have compared him to Elijah and Paul, as did Lucas Osiander in his funeral sermon for Andreae in 1590, all might have agreed with Osiander's choice of text, "I have fought a good fight, . . . I have kept the faith."[1] In a controversial age Andreae's energy and persistence made him one of the most influential among the controversial polemicists and pastors who shaped early modern Western Christendom.

Jakob Andreae the elder had served imperial troops from Bohemia to Spain before he settled down to practice his trade, smithing, in the small Swabian town of Waiblingen. There, on March 25, 1528, he became the father of a peripatetic namesake who would spend the best years of his life trying to forge a document of Evangelical reconciliation. Jakob Andreae the son suffered under the burden of his allegedly humble origins, and he retreated from the scorn of those who called him the smithy's son by walking with counts, dukes, electors, and even an emperor. Young Jakob became an Evangelical at age six when his duke, Ulrich, converted the people of his lands to Lutheranism. Jakob was withdrawn from school after only five years because his family could no longer afford the tuition. Waiblingen's mayor dissuaded the Andreaes from apprenticing Jakob to a cabinetmaker and persuaded them to apply for a ducal scholarship for their son; thus began his

---

1. Johann Valentin Andreae, *Fama Andreana reflorescens, sive Jacobi Andrea Waiblingensis . . . vitae* (Strassburg: Repp, 1630), esp. p. 402.

formal relationship with Württemberg's ruling family. After preparatory school in Stuttgart he won further ducal support for study at the University of Tübingen in 1541, completed his master of arts degree in 1545, and immediately began his theological studies. Bound by his dependence on ducal financial assistance, he remained at Tübingen, which offered a very weak theological curriculum. His only able professor was Erhardt Schnepf, who did not rank with the theological giants then lecturing at Wittenberg.[2] Andreae's formal training in theology was further weakened by its early termination, after one year, because Duke Ulrich needed personnel for his churches.

Andreae became a deacon in Stuttgart and married in 1546. His wife, Johanna Entringer, came from a prominent burgher family of Tübingen; she bore him eighteen children and managed his household—a task she carried out alone much of the time because Andreae spent so much of his life traveling. Within months of his assumption of office in Stuttgart, the city was occupied by Spanish troops, brought to Germany by Emperor Charles V for his successful campaign against the Evangelical armies in the Schmalkald War. The imperial forces stationed in Württemberg later enforced compliance with the Augsburg Interim, the emperor's plan for ecclesiastical life in the Evangelical areas of Germany, promulgated in April 1548. Many Evangelical pastors were driven from their positions. Andreae stood his ground, arguing face to face with Spanish soldiers and imperial officials over justification through faith and the Mass, until Duke Ulrich transferred him to Tübingen in late 1548. There he worked partly above ground, partly underground to keep the Evangelical faith alive in the face of imperial efforts to snuff it out. Andreae's hostility against the Roman party was shaped by his experience as a semilegal preacher in an occupied land.

Ulrich's young favorite was the last pastor to minister to him before his death in 1550, and Andreae immediately began serving his master's son and successor, Christoph. When the Truce of Passau ended the emperor's dominance in Württemberg in 1552, Christoph eagerly revived the process of making his church Evangelical. He needed personnel to do that on the parish level, and he recognized Andreae's talents for parish work. Andreae had enrolled at Tübingen for doctoral studies even though Schnepf's exile had weakened its theological faculty even further. Christoph insisted that Andreae complete his program; then he sent him to the town of Göppingen in April 1553 as superintendent of the churches in the area.

Relatively successful enforcement of the Augsburg Interim in that area and strong monastic influence there made Andreae's new charge a challenging one. Searching for proper forms for Evangelical church life and discipline, Andreae was attracted to the Genevan model. He and his brother-in-law,

2. On Andreae's life to 1568, see Rosemarie Müller-Streisand, "Theologie und Kirchenpolitik bei Jacob Andreae bis zum Jahr 1568," *Blätter für württembergische Kirchengeschichte* 60/61 (1960/1961): 224–395. On Schnepf, see Julius Hartmann, *Erhard Schnepf, Der Reformator in Schwaben, Nassau, Hessen und Thüringen* (Tübingen: Osiander, 1870).

Caspar Leyser, pastor at Nürtingen, corresponded with Calvin. Andreae briefly shared Calvin's conviction that discipline is a mark of the church and that ecclesiastical control was best centered in the pastors and leading laymen of the town. Johann Brenz disagreed; he argued for strong, centralized control over the church, exercised by the duke's ecclesiastical officials in Stuttgart.[3] He won Christoph over to his position. Andreae argued his case in correspondence and then at a synod in late 1554; he did not simply abandon his ideas to accommodate his friend Brenz or his prince. But when the decision of the synod went against him, he accepted its judgment and returned to Göppingen to continue constructing Evangelical practice and inculcating Evangelical doctrine among his people.

Andreae was successful at these tasks in his own charge, and Duke Christoph called upon him to assist with the reformation of other areas. The Religious Peace of Augsburg freed many petty princes from their fears of Roman Catholic military power; thus, after introducing reform to monastic lands near Göppingen, Andreae was invited to assist in the reformation of Wiesensteig, the Palatinate-Neuburg, and Baden-Durlach, all in 1556. Later he returned to these and many other places either to introduce the Reformation or to assist in visitations aimed at inspecting progress in the cultivation of the Lutheran faith on the popular level.[4] In 1556 in Baden he confronted representatives from the Gnesio-Lutheran party and got his first taste of the bitterness and hostility that had plagued north German Lutheranism since the Schmalkald War. Andreae felt the sting of their condemnation of Brenz for defending Andreas Osiander, propagator of a doctrine of justification which diverged from Luther's; this display of Evangelical disunity and rancor bruised Andreae's spirit. He felt that the Lutheran movement could not afford internal ill will when it was locked in battle with the Roman party for the control of the minds of the people.

Andreae worked to counter medieval concepts of the Christian faith and to present Evangelical replacements in a series of tracts that met issues on a lay level with arguments chiefly derived from the six "chief parts" of the catechism, which Andreae regarded as a reliable summary of biblical teaching. He treated the Mass, communion in one kind, the layman's use of Scripture, purgatory, monastic life, and similar subjects in such tracts.[5] In sermons on the catechism and on justification through faith and related doctrines he also laid out carefully the heart of the Evangelical faith in the

3. On Brenz's position on church and state, see James M. Estes, "The Two Kingdoms and the State Church according to Johannes Brenz and an Anonymous Colleague," *Archiv für Reformationsgeschichte* 61 (1970): 35–50 and "Johannes Brenz and the Problem of Ecclesiastical Discipline," *Church History* 41 (1972): 464–79.

4. On his concern for the laity, see Robert Kolb, "Andreae's Concern for the Laity," *Concordia Journal*, 4, no. 2 (1978), 58–67.

5. E.g., his *Einfeltiger Bericht, wie ein jeder Christ antwurten soll auss seinem Catechismo, warumb er nicht mehr zu der Mess gehe* (Tübingen: Morhart, 1558) and *Sechs Christlicher Predig von dem rechtchristenlichen und geistlichen Closterleben* (Tübingen: Morhart, 1561).

language of the common man, with illustrations and arguments suited for the barely literate and illiterate.[6] More sophisticated attacks came from Andreae's pen against Roman Catholic theologians, including the apostate Evangelical Friedrich Staphylus (a lay theologian), whose attacks on the Evangelical use of Scripture and Evangelical disunity Christoph induced Andreae to challenge. Anti-Roman polemic came easily from the pen of a pastor engaged daily in reconstructing late medieval popular belief and practice.[7]

Peace in his prince's parishes was threatened by radical sectarian "ravers" of several stripes, and Andreae was well aware of their challenge to his Lutheran faith. In 1553 he exchanged correspondence with the spiritualist Kaspar Schwenckfeld. In 1557 he participated in the examination of a Tübingen professor, Matthias Gribaldi, on charges of antitrinitarianism, and he obliged the elector Palatine, Ottheinrich, by meeting local Anabaptists in colloquy at Pfedersheim. Andreae summed up his objections to Romans and radicals alike in a series of thirty-three sermons preached at Esslingen in 1567. In them he used the catechism to examine and condemn the errors of "Papists, Zwinglians, Schwenckfelders, and Anabaptists."[8]

Duke Christoph quickly recognized Andreae's potential as an ecclesiastical diplomat. At Christoph's suggestion he was appointed one of the two Evangelical notaries at the colloquy between Lutheran and Roman Catholic theologians that Emperor Ferdinand arranged in Worms in 1557. The colloquy foundered because the Gnesio-Lutheran delegates could not in good conscience enter into discussions without a joint statement from the Evangelical collocutors that condemned certain positions held by some within the Evangelical camp. Brenz refused to comply, and the Philippist party from electoral Saxony also rejected their opponents' demands, with the result that the Lutherans entered the colloquy deeply split. Once again Evangelical disunity grieved Andreae. At Worms he apparently had cordial relations with the Philippists, including Melanchthon and Paul Eber, and later exchanged friendly correspondence with the Wittenbergers. Their princes, Elector August and Duke Christoph, agreed the next year on a common statement of faith, the brief, mildly stated "Frankfurt Recess," and an Evangelical axis linking Wittenberg and Tübingen seemed likely.

Andreae accompanied Christoph to the Reichstag in Augsburg in 1559 and represented him in Erfurt in 1561, where plans for a united Evangelical approach to the Council of Trent were discussed. Later that year he left for Paris with colleagues from Christoph's staff to add a Lutheran presence to the

6. E.g., *Zehen Predig von den sechs Hauptstucken Christlicher Lehr - Catechismus genannt -, allen christlichen Hausvättern nutzlich zulesen* (Tübingen: Morhart, 1561).

7. E.g., *Ad Friderici Staphyli confictas et calumniae plenas Antilogas Responsio* (Frankfurt am Main: Brubach, 1558) and *De Usu calicis in synaxi contra veteratorem Bartholemaeum Latomum defensio* (Tübingen: Morhart, 1568).

8. *Drey und dreissig Predigen von den fürnembsten Spaltungen in der christlichen Religion, so sich zwischen den Bäpstischen, Lutherischen, Zwinglischen, Schwenckfeldern, und Widerteuffern halten* (Tübingen: Morhart, 1568).

Colloquy of Poissy. The next year Andreae accompanied Christoph, Brenz, and others to Zabern in Alsace for an exchange with the cardinal of Lorraine and other members of the Guise family. The meeting produced nothing and helped end Christoph's hope of extensive Lutheran influence in France.

Christoph's confidence in Andreae continued to grow. In 1561 the prince called him from Göppingen to serve as theology professor, provost, and chancellor at the University of Tübingen. Even before this Andreae's talent for conciliation and theological fence-mending had attracted the duke's notice, and Christoph often put this talent at the disposal of other princes, for Christoph was not only promoting the expansion of the Lutheran Reformation in the early years of his reign, but was also promoting Evangelical unity. He feared pressure from Roman Catholic princes against the Evangelical estates and believed that doctrinal unity had to be restored among the squabbling theologians of the several Lutheran churches if they were to be freed from the serious Roman threat. Occupied in part with this concern from the late 1550s, Andreae focused his attention on the establishment of Lutheran harmony in 1568 when Christoph sent him north to aid the duke's cousin, Duke Julius of Braunschweig-Wolfenbüttel, in reforming his lands and soliciting support for a declaration of Lutheran concord. This concern consumed the better part of the last two decades of his life and resulted in the composition and adoption of the *Formula of Concord*. From 1568 to 1570 and from 1575 to 1580 Andreae, with headquarters in northern Germany, traveled extensively to woo support for his plans for concord. The *Formula* and the settlement it entailed stand as monuments to his impact upon the developing orthodoxy of the early modern period.

But his efforts and success cost him dearly. His attempts to establish order and orthodoxy had attracted invective and insult from the very beginning. During the mid-1570s Gnesio-Lutheran criticism began to subside somewhat while Philippist and Calvinist condemnation rose. Even among his colleagues, however, Andreae inspired not only respect but also envy, resentment, and disgust. His colleagues in creating the *Formula of Concord* became alienated from him as the process was completed. David Chytraeus resented Andreae's insistence on his own ideas in the composition of the *Formula*. Nikolaus Selnecker found him arrogant and domineering as they worked together in Saxony. Martin Chemnitz became angry when Andreae failed to criticize Duke Julius for having his son consecrated as bishop of Halberstadt according to Roman Catholic rites in an attempt to expand his family's power. Even his ardent princely supporter, Elector August, whom Andreae had both served and used, found his enthusiasm for Andreae had dimmed by the time Andreae's settlement was established in Saxony. The man who had invested so much of himself in his relentless pursuit of the ideal of Lutheran concord perhaps finally had to be somewhat insufferable.

Much of Andreae's last decade, spent once again at the University of Tübingen, saw his academic routine unsettled by polemics. He defended the settlement wrought in the *Formula of Concord* in a dispute between the Lutheran pastor Johann Pappus of Strassburg and the aging pedagogue, Johann Sturm, who opposed the *Formula's* introduction into that city, chiefly because of its specific condemnations of false doctrine.[9] In 1584 he tried to prevent the return of the Palatinate to the Reformed ranks after the death of the Lutheran elector Ludwig, but his theological arguments in defense of the *Formula's* theology carried no weight against the political power of the regent, Johann Casimir.[10]

In the 1580s Andreae defended the doctrine of the majesty of Christ's human nature (see chapter 3 above) and responded to attacks on it from Calvinists Lambert Daneau (see chapter 7 below), Beza (see chapter 6 below), and others, as well as from the Jesuit Gregory de Valentia. In these works he reviewed the differences that separated him from his opponents, exchanging some rather vicious personal attacks with them.[11] Andreae defended his views in face-to-face debate during his last years as well. In 1586 he journeyed to Montbéliard to meet Beza and other Reformed theologians in colloquy. The two sides could not come to agreement on the Lord's Supper, the person of Christ, baptism, the use of images, and predestination. Thus, they set in place the questions that divided orthodox Lutherans and orthodox Calvinists in succeeding generations.[12]

As he completed a report on his dispute with a lapsed Evangelical physician, Johann Pistorius, Andreae died on January 7, 1590.

THEOLOGY   Jakob Andreae's theology was shaped by greater minds within the Evangelical movement, most particularly by Martin Luther's and Johann Brenz's writings and instruction. Furthermore, Andreae's doctrinal positions developed within the context of the events that swirled around him, and on at least two occasions he altered his theological direction as controversy simmered around him. Nonetheless, his insights, developed as they were within and by his pastoral ministry and his polemical engagements, were recognized by his fellow Lutherans as helpful expressions of the Evangelical convictions they held and wished to preserve.

9. E.g., *Responsio brevis . . . contra librum Io: Sturmii, quem Antipappum quartum inscripsit . . .* (Dresden: Stöckel, 1581).

10. *Confutatio disputationis Ioannis Jacobi Grynaei de coena Domini, Heidelbergae iiii. Apr. 1584 propositae* (Tübingen: Gruppenbach, 1584).

11. E.g., *Refutatio blasphemae Apologiae Lamberti Danaei Galli, de adoratione carnis Domini* (Tübingen: Gruppenbach, 1583); *Spiegel der offenbaren unverschämbten Calvinischen Lügen . . . unnd grewlichen erschröckenlichen Lösterungen, wider die göttliche Maiestat der Menschheit Jesu Christi* (Tübingen: Gruppenbach, 1588); and *Confutatio disputationis Gregorii de Valentia, sub titulo De vera praesentia Christi . . .* (Tübingen: Gruppenbach, 1583).

12. Andreae published his version of the colloquy, *Acta colloquii Montis Bellisgartensis . . .* (Tübingen: Gruppenbach, 1587).

Andreae's theology was largely shaped by his concern that his presentation of God's Word meet the spiritual needs of the repentant sinner with
the comfort of the Gospel. His understanding of the concept of justification
changed under the impact of controversy, and its final form was shaped by
precisely that concern. In 1551 and 1553 Andreae, though only in his early
twenties, was summoned to confer with other ducal theologians on the vexing
theological problem of Osiandrism, the peculiar concept of "justification
through faith" advanced by Andreas Osiander of Königsberg in 1550.
Osiander taught that the believer is justified by the presence of divine
righteousness that is bestowed upon the believer when the divine nature of
Christ dwells in him. Osiander attacked the concept of "forensic justification"
advanced in Wittenberg and defended by Melanchthon and his students
against Osiander's new view in the early 1550s. Andreae's colleague and
friend, Johann Brenz, had become Osiander's friend while they had worked
together for reform in south Germany in the 1520s. Brenz therefore persuaded
the Württembergers to try to mediate the dispute between Osiander and his
Wittenberg foes and to strike some middle ground between the two sides.
The young Andreae, inadequately prepared by his formal training and still
maturing as a theologian, went along with this mediation attempt. Later he
turned sharply against Osiandrism. His mature view presupposed that the
merit of human works and the human will itself contribute absolutely nothing
to salvation. He stressed that the sinner is justified and absolved of sin only
through faith in the merit of the total, innocent obedience and the bitter
suffering and death of the God-man, Jesus Christ. Andreae's emphasis on
Christ's obedience, suffering, and death as the only ground for salvation
reflects his reading of both Paul and Luther and his desire to anchor the
believer's assurance of his own salvation in what God had done in his behalf.
He feared that Osiander's doctrine would drive believers to despair if they
could not feel Christ's divine presence within them, and he wanted to prevent
misrepresentation of the Gospel's comfort at all costs. [13]

Likewise, in his treatment of the doctrine of election Andreae was not
interested in pursuing the hidden recesses of God's plan for the elect with
Jerome Zanchi in 1563 at Strassburg nor with Theodore Beza in 1586 at
Montbéliard. Instead, he was concerned with questions of pastoral counsel-
ing, and he expressed his convictions in terms that dealt with the pastoral
implications of election. In 1563 he was named to an arbitration team that

---

13. For Andreae's involvement in the early Württemberg deliberations on Osiander, see the texts of
the memoranda in Theodor Pressel, *Anecdota Brentiana* (Tübingen: Osiander, 1868), Nos. 315 and 323; see
also Martin Stupperich, *Osiander in Preussen 1549–1552* (Berlin: De Gruyter, 1973), pp. 329–46, and Jörg
Rainer Fligge, "Herzog Albrecht von Preussen und der Osiandrismus 1522–1568" (Ph.D. diss.,
University of Bonn, 1972), pp. 145–53, 229–56.

This concern is evident in his treatment of Osiandrism, e.g., in his *Sechs christlicher Predig. Von den
Spaltungen, so sich zwischen den Theologen Augspurgischer Confession von Anno 1548 bis . . . 1573, nach und nach
erhaben, wie sich ein Pfarrer und Laye, so dadurch möcht verworrt seyn worden . . .* (Tübingen: Gruppenbach,
1573), pp. 1–20.

intervened in a dispute between Zanchi, a Reformed professor in Strassburg, and his colleague on the city's ministerium, the Lutheran Johann Marbach. The Strassburg Concord enunciates Andreae's view of election even though it was probably composed by another member of the team, Cunman Flinsbach. He rejected speculation that God willed man's fall into sin and predestined some men to damnation. He approached election through what the Scripture reveals about those who heed its call and believe in Christ. He believed that the promise of life to those who believe in Christ is universally valid and is appropriated through faithful use of Word and sacrament. Those who trust Christ's promise may be certain, on the basis of Christ's death for them and of the surety of God's promise in Christ, that God has chosen them as his own in eternity. They may not therefore fall into licentiousness; against that temptation Andreae pastorally proclaimed the law. But to the anxious, repentant sinner he gave assurance that God had predestined him to eternal life because of Christ's merits. [14]

Perhaps Andreae's most significant theological stance concerned the person of Christ, particularly as Christology relates to the understanding of the real presence of Christ's body and blood in the Lord's Supper. Both his pastoral concern and the force of events shaped his viewpoint in this case, too. Andreae had attempted to find a basis for solving the eucharistic disputes that had separated Zurich and Wittenberg early in his pastoral ministry. With Beza and Farel he had sought to formulate common ground on which the two sides of this dispute could agree. Their formula was rejected by comrades on both sides soon after it was concluded in 1557. [15] Two years later, in 1559, one of Andreae's colleagues in Württemberg, Bartholomaeus Hagen, was accused of Zwinglianism. In spite of—or perhaps because of—his earlier attempt to mediate Lutheran and Zwinglian positions, Andreae was appointed to the commission charged with Hagen's examination. Andreae's memorandum absolved him of teaching falsely in regard to the Lord's Supper, but warned against his understanding of Christ's ascension: that at the Ascension Christ's human nature ascended to the right hand of the Father and was located there and nowhere else. This stance disagreed with the view of Andreae's mentor, Brenz, whose position Andreae wrote into a confession drawn up at a synod in December 1559; this confession became the doctrinal standard for the clergy of Württemberg. [16] The position that he incorporated into this Stuttgart

14. On this dispute see James M. Kittelson, "Marbach vs. Zanchi, The Resolution of Controversy in Late Reformation Strasbourg," *Sixteenth Century Journal* 8, no. 3. (1977): 31–44.

15. Related materials are found in *Correspondance de Théodore de Bèze*, ed. F. Aubert, H. Meylan, A. Dufour (Geneva: Droz, 1962) 2: 66–67, 70–71, 110–11, 243–48, 253. See below, chapter 6, n. 19.

16. *Bekendtniss und Bericht, der Theologen und Kirchen Diener, im Fürstenthume Wirtenberg, von der warhafftigen gegenwertigkeit, des Leibs und Bluts Jesu Christi im heiligen Nachtmale* (Magdeburg: Kirchener, 1560). On Brenz's view see Otto Fricke, *Die Christologie des Johannes Brenz im Zusammenhang mit der Lehre vom Abendmahl und der Rechtfertigung* (Munich: Kaiser, 1927), and Martin Brecht, *Die frühe Theologie des Johannes Brenz* (Tübingen: Mohr, 1966), pp. 64–111.

confession remained a key element in Andreae's public presentation of his faith for the rest of his life.

Brenz and Andreae taught that through the personal union of Christ's divine and human natures the attributes of the Son of God, particularly his divine majesty and his omnipotence, are communicated to or shared with his human nature. In the one person Jesus, Andreae taught, are united two distinct natures, which remain unmixed and undiminished alongside each other, retaining their own essences and characteristics. However, these natures do share their attributes with each other. He based his position on Colossians 2:9, "In him the whole fullness of the Godhead dwells bodily," among other passages. Mocked as a Ubiquitist because he claimed that Christ's human nature is omnipresent, and condemned as a Eutychian because he was misrepresented as teaching that the human nature is subsumed into the divine nature, Andreae doggedly persisted in reminding his opponents that Luther, too, had taught that Christ's human nature could not be circumscribed at some heavenly location at God's right hand because it was in Christ's person able to be present everywhere. He persevered in the propagation of this concept, in the face of criticism from Lutheran Philippists and from the Calvinists and Jesuits alike, not just because his friend Brenz had defended the position, nor only because he found it a helpful basis for defending his mature view of the substantial sacramental presence of Christ's body and blood in the elements of the Lord's Supper. As the concept slowly claimed his mind at the end of the 1550s, he found in it a source and confirmation of the Gospel's comfort. For in the personal union with the divine nature, Christ's human nature, which has experienced fully the tribulations common to mankind, can sympathize with and act in behalf of the believer with the omnipotence and omniscience at the command of the one who is both God and man. [17]

Andreae's view of Christ's person was connected with his more general affirmation that God works his saving will by using the created order in a direct way: that God has become a human being in Jesus Christ and that forgiveness of sins is conveyed by baptismal water comprehended in God's Word and by Christ's body and blood distributed and received in sacramental bread and wine. He taught that not only the elect but also the unrepentant unbeliever receive Christ's body and blood—essentially, sacramentally present—in the Lord's Supper; but without faith the communicant receives judgment, not blessing, from the sacrament. To the anxious but repentant sinner Andreae gave the assurance of God's unfailing grace in both sacraments. The believer can rely on God's pledge of salvation in baptism and in the Lord's Supper, Andreae proclaimed to those who needed the Gospel's consolation. His proclamation of the law to the arrogant and secure avoided such statements, in line with his general pastorally oriented, dialectical presentation of his message.

17. See, e.g., those tracts mentioned in note 11 or in the *Sechs Predig* (n. 13 above), pp. 75–99.

Though the meanness of polemical exchanges sometimes obscured that orientation, Andreae's pastoral concern, absorbed from Brenz and Luther, was the driving force that kept Andreae on the road in search of Lutheran unity for more than a decade.

ROLE IN THE   Andreae's impact upon early modern Western Christen-
CHURCH   dom, specifically German orthodox Lutheranism, arose
              out of his creative churchmanship. In two areas, the doc-
trinal and the political, he shaped the outline of ortho-
doxy, though he did so neither because of his own theological depth nor because of his organizational genius. He became the architect of Lutheran orthodoxy because he combined the ideas of others with his own driving energy. He was not a creative thinker, but he formulated the concepts of other Evangelical theologians in such a way that he was able to overcome differences which separated them. Having cooperated in satisfying the longing for concord that moved both theologians and princes, he was able to assist both the shaping of a common confession for German Lutherans and the establish-ment of models for the structure of church government among them that would last throughout the modern period.

Andreae spent much of his career in search of Evangelical unity. His inclination in that direction matched that of his prince, Duke Christoph, who entrusted to him a number of missions in behalf of local as well as empire-wide concord among Evangelicals. His first tract, composed in 1557 with Christoph's encouragement, embodied his attempt to overcome differences regarding the doctrine of the "real presence" of Christ's body and blood in the Lord's Supper; it offered "instructions for the simple Christian to find his way through the wearisome discord over the sacrament."[18] This was only one of a number of printed works that dealt with the problem of Evangelical disunity to come from Andreae's pen in the 1550s and 1560s; these tracts minimized the extent of that disunity and pointed toward solutions for the problems which disunity caused.[19] Andreae's services as arbitrator were offered by Christoph not only to the city council at Strassburg in 1563. The previous year he had also taken part in a mission to Weimar, the stronghold of the Gnesio-Lutheran party, in an attempt to mediate a dispute over the role of the human will in conversion. This dispute involved two antagonistic colleagues at the University of Jena, Matthias Flacius Illyricus (see chapter 2 above) and Viktorin Strigel. Duke Johann Friedrich the Middler had already exiled Flacius and his key supporters on the faculty. Andreae's task was to work out a reconciliation between Strigel and the ducal Saxon clergy, largely sympa-

18. *Kurtzer und einfältiger Bericht von des Herren Nachtmal, und wie sich ein einfältiger Christ in die langwirige zwyspalt . . . schicken soll* (Augsburg: Gegler, 1557).

19. E.g., *Bericht von der Einigkeit und Uneinigkeit der christlichen Augspurgischen Confessionsverwandten Theologen . . .* (Tübingen: Morhart, 1560).

thetic to Flacius. Andreae and a colleague from Württemberg did formulate a statement to which Strigel could agree; it stated that God alone effects conversion but does so through a human modus agendi. Within a short time Andreae experienced disappointment with this Philippist sympathizer and complained that the next year Strigel had embraced the synergistic position which Flacius had accused him of defending. Andreae felt that he had been duped.

The ground for his future alienation from the entire Philippist party was laid in 1564 when Andreae joined other members of Christoph's ecclesiastical staff in a colloquy at Maulbronn with theologians from the Palatinate (see chapter 8 below). Since Elector Frederick III's accession in 1559, his church had drifted toward its own brand of Reformed theology, summarized in the Heidelberg Catechism of 1563. Christoph, alarmed by the prospect of another doctrinal division within the south German Evangelical movement, called for a colloquy to resolve differences between his theologians and Frederick's. However, differing views of the Lord's Supper and the person of Christ divided the two sides at Maulbronn, and the colloquy only exacerbated their division. [20] In the wake of Maulbronn Paul Eber and his colleagues at the University of Wittenberg publicly disagreed with the position represented there by the Württembergers on the communication of divine attributes to Christ's human nature, and Andreae expressed his disapproval of the Wittenberg critique in letters. This disagreement did not seem to cast a shadow, however, over Andreae's relationship with the Wittenbergers four years later as he began the biggest project of his career.

In 1568 Duke Christoph's ecclesiastical handyman was sent to aid the duke's cousin, Julius of Braunschweig-Wolfenbüttel, in the reformation of his lands. To convert his church from the faith of his arch-Roman Catholic father, Heinrich, Julius put together a team of theologians borrowed from the city of Braunschweig (Martin Chemnitz), from Saxony (Nikolaus Selnecker), and from Württemberg (Andreae). When Andreae left Tübingen in late 1568, he carried with him his duke's commission to campaign for Lutheran unity in north Germany. Duke Christoph died soon after Andreae departed, but during the next two years his son-in-law, Landgrave Wilhelm of Hesse, and Duke Julius supported Andreae's efforts to create that unity. From Julius's court Andreae set out in early 1569 on a mission that took him to the courts of nearly every Evangelical prince in the empire, and to the imperial court in Prague, as well as to most of the Lutheran cities and universities in Germany. He took with him a confession of five brief paragraphs which he had composed as a statement upon which unity could be constructed. His "Confession and Brief Explanation of Certain Disputed Articles" treated justification, good works, the freedom of the will, adiaphora, and the Lord's Supper in

20. For the Württemberg view of the colloquy, see *Epitome Coloquij inter . . .D. Friderici Palatini Electoris, & D. Christophori Ducis Wirtenbergensis Theologos, de Maiestate hominis Christi deque vera eius in Eucharistia praesentia* . . . (n.p., 1564).

such cursory fashion that it had no hope of solving the complex doctrinal disputes that were tearing north German Lutheranism apart. At this point Andreae did not take seriously the depth of the differences separating the two north German parties, Philippists and Gnesio-Lutherans,[21] and he was working with an approach to Lutheran unity much like that the Philippists favored: a brief, general confession that did not arouse passions by being too specific on the issues under debate.

Andreae's diplomatic missions to the Evangelical estates met with mixed success. He was not trusted in many circles, particularly among the Gnesio-Lutherans. When he visited the ducal Saxon court in 1569, two of Duke Johann Wilhelm's theologians attacked him vigorously for error and duplicity. On the other hand, the Philippists viewed him as unreliable, egocentric, and in error on the person of Christ. Nonetheless, Andreae felt that he had established momentum toward Lutheran unity by getting most Evangelical governments to express interest in his mission if not full approval of his confession. So he prevailed on Landgrave Wilhelm and Duke Julius to sponsor a synod of representatives from several Evangelical lands at Zerbst in May 1570 in order to proclaim Lutheran concord. At Zerbst tensions between Andreae and the Wittenbergers barely rippled the deceptively calm surface of their relationship; those tensions exploded in the succeeding months. In Wittenberg the next month Andreae criticized the faculty's view of the relationship between Christ's divine and human natures. They tried to assure him that they did not mean what he understood by their condemnation of the concept that all divine virtues are poured into Christ's humanity. However, when Andreae announced soon thereafter that the Wittenbergers agreed with his position, they denied it, and he turned bitterly against them and their double-talk. The general lack of enthusiasm for Andreae's confession, the failure of the synod at Zerbst to take decisive action, and his own alienation from the electoral Saxon theologians at Wittenberg doomed Andreae's first attempt to construct concord.

He returned to Württemberg in December 1570 and during the next three years served Duke Ludwig's government as he continued his teaching and administrative duties at the University of Tübingen. In 1573 he once again turned his attention to the problem of disunity among the Lutherans, and he once again approached the problem with an analysis of its facets in terms designed to explain them to lay people. His *Six Christian Sermons on the Divisions Which Have Continued to Surface among the Theologians of the Augsburg Confession* treated ten disputes, adding to those dealt with in his confession discussions on original sin and on several disputes over law and gospel, and substituting for his treatment on the Lord's Supper one on the person of Christ. The *Six Sermons* marked the beginning of Andreae's bid for

21. On the differences between the two parties, see Robert Kolb, "Dynamics of Party Conflict in the Saxon Late Reformation, Gnesio-Lutherans vs. Philippists," *The Journal of Modern History* 49, no. 3 (1977): D1289–1305.

Gnesio-Lutheran support, for it represented a significant alteration in his strategy for reaching Lutheran concord. In this volume he rejected the Wittenbergers' understanding of the person of Christ in decisive fashion, with virulent personal attacks upon the party. At the same time he abandoned his belief that brief, general statements could solve the doctrinal problems besetting Lutherans, as the Philippists had maintained. Andreae adopted the Gnesio-Lutheran approach to unity through specific condemnations of false teaching and false teachers. The text of these sermons, with two exceptions, did not mention who was propagating the false doctrines being condemned. However, these theologians were named in the margins alongside the text. The exceptions were condemnations of the Wittenberg theologians by name in sermons on the definition of the Gospel and on the person of Christ. Not only did Andreae's sermons comply with the Gnesio-Lutheran insistence that false teachers be condemned, they also judged that the main body of Gnesio-Lutherans, led by Johann Wigand (see chapter 2 above) and Tilemann Hesshus, held the correct position on each issue under consideration. With Wigand and Hesshus, Andreae condemned on the one hand the view of their erstwhile comrade, Flacius, on original sin and on the other Philippist approaches to the freedom of the will, adiaphora, and the person of Christ. Andreae had come to the conclusion that the Wittenbergers were indeed trying to subvert Luther's gospel, and he decided that Lutheran concord could be attained by confessing in specific detail what he believed to be both Lutheran and scriptural on each of the issues under dispute.[22]

Thus, he finally created a document, in the *Six Sermons*, that conceded relatively little to the Philippists at points on which they and the Gnesio-Lutherans disagreed. He did have to compromise on some of his own expressions and views as he developed the *Six Sermons* into the *Formula of Concord*, but the basic stance set forth in the *Six Sermons* remained. Upon publication of this work Andreae sent copies to several north German theologians. Their reservations about him and the lay-oriented approach to doctrinal questions in the *Six Sermons* prevented ready acceptance of the book, but Martin Chemnitz and others urged Andreae to redraft and present his ideas in theses and antitheses so that theologians could work with them easily. Andreae composed a new document, his "Swabian Concord," and sent it to Julius and Chemnitz in March 1574.[23] Its narrative presentation treated election, the Lord's Supper, and the errors of Anabaptists, Zwinglians, Antitrinitarians, and Schwenckfelders, as well as the issues treated in the *Six Sermons*. Andreae chafed for nearly two years while Chemnitz and David Chytraeus of Rostock revised his text and circulated their revision throughout north Germany. In the meantime the princes of Württemberg, Henneberg,

22. The title is given in n. 13; the text is translated in Robert Kolb, *Andreae and the Formula of Concord, Six Sermons on the Way to Lutheran Unity* (St. Louis: Concordia, 1977), pp. 61–120.

23. This text was edited by H. Hachfeld, *Zeitschrift für die historische Theologie* n. s. 30 (1866): 234–301.

and Baden tried to get the drive for concord moving again by having two of Andreae's colleagues on Duke Ludwig's staff draw up another formula for concord, the "Maulbronn Formula."

In early 1576 August of Saxony broke the logjam of good intentions, suspicion, and poor planning blocking Lutheran concord. In 1574 he had discovered that some of his most trusted Philippist advisers had been endeavoring to alter the doctrinal position of his church on the Lord's Supper, moving it toward a spiritualistic understanding of the real presence. Enraged by what he considered their treachery and betrayal, he exiled many of the party of his chancellor, Georg von Cracow, and his personal physician, Caspar Peucer, and he jailed these two and two others. The previous year August had assumed control of the lands of his cousin, Johann Wilhelm of Ducal Saxony, whose death left his minor children under August's jurisdiction. August wreaked vengeance on Johann Wilhelm's theological establishment, the stronghold of Gnesio-Lutheranism, which had been so critical of him and his theologians for a quarter century. Thus, by late 1574 the political strength of both the Gnesio-Lutheran and the Philippist parties had been diminished significantly. Furthermore, August was determined to create a doctrinal standard that would maintain Luther's faith in August's lands. At a meeting at Lichtenberg in February 1576 his ecclesiastical advisers, among them Nikolaus Selnecker, urged August to call Andreae and other prominent theologians to assist in that project. With a leave of absence from his duties in Tübingen, Andreae embarked, taking his family with him, upon a Saxon sojourn that lasted through 1580.

At the elector's invitation, Chemnitz and Chytraeus met with his own theologians, Andreae and Selnecker, and with two representatives from Brandenburg, Andreas Musculus and Christoph Körner, at Torgau in May 1576. Though Andreae favored the Maulbronn Formula in an extensive memorandum to August offering guidelines for a statement of concord, the group used the text of the Chemnitz-Chytraeus revision of Andreae's "Swabian Concord," the "Swabian-Saxon Concord," as the basis of their formula. They were not in full agreement and debated several issues, including the person of Christ, quite hotly among themselves, but finally they composed a document that they believed could unite divided German Lutherans. Because Andreae and others had pleaded for a shorter document— more easily comprehended by lay people—and to provide August with a brief overview of their work, Andreae wrote a summary of the "Torgau Book." This summary became the "Epitome" of the *Formula of Concord*.[24]

The "Torgau Book" was circulated among the Evangelical estates of the empire and elicited varying reactions. Some approved it, some suggested revisions, others rejected the effort of the Torgau Six. So Andreae, Chemnitz,

---

24. The "Epitome" and the "Solid Declaration" of the *Formula of Concord* are found in *Die Bekenntnisschriften der evangelisch-lutherischen Kirche* (Göttingen: Vandenhoeck & Ruprecht, 1967). pp. 735–1135.

and Selnecker met again in Bergen Abbey, near Magdeburg, in March 1577 to sift through the critiques they had received. Two months later their three comrades joined them to complete the revision of the "Torgau Book." Overcoming their differences on the person of Christ and the third use of the law, they produced the "Bergic Book," which became the "Solid Declaration" of the *Formula of Concord*.

Now Andreae began the process of selling this *Formula* to the Lutheran churches of Germany. He spent the next three years writing memoranda and visiting churches, trying to convince others to accept the *Formula*. He started with a visitation of Saxon schools and churches, in which he ran into surprisingly little difficulty in inducing pastors and teachers to subscribe to the *Formula of Concord*, although he continued to encounter Philippist opposition throughout his stay in Saxony.

Andreae also had to deal with objections to the *Formula* from outside Saxony. August had adopted the Concordianist movement as his pet project, and his initial reaction to the proceedings at Bergen had been very favorable. However, when criticism of the *Formula* mounted, Andreae had to work hard to prevent August from sending his theologians once again to the conference table to revise the *Formula* one more time. Andreae began another round of travel to meet with opponents of the new document and to recruit support for it. He met with Flacius's friend, Cyriacus Spangenberg, in September 1577 to attempt to convince him that the *Formula's* statement on original sin was correct. He failed. Throughout 1577 and 1578 Andreae met with representatives of governments friendly and hostile to the *Formula* in attempts to smooth the path of its acceptance, with varied results.[25]

Andreae believed that the effectiveness of the *Formula* depended on its publication, and so he pressed for a printed edition of the *Formula* and other Lutheran confessional documents which would replace the *Corpora doctrinae* of each land that had its own confessional collection. He composed a preface for such a volume, later revised by others. On June 25, 1580, on the fiftieth anniversary of the presentation of the Augsburg Confession, the *Book of Concord* was published, signed by the three secular electors of the empire, Saxony, Brandenburg, and the Palatinate, as well as nearly fifty princes, thirty-five imperial cities, and about eight thousand pastors. Andreae's efforts at conciliation had excluded some of Flacius's followers on one side and some Philippists on the other. However, most Gnesio-Lutherans and many Philippists, along with many not affiliated with either party, agreed that the *Formula of Concord* was a suitable expression of the biblical message which Luther had proclaimed.

When he was not traveling to shore up the Concordianist movement during his Saxon sojourn, Andreae was working to offset Philippist influence in Saxony. In sermons and an occasional tract he recalled with horror the

---

25. Documents relating to Andreae's activities in this effort are found in Leonhard Hutter, *Concordia Concors* (Wittenberg: Berger, 1614), lvs. 75–256.

perfidy of the "crypto-Calvinist" party and its efforts to subvert the teaching of the Augsburg Confession. He hailed August as the great deliverer of the truth that Luther had taught. He denied that he was campaigning against Melanchthon although he did point out that Philip had not always confessed the truth forthrightly and correctly. He defended his belief that within Christ's person his human nature shares divine omnipotence and other divine attributes communicated by his divine nature. As August's agent he visited Peucer's cell to persuade him to recant his "Calvinism"; Peucer refused.[26]

Andreae's service in Saxony not only involved establishing doctrinal orthodoxy; he also assisted in the consolidation of the relationship between church and state that had been developing in Saxony under the Philippists. To do so came quite naturally to him since the Saxon system of rather firm control of the church by the prince was very similar to that to which he had become accustomed in Württemberg. He set guidelines for the behavior and supervision of the Saxon clergy and made other provisions in the realm of ecclesiastical practice that gave the prince tighter control of the church. He also played an important role in a reform of Saxon education on the university and secondary levels, instituting closer supervision of instructors and increasing the number of government-supported scholarships available. In helping establish the pattern of princely dominance of the Lutheran churches in north Germany, Andreae disagreed with his Gnesio-Lutheran friends, who had generally taken a stance of independence over against the prince. Princes probably would have constructed and cultivated this pattern without Andreae's assistance, but he was in fact one important agent in the actual development of the system of princely control of the church.[27]

Jakob Andreae's energetic pursuit of concord ground down his body and earned him the hostility of scores of prominent German ecclesiastical and political figures, but his persistence erected a monument to him in the form of the settlement that determined the shape and content of orthodox Lutheran life and thought. He presided over the end of the era in which Luther's heirs struggled to define Luther's message for their people and thereby opened the door to the settled Lutheranism of the orthodox period.

---

26. Andreae described various aspects of his Saxon service in his *Fünff Predigen von dem Wercke der Concordien* . . . (Dresden: Bergen, 1580); related materials are found in Hutter.

27. See n. 3 above.

5

hEINRICh BULLINGER

1504–1575

ROBERT C. WALTON

LIFE   Heinrich Bullinger was the fifth and youngest illegitimate
        son of the dean of the Chapter of Bremgarten in Aargau,
        a region under the joint administration of the Swiss Con-
federacy. His father, Heinrich, gladly paid the customary concubinage fees to
his friend the bishop of Constance in order to live at peace with Anna
Wiederkehr, the daughter of a well-to-do Bremgarten miller and town
councilor. Heinrich senior had inherited a good income from land; he belonged to the local establishment and spent much of his time hunting and
entertaining. Bullinger grew up in a household full of hunting dogs and local
dignitaries, an experience that did him no harm when he became the bishop
(*antistes*) of Zürich at age twenty-seven in 1531. The genuine piety and
devotion to the church he learned from both of his parents were even more
important for his future career.

When he was twelve years old, his father sent him to school at Emmerich
in the duchy of Cleves, where he joined his brother, Johannes, and was
introduced to the new Italian curriculum. While at Emmerich, he was also
influenced by the piety of the Brethren of the Common Life which was well
represented among the faculty of St. Martin's School, though the school itself
was not controlled by the brethren. Another experience which broadened his
awareness of the world around him was that he and his brother were compelled
by their father to beg for their room and board, to make them aware of the
plight of the poor. In doing this Heinrich senior followed a typical late
medieval practice. For instance, in later life Luther spoke of having to beg for
his bread when at school.

The experience of begging did have a lasting effect upon Bullinger, but
it did not help him to understand the radical economic changes caused in the
Zürich countryside by the continuing growth of population and the inflation

69

that typified Europe's economy in the sixteenth century. His problem was that in his youth Bullinger knew well a late medieval rural world in which, due to a relative scarcity of labor, even the day laborer earned enough to support his family with a slight margin of comfort. That world changed radically during the course of the sixteenth century, but Bullinger's economic attitudes remained those of his youth, reflecting the views of the wealthy rural upper strata of the Swiss cantons at the end of the medieval period. The tendency to identify worldly success with a "state of grace" prevalent in some of his early theological writings, though later somewhat modified, characterizes his attitude towards the poor, even though he always sought to provide charity for the poor and, as economic conditions worsened, the chance for them to work in Zürich's nascent textile industry.

In the summer of 1519 Bullinger entered the University of Cologne, one of the few remaining citadels of the *via antiqua*, with the intention of becoming a Carthusian monk. By the time he received his master of arts degree in 1522, he had been thoroughly introduced to humanism and had been led, like Luther, through studies of Peter Lombard to the Church Fathers and the Bible. As a student, Bullinger read the works of Erasmus and Faber Stapulensis, as well as Luther's early writings, which at first did not greatly impress him. The 1521 edition of Melanchthon's *Loci* was what convinced Bullinger that salvation was the result of God's grace. Melanchthon set him on the road to becoming a reformer and was to be a lifelong influence on Bullinger.

Some months after he returned home in 1522, he found employment in Zürich's territories. The abbot of Kappel, Wolfgang Joner, hired him as the Latin teacher at the newly founded Kappel Cloister School. Before consenting to go to Kappel, he told Joner that he would not accept the position if Joner required him to attend mass. Joner finally agreed that Bullinger was to be free to worship as he saw fit. Bullinger's unwillingness to participate in the Mass, the central cultic rite of the medieval church, indicates that he had already broken with the doctrine of transubstantiation and the medieval church's understanding of ordination as a sacrament. Whether at this time he believed in some form of the real presence as Zwingli still did is hard to say, but it is quite probable that he did not. Indeed, Bullinger may well have influenced Zwingli's subsequent abandonment of the belief in Christ's real presence in the elements of the Lord's Supper. He certainly anticipated Zwingli in another important way: Bullinger introduced an up-to-date classical curriculum into the Trivial school[1] at Kappel and then insisted that the monks required a basic theological education. To achieve this end Bullinger established a daily series of exegitical lectures that eventually replaced the traditional services and prayers performed by the monks. Bullinger lectured in the vernacular and provided a discussion period at the end of the lectures. His lectures were also open to the cloister's servants and nearby residents. In estab-

---

1. So named for the three disciplines or "ways," *triplex via*, which formed the basic curriculum.

lishing these lectures, Bullinger anticipated by a good two years Zwingli's decision to begin a similar series of exegetical lectures that he called "the prophesying" for the benefit of Zürich's pastors. As Zwingli's successor in Zürich, Bullinger perfected the prophesying, and it was then imitated everywhere Reformed churches were founded in Europe.

After his initial success at Kappel, Bullinger's career advanced rapidly. At Zwingli's request, he participated in the Bern disputation of 1528 as part of Zürich's delegation. In the following year he finally convinced his father of the correctness of the reform program, but because the old man proclaimed his advocacy of reform from the chancel he lost his post as people's priest[2] in Bremgarten and was forced to leave the town with his concubine. He later returned, a married man, to take a parish in a village near Bremgarten. Heinrich senior was able to return because Zürich's political pressure soon opened all the territories jointly administered by the Confederates to the preaching of advocates of reform. Gervasius Schuler became Bremgarten's new people's priest, and Bullinger joined him, in the middle of May 1529, to help guide the progress of reform in his hometown. Young Bullinger was successful and well liked at Bremgarten, and the town councilors were determined to keep him. When Zwingli invited him to join the delegation that was to travel to Marburg in Hesse to discuss and, if possible, reconcile the theological differences between Zwingli and Luther so that the German Protestants could ally themselves with the Swiss, the Bremgarten council refused to give Bullinger permission to accompany Zwingli.

Zwingli's eagerness to have Bullinger with him indicates the high regard in which Bullinger was held, both by the Zürich reformer and by his supporters. This regard had been greatly enhanced by Bullinger's literary production. His early works laid down the outlines of his mature theology and were the first volumes in what was to be an amazing flood of often repetitious but enormously important and very widely read theological works.

During his first year at Bremgarten, Bullinger married a Züricher, Anna Adlischwyler, despite the opposition of her mother (who wanted a richer husband for her wealthy daughter). The two long love letters he wrote during the difficult courtship anticipate the ideas about the role of the partners in a Christian marriage that he developed more fully in his treatise *On Christian Marriage*, which appeared in 1540. Anna was the mother of his eleven children, and she served her husband loyally until her death.

Zürich's defeat and Zwingli's death in the Second Kappel War (October 1531) changed Bullinger's life. During the meetings of the Swiss Confederates held at Bremgarten in the summer of 1531, Bullinger, unlike his father and brother Johannes, preached in favor of peace and reminded the representatives of the confederacy of their common heritage. His preaching did not prevent either the war or the recatholicization of Bremgarten, but it

2. The "people's priest," or *Leutpriester*, was especially charged with preaching. He was not, ordinarily, the parish priest.

did make it possible for him to save his household goods, which were not plundered by the victorious Catholics as were those of his father and brother. However, neither he nor the rest of his family were allowed to return to Bremgarten. All of them lived the remainder of their lives in exile.

In the aftermath of the disaster, Bullinger was simultaneously called to head churches at Basel, Bern, and Zürich. He chose to be Zwingli's successor, as soon as the Zürich magistrates guaranteed him the right to preach the Gospel freely and promised to enforce the Morality Ordinance of 1531. After that, Bullinger devoted his attention to the consolidation of the Zürich church. His work guaranteed the survival of Zwinglian Protestantism in Switzerland, which in turn made possible the introduction of the Reformed faith in the French-speaking areas of the Confederacy.

Bullinger's initial struggle in Zürich, concerning the right to preach the Gospel, was the result of the demands of the canton's country districts contained in the Meilan articles of 1531. The country men demanded that the clergy confine their preaching to the sphere of religion and also insisted that the clergy not criticize publically the conduct of their parishioners. Had their wishes been heeded, Zwingli's basic conception of the responsibilities of the prophet and the magistrate in the government of a unitary Christian society (*res publica christiana*) would have been abandoned. The prophet was to proclaim the Gospel and to correct the conduct of flagrant sinners, first by private and then by public admonition (*correctio*). Sinners were to be ostracized if they did not mend their ways. The right to excommunicate, i.e., to coerce miscreants, was reserved to the magistrate.

As a bishop, Bullinger spent a great deal of time fighting what he believed were false doctrines. For this reason he waged a lifelong struggle against the Württemberg reformer, Johannes Brenz, and his doctrine that Christ's body was ubiquitous (see chapter 4, p. 61). For Bullinger, there could be no *communicatio idiomatum* (communication of attributes) between Christ's divine and human natures. Christ's body remained in heaven while his spirit was present for the believer when he took part in the Lord's Supper. The Council of Trent was also the object of his concern and his vituperation, as were the heretical tendencies of men like Michael Servetus, whose execution in Geneva Bullinger heartily approved.

His desire for accommodation with his fellow Protestants is revealed both by his willingness to negotiate with the Lutherans at the time the Wittenberg Concord was framed (1536), and by the great care he exercised to prevent disagreements between Zürich and Geneva over such matters as the terminology to be used in describing Christ's presence in the Eucharist and the question of church discipline. The First and Second Helvetic Confessions (1548 and 1566) were triumphs of his moderate approach to the definition of theological truth. His caution about expressing the full rigor of the doctrine of double predestination was not appreciated at Geneva, but it was motivated by his hope for harmony, as well as his pastoral concern, and not by a basic disagreement with double predestination. Bullinger's old age was soured by the ongoing and ever more bitter conflict with Geneva over the question of church discipline. He never got over the failure, at the end of the 1560s, of his disciple, Thomas Erastus, to introduce into the polity of the Reformed Church of the Rhineland Palatinate the Zwinglian version of church discipline, which put all coercive power into the hands of the magistrate.

In the midst of all his pastoral concerns Bullinger loved his children and guided their education and careers with great care. He also took pleasure in his wine, carefully recording the fate of each year's vintage in his diary, and he enjoyed his friends in the Innkeepers' Guild, which he joined when he became a citizen of Zürich.

From the death of Zwingli in 1531 to his own death on September 17, 1575, Bullinger guided the church and schools of Zürich, a city that became a major center of Reformed life and doctrine.

THEOLOGY   Bullinger's use of patristic, medieval, and humanist sources to expound his theology was eclectic. Lorenzo Valla and, to a lesser extent, Marsilio Ficino and Jean Gerson were responsible for Bullinger's idea that the primitive church was the norm by which the church of his own day was to be judged and reformed. In his opinion, the primitive church and the Church Fathers, especially those of the second century, remained true to the authority of the Scripture, and the fall of the church came after the time of Gregory the Great.[3]

Like Zwingli before him, Bullinger laid great stress upon the doctrinal statements that emerged from the first four ecumenical councils. Both the *Decades* and the Second Helvetic confession begin with them. Bullinger included these creeds in order to demonstrate that the doctrines he expounded, and to which his church adhered, were in conformity with the teachings of the early church. Indeed one of his major arguments was that the Swiss Reformed churches, and their sister churches elsewhere in Europe, stood in a line of doctrinal succession guaranteed by God, which reached back to the early church and before it to the very beginning of the world itself. In advancing this argument, Bullinger rejected the conception of apostolic succession propounded by his traditionalist opponents. Only those individuals and churches that had maintained the doctrine given by Christ to his apostles were "true" and "orthodox." In arguing the "antiquity" and "catholicity" of Reformed theology, Bullinger not only employed a conception of normative orthodoxy he had derived from Tertullian, Valla, and Ficino, but he also followed closely the apologetic of the Lutherans in the empire.[4]

3. Joachim Staedtke, *Die Theologie des jungen Bullingers* (Zürich: Zwingli Verlag, 1962), pp. 36–38, 39.

4. Jaroslav Pelikan, *Luther the Expositor*, companion volume to *Luther's Works* (St. Louis: Concordia, 1959), pp. 74–75.

The terminology and dogmatic content of his theology were derived from the Bible and the Church Fathers, especially from Tertullian. Bullinger's conception of the person and work of Christ, his consideration of the centrality of Christology in the salvation event, and his use of the idea of a covenant were in very large part derived from Irenaeus and also from Zwingli. Cyprian influenced him less and Athanasius more, and he was influenced by Cyril's opinions on the integrity of Christ's divinity in the flesh. Bullinger's lifelong struggle against the externals of the late medieval cult were in part motivated by what he had learned from Lactantius. He remained indebted to Augustine for his explanation of the doctrine of the Trinity, his view of the work of the Holy Spirit, and his belief in predestination, as well as for his doctrine of the Lord's Supper.

Bullinger had studied the scholastics of both the *via antiqua* and the *via moderna*[5] more carefully than his critical remarks about them sometimes indicate. Aquinas certainly influenced his definition of natural law and its function in the conscience of individuals and the government of society. Bullinger's basic hermeneutical principle of letting difficult biblical passages be interpreted by other passages from the Scripture was derived from Augustine and Gerson.[6]

Bullinger knew and employed all of Luther's early works, and they certainly influenced his own theological development. Indeed, a careful study of Bullinger's relationship to Luther and especially to Melanchthon, whose *Loci* played a decisive role in the final stages of his break from Rome, is a special *desideratum*. That Bullinger was much influenced by Erasmus and Faber Stapulensis cannot be denied, though it is equally obvious that he rejected Erasmus's belief in free will. Bullinger and Erasmus were no doubt one in their mutual indebtedness to the conception of piety, which they both learned from the Brethren of the Common Life.[7]

Above all, Heinrich Bullinger was Zwingli's disciple and heir. This does not mean that he was merely the Zürich reformer's follower, for he modified and matured Zwingli's theology. The maturation of the Zwinglian inheritance that occurred under Bullinger's direction are among the most fascinating aspects of Bullinger's work, and they represent his greatest theological achievement. Susi Hausammann has observed in her consideration of Bullinger's doctrine of justification that even though Bullinger was influenced by others, he had a way of employing their thought to make his own unique formulation.[8]

---

5. The *via antiqua* was the tradition stemming primarily from Aquinas and Scotus. The *via moderna* looked principally, though not exclusively, to Ockham.

6. Susi Hausammann, *Römerbriefauslegung zwischen Humanismus und Reformation: Eine Studie Heinrich Bullingers Römerbrief Vorlesung von 1525* (Zürich: Zwingli Verlag, 1970), pp. 129–30.

7. Staedtke, pp. 22–26, 46–50.

8. Hausammann, *Römerbriefauslegung*, pp. 53–55, 84–87, 124–25, 127–30, 155–61.

The idea of the absolute sovereignty of God is generally regarded as the hallmark of Reformed theology. Even a cursory glance at Bullinger's major theological works reveals how completely he justifies this assertion. Indeed, the whole of Bullinger's religious thought can be interpreted and understood only in terms of his doctrine of God, the Sovereign Lord and Creator.

The God he worshiped, and in whose service he labored as a Reformed bishop and theologian, was the God of the Niceno-Constantinopolitan Creed, whose plan of salvation for humanity was revealed in the Son and Savior, the Christ of the Chalcedonian formula: truly God, truly man.[9] Although his theology was the product of a response to the challenges he faced as a mentor and guide of Reformed Protestantism within and beyond the Swiss Confederacy, nevertheless it evolved with remarkable consistency into a careful commentary upon the significance of the triune God for the faith and life of the church.

The role of scripture, prayer, ministry, and sacraments in the church, the doctrine of the church itself, as well as the central question of the relationship between the clergy and the Christian magistrate in a Christian society—all depended upon Bullinger's doctrine of God. The same can be said of his use of the idea of the covenant (see below, pp. 79–80), which is often misunderstood and overemphasized. His cautiously stated but nevertheless firmly and consistently maintained doctrine of double predestination is also the logical consequence of his understanding of the love and power of God the Creator.

When one considers Bullinger's doctrine of God and the relationship of his mature theology to it, it is striking how completely the Zürich *antistes* had made Zwingli's pneumatology his own. The working of God, the Spirit, in every aspect of the life of the church in this world was indeed the constitutive element in his clearly enunciated trinitarian theology.[10] The Spirit acted among men visibly and invisibly. In its invisible form, "he is daily watering us with his grace, and bringing faith, hope and charity unto us." Bullinger denied that the Spirit could be limited to any one place, and he was at pains to demonstrate that the same Spirit that inspired the patriarchs, the prophets, and the apostles inspired the church of his own day. As he undersood it, "the

9. Heinrich Bullinger, *Das Zweite Helvetische Bekenntnis Confessio Helvetica Posterior*, German trans. by Walter Hildebrandt and Rudolf Zimmermann, (Zürich: Swingli Verlag, 1966), pp. 23, 49. Hereafter referred to as HB 2. *The Decades of Henry Bullinger, Minister of the Church of Zürich*, ed. Rev. Thomas Harding, 5 vols. (Cambridge: Cambridge University Press, 1848), *Decades* IV, Sermon VI, 238–54, 259–62. Hereafter referred to as *Decades* with number and sermon number. The references to the Latin edition of the *Decades, Sermonum Decades quinque, de potissimis Christianae religionis capitibus, in tres tomas digestae, authore Henrycho Bullingero ecclesiae Tigurinae ministro* (Tiguri: In officina Christoph. Froschaueri, 1552), are given in parentheses. (D, pp. 228b–233b.)

10. G. Locher, Die Lehre vom Heiligen Geist in der Confessio Helvetica Posterior," *400 Jahre Confessio Helvetica Posterior*, ed. Joachim Staedtke (Zürich: Zwingli Verlag, 1966), pp. 300, 307, 311. Hereafter referred to as "Die Lehre."

Father by the Spirit worketh all things through the Spirit." He used it to protect the church from error and to bind it together: "the mystical body of Christ is united by the Holy Ghost."[11] This conception of the work of the Spirit was essential to Bullinger's assertion that the orthodox teaching of the church was based upon the eternal and unchanging word of God, and it was also central to his understanding of God's covenant as a single and unchanging covenant that contained in God's promise to Abraham the epitome of the message of the Gospel.

For Bullinger, knowledge of God depended upon God's revelation. Though he did believe that God revealed himself in nature and in that special creature created in God's image, Bullinger maintained that the only full and proper knowledge of God came from God's word: "God cannot rightly be known but by his word; and that God is to be received and believed to be such an one as he revealeth himself unto us in his holy word." In making this assertion Bullinger was also careful to say that although God normally used the preaching of his word to instruct people about his will for them, he was by his very nature free to choose other means of communication if he desired to do so.[12]

Normally, God spoke to the church and its members through preaching, which Bullinger asserted was "the word of God itself."[13] Following Romans 10:30–17, he argued that the faith of the believer could only be awakened and developed by hearing the proclamation of the word. As the word was preached, the Holy Spirit caused the preacher's exposition of it to become the Word of God itself. The Holy Spirit, not the minister, was responsible for ensuring that the preacher's words were so employed that his hearers understood the sermon.[14]

As God's word, the Scripture naturally shared the properties which were common to God. It was "true, just, without deceit and guile, without error or evil affection, holy, pure, good, immortal and everlasting." Because it possessed these properties, the Scripture was also self-authenticating.[15]

Like Zwingli before him, Bullinger employed the text of 2 Corinthians 3:6 to distinguish between the letter and the Spirit of the Word. This distinction was common enough to the reformers, who derived it from St. Paul (Romans 2:27–29; 2 Corinthians 3:6) and from St. Augustine.[16] It

11. *Decades* IV, Sermon VIII, pp. 307–09, 310–13, 314, 319. (D, pp. 244a–245b, 246a–246b.)

12. HB 2, pp. 8, 19. *Decades* IV, Sermon III, p. 125. (D, pp. 204a–205a.)

13. *Decades* V, Sermon III, p. 95; (D, p. 292b) "Die Lehre," p. 322. Cf. *Decades* I, Sermon I, p. 37 (D, p. 7a) and *De Scripturae Sanctae authoritate, certitudine Firmitate et Absoluta perfectione* (Tiguri: in Officina Froschoveriana, 1538), p. 8a. Hereafter referred to as HB, *SS*.

14. ". . . Fides ex auditu est, auditus autem per verbum dei . . ." HB, *SS*, pp. 16b–17b; HB 2, pp. 17–19; Hausammann, p. 57.

15. *Decades* I, Sermon I, p. 37 (D, p. 1a); cf. E. Egli, Finsler, W. Kohler, eds., *Huldreich Zwinglis Sämtliche Werke*, 14 vols. (Zürich Leipzig: Berichthaus Verlag, 1901) 1: 341. Hereafter referred to as Z.

16. *De Doctrina Christiana*, 3: 9.

was of particular importance for Bullinger when he discussed the sacraments. The *letter* referred to external things, especially the teaching of the law, which, Bullinger asserted, was destructive and caused sin if the *Spirit* was absent and there was no faith in the heart. The Spirit's realm of activity was the inner man. His heart and soul were able to receive "the inspiration, revelation and doctrine" that Bullinger identified with the Spirit.

Yet the *antistes* did not lack respect for the written word. Bullinger viewed it as God's instrument and he was very careful to deny that the canon of Scripture had, as his traditionalist opponents claimed, been established by a decision of men, or of the church. The Scripture had its origin in the living voice of God, whose Spirit guided the development first of the oral tradition and then of the written record of the Word, and finally guided the formation of the canon itself. The Holy Spirit guided Moses' hand and caused the fathers to know which books should be retained in the canon and which rejected.[17] The canonical books provided the church with the sum and substance of "orthodoxy," that is, with all that was necessary for teaching the faithful "saving" doctrine and informing them about the conduct God required of them. They also provided the church with the norms for instituting reform whenever necessary. However, the dynamic of the canonical Scripture depended not upon a jot-and-tittle formula like the one added to the Second Helvetic Confession in the *Formula Consensus* of 1675.[18] The key to the authority of Scripture was the dynamic action of God's Spirit.

The Holy Spirit was the key to the proclamation of the Gospel by the clergy. Like Zwingli, Bullinger believed that the members of the congregation were taught by God *(theodidacti)*. Paraphrasing St. Paul, he said that the ministers preach and write with ink, while the Spirit moves the heart. Without the working of the Spirit, the preaching and hearing of the Word remained an external form; those without faith could not receive the inward fruit of the Word. Even where the minister was an evil man, the Spirit could use his words to good effect.[19]

Nevertheless, Bullinger gave the preaching of the ministers or "prophets" to use the term Zwingli and Bullinger borrowed from the early Luther, a central place in the life of the visible church. When they preached, they united all the members of the visible church (one could say "visible particular churches," which is what Bullinger meant) and brought them into the unity of the body of Christ. He asserted repeatedly that "the ministry is of the Lord, and through it he worketh our salvation." For this reason he called the ministers "saviors."

17. *Decades* I, pp. 39–43, 46–47 (D, pp. 1b–3b, 4a–4b); HB, *SS*, pp. 3b, 7a–7b, 8a–8b, 11b–12b; *Decades* IV, Sermon VIII, p. 299. (D, p. 243a).

18. HB 2, pp. 17–19; *Decades* IV, "On the Reforming of Churches," pp. 119–22 (D, pp. 203a–203b); HB 2, p. 152.

19. *Decades* V, Sermon I, p. 22; cf. *Decades* V, Sermon VIII, p. 353. (D, pp. 275a–275b; p. 349a).

The ministers were, he maintained, chosen by God through the Spirit and were thus "Spirit-filled men." In ordaining them, the church confirmed this choice and it was obliged to seek signs of the gifts of the Spirit, one of which was a high standard of conduct. It was necessary for the minister to have a good education so that he could expound the Scripture in a proper literal sense. The power of the keys the minister received at ordination had nothing to do with the claims to authority made by the pope and hierarchy of the Roman Church. The Gospel itself was the key to heaven. When the minister preached the Gospel, he bound and loosed, opening the gates of heaven to those who believed the word and closing them to those who rejected the Gospel.[20]

The sacraments of Baptism and the Lord's Supper also depended upon the Holy Spirit. Bullinger stated repeatedly that they were "not simple or bare signs but ceremonies or religious actions." Speaking of the Lord's Supper, he explained that Christ's words "This is my body, this is my blood" could not be used to demonstrate "a corporal presence . . . in the supper." They had to be understood

> mystically and sacramentally: so that the body and blood of Christ do abide in their substance and nature, and in their place, I mean, in some certain place of heaven; but the bread and wine are a sign or sacrament, a witness or sealing, and a lively memory of his body given and his blood shed for us.

The purpose of the words of institution was "to signify, and by signifying to bear witness, and to admonish. . . ." As Bullinger understood it, not everyone could profit from participation in the sacraments. To prove this pont he cited St. Augustine, who had said that "the fountain of regeneration is common to all . . . ; but inward grace, whereof they are sacraments, whereby the members of Christ with their head are born anew, is not common to all."[21] There can be no doubt that his conception of the sacraments presupposed the doctrine of election. Those who had not already received faith through the quickening of the Holy Spirit were not moved by the Spirit and born anew when they took part in the Supper, or, for that matter, when they were baptized. For those without faith, the sacraments remained outward "signs" or "marks" of

---

20. Z, 1: 349, 350–51, 352, 353, 375, 376, 397; *Decades* I, Sermon I, p. 43; Sermon IV, pp. 84–85, 87, 90; *Decades* V, Sermon III, pp. 126–127; Sermon I, pp. 22–23; Sermon III, pp. 101–02; *Decades* I, Sermon I, p. 49; *Decades* III, Sermon V, pp. 133, 148; *Decades* V, Sermon IV, pp. 128–29; Sermon III, p. 95; Sermon IV, pp. 147–49, 150, 160 (D, pp. 2b, 11b–12b, 229b, 275a–275b, 294a, 4a, 113a, 299b–300a, 292a, 303b–305a, 307a); "Die Lehre," pp. 300, 307, 311; Fritz Busser, "De Prophetae Officio," *Festgabe Leonhard von Muralt* (Zürich: Verlag Berichthaus, 1970), pp. 245–57; Hausammann, pp. 197–98.

21. *Decades* V, Sermon VI, pp. 252, 253–54, 264; as quoted from A. Augustinus, *In Psal. LXXVII, Enarrationes* by H. Bullinger, *Decades* V, Sermon VII, pp. 300–01; cf. *Decades* IV, Sermon VII, pp. 275–80 (D, pp. 328a–330a, 338b, 236b–237b).

membership in the visible church, since they had never received the quickening of the Spirit that made them members of the church triumphant. The true church was known only to God, who enabled the believer to bring forth good works, the "fruits of the Spirit."

Bullinger's assertion that the sacraments "do neither confer nor contain grace" was motivated by his desire both to affirm God's sovereign freedom and to avoid the confusion between the *sign* and the *thing signified*, which had led the medieval church to objectify the sacraments as channels of grace which justified the participant. Bullinger believed that the Scriptures and the Fathers taught salvation by faith, and he was at pains to maintain the integrity of this teaching against the danger of a false interpretation of the sacraments. To maintain it, he had to demonstrate that

> the Lord did not institute the sacraments or sacrifices that, being offered, they might give grace or justify us; but to be witnesses of the grace of God; and that by them his people might be kept, and drawn in due order, from idols and heathenish worship, and led to Christ.[22]

This interpretation also permitted him to defend, as Zwingli had done before him, what he believed to be the integrity of Christ's divine and human natures and to refute the Lutheran teaching that Christ's body was ubiquitous, which had been developed by the Swabian reformer Johannes Brenz. Christ, Bullinger asserted, was "everywhere according to the nature of his Godhead, and is contained in place [heaven] according to the nature of his manhood." When speaking of Christ, it was proper that there should be an "alloeosis," that is, "a mutual giving or an interchanging of properties," but Bullinger warned that it was false to "extend his humanity [as far as] his divinity is extended." The human body of Christ could not in all respects be made equal with his Godhead;[23] it must remain circumscribed and localized according to the nature of bodies.

It is important to understand Bullinger's idea of the relationship between grace and the sacraments. At creation God had promised man his grace, and God kept and keeps his promises. In so saying, Bullinger was also explaining what he meant when he talked about God's covenant. To him, "true religion" was a "friendship, a knitting, and a unity [or a league] with a true, living, and everlasting God; unto whom we being linked by a true faith do worship . . . , and serve him alone." Salvation and faith were basic to any definition of religion, ". . . which elsewhere is called in scripture a league or covenant . . . . For as they which be confederate are united and made one by a league; so God and man are knit together by religion." As Peter Walser[24] has observed, the *covenant* idea was not really a basic principle of Bullinger's

---

22. *Decades* V, Sermon VII, pp. 302, 316 (D, pp. 338b–339a, 341a).
23. *Decades* IV, Sermon VI, pp. 266, 270, 271 (D, pp. 234b–235b).
24. *Decades* IV, Sermon V, pp. 231–32 (D, p. 227a); Peter Walser, *Die Prädestination bei Heinrich Bullinger* (Zürich: Zwingli Verlag, 1957), p. 244.

theology. Bullinger used the term as a synonym for the word "religion." In other words he used it to refer to a general relationship between God and mankind. As is clear from his use of the terms *confederation* or *league* as equivalents for covenant, Bullinger's model for the idea of the covenant was a political one, derived from the loose patterns of alliances sworn to by the Swiss Confederacy. Neither *De Testamento* nor *Der alte Glaub* develop a full covenant theology. When comparing Bullinger's use of the covenant idea with that of Cocceijus, Gottlob Schrenk[25] noted just how loosely Bullinger employed the term but, nevertheless, he overemphasized Bullinger's role as a covenant theologian.

What Bullinger sought to do was not to develop a theology of the covenant but to emphasize the constancy and reliability of God's commitment to men and to remind them of their obligation to serve God. Part of that obligation was fulfilled by participation in the sacraments. To those able to receive him, God communicates with increasing frequency as they "grow in faith." Their reception of his communication is naturally spiritual; certainly it does not occur first when the believer receives the sacraments, "as if he should pour out himself into us by them, as it were by conduit pipes." Bullinger used this statement to illustrate that God is bound to no means. But he also added that, when the believer partakes of the sacrament, he receives God "after a special manner . . . proper unto the sacraments," which permits him to grow "spiritually and by faith." Thus he concluded that the sacraments do not give grace but rather witness to the truth and confirm God's good will and strengthen the faith of the believer.[26] His conception of the sacraments represents a fuller elaboration and further development of the position Zwingli had taken in the *Ratio Fidei* of 1530.

Baptism and the Lord's Supper were the successors of circumcision and the passover, which had been part of the ceremonial law. They had prefigured Christ and were both "outward" and "inward." God used circumcision to present the Israelites with a visible reminder that he had renewed his covenant with men. The passover served to remind them of what God had done for them and was also a "type" of Christ.[27] The ceremonial law was abrogated by Christ, who instituted Baptism and the Supper to replace the ceremonies that had prefigured him. The new sacraments presented signs—water, bread, and wine—signifying invisible and heavenly things which can be seen with "the eye or mind of faith" but not with the bodily eye. Thus, Christ's body remained in heaven during the supper, but it could be seen by the eye of faith as the believer ate Christ "mystically and sacramentally" in faith.[28]

25. Gottlob Schrenk, *Gottesreich und Bund im älteren Protestantismus* (Darmstadt: Wissenschaftliche Buchgesellschaft, 1967), pp. 40–44.

26. *Decades* V, Sermon VII, pp. 315–16, 317–18 (D, pp. 341a–342a).

27. *Decades* III, Sermon VI, pp. 175, 177, 178, 179 (D, pp. 112b, 113a–113b).

28. *Decades* V, Sermon VI, p. 251; *Decades* III, Sermon VI, p. 184. For a clear definition see *Decades* V, Sermon VIII, pp. 367–68; Sermon IX, p. 403 (D, pp. 262a, 115b, 359a–359b, 361a–361b).

Outward or visible signs of membership in the church, the sacraments also served as proofs of citizenship in the civic community. On the practical level this development was logical in an urban commonwealth like Zürich, but there was also a good theological reason for it. When speaking of the moral law, which was summarized in the Ten Commandments, Bullinger stated that the two tables of the Decalogue were the bases for all true good works and the guide for the lives of all men in the world, because all law had to be referred to the Decalogue "as to the eternal mind or will of God."[29] The judicial laws, enacted by the magistrate and covering the whole scope of public life, could not but reflect "the substance of God's laws."[30] Bullinger's concept of the law was typically medieval in that he believed that all society was under God's law and was obviously both unitary and theocratic.

Bullinger assumed that the magistrate was a Christian, had been "ordained of God and is God's minister." His most famous statements on the subject of the Christian prince were made to Edward VI of England, whom he hailed as a new Josiah and whom he advised to submit his kingdom to the "rule of God's holy word." When Edward did this, he would, Bullinger assured him, be guided by the Holy Spirit in all his actions. Indeed, Bullinger believed that all "regenerate" rulers received the same guidance. His conception of the relationship between the Godly ruler and the minister was typically Zwinglian:

The politic magistrate is commanded to give ear to the ecclesiastical ruler, and the ecclesiastical minister must obey the politic governor in all things which the law commandeth . . . the subjection and duty which they owe is to the Lord Himself.

Believing in the Christian ruler who heeded the words of the prophet and was guided by the Holy Spirit,[31] Bullinger left to the ruler the responsibility for "ordering rightly matters of religion," and the right "to make trial of doctrines and to kill those that do stubbornly teach against the Scripture."[32] In this theological system the visible church was under the supervision of the Christian magistrate.

Following Zwingli's definition, Bullinger explained that the true church was invisible. The visible church referred both to the universal church in the world and to its particular component churches.[33] The visible church was the church militant, the kingdom of grace. It was a mixed body, containing in good biblical and Augustianian terms the wheat and the tares,

29. *Decades* III, Sermon VII, p. 220; *Decades* II, Sermon VII, p. 342; *Decades* III, Sermon IX, p. 353 (D, pp. 132b, 66a, 160b).

30. *Decades* III, Sermon VIII, p. 280 (D, p. 145a).

31. *Decades* III, Dedication to Edward VI, p. 14; cf. *Decades* IV, "On Reforming the Churches," pp. 121–22; *Decades* IV, Sermon VII, pp. 277–78; *Decades* II, Sermon VII, p. 329; cf. Z, 14: 420, 424 (D, pp. 88a–88b, 203a–203b, 237a–237b).

32. *Decades* II, Sermon VI, p. 380; Sermon VII, pp. 323–25, 334, 337–38 (D, pp. 62a–62b, 64a, 65a).

33. Z, 2: 56–58.

the "elect" and the "hypocrites," who could not be separated in this life because they shared the outward signs of membership in the church; they heard the Word preached and participated in the sacraments. The wheat, the elect, were endowed with "faith and true obedience," the "inward marks," which allowed them to show the fruits of faith and made them pleasing to God. They were members of the church triumphant, the true church, which was invisible and known only to God. Bullinger referred to the true church as "the Kingdom of God," "the true church of the elect," and "the congregation of the saints."[34]

The church militant was constantly at war with the kingdom of the world, headed by Satan. Satan's kingdom was made up of "unfaithful apostates" who, "through their own proper malice," revolted from God and appointed Satan as their king. Their fate was "everlasting punishment in the world to come."[35]

Bullinger's twofold definition of the church and the distinction he made between the elect, who were able to demonstrate the "fruits of faith," and the hypocrites, who could not, were directly related to his doctrine of election. But no matter how cautiously he expressed it, the idea that there were "fruits of faith" moderated the rigor of his predestinarianism. His description of the kingdom of Satan and the choice its members made between serving God and Satan placed the responsibility for their wickedness upon them and not upon God; it also cautiously assumed that some were doomed to eternal damnation.

Bullinger's discussions of the authority of the visible church and the function of the clergy were largely devoted to a refutation of papal claims to authority, especially that the pope was the possessor of *plenitudo potestatis* (fullness of power). Bullinger flatly refuted the validity of the apostolic succession. Citing Tertullian, he maintained that the only "lawful succession" was one which upheld the purity of doctrine of the Scriptures and the Apostles.[36]

The authority granted to the church in the world was limited. Bullinger explained that there were two kinds of power: one was "free and absolute," the other, "which is limited, . . . is also called ministerial." "Absolute power" was reserved to Christ the King. "Ecclesiastical jurisdiction," or "ministerial power," was the authority Christ, the true head of the church, permitted the church to exercise through "her ministers." The visible church should be governed by ecclesiastical laws derived from Scripture and not by the traditions of men, "invented at their own choice. . . ."[37] Like the Christian commonwealth, the magistrate, or the prince, the church in the world was subject to and limited by the law of God.

34. *Decades* IV, Sermon IV, pp. 275–76, pp. 276–80; *Decades* V, Sermon I, pp. 5, 7–8, 8–9, 19–21, 23; HB 2, pp. 77–87 (D, pp. 236b–238b, 271a–272b, 274b, 275b).

35. *Decades* IV, Sermon VII p. 281; *Decades* V, Sermon I, pp. 8–11, 12–16 (D, pp. 258a, 272a–274b).

36. *Decades* V, Sermon I, pp. 28, 32 (D, pp. 276b–278a).

37. *Decades* V, Sermon I, pp. 41–42, 43; *Decades* II, Sermon I, p. 207 (D, pp. 280b–281a, 38a–38b).

The church's functions were, first, "at certain times, in a certain place," employing an "appointed order," to celebrate the sacraments, "according to the laws and received custom of the church." The church baptizes infants and administers the Lord's Supper. The visible church is responsible for ordaining ministers and consulting the Scripture, in order to decide between divergent interpretations of doctrine. When it performed these functions properly, the church was said to be guided by the Holy Spirit.[38]

With the aid of "judges conveniently appointed," the church considered marriage cases, which fell to her jurisdiction as a part of her right to order "ecclesiastical matters." Excommunication was also part of her general responsibility to correct, to admonish, and to punish members of the church. This responsibility, along with that of judging marriage cases, was to be exercised by the particular visible church. However, Bullinger carefully qualified the power to excommunicate by saying that it should be used to "edify, and not destroy . . ." and should be "limited with the rule of the Word and of love. . . ."[39]

In fact a close look at his exegeses of Matthew 16:13–18, Matthew 18:15–18, and 1 Corinthians 5 reveals that from the very beginning of his career at Zürich Bullinger was unwilling to bar anyone from hearing the Word preached or from participating in the sacraments, unless the individual himself believed that he was unworthy and excluded himself. Bullinger defined the Lord's Supper as a "joyous public expression of faith that Christ's blood had been shed for sinners," and he argued that to bar sinners from the Supper meant that Christ's blood had been shed in vain. He maintained that major crimes such as murder, incest, blasphemy, and drunkenness were to be dealt with by the Christian magistrate who presided over the affairs of the Christian Commonwealth. He defined the exercise of excommunication by the particular church in terms of a public "censure" or "correction" imposed in order to persuade the miscreant to mend his ways. The church was to separate the sinner from Christ's body by ostracizing him. Bullinger's handling of the problem of excommunication represented a further development of the position first ennunciated by Zwingli.[40] Bullinger's conceptions of the use of excommunication and of the sphere of the visible church's authority differed sharply from those of Calvin and Beza. These differences were long an underlying cause of friction between Zürich and Geneva.

---

38. *Decades* V, Sermon I, pp. 43, 44 (D, p. 281a).

39. *Decades* V, Sermon I, p. 46 (D, p. 281a).

40. H.B., *In Sacrosanctum Jesu Christi Domini nostri Evangelium secundum Matthaeum, Commentariorum libri XII* (Tiguri: Apud Forschorverum, 1542), pp. 53a, 175a–75b; HB, In priorem D. Pauli, *Ad Corintheos Epistolam, Heinrich Bullingeri Commentarius* (Tiguri: Apud Christoph. Froscho, 1534), pp. 45a–45b, 47b–48b, 49a–49b; HB to P. Dathenus, June 1, 1570, and also HB to Erastus, Oct. 17, 1568, both printed in T. Erastus, *Explicatio Gravissimae Quaestiones utrum Excommunicatio* (Pesclavii: Apud Boacium Sultaceterum, 1589), pp. 355ff, 358–59; cf. Bullinger to Berchtold Haller, July 6, 1531, in *Heinrich Bullingers Werke, Erster Abteilung Bibliographie*, ed. Fritz Busser, 2 vols. (Zürich: Theologischer Verlag, 1977), section 2 (correspondence), 1:207–09, 210–14; cf. Z, 4:32, 5:727.

According to Bullinger, the message of the Old and the New Testaments was the same: God wished "well to mankind" and had created man in his own image, so that he could enjoy "all the good gifts of God." Man did not accept this message: ". . . by means of the devil and his own proper fault, [man] fell into sin, misery, and death, changing his likeness to God in the similitude of the devil." God did not allow man's fall to be final, and so he started over again to "free man from evil" and to restore him to the likeness of the image of God.[41]

He decided to restore him by means of the Word Incarnate, "so by dying in the flesh, he cleansed, sanctified, and delivered mankind. . . ." Christ, the high priest, propitiated God and made sinful man's justification possible. God was not willing to impute righteousness to him "without works."[42]

Was God's grace available to all? The answer is no. The theme that some were excluded from becoming co-heirs of Christ in eternity runs like a red thread through Bullinger's theology. The question remains, was Bullinger a double predestinarian? The answer is a cautious yes. Bullinger believed that this is what the Bible said: "[God,] by his eternal unchangeable counsel, hath fore-appointed who are to be saved, and who are to be condemned." The end of this decision was "Christ, the Son of God," in whom "God hath chosen us . . . before the foundation of the world." In developing this doctrine he was careful to say that man was responsible for his own fall. God knew of it in advance and God permitted it but did not cause it. From a pastoral perspective, what was striking about Bullinger's doctrine is that he believed faith was a "sign of election," which could be applied to cities as well as individuals, and that he left an important place for worship and prayer in the life of the believer.[43] Bullinger viewed the ability to worship, pray, and to do good works as signs of faith, or grace. In this he differed from Calvin, who was far more cautious in equating the claim that one had faith or any other human action with a "sign of election."

In Bullinger's theology the Third Person of the Trinity was the constitutive element in word, sacrament, church, and society. Bullinger's system left no place for the independent action of any human agency; all were subordinated to a sovereign God. His conception of the relationship between God and his earthly instruments reveals the extent of the Reformed reaction against the structure, sacraments, and theological teachings of the Roman Church.

41. *Decades* I, Sermon I, 38–39, 39–40, 42 (D, pp. 2a–3a).

42. *Decades* I, Sermon I, pp. 42–43; HB 2, pp. 69–71; *Decades* I, Sermon VI, pp. 114–15 (D, pp. 3a–3b, 17a–17b).

43. *Decades* III, Sermon IX, pp. 321–22, 329–30; *Decades* V, Sermon VII, pp. 300–25; *Decades* VI, Sermon IV, pp. 179, 183, 184, 185–87; *Decades* III, Sermon IX, pp. 330, 336, 337 (D, pp. 154a–154b, 156b–157b, 338b–347a, 216b–218a, 156b–158a); HB 2, pp. 43–46, 65–66, 71–72. Peter Walser, pp. 130–133, 169, 180, 191–93; *Ioannis Calvini Opera Quae Supersunt Omnia*, ed. G. Baum, E. Cuntz, E. Reuss (Brunsvigae: Apud C. A. Schwetschke et Filium, 1875), col. 14, 483, 490.

ROLE IN THE
CHURCH

In his own day Heinrich Bullinger was among the most important Protestant theologians in Europe. His *Decades* of sermons were at least as important as Calvin's *Institutes of the Christian Religion* and Beza's *Confessio Christianae Fidei* in the development of the life and thought of the European Reformed churches. Indeed, in countries like Holland, the *Decades* were more widely read by the laity than the *Institutes*. Fritz Büsser, director of the Institute for Swiss Reformation History in Zürich, has recently compared the volume of Calvin's and Bullinger's theological writings.[44] Three years before Calvin's commentary on Romans appeared in 1540, Bullinger had published the first of the seven Latin editions of his *Commentaries on the Pauline Epistles*. Taken as a whole, his biblical commentaries were far more numerous than Calvin's and probably more widely read. The same can be said of his other major theological works, such as the *Summa Christlicher Religion* and the *Catechesis pro adultioribus scripta*.

Among his other lasting works were his *Treatise on Christian Marriage* which was one of the first Protestant works to consider the subject of marriage. His *History of the Reformation* helped to set the tone for the Protestant interpretation of the Reformation as a response to the degeneracy and corruption of the Roman Church. Along with his *The Origins of the Anabaptists* (1560) and the earlier *About the Shameless Wickedness of the Anabaptists* (1531), the *History of the Reformation* helped form the normative view of Anabaptism, a view that has only recently been challenged. Limitations of space prevent the mention of his numerous polemical works against Lutheran and Catholic opponents.

Bullinger successfully defended and in fact clarified the basic Zwinglian definition of the function of the priest and magistrate. In his early years at Zürich he made his position clear in his exegeses of Matthew 16:13–18, Matthew 18:15–18, and 1 Corinthians 5, as well as in his oration *Concerning the Prophet's Office (De prophetae officio)*, delivered as a memorial to Zwingli's memory at the end of January 1532 and in *Concerning the Appointment and Function of Bishops Who are Ministers of the Word of God (De Episcoporum, qui verbi dei ministri sunt, institutione & functione . . .)*, printed in 1538. The *De Episcoporum* was published together with *Concerning the Authority of Scripture*, a natural development because Bullinger assumed that the Scripture was the basis for the bishop's authority. The two works were dedicated to Henry VIII of England. In the *De Episcoporum* Bullinger cited Marsilio of Padua

---

44. Fritz Büsser, "Bullinger, Nicht Calvin," *Neue Züricher Zeitung (NZZ)* 6/7, no. 261 (Nov. 1976): 59; "Heinrich Bullinger und die Zürcher Reformation," *NZZ* 10/11, no. 34 (Feb. 1979): 76. For the comparison of the volume of Bullinger's and Calvin's works, see Fritz Büsser, *Heinrich Bullingers Werke*, 2:250–59, and *C.R.*, 59:449–54. The volume of Bullinger's works is considerably greater. For the remarkable spread of the *Decades*, see Walter Hollweg, *Heinrich Bullingers Hausbuch*, vol. 8 of *Beiträge zur Geschichte und Lehre der Reformierte Kirche* (Neukirchen: Verlag der Buchhandlung des Erziehungsvereins, 1956), pp. 69ff, 77ff, 82ff, 147ff, 178ff, 186–91.

frequently and revealed clearly the Marsilian basis of his conception of the two offices. The terminology for his general discussion of this problem was derived, as was Zwingli's, from Erasmus's *Paraphrases of the New Testament* and his *Annotations*. The ideas developed in these works formed the basis for Bullinger's conception of his own function as a Reformed bishop and reveal why Bullinger basically differed from Calvin and Beza on the question of church discipline and why he later supported the English bishops against Thomas Cartwright.

Bullinger stood at the head of a group of pastors and teachers at the Zurich school and theological seminary, the Carolinum. At various times this circle included Conrad Pellikan, Leo Jud, Rudolf Gwalter, Caspar Megander, and Peter Martyr Vermigli, all well-known and productive theologians. It follows that under Bullinger's direction Zürich was a center for theological education attracting students from all over Europe. For the first decade and a half after Zwingli's death, it was the only Reformed center of first intellectual rank in all of Europe. The curriculum of the Carolinum and the prophesying, at which the central themes of Reformed biblical theology were discussed, provided the model for the education of the Reformed clergy throughout Europe. Bullinger's five *Decades*, in which the doctrines of Reformed theology were considered in the form of sermons, were probably first presented to and then discussed by the students and pastors gathered to take part in the prophesying.

Another of his lasting achievements was that masterpiece of irenic and practical theology, the Second Helvetic Confession. It was originally composed as part of Bullinger's last will and testament and was used to aid the elector Frederick III in defending his right to embrace the Reformed faith before the princes of the empire at the Diet of Augsburg in 1566. Though it was never adopted in the palatinate, the confession formed the basis for the union of the Swiss churches, including Geneva, and promoted the strengthening of Protestantism in the Swiss Confederacy. It continues to be an official confession of the small Reformed Church in Poland, of the larger, more influential Reformed church of Hungary, the Siebenburgen, and of the bishoprics of Klausenburg and Grosswardein.

The remnant of Bullinger's correspondence now at Zürich consists of about 12,000 letters, which far exceed what Melanchthon, Calvin, or Beza left behind. These letters testify to Bullinger's importance in the history of the Reformation of the sixteenth century. At the present, the most important printed collection of letters are the *Zürich Letters*, which catalogue Bullinger's relationship with England from the time of Henry VIII to the reign of Elizabeth. They reveal that, during the Marian exile, Zürich hosted a group of Englishmen including the future bishops Cox, Parkhurst, Sandys, and (briefly) Jewel, as well as Francis Russell, second earl of Bedford. These men returned to England under Elizabeth to become prominent in the Church of England. The correspondence shows Bullinger at work to prevent the spread of Brenz's doctrine of ubiquity in the Elizabethan church and reveals how strongly he opposed Cartwright's Presbyterianism. The unprinted correspondence between him and Thomas Erastus in the Palatinate shows, among other things, that Bullinger was Erastus's mentor and could be called the true father of Erastianism. Bullinger's letters also reveal how important his role was in protecting Calvin and Beza at Geneva from the wrath of the Bernese. Indeed, it is not too much to say that without Bullinger's steadying hand, Geneva might not have become the center of an international Calvinist movement. His moderation and good sense are everywhere apparent in his correspondence. The letters tell us that he was the wise fox of the Reformed churches.

Why is Bullinger not better remembered? It is hard to explain this fact, because he deserves to be better remembered than he is. If anything, Bullinger spoke too directly to the time in which he lived. And, like Erasmus, he suffered the fate of moderate men of his day, eclipsed by more fanatic friends and supporters as Protestantism became more rigid in the face of the Counter-Reformation. At the Synod of Dort in 1618, the Swiss delegates had to defend his writings against the charge that they were Arminian. Times had changed and Bullinger had been unlucky.[45]

45. The bulk of the information in the portions of this essay which have not been footnoted has been derived from the following sources:

Fritz Blanke, *Der junge Bullinger* (Zürich: Zwingli Verlag, 1942).

Andre Bouvier, *Henri Bullinger: Reformateur et Conseiller Oecumenique le Successeur de Zwingli* (Neuchatel/Paris: Librairie E. Droz, 1940).

G. W. Bromiley, ed., *Zwingli and Bullinger*, vol. 24 of *The Library of Christian Classics* (Philadelphia: The Westminster Press, 1953).

Heinrich Bullinger, *Diarium (Annales vitae) der Jahre 1504–1574*, ed. Emil Egli, vol. 2 of *Quellen zur schweizerischen Reformationsgeschichte* (Basel, 1904).

Ulrich Gäbler and E. Herkenrath, eds., *Heinrich Bullinger 1504–1575 Gesammelte Aufsätze zum 400. Todestag*, 2 vols., vols. 7 and 8 of *Zürcher Beiträge zur Reformationgeschichte* (Zürich: Theologischer Verlag, 1975).

David Keep, ed., *Henry Bullinger 1504–1575: British Anniversary Colloquium, 1975* (Woodbury, Exeter: D. J. Keep, 1976).

Ernst Koch, *Die Theologie der Confessio Helvetica Posterior*, vol. 27 of *Beiträge zur Geschichte und Lehre der Reformierten Kirche* (Neukirchen: Neukirchener Verlag des Erziehungsvereins, 1968).

Carl Pestalozzi, *Heinrich Bullinger. Leben und ausgewählte Schriften*, V. Theil, *Leben und ausgewählte Schriften der Väter und Begrunder der reformierten Kirche* (Elberfeld: Verlag von R. L. Friderichs, 1858).

Joachim Staedtke, *Die Theologie des jungen Bullinger*, vol. 16 of *Studien zur Dogmengeschichte und syst. Theologie* (Zürich: Zwingli Verlag, 1962).

6
THEODORE BEZA
1519–1605
JILL RAITT

LIFE

Burned in effigy in the Place Maubert and declared an outlaw by the Parlement of Paris for fleeing to Geneva with the wife he had secretly married during his years as a humanist, Theodore Beza was determined to live and die in the "true religion." Who was this ardent, gifted refugee?

Baptized Dieudonné de Besze, Theodorus Beza Vezelii, as he often signed his Latin works, was born on June 24, 1516, at Vézelay, France. His father, Pierre de Bèze, who successfully petitioned to be readmitted into the French nobility in 1551, served as King's bailiff at Vézelay. Theodore's mother, Marie Burdelot de Bèze, who also came from the lesser nobility, bore four sons and three daughters, of whom Theodore was the youngest. The lad scarcely knew his mother, who died not long after the sickly child was taken to Paris by his uncle Nicholas. Theodore gained sufficient strength to be sent to Orléans to study in the home of the humanist Melchior Wolmar,[1] student of William Budé and Lefèvre d'Etaples. Wolmar's influence on Beza was profound. Not only did he learn to write elegant Latin and Greek and begin his study of law; more importantly, he began to imbibe "true religion." Later Beza wrote to Wolmar that he celebrated December 9, 1528, as a "second birthday," since on that day he had entered Wolmar's home.[2]

In 1530, Marguerite of Navarre invited Wolmar to the University of Bourges, and Beza accompanied him to that refuge for scholars influenced by

---

1. Melchior Wolmar early moved beyond both Lefèvre d'Etaples and William Budé, openly becoming Reformed. He was also a friend of the young Calvin during the latter's stay at Orléans. In fact, as Parker puts it: "According to some writers it was he who won Calvin for the evangelical faith. This also is not impossible." T. H. L. Parker, *John Calvin: A Biography* (Philadelphia: Westminster Press, 1975), p. 18. Although neither Calvin nor Beza mention meeting in Orléans, they could easily have done so in the home of Wolmar, although Beza was ten years Calvin's junior.

2. *Theodori Beza Vezelii volumen primum Tractationum Theologicarum*, . . . Editio secunda ab ipso Auctore recognita. (Geneva: Eustathius Vignon, 1582), p. B. ii recto: "Ita igitur factum ut ad te pervenirem anno Domini 1528, Nonis Decembries: quem diem ego non aliter quam alterum natalem merito soleo celebrare." (Hereafter cited as *T.T.* plus volume and date.)

and influencing the nascent French Reformation. When in 1535 Wolmar no longer felt safe in Bourges and left for Tübingen, Pierre de Bèze ordered his son to return to Orléans to his legal studies. Beza complied, but not with grace, since his greatest desires were to study classical poetry and to enjoy the company of humanists. He joined the sodality formed around the poet Jean de Dampierre[3] and in that stimulating environment, he began writing the Latin verses that would be collected in his first publication, *Poemata*.[4]

In 1539, newly licensed in civil law, Beza moved to Paris. After several months there, he prevailed upon his father to allow him to leave the practice of law and devote himself to humanist studies. When his brother Audebert died in 1542, Beza added to his benefices that of Saint-Eloi-lès-Longjumeau.[5] His income from the Roman church was a real obstacle to his increasingly Reformed tendencies, but it was not his only temptation. Describing this period to Wolmar, Beza wrote:

> In order not to be vanquished by evil desires, I married, but secretly, telling only two or three friends who shared my convictions. I married secretly both to avoid scandal and in order not to lose that cursed money which I received from my benefices. But I did it with the formal promise that as soon as I could, having rejected all obstacles, I would take my wife into the Church of God and there confirm my marriage openly. Meanwhile I would not take any of the sacred orders of the papists.[6]

Beza's conversion, begun in Wolmar's home, was furthered in 1535 by his reading of Bullinger's treatise, *De origine erroris in Divorum ac simulacrorum cultu*.[7] Between 1535 and 1548, Beza grew convinced that he must renounce the Roman church, but he temporized until an illness brought him near death. Upon his recovery he set out for Geneva with his wife, Claudine Denosse, arriving on October 24, 1548.[8]

France, however, would not let her promising young humanist go so lightly. On April 3, 1549, parlement decreed Beza an outlaw and confiscated his goods, and on May 31, 1550, it ordered him burned in effigy and

3. When de Dampierre died in 1545, Beza eulogized him in "In Obitu Joannis Dampetri." See H. Meylan, "Bèze et les Sodales d'Orléans, 1535–1545," in *Actes du Congres sur l'ancienne Université d'Orléans* (Orléans: Comité d'organisation des journées universitaires d'Orléans, 1962), pp. 95–100.

4. Published by Conrad Badius for Robert Etienne in Paris in 1548. See Frédéric Gardy, *Bibliographie des oeuvres. . . .de Théodore de Bèze* (Geneva: Librairie E. Droz, 1960), pp. 1–17. (Hereafter cited as Gardy.)

5. Jacques Pannier, "Le Prieuré et la Seigneurie de Longjumeau au milieu du XVIe siècle: Théodore de Bèze et Michel Gaillard," in *Société de l'histoire du Protestantisme français*. 47, (1898): 393–413.

6. Quoted in Paul-F. Geisendorf, *Théodore de Bèze*, 2nd ed. (Geneva: Alexandre Jullien, 1967), pp. 26–27.

7. Basel, 1529.

8. *T.T.*, Vol. 1, B.iii: " . . . ut Christum sequar, meque una cum mea coniuge Genevam in exilium voluntarium recipio. Itaque anno Domini 1548. 9. Cal. Novembris in eam urbem relicta Aegypto ingressus . . ."

confiscated his goods, the latter sentence lifted only in 1564 when he had become a diplomat of considerable importance.

There was no employment for Beza in Geneva in 1548, but Pierre Viret[9] invited him to the Academy at Lausanne, where Beza taught Greek and later took his turn as rector. [10] Added to these duties he gave lectures on the Epistle to the Romans to other French refugees, continued Marot's translation of the Psalms, [11] engaged in theological disputations, and wrote two humanist works (*Abraham sacrifiant*[12] in 1559 and *Alphabetum graecum*[13] in 1554). In 1555, contrary to Bern's prohibitions, Beza published his *Tabula praedestinationis*[14] in defense of Calvin's doctrine of predestination. Bern neither supported the Genevan doctrine nor allowed argument about the subject, but the fires of debate were kept burning as Calvin and Beza responded to the attacks of Jerome Bolsec[15] and Sebastian Castellio. [16]

More indicative of Beza's basic work during the 1550s was his translation of the New Testament into Latin, published together with his *Annotations* in 1556. [17] In 1558, Beza prepared for his Roman Catholic father the *Confession de la foi chrestienne*, a widely used statement of beliefs published in French in 1559 and in Latin in 1560. [18]

In addition to his academic duties, his publications, and his involvement with France and her refugees, in 1557 Beza also undertook his diplomatic journeys, with his mission to gain support, among German princes for the French Protestants. [19] For the next thirty years, these efforts at diplomacy were to be frustrated by differences between Lutheran and Reformed theologians concerning the Lord's Supper. Beza was also frequently called to France between 1560 and 1572 to assist the growing Reformed churches there. [20]

9. Pierre Viret (1511–71), one of the reformers of Geneva, who then assisted in the reform of Lausanne, where he lived 1536–58.

10. Geisendorf, *Théodore de Bèze*, pp. 54–64.

11. See below, n. 60.

12. See below, n. 58. See also Gardy, pp. 19–32.

13. See Gardy, pp. 41–44.

14. See Gardy, pp. 47–53.

15. Jerome Bolsec (d. 1584) had been a Carmelite friar. He became a Protestant and then, after his altercations with Calvin, reverted to Roman Catholicism.

16. Sebastian Castellio (1515–63) was a professor in the Geneva Academy who held that the Song of Songs was a true love poem and not an allegory. He was dismissed and moved to Basel where he wrote against the burning of Servetus, *De haereticis an sint persequendi* . . . . (Basel? 1554).

17. See below, n. 56.

18. See below, n. 34.

19. Although Beza and William Farel thought that they had brought home a successful accord from the meeting with Lutheran theologians, which took place not at Worms, but at Göppingen, their illusion was shattered by the outrage of Geneva's closest allies in Zürich. Bullinger would not tolerate the use of the word "substance" to describe the mode of Christ's presence. It took a contrite letter from Beza and an adroit letter from Calvin to appease the angered Zürichers. Cf. Raitt, *The Eucharistic Theology of Theodore Beza* (Chambersburg, 1972), American Academy of Religion Studies in Religion, no. 4, p. 3.

20. Geisendorf, *Théodore de Bèze*, pp. 125–225, 292–315.

Meanwhile, both Beza and Viret were suffering at Lausanne under the heavy hand of Bern, which did not appreciate their outspoken advocacy of Calvin and the Genevan church. In 1558 the tensions proved too much, and both men left Lausanne. Beza, now thirty-nine years old, arrived at last where he had long desired to be, beside Calvin in Geneva. His arrival coincided with Calvin's victory over dissident parties and his determination to establish an academy at Geneva. Beza was presented as the Academy's first rector in June 1559, assisting Calvin as well with lectures in theology.

But the fifteen sixties were to prove even more active than the turbulent days at Lausanne. Beza was soon summoned to Poissy where Catherine de Medici hoped to unite her fractured kingdom by means of a colloquy between Roman Catholic and Reformed.[21] But the colloquy, so promising at the outset, soon came to grief over the doctrine of the Lord's Supper. Beza stayed on in France, first at Catherine's invitation and then, when the Wars of Religion broke out, riding at the side of Coligny and Condé as treasurer and adviser. After the uneasy Peace of Amboise in 1563, Beza at last was able to return to Geneva.

The burden of Beza's duties in the Academy and the Church of Geneva and his polemical and biblical work was made heavier in 1564 when he was designated by the dying Calvin as his successor. Beza reluctantly accepted the post of "Moderator of the Venerable Company of Pastors of Geneva," a position that he held until 1580.[22] Nor were his duties effectively lightened when he persuaded the company to allow him to step down; he continued to be the city's foremost councilor and pastor until a few years before his death in 1605.

The forty years of consolidation following Calvin's death contained no moments of brilliance such as Poissy and no months of danger equal to riding beside Condé and Coligny.[23] Nevertheless the achievements of those forty years were monumental. Calvinists were able to avoid the theological conflicts that beset Lutherans after the death of Luther, with Beza building solidly on the firm foundations laid by Calvin.[24] The teaching of theology was one of his first concerns, and Beza remained the only regular professor of theology at Geneva from 1564 to 1595.[25]

Following the publication in 1577 of the *Formula of Concord*, French Reformed refugees in the lands of Lutheran princes were subjected to

21. Raitt, *Eucharistic Theology*, pp. 31–41. Cf. Donald Nugent, *Ecumenism in the Age of the Reformation: The Colloquy of Poissy* (Cambridge: Harvard University Press, 1974).

22. Tadataka Maruyama, *The Ecclesiology of Theodore Beza: The Reform of the True Church* (Geneva: Librairie Droz, 1978), pp. 125–26.

23. Geisendorf, p. 244.

24. The degree to which he may be responsible for Calvinist orthodoxy is now, as then, a matter of scholarly debate. Cf. Raitt, *Eucharistic Theology*, p. viii and below, p. 104.

25. Paul-F. Geisendorf, *L'Université de Genève, 1559–1959* (Geneva: Alexandre Jullien, 1959), p. 64.

increasing pressure to conform to Lutheran discipline.[26] In 1586, the Colloquy of Montbéliard was called to settle this problem in the duchy of Württemberg. The principal disputants were Beza and Jakob Andreae (who, with Martin Chemnitz, was an author of the *Formula*).[27] The chief point of debate was the Lord's Supper. But by 1586, the dispute had turned into a Christological argument, owing to the Brenz-Andreae insistence upon the ubiquity of the human nature of Christ.[28]

Nor were church-state relations in Geneva always harmonious. Beza's duties as moderator of the Genevan church included his participation on the city council and therefore involved continual mediation between magistrates and pastors. Two major issues were usury on the one hand and the right to preach without government restraints on the other.[29] Several times Beza threatened to resign in order to preserve what he considered to be the right balance of authority.

Beza's advice continued to be sought outside Geneva. In 1571 he was called to La Rochelle in France, where he was elected president of the synod that established the French Confession of Faith.[30] The English nonconformists, the Scottish Presbyterians, the churches of Orange, the pastors of Poland, Hungary and Czechoslovakia—all appealed at one time or another to Beza, soliciting his advice and authority in their struggles against Anglicans, Roman Catholics, Lutherans, Anabaptists, and the forerunners of Unitarianism.[31]

Beza's last years were financially difficult. In 1597 he sold his library to Count de Zastrizill in Poland. In 1598 his books, containing many from Calvin's own library, were removed to the Gotha library.[32] Yet his advice was still sought by royalty. In 1600, Henry IV, campaigning against Savoy, camped outside Geneva. When he requested Beza to visit him, the eighty-one-year-old councilor rose from his sickbed and rode out to see Henry, who called him "Father" as he had since his childhood at Nérac.

Beza's last extant letter was written in October 1603. He died on October 13, 1605. In 1598, he witnesssed to his lifelong determination

26. Jill Raitt, "The French Reformed Theological Response," in *Discord, Dialogue, and Concord: Studies in the Lutheran Reformation's Formula of Concord*, ed. L. W. Spitz and Wenzel Lohff (Philadelphia: Fortress Press, 1977), pp. 178–90.

27. See chapters 1 and 2 above.

28. Raitt, "French Reformed Theological Response," pp. 185–88. Also see chapter 4 above.

29. *Registres de la Compagnie des Pasteurs de Genève*, ed. O. Labarthe and B. Lescaze (Geneva: Librairie Droz, 1974), 4(1575–82): xii, 419–25, nos. 62–64. (Hereafter cited as *Registres.*)

30. After this synod Peter Ramus contested both anti–Congregationalist decisions and the use of that banner word "substance" with regard to Christ's presence and wrote angrily to Bullinger on both points.

31. Geisendorf, *Théodore de Bèze*, pp. 283–92.

32. Ibid., p. 415.

to remain faithful to those great leaders of the Reformation, "especially the late John Calvin."[33]

THEOLOGY   Beza has no systematic work to compare with Calvin's *Institutes of the Christian Religion*. The nearest is his *Confession de la foi chrestienne* of 1559. After the Latin edition of it in 1560, this work remained unrevised through its many subsequent editions and translations during Beza's lifetime[34] and thus it appears that Beza was satisfied with it as a short statement of his theology. *Quaestionum et Responsionum Christianorum libellus*, the first part of which appeared in 1570 and the second in 1576,[35] may also be regarded as a systematic arrangement of his theology, although it is not free of polemical issues and arguments.

The basic arrangement of the *Confession* is credal: first dealing with the Trinity and then, successively, with the Father, Jesus Christ, the Holy Spirit, the Church, and the Last Judgment. Under the Trinity heading, Beza discusses God the Creator, who determines within himself, in an eternal *now*, all that shall be. But in this timeless decree, the all-powerful, just, and merciful God includes the temporal action of secondary causes, which, by acting according to their created natures, work together to glorify God.[36] This principle of causes or instruments, inherited from scholastic philosophy and used by Calvin, plays a key role in Beza's theology.

Thus in his theology of the fall, Beza stresses that the natural faculties of mankind were not stripped away in the fall; not even free will was destroyed "if you add this, that all of these faculties were nothing but darkness and hatred for God." One must further qualify free will as the power of acting spontaneously rather than by coercion; it is no longer the power to choose between good and evil. So the definitive human faculties remain, and through them, however warped by the fall, God's glory is achieved necessarily, but freely, that is, spontaneously. No one is coerced into sin, hence God cannot be charged as the author of sin. Beza wrote in the *Quaestionum et Responsionum . . . libellus*:

33. *Annotationes maiores in Novum Dn. Nostri Iesu Christi Testamentum. II: Ad Galatas III:18* (pp. 329a, lines 1–38.) ". . . D. I. Calvinum, meum in Domino parentem, (cuius est apud me memoria, sicuti esse debet, ut vel ob hoc pene unum mihi in hac vocatione vivendum putem, quod illius memoria in tantis tempestatibus regi possim, nedum ut ab eo in doctrina ipsa dissentiam). . ."

34. Published by Badius in Geneva. See Gardy, pp. 60–80, for the translations into Latin and then the major languages of Europe previous to 1564.

35. Published in Geneva and found in *T.T.*, vols. 1 and 3, (both 1582) respectively (henceforth abbreviated *Q.R.*).

36. See *Confession* II, v and III, v; and *Q.R.* I, 678: "Primum, animalia et ratione predita instrumenta (cuiusmodi sunt Angeli et homines) sic agi a Deo opifice, ut etiam ipsa interiore suo motu spontaneo agant, ac proinde ad unam edendam actionem duae concurrant causae, Deus videlicet seiunctus ab instrumento, et tamen instrumento tribuens sese movendi principium: et ipsum sese movens instrumentum."

You must remember that Coercion differs from Necessity since many things are simultaneously necessary and voluntary, as, you must agree, was the death of Christ. But nothing can be both coerced and voluntary . . . .[37]

Sinners therefore sin *necessarily* since nothing escapes God's decree. But they do so *voluntarily*. No one forces them; sin is simply attractive to corrupt human nature. Only grace, won by Christ the Mediator, truly liberates them by freeing them from the spontaneous inclination to sin. In fact the Holy Spirit bestows not only the gift of justification, but the beginning of sanctification, that is, the true liberty of the children of God.

In moving to an understanding of the second person of the Trinity and therefore of Christ, Beza followed Calvin in his emphasis on Christ's soteriological work as Mediator. It was in heated polemics with the Württemberg Lutherans[38] that Beza developed his later Christology, asserting what Calvin refused to define—namely, that the hypostatic union is the assumption of an apersonal human nature into the person of the Logos.[39] With Calvin, Beza fought constantly to make a clear distinction between the two natures and their properties, not allowing their direct communication from nature to nature as the Lutherans taught (see chapter 3). Rather, Beza insisted that the properties refer to the composite person, the God-man Jesus Christ. The God-man corresponds to Chemnitz's "first genus," but Beza fought against the "third genus." Thus, one may say that this man is God, but one may not say that this humanity is the divinity. So one may say that God died on the cross, but one may not say that the divinity died on the cross. Nor can the humanity be endowed with divine attributes, such as ubiquity, without ceasing to be truly human. On the contrary, the body of Christ is ascended to heaven, and there it remains, located and circumscribed as are all human bodies, until the second coming. It cannot, therefore, be present as a natural body in, under, or with the bread and wine in the Lord's Supper. This problem of the *communicatio idiomatum*, or the "communication of properties," became a major point of controversy in the era between 1560 and 1600 and led not only to the label "extra-calvinisticum"[40]—since Calvinists taught that Christ acted even *extra carnem* or outside the flesh—but also to the *kenosis* arguments of the seventeenth century. The debate centered around the extent of Christ's powers as the man-God and the Lutheran teaching that he "hid" them at his incarnation in order to manifest them at his ascension. The debate turned on the phrase found in Phil. 2:5–11, *forma servi*, "form of a servant," which Beza

---

37. *Q.R.* I, 665.

38. Primarily with Andreae, after Brenz's death in 1570.

39. Jill Raitt, "The Person of the Mediator: Calvin's Christology and Beza's Fidelity," in *Occasional Papers* no. 1, American Society of Reformation Research, 1977, pp. 53–80.

40. For a fine study of this term see David Willis, *Calvin's Catholic Christology: The Function of the So-Called Extra Calvinisticum in Calvin's Theology* (Leiden: E. J. Brill, 1966).

insisted referred to human nature, and therefore the *forma servi* could not be laid aside even in Christ's glorification. The Württembergers and Chemnitz took *forma servi* to mean Christ's state of exinanition, or "self-emptying," which consisted in the laying aside of his majesty in the Incarnation, a majesty to be resumed in glory, thereby ending the condition of *forma servi*.[41]

In the Christological section also falls Beza's view of the work of redemption. His doctrine of justification follows Calvin's, which does not differ from Luther's doctrine of *sola fide*.[42] But Beza also tried to answer the problem of grace alone in relation to the human will and understanding. His questioner asks:

Q. Thus in the reception of first grace men remain merely passive [$\pi\alpha\theta\eta\tau\iota\kappa\tilde{\omega}\sigma$], nor are they co-workers [$\sigma\acute{v}\nu\epsilon\rho\gamma o\iota$] with God.

R. Certainly if you look to the order of causes and that first beginning of grace, by which God remakes us, we must confess that it proceeds wholly from God, who first loved us while we were yet enemies, and is therefore only received by us. If, however, you consider the instant of time in which God works in us as simultaneous with that moment in which we are enabled to will to receive it, then we do will to receive it. Otherwise grace would be empty. Therefore those who oppose this mode of cooperation [$\sigma\upsilon\nu\epsilon\rho\gamma\epsilon\acute{\iota}\alpha\nu$] oppose the grace of God . . . since this very cooperation is the gift of God's grace.[43]

Beza thereby affirms the Reformation doctrine of *sola gratia* and indeed of the corruption of the faculties, which, by their nature, could achieve nothing. But once endowed by grace, the mind and will are healed and made capable of meeting the grace offered. By "one grace," Beza emphasizes, we both know and will simultaneously, and, through grace, want to receive grace.[44]

The Holy Spirit, whose activity is stressed as the continuing work of Christ after the Ascension, uses instruments to implement Christ's primary agency. The initial "secondary cause" or "instrument" is Christ's humanity,

---

41. This debate is reported at great length by both sides several times over. For Beza's reports, see Gardy, pp. 197–99. For Andreae's version, see above, chapter 4, n. 13.

42. *Q.R.* I, 671.

43. *Q.R.* I, 666: "Ergo in primae gratiae receptione homines sese habent merè $\pi\alpha\theta\eta\tau\kappa\tilde{\omega}\sigma$, nec sunt gratiae Dei $\sigma\acute{v}\nu\epsilon\rho\gamma o\iota$. R. Sane si spectes ordinem causarum et primum illud initium gratiae, qua nos refingit Dominus, fateri necesse est illam a Deo in solidum proficisci, qui nos prior diligit adhuc inimicos, a nobis vero duntaxat recipi. Sin vero temporis punctum quo Deus in nobis agit consideres, simul eodemque momento nobis datur ut possimus velle recipere, et volumus recipere: alioqui inanis esset gratia. Itaque qui istiusmodi $\sigma\upsilon\nu\epsilon\rho\gamma\epsilon\acute{\iota}\alpha\nu$ quasi gratiae Dei repugnantem oppugnant, multis modis imperitiam suam produnt, quum haec ipsa $\sigma\upsilon\nu\epsilon\rho\gamma\epsilon\iota\alpha\nu$ sit gratiae Dei donum, ita illi cooperans, ut sit quidem ordine causarum posterior, sicut effectum efficientem causam subsequitur, ac proinde omnia in solidum uni gratiae Dei accepta ferantur. . . ."

44. Ibid.

first in incarnation and thereafter in sacrament. The second instrument is faith, which is created and bestowed by God on the elect—that is, on those whom God, from all eternity, chose to be the instruments of his glory, giving them to Christ irrevocably to be saved from the *massa damnata*. Faith is a gift enabling the elect to hear efficaciously the word of God and to receive it sacramentally. It differs from historical faith, which even devils possess and which assents to the facts of Jesus's life without trusting in his saving work. Historical faith is not, of itself, efficacious for salvation.

The third instrument used by the Holy Spirit is the preaching of the Gospel, through which faith is given so that it may not only be heard, but grasped and applied to oneself. The sacraments are also instruments of the Holy Spirit, who, in the elect, makes good the promise of which the sacraments are visible signs. When Christ offers himself to communicants in the Lord's Supper, it is the Holy Spirit who prepares, by faith, the mouth of the soul to receive him. Without interior preparation, the communicant has no means to eat Christ and so receives only the signs, the bread and the wine. Nor does the Holy Spirit bypass the human endowment of intelligence, for as Beza explains it, the gift of faith prepares the mind to grasp the analogies presented by the sacraments. In baptism these are washing and rebirth. In the Lord's Supper, the signs point to and, by the power of the Holy Spirit, make present and available the crucified and risen body of Christ with all its benefits of salvation and sanctification. But since the body of Christ is ascended, the Holy Spirit, through faith, lifts the soul to heaven, there to be joined in a mystical marriage with Christ and to eat and drink his body and blood according to Christ's own institution.[45]

In the second part of *Quaestionum et Responsionum*, Beza supported the Reformed doctrine of the Lord's Supper.[46] In doing so, he moved again beyond Calvin's doctrine by arguing for *relation* rather than *substance* as the most suitable category to describe the mode of Christ's presence through the instrumentality of the bread and wine in the liturgical action. Through and during their use in the Supper, the bread and wine acquire a new relation to the body and blood of Christ, so that they may be the sacramental means through which Christ offers himself, by the power of the Holy Spirit, to the faithful.[47]

Beza's doctrine of baptism in harmony with Calvin's retains the same sacramental principles, even though it brings them into conflict with the received tradition. Since faith is given only to the elect, baptism does not, ipso facto, ensure that one is adopted by God and effectually regenerated in the Spirit. In addition, faith comes by hearing, so that while the faithful

45. See Raitt, *Eucharistic Theology*, especially pp. 41–68.
46. *Q.R.* II, 335:49; Raitt, *Eucharistic Theology* p. 62.
47. This doctrine is further elaborated in Beza's last effort to reconcile Lutherans to Reformed Eucharistic doctrine: *De controveresiis in Coena Domini . . .* (Gardy, pp. 211–12.)

community integrates the newly baptized infant into itself, often the effects of baptism are not realized until adolescence or even until the moment of death, when the preached word may at last meet the faith given at that moment by the Holy Spirit. This doctrine also means that no individual can be pronounced reprobate, but hope and charity must always be the guides in one's dealings with everyone. But the more immediate problem for the reformers was the baptism of moribund infants by midwives. Since in Lutheran and Roman Catholic doctrine some form of baptism was necessary for salvation, such emergency baptism was allowed. But for the Reformed, God's election was essentially independent of anything men and women may do. Emergency baptism was therefore unnecessary and involved what Calvin and Beza considered an abomination—the usurpation by women of an office reserved to ministers. Since not even laymen may baptize, for laywomen to administer baptism was a double blasphemy.[48]

One may well question the Reformed doctrine of the sacraments, for with regard to baptism it seems to be undercut by the doctrine of election. What saves it, however, is Beza's insistence on the traditional doctrine that God uses secondary causes, although he is not bound by them. God will not, ordinarily, bypass the normal activity of his creation, and therefore men and women must use their minds, wills, and affections in a godly manner insofar as these natural faculties are gifts from the Holy Spirit to be so used. Hence the ordinary way for the elect to pursue a godly course is to be baptized, attend church, hear the word, awaken to the fact of the security of God's promise with regard to oneself (i.e., to the fact of one's election), receive the Lord's Supper, and strive to live according to the commandments. By these means, the old man dies more and more as the new man increases in Christ, that is, in *sanctification*.[49]

Sanctification is given inseparably with justification but is distinguished from it in the same way growth is distinguished from birth. According to Beza, sanctification is twofold. Its origin is the imputation of the justice of Christ, in whose immaculate human nature the sanctification of the elect is rooted. But once an individual is so justified, a real change occurs by means of a new habit given through the grace of the Father and the power of the Holy Spirit, which joins one to Christ.[50] Just as a parent plans the path of a toddler, encourages it to walk, and even supports it, so the Holy Spirit guides and sustains the faithful in good works. By this activity of the Holy Spirit, the old Adam dies and the new Christain grows stronger in Christ. Never, however, does this toddling sanctification reach perfection. Never

48. *Q.R.* II, 347: 140–41.

49. On the relation between predestination and the sacraments, see the fine study by Peter Fraenkel, *De l'Ecriture à la Dispute*. Lausanne, 1977, vol. 1 of *Revue de Théologie et de Philosophie*, pp. 27–28.

50. *Q.R.* I, 671–72: "Q. Ais igitur hanc posteriorem santificationem non esse quiddam extra nos, et sola imputatione nostrum, sed novum esse habitum vere nobis insitum et inhaerentem ex Patris caelestis mere gratia, et Sancti Spiritus virtute, nobis in Christo collatum. R. Aio."

may one stand in one's own justice before God, as the imputation of Christ's righteousness always is necessary for salvation.

Another case of distinction without separation Beza makes is that between the eternal decree of predestination and its execution. The two belong together as do the sun and its rays, but in the same way, they can be distinguished. So *in the decree*, God wills the election of some men and women from every race and nation—a decree of election which is Calvin's and Beza's interpretation of God's will to save all mankind. This decree of election is metaphysically prior as cause[51] to all its consequences (such as the creation and fall.) For this reason, this doctrine of predestination is called *supralapsarian*. Beza teaches it explicitly; it is implicit in much of what Calvin teaches, and Calvin never corrected Beza's doctrine, but rather approved it. *In the execution* of the decree in time, actual nameable individuals are the object of trinitarian action, either for salvation or damnation. The elect are given to Christ and guided by the Spirit, until all are lifted in Christ to the Father. Of the elect, the humanity of Christ is the first, so that in the man-God all the elect are gathered to be justified and sanctified.[52]

A beautiful example of Beza's understanding of predestination as a doctrine of comfort occurs in a letter of condolence to Gaspard de Coligny on the death of his wife Charlotte de Laval:

> But the sovereign remedy is that which you have taken, namely the power, the wisdom, the good will of the Lord: power to assure you that he lacks no means; wisdom to enable you to understand well that he knows better than anyone, even you, what is best for you and yours; good will which is proper to God's elect, namely, that he who has chosen us by his eternal and unchangeable council (to which our vocation is an infallible witness resounding in our ears by the preaching of his word accompanied by his sacraments and in our hearts through the Holy Spirit), and since he can do all, he wishes nothing and consequently does nothing except for the salvation of his own.[53]

Beza adds that Coligny should apply this comfort not only to the loss of his wife but to the terrible situation in which the Huguenots, and especially their leaders, find themselves.

In the actualization of the decree, the church serves as the organ for the preaching of the word and the administration of the sacraments. From it come men called to the ministry who serve the church in one of four offices: as deacons, who administer the hospitals and the funds given for charity; as elders, who share with the pastors the government and oversee the discipline

---

51. But it is not prior temporally, since it is an eternal counsel.

52. *De praedestinatione doctrina* . . . (Geneva: Vignon, 1582.) Reprinted in *T.T.*, vol. 3: see p. 406; pp. 438–40.

53. Translated from *Correspondance de Théodore de Bèze*, vol. 9 (1568), collected by H. Aubert; ed. H. Meylan, A. Dufour, C. Chimelli, B. Nicollier (Geneva: Librairie Droz, 1978), pp. 97–98.

of the church and its faithful; as pastors, who preach and administer the sacraments; and as teachers, whose primary duty is to see to the correct interpretation of Scripture. In the church of Geneva, the last two categories frequently overlapped as they did for Calvin and Beza themselves. Since the episcopacy was not of divine institution, Beza preferred that it not be introduced. But neither did Scripture prohibit it. Therefore, he ruled, it was allowable where the peace of the church required it, as in Elizabeth's England.[54]

As for the sacraments rejected by all the reformers, the Genevan church retained the right to oversee the areas of life these sacraments had touched. Penance remained in the form of the pre-communion declaration of conscience to the minister and the application of God's promise of forgiveness. Ordination was replaced by a vote of the pastors and elders and installation in a parish. Marriage was regulated by civil and ecclesiastical ordinances. The dying were comforted by the clergy, who prayed with them and who could celebrate the Lord's Supper in their presence if a number of the faithful were also present.

So in Beza's Geneva, by the redeeming power of Christ and through the agency of the Spirit, the unchangeable providence of God, using as instruments the humanity of Christ, faith, preaching, sacraments, and the forms of ministry established in the church, provided for every stage of a Christian's development, from birth to death.

ROLE IN THE CHURCH   Certain areas of Beza's work have long been recognized due to their focus in particular texts. His role in the history of biblical texts and exegesis was established through his discovery of the *Codex Bezae*[55] and his series of New Testament *Annotations*,[56] culminating in the 1588 *Bible de Genève*.[57]

Moreover, Beza has also been recognized as a poet and the originator of a new genre of drama, the biblical tragedy later utilized by Racine. Of Beza's *Abraham sacrifiant*, Mario Richter writes:

---

54. W. Nijenhuis, *Ecclesia Reformata: Studies on the Reformation* (Leiden: E. J. Brill, 1972), pp. 130–87, introduces the text of Beza's treatise *De triplici episcopatu* (on pp. 130–39) and then reproduces the text in Latin and English. On this question, see especially pp. 160–67.

55. M. Metzger, *The Text of the New Testament: Its Transmission, Corruption and Restoration* (New York; Oxford University Press, 1965), p. 105.

56. *Iesu Christi D.N. Novum testamentum, sive Novum foedus. Cuius Graeco tertui respondant interpretationes duae. Una vetus: altera, nova, Theodori Bezae, diligenter ab eo recognita* (Geneva, 1565) (second and critial edition, which was revised in 1582, 1588, 1598).

57. *Registres*, 5 (1583–88, ed. O. Labarthe and M. Tripet, (Geneva: Librairie Droz, 1976), pp. 337–51.

His Abraham is not, then, so much a reprise of the medieval mystery play as it is an original invention of a new kind of theatrical and popular representation through the utilization of distinctly classical elements absorbed during a long and impassioned humanist training.[58]

Enjoyed and played in its own day, translated, and still produced in the twentieth century, this play has been called by some scholars the first French tragedy.[59]

In his preface to *Abraham sacrifiant*, Beza prayed that his humanist friends in Paris might also learn that "it is better to sing a canticle to God than to petrarchize a sonnet." With regard to Beza's translations of the Psalms, common opinion ranks them below the translations of Marot. A number of reasons are advanced: Beza wrote them while at the same time working on other major works (such as his New Testament *Annotations* and translations) and during periods of great activity in the Lausanne school.[60] But beyond these reasons, Beza's purpose was to provide the French Reformed with models of serious and pious poetry and, above all, to be faithful to the biblical text, and in the latter two endeavors, Beza was eminently successful. The Huguenot Psalter provided a source of inspiration and encouragement to the embattled Reformed forces during the Wars of Religion and was carried into exile with them to Europe and America.

Finally, Beza's *Du droit des Magistrats sur leurs subiets* is an important text in political history.[61] At the time, it inspired the Huguenots after the massacre of St. Bartholomew's Day in 1572. It was published anonymously in 1574, the Genevan authorities fearing political repercussions from Paris should the author be known. Beza's thesis was that the authority of kings is originally derived from God through popular election, and therefore sovereignty must remain responsible to the people under God. When a king abuses his power and plays the tyrant, the people need not seek redress through princely leaders, but may overthrow the tyrant under the leadership of their elected magistrates. Beza had departed from contemporary political theory and from the firm injunctions of both Luther and Calvin in this regard.

Beza was not, however, a revolutionary in his own godly city. Geneva's unique balance between the governing authority of the city's councils—

58. *Dizionario critico della Letteratura francese*, vol. 1, p. 135: "L'*Abraham* non e, dunque, tanto una represa dei misteri medievali, quanto piuttosto l'invenzione originale di un nuovo genere di rappresentazione teatrale e popolare attraverso l'utilizzazione di elementi squisitamente classici, assorbiti durante un lungo e appassionato eservizio umanistico."

59. This judgment is not seriously disputed by its strongest critic, C. R. Frankish, who only questions it lightly.

60. Michel Jeanneret, *Poesie et tradition biblique au XVIe siècle* (Paris: Librairie José Corti, 1969), pp. 88–105.

61. An excellent critical text with notes and ample introduction concerning the history of the text and its ideas is that edited by Robert M. Kingdon (Geneva: Librairie Droz, 1970).

increasingly concentrated in the Small Council—and the moral suasion of the Company of Pastors was particularly effective during the nine years of Calvin's ascendancy (1555–64).[62] After Calvin's death, the magistrates began the slow alteration of that balance in their favor, and Beza did not wish to dominate Geneva as had Calvin. He refused to be moderator for life of the Company of Pastors and changed the office to one filled by an annual election. In 1580, the charge became hebdomadally rotated among the pastors. Beza made no objection to being given a lower seat on the council than Calvin had had, nor did he object to the reversal of precedence on civic occasions when the magistrates walked ahead of the pastors.

In fact, the Ordinances of Geneva bound the pastors to obey the magistrates, who, in turn, vowed to obey the Gospel. The interpreters of the gospel were the pastors, who believed they had the duty of correcting the moral behavior of all residents of Geneva. Here the conflict began. The pastors considered many social matters to be also matters of morality: usury; behavior on Sundays, at parties, and in taverns; the price of grain when it rose beyond the ability of the poor to pay for it; proper dress. The only means of correcting faults along these lines was denunciation from the pulpit. Increasingly, the magistrates resisted this practice, particularly when one of their number was the culprit publicly denounced.[63]

On these matters, Beza took a strong stand, protecting the pastors' prerogative, calming the overzealous among them, and raising his voice in protest against immoral practices of the most powerful magistrates. Beza was unable, however, to maintain the balance, and by 1600 the magistrates became the most powerful men in the city. Beza had succeeded Calvin, but no minister succeeded Beza as the city's foremost citizen.

Beza's influence on the Genevan Academy, however, was profound, first as its rector and then as its only regular professor of theology from Calvin's death until 1595. In the academy, as in the city, Beza's voice was often decisive—for example in the appointment of professors of law (1566) and of medicine (1567)—but especially with regard to theology. The most serious crisis for the academy occurred in 1586 when Charles Emmanuel of Savoy, long covetous of Geneva, blockaded the city. Dependent upon large numbers of foreign students, the school was reduced to penury and near starvation since returning students could not enter Geneva. In spite of impassioned pleading by the Company of Pastors and especially by Beza, the school was closed. But

---

62. See E. William Monter, *Calvin's Geneva* (New York: John Wiley and Sons, Inc., 1967).

63. For the minutes of these actions, with explanatory notes, see *Registres*, vol. 4 (1575–82). Editors Labarthe and Lescaze argue that the ministers maintained the balance. My reading of the material, however, leads me to agree with older interpreters who find the magistrates slowly gaining over the ministers. Cf. Amadée Roget, *Histoire du peuple de Genève depuis la Réforme jusqu'à l'Escalade*, vol. 7 (Geneva, 1887); Albin Thourel, *Histoire de Genève depuis son origine jusqu'à nos jours*, . . . (Geneva, 1833); Eugene Choisy, *L'État chrétien calviniste à Genève au temps de Théodore de Bèze.* (Geneva, n.d.); E. William Monter, "Pew and Pulpit."

Beza refused to allow a lack of funds to end so great a work and continued to give his courses, doubling them, in fact. Somehow the necessary funds were raised, and in 1587 the professors were recalled to their chairs.

Beza continued to guide his students; indeed, the bulk of Beza's correspondence with French churches deals with the supply of pastors, the conduct of those sent and of their parishes, and the solution of both theological and practical problems.[64]

But Beza's concerns spread far beyond France. The Reformed of the Low Countries looked to Geneva not just for good counsel. They also looked to Geneva for training of ministers until Leiden University was established, at which time Geneva sent its most promising younger theologian, Lambert Daneau,[65] to join the new faculty. Between Geneva and Poland correspondence was equally heavy.[66] Hungary, too, received counsel and a welcome for its students in Geneva.

England's relations with Geneva were cool under Elizabeth, in spite of all Beza did to win her favor.[67] But it was to England, to Lord Burghley, that Beza sent his biblical discovery, the *Codex Bezae*. The unsettled relations between the English establishment and the nonconformists kept the situation tenuous. The nonconformists sought Beza's support for their antiepiscopal policy, while Beza himself sought military and moral support from Elizabeth against Lutherans and Roman Catholics. Relations with Scotland were better, although once he left Geneva, John Knox tended to go his own way. In fact, his *Monstrous Regiment of Women* was one of the chief factors alienating Elizabeth from the Genevans.[68]

Beza's contacts with German cities arose out of his efforts to persuade Protestant princes to send troops to aid the Protestants in France and out of his correspondence with Reformed congregations in German lands. His efforts to help French Protestants were only partially successful as all German princes had to balance support of the Huguenots against the growing ascendancy of the Guises and their relation with the empire. After 1566 only the stubbornly loyal Johann Casimir continued to supply the French with troops.

Beza's correspondence with Reformed areas inside the German territories of the empire dealt chiefly with practical problems arising out of the Peace of Augsburg (1555), in which only the Roman Catholic and Lutheran faiths were officially recognized and the principle *cuius regio, eius religio* was adopted. The problems grew steadily worse for the Reformed through the Diet

64. Robert M. Kingdon, *Geneva and the Coming of the Wars of Religion in France, 1555–1563* (Geneva: Librairie Droz, 1956), and by the same author, *Geneva and the Consolidation of the French Protestant Movement, 1564–1572* (Geneva: Librairie Droz, 1967).

65. See below, chapter 7.

66. See Nancy Conradt, *"John Calvin, Theodore Beza and the Reformation in Poland"* (Ph.D. diss., University of Wisconsin, 1974).

67. Geisendorf, *Théodore de Bèze*, p. 291.

68. Ibid.

of Augsburg in 1566 to the imposition of the *Formula of Concord* after 1577. Could Reformed communities accept baptism and communion from Lutheran ministers in areas where Reformed ministers were limited to preaching? Could they accept arbitrary changes imposed on their liturgy? Beza dealt with these questions on a case-by-case basis in an effort to prevent the total proscription of the Reformed. In 1566, such a condemnation was averted due to the energetic efforts of Beza and Bullinger to organize the Reformed of England, Scotland, France, the Lowlands, and Poland to endorse Bullinger's Second Helvetic Confession and to exert political pressure on Emperor Maximilian. But after 1577, German Lutheran princes seconded the efforts of Lutheran theologians to force the endorsement of the *Formula of Concord* in their territories.[69]

In fact, it is partly attributable to Beza that Calvinists were able to avoid the internal conflict experienced by the Lutherans. The *Harmony of Confessions*, assembled by Jean François Salvard in 1581,[70] was accomplished with Beza's encouragement and allowed for Reformed communities to maintain their own church discipline and credal formulation within the larger scope of commonly shared Reformed principles. Thus, there was no need for a Reformed *formula concordiae* to cement amicable relations.

Two related issues form the basis of the major question in current Beza scholarship: his doctrine of predestination and the role it plays in his doctrinal development. The major question is the degree to which Beza fostered an orthodox scholasticism. In his full-length study of Beza's theology, *Vernunft und Offenbarung bei Theodor Beza*,[71] Walter Kickel argues that Beza's doctrine of predestination (1) distorts the less rigid teaching of Calvin and (2) serves as a principle from which a system of theology is derived. This, then, leads to a scholastic orthodoxy that subverts the more biblical and humanist base of Calvin's theology. On the other side, scholars who are examining the whole corpus of Beza's work see Beza's contribution to the Reformed tradition not as deleterious but as an inevitable development, the effort to stabilize and thus to maintain Calvin's basic theology. These scholars are also seeking to understand better the whole period of the late reformation in order that the full impact of Beza's work can be better assessed. What cannot be disputed is that Theodore Beza, the foremost pastor and theologian of Geneva from 1564 until 1599, was a primary shaper of the Reformed tradition.

69. Raitt, "French Reformed Theological Response," pp. 178–79.
70. *Harmonia confessionum fidei* . . . (Geneva: Petrus Santandreanus, 1581).
71. Neukirchen-Vluyn, 1967.

7
LAMBERT DANEAU
1530–1595
OLIVIER FATIO

Translated by Jill Raitt

LIFE   Little is known about the childhood and the education of Lambert Daneau (Lambertus Danaeus).[1] He was born around 1530 at Beaugency-sur-Loire into a family of the lesser nobility. After attending the schools of Orléans, Lambert was sent to Paris around 1547 or 1548 where he studied with the hellenist Adrien Turnèbe. One may surmise that he also attended the courses of other royal lecturers and there acquired the humanist knowledge and methods in grammar, logic, rhetoric, physics, history, and geography of which he would make such extensive and pertinent use in his work as a theologian.

From 1553 to 1557 Daneau undertook legal studies at Orléans, where he obtained his license in civil law. After two unsuccessful efforts to become a professor of law there, he left for Bourges, where he remained until 1559; it was probably at Bourges that he obtained his degree of doctor of law. He was particularly impressed by two professors: François Hotman, whom he would meet again in Geneva after the Massacre of St. Bartholomew, and Anne du Bourg, whose martyrdom would determine Daneau's religious vocation.

As a lawyer in Orléans, Daneau frequented the literary circle of jurists and of humanists, whose preoccupations were juridical as well as philological, rhetorical, historical, ethical, and religious. From this period there exists an unedited treatise by Daneau dated 1560: *De Jurisdictione omnium judicum dialogus.*[2] In it Daneau employed the dialectical method so characteristic of his theological works.

---

1. For the few documents that yield some information about Daneau's early years see Paul de Félice, *Lambert Daneau, pasteur et professeur en théologie, 1530–1595. Sa vie, ses ouvrages, ses lettres médites* (Paris: Fischbacher, 1882), pp. 1–23; and Olivier Fatio, *Méthode et théologie. Lambert Daneau. Les débuts de la scolastique réformée* (Genève: Droz, 1976), pp. 1–3.

2. (Bern: Burgerbibliothek), Cod. Bern. 284.

Almost nothing is known about Daneau's religious convictions before his arrival in Geneva. It is probable that he grew up in an Evangelical environment. Among his friends at Orléans, in following the courses of the royal lecturers at Paris, and then at the Universities of Orléans and Bourges, he must have been in contact with Evangelical ideas. In any case, if one is to believe the autobiography contained in his 1576 dedication of his commentary on Augustine's *De haeresibus ad Quodvultdeum*,[3] Daneau was only faintly attracted toward the Evangelical movement. It was the martyrdom of Anne du Bourg, burned at the stake in Paris on December 23, 1559, that inflamed Daneau and determined him to go to Geneva, where he arrived in 1560. In fact, this tardy dedication dramatizes and telescopes events by presenting as a kind of conversion what may have been in reality a desire to deepen his knowledge of theology—a desire common to many humanists at that time—quickly followed by a total consecration to theology.

In Geneva the thirty-year-old laywer began to follow the sermons and classes of Calvin. As a result, he decided to give up his legal career and to dedicate himself to theology. He was conquered not only by Calvin's doctrine, but also by the ecclesiastical and civil order that this very doctrine had engendered in Geneva. He would become the instrument and advocate of this ideal "model."[4]

Daneau would willingly have remained in Geneva where, it seems, he taught philosophy for a time. But the company of pastors decided otherwise, and he was one of the many pastors sent into France to "shape up" the Reformed church.[5] Daneau became minister of the church at Gien from 1562 to 1572.[6] During these ten years the Wars of Religion troubled all of France, and Daneau had to take refuge at Orléans from September 1562 to April 1563 and again at Sancerre in 1568. On his return to Gien, he was imprisoned. Twice his library was confiscated.[7] But in spite of the extent and harshness of his ministerial tasks at Gien, his intellectual ardor began to bear fruit. It is during this period that Daneau acquired a good part of his astonishing patristic learning and knowledge of St. Augustine in particular. It is equally during his stay at Gien that Daneau conceived the first project of his *Isagoge*, an introduction to the commonplaces of theology treated according to the dialectical method.[8] His other works published between 1564 and 1566 consist of translations of the polemical and moral treatises of Tertullian and

---

3. Lambert Daneau (hereafter abbreviated as LD), *Augustini liber de haeresibus ad Quodvultdeum commentariis illustratus* (Geneva, 1576), fol. a ii verso.

4. Fatio, *Méthode*, pp. 5–6.

5. LD, *Augustini liber de haeresibus*, fol. a iii and verso.

6. Félice, *Daneau*, pp. 43–69; Fatio, *Méthode*, pp. 7–14.

7. Cf. Daneau's letter to J. Simler, Mar. 23, 1576, in Félice, *Daneau*, p. 314.

8. Cf. Daneau's letter to P. Daniel, Sept. 8, 1564, in Félice, *Daneau*, p. 266. See also pp. 268, 272–73, 288–89.

Cyprian on the dress of women and on idolatry.[9] In these works Daneau's taste for patristics and philosophy was joined with his pastoral concern for morality and the practical application of the Word of God.

Among the Reformed churches in France Daneau acquired such a reputation that the Synod of La Rochelle, on April 17, 1571, designated him as one of the ministers charged with drawing up a response to the books of the "adversaries."[10] Thus his name was included with the best-known pastors of the kingdom. This period of activity, so full of promise, was brutally terminated by the St. Bartholomew's Day Massacre in 1572. He returned to Geneva and there grew from a pastor who occasionally had time to attend to the study of theology, morals, and apologetics, into an internationally recognized theologian.

Daneau arrived in Geneva at the end of September 1572[11] and was given the parish of Vandoeuvres in November.[12] He was also given the post of "lector in theology" at the academy, a position created to give some assistance to Theodore Beza.[13] On the following June 25, Daneau was named pastor of St. Pierre, the fine old church in the heart of Geneva.[14] But in spite of his important pastoral and professorial functions, Daneau did not play a primary role in the Genevan church, which was effectively directed by Theodore Beza and Jean Trembley. This is partly explained by Daneau's position as a refugee. A good number of the French refugees remained withdrawn from the life of the church and state of Geneva. Nevertheless, Daneau counted among his friends Theodore Beza, whom he respected as his teacher, the lawyer François Hotman, and the pastors Antoine de Chandieu, Simon Goulart and Jean François Salvard, with whom he collaborated on the 1581 edition of the *Harmonia confessionum fidei*.

When in July 1576, doubtless because of the Edict of Beaulieu, the church of Gien asked Daneau to return, he refused on account of ill health.[15] In fact, poor health forced him to relinquish his pastoral charge and to reduce his

---

9. During this period Daneau translated *Traité de Tertullian touchant l'Idolâtrie* (Orléans, 1565); *Deux Traictez de Tertullian. L'un des Parures. L'autre des Habits des femmes Chrestiennes.* (Paris, 1565); *Deux traittez de S. Cyprian. L'un contre les Ieux. L'autre par lequel il monstre que l'homme chrestien ne doit voir spectacles publics* (La Rochelle, 1566); *Traité de S. Cyprian du mal qu'apporte l'Envie et Jalousie. Item, un autre traité touchant la discipline et les habits des filles* (Orléans, 1566). Cf. Fatio, *Méthode*, bibliography 1, 2, 4, 5.

10. Jean Aymon, *Tous les synodes nationaux des Eglises réformées de France*, 2 vols. (The Hague, 1710), 1, p. 108; and John Quick, *Synodicon in Gallia reformata or the Acts of those famous national councils in France*, 2 vols. (London, 1692), 1, p. 99.

11. Paul Geisendorf, ed., *Le livre des habitants de Genève*, 2 vols. (Geneva: Librairie Droz, 1963), 2, p. 29; Sept. 29, 1572.

12. *Registres de la Compagnie des Pasteurs de Genève*, 5 vols. ed. O. Fatio and O. Labarthe (Geneva: Librairie Droz, 1969), 3, p. 90.

13. *Registres*, vol. 3, pp. 90, 93, 94.

14. *Registres*, vol. 3, p. 138.

15. *Registres*, vol. 4, ed. O. Labarthe (Geneva: Librairie Droz, 1974), pp. 59–60.

teaching.[16] But his difficulties did not impede the intensive labor to which a prodigious literary production bears witness. Daneau, encouraged by Beza, who was anxious to find well-qualified champions of Calvinism, published in less than eight years (1573–81) some twenty-seven works, nearly all of which are important volumes.[17] Among them are the moral treatises: *Les Sorciers, Brève remonstrance sur les jeux de sort* (1574); editions of St. Augustine's works, with abundant commentary;[18] a commentary on Peter Lombard's first book of the *Sentences* (1580); works on methodology like *Elenchi haereticorum* (1573) or *Methodus tractandae sacrae scripturae* (1573); a commentary on 1 Timothy (1577); a *Physica Christiana* (1576) and an *Ethice Christiana* (1577); and a series of polemical works against the ubiquitarians[19] and the papists.[20]

This intensive activity brought Daneau into the network of Reformed theologians whose principal centers were Geneva, Zürich, Basel, Heidelberg, and, temporarily, Neustadt-an-der-Hardt. From 1576 on, Daneau became equally well known as the implacable pursuer of the ubiquitarians. From this date until 1584 he responded, in eight works, to all the great Lutheran theologians: Nikolaus Selnecker, Lucas Osiander, Stefan Gerlach, Jakob Andreae and Martin Chemnitz. Raised to the first rank of Calvinist polemicists, he showed himself to be firm and persevering, capable of tenacious enmities and of a vehement and violent oratory that was truly awesome.

Through his publications, his contacts, and his polemical activity, Daneau made a name for himself at Geneva. It is not, therefore, surprising that in May 1579, on the advice of Jerome Zanchi and Daniel Toussaint, he was considered as a candidate for the chair of theology at the University of Leiden, a chair left vacant by the departure of William Feugueray. But neither the government of Geneva nor Beza, who was ill, wished to let him go. Nevertheless, the magistrates of Leiden returned to the charge at the end of 1580, and this time Daneau received authorization to leave Geneva in spite of the profound regret of Beza. Daneau was given Genevan citizenship on January 16, 1581, and left the city on the following February 10.[21]

The Genevan years had been decisive for Daneau: they had allowed him to acquire control of his extraordinarily extensive knowledge and to bring his theological thought to maturity. He had arrived with a certain limited

16. Olivier Fatio, *Nihil pulchrius ordine. Contribution à l'étude de l'établissement de la discipline ecclésiastique aux Pays-Bas (1581–1583)* (Leiden: Brill, 1971), p. 15.

17. Fatio, *Méthode*, bibliography 8–80.

18. *Augustini Enchiridion commentariis illustratus.* (Geneva, 1575); *Augustini de haeresibus*; *Paratitla in Augustini tomos duos praecipuos* (Geneva, 1578).

19. Among these pamphlets are *Antiosiander* (Geneva, 1580); *Examen libri de duabus in Christo Naturis a Martino Kemnitio conscripti* (Geneva, 1581).

20. *Response chrestienne à Matthieu de Launoy et Henry Pennetier* (Geneva, 1578) and *Ad novas Genebrardi calumnias responsio* (Geneva, 1578).

21. See Fatio, *Nihil pulchrius*, pp. 15–22, for the sources for this period of Daneau's life.

reputation and he left after being elevated to the rank of a renowned Calvinist theologian.

In calling Daneau, the curators of the University of Leiden and the burgomasters of the town hoped to contribute to the reputation of their new university. In fact, they would receive a doctor of the Reformed church, who conceived of his teaching duties as a ministry and subordinated them to ecclesiastical needs. The confrontation would not be long in coming between a magistracy with caesaro-papist tendencies and a professor trained in a presbytero-synodal form of the church such as Calvin had conceived for France.

In May and June of 1581 Daneau participated in the national Synod of Middelburg and took part in the interrogations of Pastor Gaspard Coolhaas, declared adversary of Reformed ecclesiastical discipline, who was firmly supported by the magistracy of Leiden. In a work showing the necessity of a visible church, Daneau confronted the magistracy of Leiden and Dirck Coornhert, its ideologue and partisan of an individualistic Christianity constituted as such in its very institutions.[22]

In July of 1581 Daneau was engaged in a test of strength with the magistracy of Leiden over the appointment of elders and deacons to form a consistory in the French-speaking community for which he was preacher. He appointed them without consulting the civic authority, in spite of the latter's recognized rights.[23] The conflict reached its peak in February of 1582, when the magistracy of Leiden, after having compared the Genevan discipline favored by Daneau to the Spanish Inquisition, accused him of wanting to place upon the churches a new yoke as insupportable as that of the papacy. Daneau, cut to the quick, offered his resignation on February 28, 1582.[24]

Nothing could retain him, neither the affection of his students nor the support of the prince of Orange, who affirmed in March that "without Daneau, the theology faculty would be empty."[25]

His sojourn at Leiden seemed to be a failure. Could he have acted otherwise? He did not understand Dutch and held in little esteem the country's intellectual development. In addition he had been taken up in the

22. See Fatio, *Nihil pulchrius*, for the details of this crisis, which resulted on the one hand in the excommunication of Coolhaas (1534–1615), pastor of Leiden from 1574, by the provincial synod of Haarlem, and on the other hand in the dismissal of Daneau. In the same volume, one will also find an analysis of Daneau's response to the famous Dirck Coornhert (1522–90), moralist, politician, latitudinarian, and man of tolerance. LD, *Ad Libellum ab anonymo quodam libertino recens editum, hoc titulo, de externa seu visibili Dei Ecclesia, ubi illa reperiri possit, et quaenam vera sit etc. seu potius, adversus externam et visibilem ecclesiam* (Geneva, 1582). Cf. Fatio, *Méthode*, bibliography 90.

23. Cf. Leiden, Gemeentearchief, Gerechtsdagboek A (Secretariearchief no. 9248), fol. 145, July 11, 1581, published in Fatio, *Nihil pulchrius*, p. 171, n. 1.

24. P. C. Molhuysen, *Bronnen tot de geschiedenis der Leidsche Universiteit*, vol. 1 (The Hague, 1913), pp. 27–28; and Fatio, *Nihil pulcherius*, pp. 83–89.

25. William of Orange to the University of Leiden, Mar. 10, 1582, in Molhuysen, *Bronnen*, d. 86, p. 99.

larger issue of the establishment of the Reformed church, which, although authorized and rooted in the Low Countries, was far from being understood according to Daneau's conception of the whole church. This conflict between two conceptions of the church and its relations with the state, in fact between two conceptions of society, continued after Daneau's departure.

These troubled circumstances, however, did not interfere with Daneau's unwearying intellectual activity. He found time at Leiden to prepare, and probably to teach, the beginnings of his great theological work, the *Isagoge de Deo*, which was published in 1583 by Vignon in Geneva.[26] It should be noted also that among his students was the celebrated Arminius, whose gifts Daneau praised publicly.[27]

Daneau left Leiden for Gand where, enjoying the excellent atmosphere of this Reformed haven, he taught in the Calvinist academy from May 1582 to May 1583.[28] He then answered a call to southern France to teach theology at Orthez. In 1583 he occupied the principal chair of theology in the academy, which had nearly 600 students. At the same time, he performed ministerial duties and seemed to enjoy the tranquility of Orthez after his embattled stay at Leiden.[29] During the seven years at Orthez, Daneau was able to finish his *Isagoge*, publishing *De salutaribus Dei donis erga Ecclesiam* in 1586 and *De homine* in 1588.[30] In addition, he published a commentary on the minor prophets in 1586[31] and an explanation of the Apostles' Creed in 1587.[32] Through correspondence he maintained his bonds of friendship with his teachers and friends such as Beza in Geneva and Rudolf Gwalter in Zürich. In 1591 Daneau moved the university to its new home at Lescar. One year later he left Béarn to become pastor at Castres.[33] There he wrote a refutation of Bellarmine's work, which was published posthumously in 1596 and 1598,[34] and a work on Christian politics that appeared in 1596.[35] The year of his death, 1595, Daneau synthesized his thought for the last time in *Compendium sacrae theologiae*, published at Montpellier.[36]

26. LD, *Christianae Isagoges ad Christianorum Theologorum locos communes libri II* (Geneva, 1583). (Fatio, *Méthode*, bibliography 106). Cf. Fatio, *Nihil pulchrius*, p. 95.

27. P. Bertius, *Oratio in obitum D. Iac. Arminii*, (1609), cited in Fatio, *Nihil pulchrius*, p. 186, n. 12.

28. On Daneau's years at Gand, see Fatio, *Nihil pulchrius*, pp. 98–102.

29. Félice, *Daneau*, pp. 118–133. Cf. Daneau's letter to Gwalter, Dec. 11, 1584, published in Fatio, *Méthode*, pp. 122*–123*.

30. Fatio, *Méthode*, bibliography 116 and 122.

31. LD, *Commentarii in Prophetas Minores* (Geneva, 1586). Fatio, *Méthode*, bibliography 118.

32. LD, *Symbolici Apostolici explicatio* (Geneva, 1587). Fatio, *Méthode*, bibliography 120.

33. Félice, *Daneau*, pp. 126–27.

34. LD, *Ad Bellarmini disputationes theologicas responsio* (Geneva, 1596), and *Ad tomum secundum controversiarum Bellarmini responsio* (Geneva, 1598). Fatio, *Méthode*, bibliography 132 and 135.

35. LD, *Politices christianae libri septem* (Geneva, 1596). Fatio, *Méthode*, bibliography 133.

36. LD, *Compendium sacrae theologiae* (Montpellier, 1595). Fatio, *Méthode*, bibliography 128.

THEOLOGY   The reader of Daneau's works is less struck by the originality of his thought than by the range of his interests and erudition, by the diversity of his points of view, by the order and elegance of his reasoning. Daneau is a universal mind. Inspired by a vast encyclopedic plan, he undertook to found on Holy Scripture a number of recognized areas of knowledge, in order to integrate secular influences into the Reformed churches and academies. He added thereby to his theological and polemical works a *Physica christiana* (Geneva, 1576 and 1580); an *Ethice christiana* (Geneva, 1577); a Christian history, *Vetustissimarum primi mundi antiquitatum libri IIII* (Geneva, 1590); and a *Politice christiana* (Geneva, 1596). In doing this, Daneau is typical of scholars of the developing Reformed academies, who tried to extend to every aspect of knowledge the specific mark of Calvinism.

In Calvin and Beza, Daneau recognized his masters. But by the multiplicity of his interests and above all by his plan to base all knowledge on Scripture, he ventured into territory toward which his masters themselves had not turned. In more than one case, he was obliged to supplement their silence by direct borrowings from the Fathers, from Augustine through the middle ages to contemporaries such as Melanchthon, Peter Martyr Vermigli, Zanchi, Pierre Viret, and Chandieu. In order to synthesize his thought and to enlarge his points of view, he looked to a theologian who influenced his thought almost as much as Calvin and Beza, Andreas Hyperius.[37] To this name must also be added those of Niels Hemmingsen, the Danish crypto-Calvinist, and Johann Jakob Grynaeus of Basel. In short, Daneau's theology was eclectic. Nevertheless this man at the crossroads had succeeded in giving to his thought an order that is the expression of an intellectual energy and of an activity that never weakened to the end of his days. More than the term "orthodox," which brings with it a notion of rigidity and absence of imagination, the term "scholastic" applies to Daneau's work. In fact, he tried to present to his students in the most synthetic and accommodating manner both a theological understanding, which he considered admirably developed by Calvin and Beza, and the extension of this understanding to other areas of study. Why, then, should scholars criticize the rational framework to which he resorted as a corruption of the existential discoveries of the Reform?[38] It would be better to recognize it as a pedagogical support favoring the presentation of ideas easily put to use and corresponding to the process of scholarly transmission and the establishment of the Reform.

---

37. Note, for example, the influence of Hyperius's *De Theologo, seu de ratione studii theologici libri IIII*, 3rd ed. (Strasbourg, 1562) on Daneau's *Methodus sacrae scripturae tractandae*, (Geneva, 1579). Cf. Fatio, *Méthode*, pp. 64ff.

38. Ernst Bizer, "Frühorthodoxie und Rationalismus," in *Theologische Studien*, no. 71, Zürich, 1963, pp. 6, 15, 60–63.

Instead of describing some of Daneau's theological positions, it seems more useful to show the constitutive elements of his thought.

Before being a commentator on Scripture, Daneau was a man gifted at presenting a systematic construction. He was a professor who presented a summation of a problem in the briefest and most comprehensible manner, and at the same time exposed the roots of heresies. To accomplish this double objective, which corresponded, he thought, to the true method of teaching theology, that is, to affirm a doctrine and to refute its contrary (compare 2 Timothy 3:16 and Titus 1:9), Daneau needed an instrument that would assure both rigor and rationality. He found it in dialectic, the science of argumentation and reasoning, which provided him with the basis of his method.[39]

This dialectic is the Ciceronian Aristotelianism of Johannes Caesarius, of Johann Sturm, and, above all, of Philip Melanchthon. It points out that the most direct way to present the matter is to advance by posing questions (*an sit, quid sit, quis sit*, etc.) the responses to which are contained in the different dialectical *loci*, such as, for example, definition, gender, species, difference, cause. The first important work that Daneau published, *Elenchi haereticorum* (1573), provided a method intended to refute the arguments of heretics. This entire work was inspired by the *Topica theologica* (1564) of Hyperius.

Inspired by the refutations of Aristotle, Daneau taught that one passed through the discovery, analysis, and refutation of sophistries, that is to say, those places where erroneous arguments result in erroneous conclusions. Thanks to this dialectic, Daneau presented a universal method for exposing the corruptions inflicted by heretics on theological teaching and reestablishing it in its true form. He intended to furnish an instrument that would be valid against all heretics, by attacking the construction of their paralogisms without having to know each point of their doctrines.[40] He justified his method by the fact that Revelation itself utilizes logical categories. Is there, he asked, a dialectician more rigorous in argumentation or more keen in refutation than Paul?[41] To Daneau, prophets and apostles, under the direction of the Holy Spirit, are the greatest rhetoricians and dialecticians. The heretic, by contradicting the Gospel, commits therefore faults of logic and of rhetoric; his language is made up of confused propositions reducible to paralogisms. At the very instant that the heretic thinks he has overthrown the faith, he is constrained by logic. Dialectic comes therefore to support the confession of faith.

---

39. LD, *Elenchi haereticorum* (Geneva, 1573), p. 1, and *Methodus sacrae scripturae tractandae*, pp. 4 and 33.

40. LD, *Elenchi*, pp. 2, 3, and 5.

41. LD, *Elenchi*, p. 10.

In the face of the reluctance of certain theologians, those of Zürich, for example, to use dialectic in theology,[42] Daneau responded carefully utilizing the distinction between matter and form: dialectic does not give the substance of the faith to teaching; only Scripture contains true doctrine. On the other hand, the form of theology, that is to say, "the method and the manner of teaching and defending the faith," can be aided by the art of Aristotle and the dialecticians. Following Melanchthon and Beza, Daneau affirmed that dialectic is a gift of God; it must be used as a servant, as an instrument facilitating reasoning.[43] In his treatise *Transubstantiation* (La Rochelle, 1589), Daneau wrote: "As thus the true God is the author of the nature possessed by each thing, and notably of that reason by which man differs from brute beasts, and by which he discourses, argues and concludes from premises which are afforded him, he sees the consequences of things and separates the true from the false, certainly it must be said that anyone who rejects this conclusive reason, rejects also the wisdom of God of which the reason of man is a spark, a small flame, or a ray or streamlet."[44]

This taste for methodology is found again in the manner in which Daneau approaches biblical exegesis. *Methodus tractandae scripturae* (1579) proposes to the pastor and to the professor the way to explain Scripture. For each verse, Daneau proposes to begin with the rhetorical, dialectical, and theological *loci*. [45] The rhetorical locus makes apparent the type of liaison that unites a passage to its context and, at the same time, the frame of the theological explanation. The dialectical locus searches out the type of argument used by the author of the scriptural passage. As for the theological locus, it allows one to express the theological content of the text, and it comprises many stages: *summa, divisio membrorum, collatio locorum similium et dissimilium, explicatio verborum.*[46] In a manner that foreshadows Puritanism, Daneau's method insists finally on practical application and moral exhortation which ought to follow the exposition of a theological locus. In practical terms the exposition of the theological locus does not suffice to teach that which is necessary for the instruction, edification, correction, and consolation of the Christian.[47]

Daneau's method holds to a strict plan patently drawn from the popular and learned methods of teaching proposed by Hyperius in *De Theologo.*[48] The plan does not provide a key to interpretation but proposes a way to move

42. Bullinger's letter to Beza, Dec. 1, 1568, in *Correspondance de Théodore de Bèze*, (9 vols.) (Geneva: Librairie Droz, 1978), 9, p. 197.

43. LD, *Elenchi*, pp. 9–11.

44. LD, *Deux traitez. L'un de la Messe et de ses parties. L'autre, de la transsubstantiation du pain et vin de la Messe* (La Rochelle, 1589), p. 197.

45. LD, *Methodus sacrae scripturae tractandae*, p. 12.

46. Ibid., pp. 30–34.

47. Ibid., p. 35.

48. Hyperius, *De Theologo*, p. 398.

through the explication of a text. It indicates the steps of this path without saying anything about the content of the exegesis, a task that belongs to theology. Its end is to formalize the project expressed in the preface of Calvin's commentary on Romans: to explain the biblical text in a continuous manner without skipping anything.[49]

The content of Daneau's exegesis is found in the few commentaries that he published: In *Priorem Epistolam ad Timotheum commentarius* (Geneva, 1577), a veritable treatise on ecclesiastical discipline (to which we will return); *Orationis Dominicae Explicatio* (Geneva, 1582); *In Ev. secundum Matthaeum commentarii brevissimi* (Geneva, 1583); *In tres Joannis et unicam Judae Epistolam* (Geneva, 1585); *In prophetas minores commentarii* (Geneva, 1586); *Quaestionum in Ev. secundum Marcum liber unus* (Geneva, 1594).[50] Daneau followed Calvin's exegesis in general, while paying considerable attention to Beza's *Annotationes*. Nor did he neglect Hemmingsen, Melanchthon, or Erasmus. But the formal framework in which his commentaries were written prevented his exegesis from being a repetition of those authors just cited. It should be noted that the hermeneutic that dominates the commentary on the minor prophets is very close to that of Calvin, in the sense that it allows the text of the Old Testament to retain its historical density. Attentive to the development of the history of salvation and to the paradigmatic signification that each of its moments could take for the present situation, Daneau refused to move at once to a Christological interpretation of the prophetic texts.[51]

Another characteristic of the thought of Daneau is that reference to the fundamental authority, Scripture, is accompanied by numerous references to diverse authorities. These certainly do not constitute a second source of revelation, but they illustrate, or even prove, theological affirmations.

Daneau was a connoisseur of the Greek and Latin classics, from whom he drew an encyclopedic knowledge of geography, physics, schemes of logical thought, ethics, and politics. Certainly he affirmed that the word of God surpassed infinitely these pagan luminaries, and it is on this basis that he intended to build his *Ethice christiana*, his *Physica christiana*, and his *Politice christiana* in order to grasp the influence on Christians of the *Nicomachean Ethics*, the *Physics*, and the *Politics* of Aristotle.[52] But it is evident that these works of Daneau owed much to the structures of those of his illustrious predecessor.

The Church Fathers retained his attention, in particular Augustine, whose *Enchiridion* he edited and commented upon (Geneva, 1575), followed

---

49. John Calvin, dedicatory letter to S. Grynaeus in the "Commentaire aux Romains," in *Calvini Opera*, vol. 10, (C.R. 38) 2, cols. 402–06.

50. Fatio, *Méthode*, bibliography 55, 85, 105, 115, 118, 127.

51. Compare the exegesis of Mic. 2:13 in Calvin (*Calvini Opera*, vol. 43, [C.R. 71] cols. 315–318) and in LD, *Commentarii in prophetas minores*, pp. 538–540.

52. See, for example, LD, *Physica christiana pars altera* (Geneva, 1580), fol. q. ii–iii verso, dedicatory epistle to Peter de Sborow, palatine of Cracovia.

by *De haeresibus ad Quodvultdeum* (Geneva, 1576).[53] Contrary to the reformers of the first generation, Daneau did not first seek in Augustine an anti-Pelagian and anti-Donatist theologian. His personal preoccupations caused him to see first in Augustine the man of theological method and the systematician, then as the adversary of heresies, and finally as the exegete.[54] Daneau gave, therefore, in the *Enchiridion*, a systematic work par excellence, a commentary that is the first expression of a theology in which the influence of Calvin and Beza appears. Thus chapters 33 to 35 of Augustine, dedicated to the incarnation and the work of the mediator, furnished Daneau with the occasion to treat the hypostatic union in a manner that reflected the theology developed by Beza in his battle against the ubiquitarian Lutherans.[55]

Daneau distinguished himself from his contemporaries by his interest in scholasticism, for which he felt, at the same time, aversion and fascination. One is aware of these two attitudes in his commentary on the first book of the *Sentences* of Peter Lombard, *In Petri Lombardi librum primum sententiarum commentarius* (Geneva, 1580).[56] He expressed aversion for a theology that is contained in tedious questions and that, by distancing itself from Scripture, allows itself to be invaded by Aristotelian philosophy. But he is fascinated by a method whose application resulted in clear and rational constructions; he has admiration also for some of the elements of truth still present in this theology justified by numerous proofs drawn from St. Thomas, Durand de Saint-Pourçain, from canon law, or from Nicholas of Lyra.[57]

These multiple influences were brought together and carefully ordered in the *Isagoge*, Daneau's great theological work. The witness par excellence to his eclecticism and his dedication to system, it presents an original synthesis, while at the same time it covers all the theological loci, from the doctrine of God to that of eternal life. The *Isagoge* ought to be considered as an introduction to theology, prepared by a professor for his students.[58] It also helped to stabilize Reformed academies, many of which had, at this time, a precarious existence. In many of them, professors remained only a short time. Daneau's career is itself an excellent example of this instability. The *Isagoge* appeared then as a manual that presented, at a high level of popularization, a means of learning theology outside of an academic setting. As a Reformed version of the *Sentences*, it allowed ministers or doctors who had already finished their formal education a means of refreshing their understanding of theological principles.

---

53. Fatio, *Méthode*, bibliography 28 and 40.

54. See "De methodo librorum Augustini, et de eorum evoluendorum ratione" in LD, *Augustini Enchiridion*, fol. **i verso–** iii.

55. Fatio, *Méthode*, pp. 113–116.

56. Ibid., bibliography 75.

57. LD, *In Petri Lombardi librum primum sententiarum commentarius* (Geneva, 1580), fol. ** i verso–fol. ** iiii. Cf. Fatio, *Méthode*, pp. 129–130.

58. In this regard, see Daneau's prolegomena in *Compendium sacrae theologiae*, fol. i recto and verso.

From 1564 to its publication between 1583 and 1588, Daneau labored over this work. It has five parts—*De Deo, de angelis, de homine, de Ecclesia, de salutaribus Dei donis erga Ecclesiam*—which Daneau, as usual, had visualized in a great diagram. The last part is constructed according to Beza's diagram of the *Summa totius christianismi* (1555),[59] which "geometrically" organized the stages of the history of salvation and of reprobation as functions of the divine decree.

In order to treat each theological locus, Daneau utilized the dialectical questions: *an sit, quid sit, qualis sit, etc.*[60] This dialectical structure led him to present a description of God *in se* in order to answer the question *quid sit.*[61] Calvin had eschewed describing the essence of God (*Institutes* I, 13, 1) so Daneau borrowed from the Calvinist Zanchi his plan for describing the divine essence according to its attributes. More distantly, he followed the *Summa theologica* of St. Thomas and *The Orthodox Faith* of John Damascene. He remained, nevertheless, more reserved than Zanchi with regard to metaphysics and in particular to the Thomist definition of God as *ens simplicissimum.*[62] Zanchi began his own doctrine of God with definitions in the light of which he understood Scripture. Never did he see the least opposition between metaphysics and exegesis. Daneau, on the other hand, presented a less speculative theology in spite of its method and its rationalizing character. He made a point of beginning with Scripture and then aligning his points with certain metaphysical elements. Nor did he always find it easy to bring about such a conciliation. Pulled between Calvin and the new school of someone like Zanchi, he opted for prudence and worked out a theology with a remarkable formality, but he was very hesitating and ill at ease to be thus at the juncture of two worlds.

But in the final part of *Isagoge, De salutaribus Dei erga Ecclesiam*, there is no trace of uncertainty. Daneau could base himself here on both Calvin and Beza in speaking of the decree of God, of its realization either through justification and sanctification or though reprobation and hardening. In the *De homine*, a rich anthropological chapter, Daneau utilizes a multiplicity of sources from St. Thomas and Aristotle, passing through Beza, Martyr, and Melanchthon to Grynaeus.[63] As an eclectic work, *Isagoge* echoes some of the diverse points of view of Calvinist theologians in the second half of the sixteenth century.

59. Frédéric Gardy, *Bibliographie des oeuvres de Théodore de Bèze* (Geneva: Librairie Droz, 1960), pp. 47–53.

60. On the genesis, the plan, and the dogmatic method of the *Isagoge*, see Fatio, *Méthode*, pp. 147–150.

61. LD, *Christianae Isagoges, libri II (De Deo)* chaps. 1–8. Cf. Fatio, *Méthode*, pp. 154–165.

62. Compare LD, *Christianes Isagoges, libri II*, fol. 2 verso, 10; and Girolamo Zanchi, *De natura dei*, in *Opera theologica*, 2 vols., (Geneva, 1613), 2, cols. 63–73.

63. Johann Jakob Grynaeus, *Synopsis historiae hominis: seu, de prima hominis origine, eiusdemque corruptione, reconciliatione cum Deo, et aeterna salute, theses ducentae* (Basel, 1579), cited in LD, *Isagoges Christianae pars quinta quae est de homine* (Geneva, 1588), fol. 47–48, 69.

Daneau would summarize the *Isagoge* in 1595 in his *Compendium Sacrae Theologiae.*

To Daneau the Word of God is the foundation, not only of theology, but also, as we have said, of many other sciences, such as physics, ethics, or politics. In fact, Scripture not only contains Truth but all truths. This attempt by Daneau to found the profane sciences on Scripture brings to mind the great medieval syntheses. Daneau's method is subtle and he risks losing a hurried reader. In the *Ethic christiana* (Geneva, 1577), he employs classical terms as heavily loaded with meaning as that of *habitus*. Must one say then that he introduces into Protestant territory an ethic that is dependent on natural law or on scholastic anthropology? In fact he does not at all intend to yield to human nature a capacity to initiate moral actions or the task of fixing norms. In an authentically Calvinist sense, he constantly recalls that it is the Holy Spirit who gives the good *habitus*, then transforms it. Every moral action depends on the will of God, and man has no quality that he has not received.[64] Daneau therefore employs some classical or medieval notions without at the same time espousing their ideologies; he draws them rather into a Calvinist framework, which demands that one recall the consequences of original sin and sends the reader back to God and Scripture as the source of all moral conduct.

Daneau's work is without doubt one of the most representative in its exaltation of Scripture in all areas of knowledge and human conduct. Built for eternity, his work was nevertheless transitory. Its design and its universal pretensions could not be taken up by theologians of the following generation in an age of the more and more autonomous development of the sciences. But it endures as an exciting and unique piece of work through its attempt, sometimes equivocal or hesitating, to synthesize the Calvinist *sola scriptura* and the humanist methodology.

ROLE IN THE CHURCH   Documents are too few to measure Daneau's pastoral contribution in Gien, Geneva, Leiden, Gand, and the south of France. On the other hand, certainly his contribution strengthened ecclesiastical discipline. In 1577, he underlined the importance of discipline in a letter dedicating to William of Orange his commentary on the first epistle to Timothy, *Nihil pulchrius ordine*.[65] In the life of the church, discipline expresses the same search for method and order that Daneau exhibited in his theology. Following Antoine de Chandieu and

---

64. LD, *Ethices Christianae Libri III* (Geneva, 1577), fol. 101, 102, 106, 109.

65. LD, *In priorem Epistolam ad Timotheum commentarius* (Geneva, 1577), fol. q ii–iv. This letter to William of Orange has been published in English: *The Judgement of Lambert Danaeus, touching certaine points now in controversie, contained in his preface before his commentary upon the first Epistle to Timothie*. According to the British Museum catalogue, the work was published by R. Waldgrave, Edinburgh, 1590.

his *Confirmation de la discipline ecclesiastique, observée es eglises reformees du royaume de France*, published in 1566 in response to Jean Morely,[66] Daneau affirms the revealed character of discipline.[67] Daneau's work is made up of four long chapters, which in fact are based upon the principal parts of the *Ecclesiastical Ordinances* of Geneva of 1541, and re-edited in 1576: the election of ministers, pastors, elders, and deacons, as well as their duties; the moral censures applied to sinners by the consistory; and finally the reconciliation of sinners with the church, whether through excommunication or suspension from the Lord's Supper.[68]

In distinguishing (with the help of Aristotle) between the essential and the accidental, Daneau made precise the limits of the revealed character of the ecclesiastical order.[69] If one pretends, for example, that it is not necessary to examine the life and doctrine of a candidate for the ministry before electing him, an essential part of that election is vitiated. On the other hand, if one wishes to know when, where, and how one passes that examination, one touches only an accidental aspect of the election. The essential elements of discipline are intangible.[70] They ought to be the same in all the evangelical churches, from the beginning and perpetually. Thus in every time and place, the government of the church ought to be aristocratic and not monarchical; in each church there should be a consistory of elders elected by the community.[71]

By affirming the intangible character of the essence of discipline, Daneau was able to prevent the magistracy from changing anything whatever. In effect, the end of discipline is to establish the legitimacy of ministerial vocations and to bring church members to do penance and so return to God. But God, who gives vocations and directs consciences, is the only one who knows what laws to promulgate in these areas. Neither church nor king ought to tamper with vocation or conscience. Daneau thus safeguarded the full liberty of the ecclesiastical minister from any intrusion by civil authority.[72]

Preaching the Gospel is surely primary in the building of the church, but this primacy did not prevent Daneau from affirming that a church without sacraments and without discipline is bankrupt. By neglecting discipline, the church risks straying from God and true doctrine. Discipline protects doctrine, reforms conduct, and hold Christians in the fear and service of God. It is, in fact, the rampart and the remedy against heresies.[73]

---

66. On the problems with Jean Morely, whose Congregationalist tendencies were opposed by the Reformed churches, see the documents gathered in *Correspondance de Théodore de Bèze*, (9 vols.) vols. 7 and 8 (Geneva: Librairie Droz, 1973 and 1976).

67. LD, *In priorem Epistolam ad Timotheum commentarius*, fol. q vii verso–q viii.

68. Ibid., fol. qv and verso.

69. Ibid., fol. qv verso–qvi; pp. 169, 288–289.

70. Ibid., fol. qv verso–qvi.

71. Ibid., fol. qvi verso–qvii verso.

72. Ibid., fol. qviii and verso.

73. Ibid., fol. qq i verso, qq iiii and verso.

What has preceded should help one to understand the severity of the conflict between Daneau and the magistracy at Leiden, which intended to bring the church into submission to the state by dismantling the presbyterio-synodal organization confirmed by the Synods of Dordrecht (1578) and Middelburg (1581).

By contributing to the church's reflection on ecclesiastical discipline, Daneau gave the Calvinist churches the theological basis for their assertion of autonomy over against civil authority. He thus contributed to the determining manner and the specificity of the Calvinist Reform.

8

ZACHARIAS
URSINUS
1534–1583
DERK VISSER

LIFE   A donkey, working long days, often far into the night, in
the treadmill of the Lord: this is the self-portrait Zacharias
Ursinus painted in his letters.[1] So insistent are his complaints that his biographers, even the most sympathetic, have referred to them
as hypochondria. Thus, according to Karl Sudhoff, " [Ursinus] developed a
melancholic and hypochondriac disposition soon after his first years in
Heidelberg." A particular grievance, the "struggle" of the 1564 Maulbronn
disputation over ubiquity with Jakob Andreae, "wounded" him so deeply
that he "did not expect to be healed in this life."[2] Yet it may be more accurate

1. Ursinus to Johann Crato, June 25, 1570; Jan. 18, 1576: "Et labores pistrini mei indies mihi
graviores fiunt." *Zacharias Ursinus Briefe an Crato von Crafftheim*, Ed. W. Becker (Theologischen Arbeiten
aus dem rhenischen wissenschaftlichen Prediger-Verein, Bonn), 8–9 (1889): 79–123; 12 (1892): 41–207.
Becker has published ninety letters in chronological order from 1551 through 1570. For letters dated from
1561 to 1578, see G. A. Benrath, ed., "Briefe des Heidelberger Theologen Zacharias Ursinus (1534–
1583)," in *Neue Heidelberger Jahrbücher* 8 (1964): 93–141. These are letters dated from 1561–1578 and not
written to Crato. Among them are fifteen letters to Bullinger. See also in the same series, "Briefe des
Heidelberger Theologen Zacharias Ursinus aus Heidelberg und Neustadt a.H.," 14 (1906): 39–172. One
letter dates from 1559; the rest from 1563 to 82. They are to Crato, Joachim Camerarius, and Theodore
Beza. And again in the *NHJ* see Erdmann K. Sturm, ed., "Briefe des Heidelberger Theologen Zacharias
Ursinus aus Wittenberg und Zürich (1560–1561)," 14 (1970): 85–119. These are two letters to Abel
Birkenhain and one to Johann Ferinarius. Located in the Bibliothèque St. Geneviève in Paris, they are
part of the *Epistolae Haereticorum*, 5 vols., ms. cat. no. 1453–57.

I wish to express my thanks for their gracious assistance to Professor F. Büsser and Mr. Kurt Ruetschi,
editors of the Heinrich Bullinger Correspondence, Zürich, and to the staffs of the manuscript divisions of
the Bibliothèque St. Geneviève, Paris, and the Zentralbibliothek in Zu—rich. Special thanks are due to Mrs.
Katherine W. Kneas, Myrin Library, Ursinus College.

2. Karl Sudhoff, *C. Olevian und Z. Ursin* (Elberfeld, 1857), p. 410; Ursinus to Bullinger, June 27,
1564; J. F. A. Gillet, *Crato von Krafftheim und seine Freunde*, 2 vols. (Frankfurt: Friederichs Verlag, 1860),
2:129 and passim; Sturm, *Der Junge Zacharias Ursin, Sein Weg vom Philippismus zum Calvinismus,
1534–1562* (Neukirchen: Neukirchener Verlag, 1972), pp. 39–41 (This book is hereafter referred to as
"Sturm"). On Ursinus and the Ubiquitists see below, n. 26. See also above, chapter 4.

to think of his self-portrait as a fair description of his physical suffering and his arduous labor in service to God. And his letters reveal also that certainty of salvation that consoled him throughout his life.[3]

Although of moderate means, the Breslau family into which Ursinus was born in 1534 was sufficiently well placed that Zacharias received an excellent preparatory education. His ability and family connections also made it possible for him to go to Wittenberg, his expenses paid by several benefactors and the city council.[4]

This education was significant for the future development of Ursinus, permitting him to receive what we now would call "advanced placement." Thus the seven years at Wittenberg (1550–57) were spent mostly on work in logic, dialectics, and theology, the fields that he went on to teach in Heidelberg. But his early education was important also because the catechism he learned was written and taught by Moibanus, whose theology was apparently "Philippist" even before Philip Melanchthon had freed himself from the language of compromise required in the Augsburg Confession and its *Apologia*.[5] Although the catechisms of Moibanus have been preserved, they have only rarely been examined in connection with Ursinus's theology. More attention has been paid to a phrase Ursinus used in a letter in which he says that he was brought up in the mire of errors—*in luto erroris*.[6] The pun, as well as the contemporary context of the letter, has led to the assumption that he was referring to the Lutheran doctrine of the sacraments. It is possible, however, in the light of the limited reforms adopted in the Breslau church, to interpret the pun as referring to the ceremonial (adiaphoristic) aspects of the sacraments as celebrated in Breslau. As we shall see, Ursinus was much bothered by the Roman Catholic elements retained in the churches there.

The numerous letters Ursinus wrote to his benefactor Doctor Johann Crato permit us to glimpse the character of the student. He was clearly uncomfortable with people.[7] He switched boarding places several times, was not popular, had difficulty with his pupils, and stayed away from the more raucous aspects of student life. He developed a loyalty for Melanchthon that

3. Ursinus to Crato, Nov. 9, 1575: The fact of election gives him a certain stoic strength which others do not have, who "in omnibus consiliis fluctuant tamquam navis jactata in fluctibus . . . Stemis igitur aedificati super fundamentum Dei firmum, habent semper ob oculos illud Electionis sigillum"; Ursinus to Crato, Aug. 10, 1570: "the only firm consolation lies in God's eternal counsel." See also the discussion of Ursinus on election below.

4. Sturm, see n. 2 above. On Ursinus's ability and Melanchthon's fatherly attitude toward his charges (for one of the benefactors was Johann Crato, to whom Ursinus was introduced by Melanchthon) see the letter of Sept. 20, 1551. *Epistolae Haereticorum*, ms. cat. no. 1452–56, 3:361.

5. J. I. Good, "The Catechism of Ursinus' Boyhood", in *The Heidelberg Catechism in Its Newest Light* (Philadelphia: Reformed Church in the United States, 1914), pp. 86ff.

6. Cf. Sturm, p. 185. The pun appears in a letter to A. Birkenhain, a former fellow student of Ursinus's, written from Zürich, May 10, 1561. It probably was a student anti-authority joke.

7. Ursinus to Crato, Jan. 18, 1556; also Oct. 26, 1570, and below.

he maintained, as he did these other personality traits, throughout his life. Erdmann K. Sturm shows that these years were crucial for Melanchthon in the development of his own doctrine of the Lord's Supper, a development Ursinus followed with close attention.[8] The picture that emerges is of a precocious mind and a retiring personality. Loyalty to Melanchthon led Ursinus to espouse in his career those causes also defended by Melanchthon in his polemics against the Gnesio-Lutherans and the Tübingen theologians. This Philippism facilitated Ursinus's move to the Reformed camp when he was called to Heidelberg in 1561.[9]

In spite of the affection that Ursinus developed for Melanchthon and the regard that Melanchthon apparently had for Ursinus, the two men do not seem to have had a close personal relationship. In any case, fellow students such as Johann Ferinarius, or the polished sometime student Hubert Languet, were the sources from whom Ursinus heard of Melanchthon's private conversations on controversial issues.[10] This melting into the background was a characteristic that Ursinus exhibited even when he had become an established theologian in Heidelberg.

It appears that Ursinus had an excellent memory. At Wittenberg he took few notes. When asked by Crato for Melanchthon's precise opinions, Ursinus used the notebooks of others. His subsequent command of the texts from Scripture, the Fathers, and adversaries may have been based on this facility. In one instance Ursinus refers to his "donkey mind."[11] Aside from rhetorical modesty, he used the phrase to mock the subtlety of his adversaries' sophisms, with which he had little patience.

In 1557, after spending seven years in Wittenberg, Ursinus set out on a study trip that took him from Wittenberg to Worms and from there into the Rhine valley; into Switzerland (where he briefly visited Zürich and Geneva); into France (where he acquired the rudiments of Hebrew in Paris); and back

8. Gillet, 1:115 and passim; Sturm, pp. 39–41, on the development of Melanchthon's doctrines and their significance for Ursinus's theology, pp. 73ff, p. 82, passim. On Ursinus's admiration of Melanchthon, especially of his irenic disposition, as well as the meaning of the claim that he was Melanchthonian in his methodology, see L. Burckhardt, "Zacharias Ursinus and seine Abhängigkeitsverhaltnuss von Melanchthon", *Neue Kirchliche Zeitschrift* 37(1925): 669ff.

9. Sturm, pp. 173ff, provides extensive analyses of Ursinus's letters of 1561. Sturm sees them as critical in Ursinus's movement towards Calvinism, especially the long polemical letters to Abel Birkenhain and Johann Ferinarius of Mar. 10, 1561, and Apr. 21, 1561, which are in vol. 5 of the *Epistolae Haereticorum*. Sturm identified them as Ursinus's and had published them in the *Neue Heidelberger Jahrbücher* 14 (1970): 85–119. The *Epistolae* represent to me a source collection for a defense of the orthodoxy of Philippism against charges of crypto-Calvinism. The inclusion of the Ursinus letters, as well as the many by Languet, may mean that Philippists, at least, saw Ursinus and Languet as belonging to their faction, which in 1561 was almost certainly the case: see below, n. 16.

10. Gillet, 1:118, 178, passim; Sturm, pp. 46, 59, passim.

11. Gillet, see n. 10 above, also 2:129 on Ursinus's adversion to polemics, especially the 1557 letters to Crato, which are in 2:469ff. On his own modest estimate of his abilities see the letter to Crato of July 27, 1561.

again via Geneva, Zürich, and the Rhine valley.[12] On this trip he made a point of visiting as many known figures as possible, among whom were not only Bullinger and Calvin but also Sebastian Castellio and the theologians of Tübingen. The conversations he had on this voyage—as well as those of his trip in 1561, when he met George Cassander—are an illustration of one of his favored texts: "Examine all things and retain what is good." Although he followed Melanchthon to Worms in 1557, he apparently did not act as one of Melanchthon's assistants. There is no evidence that he actually attended any of the sessions of the colloquy that was called in yet anoth attempt to reconcile Catholics and Lutherans. It appears from the nature of the trip that he may have approached the Colloquy of Worms as a finishing graduate student does a professional meeting: as a good place to meet interesting people.

In his extensive discussion of this journey, Sturm has pointed out that Ursinus was introduced to Bullinger in a letter from Basel as a Saxon and Philippist. In view of the anti-Zwingli tone of the Worms discussions, the support from Basel may have been welcome. Nor is it strange that Ursinus was called a Philippist in this exchange, for indeed he was. We may assume that Ursinus proceeded with care, not wanting to burn his bridges to Breslau and intending to return to Wittenberg—as, in fact, he did. One is left with the impression that Ursinus used his studies as an excuse to stay off the battlefield, for once in Heidelberg, he quickly obtained his doctorate in 1562.

Soon after returning to Wittenberg in 1558 he was called to fill a teaching vacancy in Breslau. His Breslau stay has been much discussed as an important stage in his theological development. Yet the significance of the *Inaugural Oration* and *Theses*, his earliest theological statements, probably derives more from his subsequent Reformed activities in Heidelberg than from their actual content.

Erdmann Sturm has carefully analyzed the *Theses* as to their Melanchthonian and Calvinist content.[13] At the time this content probably had little public importance, for Ursinus meant the *Theses* for his own private use as a tool in his teaching. The *Theses* confirm Ursinus's earlier assertion that he had found the truth and that no coercion could make him abandon that truth or alter it. The *Theses* are often rephrased in his *Commentary* on the Heidelberg Catechism. Whether Ursinus already had moved toward Calvinism was not a question asked by his contemporaries. Melanchthon, upon reading the *Theses*, praised their *method* and expressed surprise at Ursinus's learning—had he not any previous experience of this?—saying that, "If Zacharias used his imaginative mind [*poetico spiritu*] he would survive the current tumult [in Breslau]." Melchior Adam, Ursinus's earliest biographer, calls the *Theses* "Gnesio-

12. W. H. Neuser, ed., "Das Stammbuch des Zacharias Ursinus," *Blaetter fuer Pfaelzische Kirchengeschichte* 31 (1964): 101–55; the entries made by the men Ursinus visited enabled Sturm to reconstruct the itinerary, pp. 105ff.

13. Sturm, pp. 135ff., which also contains Melanchthon's and Adam's remarks.

Melanchthonian!" If the *Theses* reflect any public participation by Ursinus in the disputes in Breslau, the authorities also must have seen them as Philippist. For when Ursinus asked for a leave of absence in 1560 to pursue his studies, they gave him a recommendation without releasing him from any future service.

Even while he was pursuing those studies in Zürich his return to Breslau remained so much of a possibility that he risked antagonizing his benefactor and friend Crato by insisting that Crato let it be known that Ursinus would not return until after he had completed his studies. It is true that Ursinus also wanted to be free to profess openly the entire Christian truth, for he stated, "If ours [i.e., the Breslau authorities] are prepared to let me teach the doctrine[s] which [are] in the churches, in which I now live . . .," he would return. This statement appears to be an admission of his adoption of Reformed theology, but in the context of his subsequent Zürich letters, this condition set for his return, like his avowed need for more study, may be seen as a means of gaining time.[14] Repeatedly he refused to be drawn into polemics by Crato because they kept him from his study. His view of the Breslau conditions is expressed in a letter to Crato on March 10, 1561, in which he relates Peter Martyr's reflection that the Danish church was still "half popish." Ursinus adds, "What must he think of ours." Obviously there was quite a distance between the Zürich Reformed church and this more than "half popish" church in Breslau.[15] But it should not be surprising that his Philippism made Ursinus receptive to the teachings of Martyr and the Calvinism of Heidelberg.

In the spring of 1561 a correspondence between the ecclesiastical authorities of Heidelberg and Zürich developed that resulted in Ursinus's going to Heidelberg in the summer.[16] He was full of anxiety about the future: "I would do anything to hide in some village in a rural district."[17]

Ursinus stayed in Heidelberg until the last five years of his life, which were spent in Neustadt as a teacher in the college established by Johann Casimir after the Lutheran reaction following the death of Elector Frederick III. Ursinus was among the last at Heidelberg to be removed from his position

14. To Crato, Mar. 10, 1561, and to Johann Ferinarius, Apr. 21, 1561, both written in Zürich.

15. It must be noted that this awareness of the "Reformation in progress" runs throughout Ursinus's *Commentary* on the Heidelberg Catechism, where his rejections of Roman errors are more frequent and more explicit than those of others, e.g. pp. 166, 168–69, 178, 288, 290, 409, and Question 80. I am using the 1956 reprint of the much issued *Commentary of Zacharias Ursinus on the Heidelberg Catechism* trans. F. W. Willard (Columbus, Ohio, 1852). The *Commentary* can be found in the works of Ursinus edited by his student Quirinus Renter: *Explicationes catecheseos Palatine, sive corpus Theologiae,* in D. *Zachariae Ursini Opera Theologica,* 3 vols., (Heidelberg, 1612), 2:46–413. Hereafter cited as *Urs. Opp.*

16. The recommendation was made by Languet at Naumburg in Jan. 1561 when as delegate of August of Saxony he met with the Palatinate delegates. See Sturm, p. 237. It is possible that Caspar Peucer was instrumental in Languet's suggestion: Languet to Peucer, *Epistolae Haereticorum,* 3:157 verso–158, Jan. 25, 1561; it may be that Ursinus refers to this interest of Peucer's when he says, "Sperabam D. Peucerum aliquid boni efficisse . . . ," to Ferinarius, Apr. 21, 1561, 5:475.

17. To Crato, July 27, 1561.

by the new elector, the Lutheran Ludwig. Possibly, Ursinus's administrative functions at the Sapience College and his retiring nature made his removal less imperative than that of such a firebrand as Caspar Olevianus. His last year in Heidelberg, which he spent without any defined duties, packing and unpacking his belongings, was a time of great anxiety. Not only did he make the decision about the second call to Bern—which, like the call of 1571, he rejected out of the loyalty to Frederick III now claimed by Frederick's son, Johann Casimir—but his strong desire was to retire to a small farm to serve the Lord in quietude. But as his savings were insufficient and as Crato missed the opportunity to show his generosity once again, Ursinus went to teach at Neustadt.[18] Here he wrote the *Admonition*, his most comprehensive work on the development of the German Reformation, as a rebuttal to the Lutheran *Book of Concord*.[19] He died, early in 1583, at the age of forty-eight, still wielding his quill in the battle for God's word.

THEOLOGY   Because he was a man who repeatedly asserted that he disliked polemics, who was hurt by the Maulbronn disputes and wounded by the struggle over church discipline in 1569–70, who had to be forced into the arena, and who preferred whenever possible to call disagreements "differences" and "semantics," it may be surprising that the bulk of his work consists of polemical writings.[20] In these his disappointment in fellow theologians sometimes shows through and he is not above punning on the names of adversaries—which then was a common rhetorical device—although in self-mockery he sometimes puns on his own

18. To Crato, Apr. 26, 1577; on the 1571 call to Bern, to Crato, Aug. 13, 1571; on the 1577 call to Bern, the letter to the Bern magistrates, Nov. 26, 1577.

19. For an assessment of the historiography, see G. A. Benrath, *Reformierte Kirchengeschichtsschreibung an der Universitaet Heidelberg im 16 und 17. Jahrhundert* Veröffentlichungen des Vereins für Pfälzische Kirchengeschichte, vol. 9, (Speyer, 1963), pp. 7ff. An analysis of the rebuttal is in Sudhoff, pp. 435ff.

20. On differences, see the discussion in the *Commentary* on the presence of Christ in the Lord's Supper; on semantics, see Sudhoff, p. 376, where he cites the 1576 *Gutachten* of the Heidelberg theological faculty (Paraphrased here): One can use the terms *substantialiter* and *realiter*, provided they are understood in a Reformed sense. It were better to use more precise terms, but peace is preferable. Also, as late as the letter to Crato, Sept. 9, 1582, Ursinus describes the differences between Beza and Melanchthon as consisting in the phraseology of definitions. The refusal to engage in polemics is strongest in the 1561 Zürich letters edited by Sturm, e.g., may 10, 1561, to Birkenhain. Yet they are almost immediately followed by the *Antopokrisis* directed against the doctrine of the Lord's Supper as espoused in Tilemann Hesshus's attack on Melanchthon's *Gutachten* for Frederick III. On the *Gutachten* see A. Kluckhohn, *Friedrich der Fromme* (Nordlingen: C. H. Beck, 1879), pp. 61ff. Melanchthon rejects transubstantiation, consubstantiation, and ubiquity, but for the sake of peace he believes it is important to find a common formula. Melanchthon's *Gutachten* is printed by Reuter in Urs. *Opp.* 3:1427–31, as *Philippi Melanchthonis judicium, de controversia Coena, ad EL. Palat. Fridericum*, and is immediately followed by the *Antapokrisis*, pp. 1431–50, from which we may assume that Reuter recognized their relationship.

name as well.[21] Yet Ursinus was always eager to find an accommodating formula. It may be that this eagerness resulted as much from his desire to be left to his studies and to his teaching as from his timidity. It is also possible that accommodation was enjoined on him as part of the avowed Palatinate policy of preventing exclusion from the religious peace of the empire. But I suggest that while these purposes were incidentally served, a genuine search for theological peace was fundamental in his method of debate. As he saw it, the first tasks of church and government alike were to remove abuses in the churches, to establish moral discipline, to teach the faithful, and to convert the erring. Polemics among theologians kept them from their ministry just as adventurous foreign policy kept the government from supporting that ministry.[22] Yet, at the same time, even his composing the Heidelberg Catechism and his use of it as a teaching device must be considered at least in part polemical.

Ursinus always maintained that he belonged, as did the Lutherans, to an evangelical church. Much of his work concentrated on showing the similarities between Lutheran statements such as the *Variata* edition of the Augsberg Confession and the Frankfurt Recess and Heidelberg Catechism.[23] Yet, later scholars have remained anxious to prove that Ursinus was a follower of Calvin and other non-Lutheran reformers. Thus A. Lang, in his exhaustive comparison of the Heidelberg Catechism and the Catechisms Major and Minor of Ursinus with those of others, found numerous examples of doctrines, sentences, and clauses that were similar to or identical with those of the

21. Thus Marbach becomes *rivum stultitiae*, to Crato, Nov. 3, 1568; on his own name, see the letter to Ferinarius, Apr. 21, 1561, when in explaining his reluctance to return to Breslau he writes "a bear is not easily tamed."

22. On the ministry of the church see the discussion of the Breslau Inaugural *Oration* in Sturm, pp. 110ff.; also the *Commentary* on Question 85 of the Heidelberg Catechism. On Ursinus's criticism of the involvement of the Palatinate church councilors in foreign policy, see his memorandum to Frederick III in Kluckhohn, *Briefe des Friedrich der Fromme* (Braunschweig: Schwetschke und Sohn, 1868–72) 2:1054ff.; on Heidelberg and the Religious Peace of the empire as established in Augsburg in 1555, see W. Hollweg, *Der Augsburger Reichstag von 1566* (Neukirchen: Neukirchener Verlag, 1964), pp. 119, passim. The Lutheran-Calvinist polemics of Ursinus's career were revived in the nineteenth century. Thus we find Karl Sudhoff, in his biography of Ursinus and Olevianus, which is otherwise a very useful work, taking a strong stand for Ursinus's Calvinism against possible Evangelical interpretations, e.g., pp. 9, 144, 118. In the United States, also, these polemics were revived in the wake of the Mercersberg Movement, see G. H. Hinkle, "The Theology of the Ursinus Movement," Ph.D. diss. Yale University, 1964), pp. 54ff and 71ff. Wulf Metz, in his thoughtful analysis of Ursinus's commentary on Questions 12–18 and their theological antecedents, accepts Ursinus's sole authorship on the basis of recent scholarship (cited below, n. 24); see *Necessitas Satisfactionis* (Zürich: Zwingli Verlag, 1970), pp. 61–88. I am inclined to agree with Metz, even though there is so far no direct evidence of authorship.

23. E.g., *Confessionis, Augustanae et Apologia; Repetitionis item, ac Francofurtensis Recessus, vera doctrina de Sacramentis, ipsissimis verbis expressa*, in *Urs. Opp.* 2:1419–27. The *Variata* was rejected by the Gnesio-Lutherans and the Tübingen theologians, but as late as 1561, it was subscribed by the Lutheran princes at Naumburg.

Genevan reformer and others. W. Hollweg, in his essay on the authorship of the Heidelberg Catechism, adds Beza's *Confession de la foi chrestienne* to the antecedents. The work of Lang has in fact become the modern starting point for these recent studies, but useful and impressive though it may be, it is nevertheless misleading. Lang indicates similarities to Melanchthon, and most modern writers on the Reformed nature of the Heidelberg Catechism overlook those studies of Calvin in which the indebtedness of Calvin to Luther is recognized. Calvin was, after all, himself a second-generation reformer. Not only did he remain a lifelong friend of Melanchthon's, but as late as 1541 he subscribed the *Variata* of the Augsburg Confession. Ursinus, who was brought up a Lutheran and who trained at Wittenberg as Melanchthon's disciple and undaunted admirer, did not in fact have to abandon much of Lutheranism to become Reformed.[24]

Ursinus cannot be categorized as belonging to any school or movement other than the evangelical church. Like Calvin, he stood with Luther in affirming justification by faith alone. He did not follow Melanchthon in the latter's synergism, for he believed man by himself could do nothing. Good works were a thanksgiving and a duty consequent upon justification. On the issue of predestination he also stood close to both Calvin and Luther and in his *Admonition* he chastised the Lutherans for deviating from Luther's position. As we shall see, he modified the doctrine of double predestination by accepting the doctrine of permission. On the meaning of the sacraments he can be placed with Calvin, but as he himself continued to argue, also with Melanchthon and in some aspects even with Luther. On the presence of Christ in the Lord's Supper, he thought like Calvin and Melanchthon, but he went so far as to accept Lutheran phraseology as long as he was allowed to give it a Reformed interpretation and as long as it excluded the doctrine of the ubiquity of Christ's human body. However, ubiquity was rejected by Melanchthon no less than by Matthias Flacius, Melanchthon's fiercest antagonist. Flacius also subscribed to the enslaved will, yet no one would make Ursinus into a Flacian. The simple fact is that none of the Christian churches subscribed to doctrines that were uniquely its own.

As the more or less official *corpus doctrinae* of the German Reformed Church was composed of the Heidelberg Catechism (1563), the *Defense* of the Catechism (1564), the Confession of the Theologians and Ministers of Heidelberg (1574), and the *Admonition* (1581)—four works either written or

---

24. A. Lang, *Der Heidelberger Katechismus und Vier Verwandte Katechismen*, Quellenschriften zur Geschichte des Protestantismus, vol. 3, (Leipzig, 1907); W. Hollweg, *Neue Untersuchungen zur Geschichte und Lehre des Heidelberger Katechismus*, (Neukirchen: Neukirchener Verlag, 1961). Also Good, "Catechism," pp. 39–79. On Calvin's indebtedness to Luther, see W. Diehl, "Calvins Auslegung des Dekalogs in der ersten Ausgabe seiner Institutio und Luthers Katechismen," *Theologische Studien und Kritiken* (Gotha, 1871): 141–62; A. Lang, *Zwingli und Calvin* (Bielefeld: Velhagen und Klasing, 1913), p. 106, goes so far as to say that Calvin's formulation of the doctrine of justification and regeneration by faith more accurately reflects Luther's theology than any other reformer's.

edited by Ursinus—there can be no doubt of his significance as a reformer who helped define the theology of a large sector of Protestantism. Determining what form this theology took may best be done by summarizing Ursinus's doctrine on the nature and meaning of the sacraments, his views of the presence of Christ in the Last Supper, and his defense of the doctrine of predestination.

Two tenets underlie the Reformed theology that Ursinus expounded. They are (1) justification is by faith alone, faith being a free gift of God to the elect; and (2) the Gospel (as found in the Scriptures) and the commentaries (of the Church Fathers and the early councils), preached by the ministers of the church, are the instruments that are required to be confirmed in this faith.

The most systematic exposition of Ursinus's theology can be found in his *Commentary* on the Heidelberg Catechism, which was published after his death by his pupil and successor David Pareus from lecture notes. We may assume that the commentary accurately represents Ursinus's explanations since Pareus's fellow students accepted his reading.[25]

At first glance it appears that Ursinus must have been dissembling when he attempts in the *Commentary* to establish the Heidelberg theology as reconcilable with the evangelical church. Thus he includes himself under the label "sacramentarian" when he discusses the accusations of the ubiquitists.[26] Among "the errors of the Sacramentarians, say they, [is] that they make the Lord's Supper consist merely in naked signs and symbols. Answer. We teach that the things signified are, together with the signs, exhibited and communicated in the lawful use of the supper, although not corporally, but in a manner corresponding to sacraments" (p. 435). He immediately goes on to treat "the general points in which the Churches, which profess the Gospel, agree and differ in the controversy respecting the Lord's Supper." In this way Ursinus defines Lutheran and Reformed churches as evangelical churches, that is, those that base their doctrine on the Gospel (pp. 100ff). It is regrettable, but not essential, according to Ursinus, that the churches differ in their understanding of the texts in some points—a point of view that could not have been developed as an expedient in the heat of Heidelberg polemics, since Ursinus had already expressed it in earlier letters.[27]

During the year after the publication of the Heidelberg Catechism, when it was attacked from several quarters, Ursinus gathered the many

25. For Reformed sources of particular points of Ursinus's theology, see Lang, *Heidelberg Kathechismus*, as well as Sturm and Sudhoff. The *Commentary* uses only passages from the Scriptures and fathers that support its own teachings.

26. The pagination refers to the 1956 reprint of Willard's translation of the *Commentary*. Ursinus deals with the doctrine of ubiquity—the omnipresence of the real body of Christ—in several places, e.g., pp. 244–47. On the Maulbronn Colloquium see Sudhoff, pp. 266ff, where he prints extensive excerpts from the minutes of the debates. The Maulbronn Protocols are given in *Urs. Opp.* 2:84–353, where they are followed by a short defense against the *cavillationes* of the Ubiquitists. (Page numbers given in parentheses in the text are from the 1956 reprint edition.)

27. To Birkenhain, May 10, 1561.

phrases used by the Lutherans in defining *sacraments* as well as the Lord's Supper into a composite definition, which reads in part as follows: "[Sacraments] are ceremonies or external, efficacious and certain signs, seals, assurances, testimonies of contract, of grace, of the will of God for us, appointed of God, to which is added the promise of grace, through which God moves the heart to believe . . ."[28] In the Heidelberg Catechism, sacraments are defined, in answer to Question 66, as: "holy visible signs and seals, appointed of God for this end, that by the use thereof he may more fully declare and seal to us the promise of the gospel, viz: that he grants us freely the remission of sin. . . ." In the exposition to Question 65, Ursinus anticipates this definition: "The word is the charter to which the sacraments are attached as seals. The charter is the gospel itself, to which the sacraments are affixed as the seals of the divine will." In the exposition of the answer to Question 66, Ursinus continues: "*The promise of the gospel* is called the promise of grace. . . ." It is a "visible sign of grace. . . . They are signs of the covenant and of God's good will toward us." No doubt, such a definition was made easier because the Lutheran definition itself is a classic one generally accepted by Roman Catholics and Calvinists alike.

Ursinus's comparison shows both a verbal and a substantial agreement with the Lutheran doctrine of sacraments in general as it was still accepted in 1563. This agreement nevertheless does not prevent him from moving away from the Lutheran doctrine of the Lord's Supper, especially where the question of the presence of Christ's body was concerned. Thus he maintained the distribution of the body and blood of Christ, not in the bread and wine, but through the Holy Ghost: "By this promise [of Grace] the bread is made the sacrament of Christ's body, and his body is made the thing signified by this sacrament; and these two, the sign and the thing signified, are joined . . . not by any physical union . . . but by a *sacramental union* . . . requiring faith of those who use it" (p. 386) "and by the Holy Ghost" (p. 388).

The commentary on the Lord's Supper comprises some sixty pages in rather small modern print. It is followed by a brief discussion of the paschal lamb, the significance of which—by using parallel columns of quotations from Isaiah, the Gospels, and Pauline texts—he firmly ties to the Last Supper. The entire exposition is a statement of a view that Ursinus developed before coming to Heidelberg, a view that he did not substantially alter and still maintained in his *Admonition*.[29] The treatment is extensive because—as in most other expositions—it deals with the numerous objections found in the writings of his contemporaries. Ursinus deals with some of these adversaries very specifically, but he rarely names them, nor does he condemn his Protestant adversaries, even by implication, for condemnation is reserved by

28. See above, n. 25.

29. Sturm on the Breslau *Theses*, pp. 146ff; Sudhoff on the *Admonition*, pp. 442ff. The *Admonition* itself in *Urs. Opp.* 2:480–696.

God (and by Ursinus) for those who partake as unbelievers, among whom are the hypocrites and reprobates.

The commentary on the Lord's Supper also provides us with insight into Ursinus's method. As always, it opens with an historical survey of the various names by which the Lord's Supper was known and their meaning. Of the various names for the sacrament, Ursinus selects the Lord's Supper, the name "the Scriptures give to it." But he also reminds the reader repeatedly of the meaning of the name *Eucharist*, that is, "thanksgiving." We may see in the Lord's Supper the division of the Heidelberg Catechism into "Misery," the state of man before the crucifixion; "Redemption," the crucifixion; and "Gratitude," after the Crucifixion. Thus the Catechism itself, through this division, symbolizes the Lord's Supper as the commemorative celebration of Christ's death on the cross.

Of the texts cited, Ursinus uses 1 Cor. 11: 23ff to render the meaning of the words of the Lord's Supper in an exegesis of the phrases used by Paul (pp. 383ff): "*He brake it*: He broke the bread which he took from the table, and distributed the one bread among many, and not some invisible thing which was concealed in the bread. He did not break his body but the bread. Hence Paul says, 'The bread which we break' (1 Cor. 10:16)." Ursinus then continues: "*This is my body*: *This*, that is, this bread: as if he would say, *this thing* which I have in my hand, which was bread. That this is the proper interpretation is evident from the following considerations: . . . 2. Paul says expressly, 'This bread which we break is it not the communion of the body of Christ?' . . . Christ, then, calls the bread his body . . ., as Augustine interprets it when he says: '*The Lord did not hesitate to say, This is my body, when he gave the sign of his body.*' " "Be it far from us," says Ursinus in almost Lutheran phraseology, "therefore, that we should say that Christ took bread visibly, and his body invisibly in the bread; for he did not say, in this bread is my body; or, This bread is my body invisibly; but, This bread is my body, true and visible, which is offered for you."

The other important phrase: "In remembrance of me," Ursinus glosses: "That is, meditating upon my benefits which I have bestowed upon you, and which this sacrament calls to your remembrance; feeling also in your hearts that I give you these gifts, and celebrating them by public confession in the sight of God, angels and men, and so giving thanks for them. . . ."

To the objection that Paul's words, "*He . . . took bread . . ., and said: Take eat, this is my body*," are in fact a gloss on the words of Christ, Ursinus retorts with Augustine's maxim. On interpreting sacramental phrases, introducing a Zwinglian note: " '*The only way by which we can determine whether a Scriptural phrase is to be taken in a proper, or figurative sense, is to see if it can be properly referred to some moral duty, or be made to harmonize with the true faith, and if this cannot be done, then we may know that it is spoken figuratively.*' " And then a little further on he produces this example: " '*Except ye eat the flesh of the Son of Man, and drink his blood ye have no life in you. Here Christ seems to enjoin a shameful crime. Hence it must be understood figuratively, as teaching us that we must partake of the passion of our Lord, and joyfully and profitably call to mind that his flesh was wounded and pierced for us"'* (p. 389).

In his comparison of the Lutheran doctrines concerning the Lord's Supper with those of the Palatinate Reformed church we glimpse something of the conciliatory nature of Ursinus. As he did not himself publish these commentaries, nor, apparently, gather his own lectures, we must assume that the running debate with Lutheran adversaries served to warn his students against errors and differences. The *disagreement,* to paraphrase Ursinus, consists of two points: (1) The interpretation of the words *This is my body*; from which follows (2) [the Lutheran insistence upon] the presence of Christ's human body and blood within the bread and wine. The *agreement,* stated in Reformed terms, consists in points that Ursinus thought more essential, especially point three: "In the supper we are made partakers not only of the Spirit of Christ, and his satisfaction, righteousness, virtue, and operation, but also of the very substance and essence of his true body and blood, given for us upon the cross, and shed for us . . . and that Christ declares and makes this known to us by this visible reception of bread and wine in the supper."

He says furthermore, in point five, that they agree "that without the lawful use"—which is defined in point seven as "by true faith and with sincere thankfulness"—"the taking of bread and wine is no sacrament, being nothing more than a vain, empty ceremony and spectacle, such as men abuse to their condemnation" (pp. 435–37).

If faith is both confirmed and strengthened by the sacraments and necessary for their efficacy, faith is also the basis of Ursinus's doctrine of the foundation and composition of the visible and invisible church. His teaching of election and predestination becomes meaningful for an understanding of his personal theology through his definition of the church as the community of saints, to which community he is certain he belongs.[30]

Those who together share in the "common passion of Christ and all his benefits" constitute the communion of saints (p. 304). Also "believers are called *saints* in three respects: by the imputation of Christ's righteousness; by the beginning of conformity to the law which is commenced in them [through the Holy Ghost]; and by their separation from the rest of the human race, being called by God to the end that they may truly know and worship him." It is their being called by God that creates the Church (p. 286), as *ecclesia* is derived from the Greek verb, "to call forth."

The visible church consists of those "who are regenerated by the Holy Ghost." They "embrace and profess the entire and uncorrupted doctrine of the law and gospel." Ursinus here refers to the parable of the wheat and tares and the parable of the net, to show that the visible church also comprises those "who are hypocrites and unregenerated, but who nevertheless consent to the

30. Above, n. 3.

doctrine and conform to the external rites of the Church." Only "the Lord knows those that are his" (2 Tim. 2:19). The invisible church is so named "because the faith and piety of those who belong to it can neither be seen nor known, except by those who possess it," who are the elect. Further on Ursinus asserts that "no one can be saved out of the Church . . . because those whom God has chosen to the end, which is eternal life, them he has also chosen to the means, which consists in the . . . call."

In consequence of this definition of the church, Ursinus teaches that the "eternal predestination of God, or of election and reprobation, naturally grows out of the doctrine of the church" (p. 293). The predestination of the election of some and the reprobation of others is defended by means of further citations from the Bible. Using the same method that he follows in all the controversial points of the Catechism, Ursinus cites and answers the many objections to both the general doctrine of predestination and the doctrine of double predestination.

From the answers to the objections an individual learns of God's majesty, which causes him "to have a greater regard for his own glory, than for the salvation of the reprobate" who "willingly falls into sin." Nor can God be accused of willing sin, for God does not necessarily "will those things that he permits . . . he merely does not prevent their accomplishment, if they do not hinder his end," that is, the end of damnation of the reprobate. Conversely God does will the means of salvation, for without his aid none would be saved, since man has lost the free will to do good (pp. 35, 56ff).

As Ursinus saw it, the doctrine of predestination was a great source of comfort, for the elect know of their election "from conversion to God, or from true faith and repentance . . . nor does every one only know his own election in particular from his faith and conversion; but he may also know in general that others are also elected." In addition Ursinus enjoins a charitable attitude even to the reprobate: "No one ought to determine anything with certainty [concerning reprobation], either concerning himself, or another before the end of life, for the reason that he who is not yet converted, may be before he dies. Hence, no one ought to decide concerning others that they are reprobate, but should hope for the best" (p. 301).

The admonition not to decide the reprobation of others may strike us as contrary to the insistence of the Palatinate disciplinists that the church may excommunicate the reprobate. Ursinus, though only a reluctant participant in the struggle, nevertheless supported the opponents of Thomas Erastus.[31]

31. The struggle between Erastians and Disciplinists involved the "ministry of the keys," i.e., the duty of the Church to guide and discipline the members of the congregation in matters spiritual as well as moral. The struggle was drawn out over five years and involved the elector's political advisers as well as other electors, particularly August of Saxony. See R. Wesel-Roth, *Thomas Erastus* (Lahr-Baden: Moritz Verlag, 1954); also Ursinus to Bullinger, Mar. 26, 1570, and Nov. 8, 1570. The Disciplinists favored a strict code that would have drawn from the State certain penal powers to permit the Church to punish moral transgressions. Alternatively, some Disciplinists would involve the State in the execution of penalties for offenses determined by the Church.

He wrote a memorandum for Frederick III in support of the power of excommunication. This memorandum is a summary of the biblical texts on the subject. It and a fuller exposition appear in the *Commentary* on Question 83. Yet, as Sudhoff points out, the church saw excommunication not as an instrument of damnation but as a means of preventing the infection of other members of the church with the errors of the reprobate.[32] Ursinus wrote that the mechanism of private examination and repeated admonition, with cause and with brotherly love, must be seen as the primary task—and preferred action—of church discipline. For Ursinus damnation was a sentence to be executed by God, not by man.

In his exposition on the answer to Question 83, Ursinus appears to have the struggle of 1569–70 in mind. This the more so, as Pareus, the editor of the *Commentary*, has inserted the theses on church discipline disputed by Peter Boquin and Boquin's student George Whithers (1568) as well as Ursinus's further remarks on that disputation that he gave for his own students in the Sapience College.

The area of church discipline is strictly limited by Ursinus to matters of morals and faith. Excommunication, the last recourse, is to be used by the church (as represented by its elders) only against the obstinate and openly wicked. In his exposition on Questions 83 and 54, Ursinus carefully separates the power of church and state. He admits that the church may receive those punished by the state for breaking the laws of the state and that the state may tolerate those who are excommunicated by the church. The magistrate inflicts punishment for crimes against its laws that may also be against God's laws, for instance, adultery. "The Church may receive them back, if they give proper evidence of true repentance."

Because the modern student is more familiar with the power of the state, the exposition to Question 83 and the inserted comments on the Boquin-Whithers disputation may be used to illustrate how apparently semantic differences may become aggravated into disagreements on substance. In the exposition itself Ursinus appears to be a moderate, contending that the ministry must be exercised with brotherly love, the penitent received. Moreover, no excommunication is to take place if it might rend the church. Yet in the inserted comments, the clear line drawn between church and state—between the church's power of excommunication and the state's physical punishment—seems to get lost in a surfeit of examples.

It is evident from Ursinus's letters to Crato that he derived his personal comfort from the doctrine of justification by faith through God's eternal election. In that sense his theology is very much a personal theology. It is personal also in that the Catechism, according to generations of its readers, speaks to them directly in what they call clear and simple language.[33] Even in

32. Sudhoff, pp. 353–54; the memorandum in *Urs. Opp.* 3:801–13.
33. Thus Sudhoff, pp. 60ff; Willard, *Commentary*, p. xiii; Good, "Catechism," pp. 21–35, passim.

his *Commentary*, which he himself considered "teaching of the more difficult character . . . belonging more appropriately to theological schools" (pp. 9–10), the personal element comes through occasionally when he drops Latin to use a German phrase, thus relating this exposition to everyday experience (pp. 109, 117, 286, 341, 450). It is a characteristic that also marks his more intimate letters, such as the one to Crato of October 26, 1570.

That to Ursinus Christianity is a guide for the personal life is further illustrated in his explanations in the catechism's section on the Ten Commandments. Like Calvin in his *Institutes* Ursinus here follows Luther's larger catechism.[34] Thus the Sixth Commandment's "Thou shalt not kill" is extended by an admonition against doing any harm or injury by physical means as well as by means of hatred, anger, or slander. But the commandment also requires positive action—that is, the preservation of a neighbor's life and safety, which can be done by humanity, mercy, and friendship. He then defines *humanity* as benevolence in mind, will, and heart towards others; while *friendship*, an aspect of *humanity*, is a true and mutual good will between good men. Here, away from the battles of theology, Ursinus provides his students with a guide for the Christian life in which empathy and charity dominate. In view of the loneliness Ursinus expressed in his letters during and after the struggle over church discipline, one feels that here speaks not a dour theologian but the man who should have had more opportunity "to walk in the meadows" or "retire to a farm" to feed his *poeticum spiritum*.[35] It may have been in his teaching that he best expressed that love for people which he could not express to his rowdy fellow students in Wittenberg or to his contentious colleagues in Heidelberg.

ROLE IN THE CHURCH   It was through his teaching also that Ursinus exercised great influence on his contemporaries. Through the Heidelberg Catechism and its *Commentary* his spirit works on into the present day. The importance of the catechism as a guide for the Christian life is well attested by its many editions and translations, even if we discount the academic and missionary translations. During the last thirty-seven years of the sixteenth century alone there were forty-three editions and translations. In all, some 207 versions have been identified.[36]

The German Reformed theologians freely drew from Calvin's *Institutes* as well as from Calvin's other writings, especially when they wanted to secure the Reformed foundations of their church. It is clear nevertheless that the use of the Heidelberg Catechism for purposes of instruction in confirmation

---

34. *Book of Concord*, ed. T. G. Tappert (Philadelphia: Fortress Press, 1959), pp. 365ff. On Calvin and Luther's exposition of the Decalogue, see above, n. 25.

35. To Crato, Sept. 19, 1569; June 20, 1577.

36. D. Nauta, "Die Verbreitung des Katechismus", *Hanbuch zum Heidelberger Katechismus*, ed. L. Coenen (Neukirchen: Neukirchener Verlag, 1963), pp. 39–62.

classes and as the basis for regular sermons, kept Ursinus's *Commentary* as an important foundation of Reformed theology. Subsequent generations produced their own commentaries, but they all made extensive use of the *Commentary* as well as other of Ursinus's works, chief among which was the *Admonition*.[37] The latter became even more significant in the nineteenth century in the staving off of Evangelical ecumenism.[38]

The significance of Ursinus as author and chief editor of the *corpus doctrinae* of the German Reformed Church has been well established. No doubt his German background and education played an important role. His frequent injections of German phrases into his letters, his translation of Calvin's catechism into German and his redaction of the German edition of the Heidelberg Catechism confirm his familiarity with the German cultural and religious heritage. As we have seen, much has been said about the nature of Ursinus's Reformed theology—whether it was Philippist, Calvinist, syncretist—resulting from Ursinus's method of examining all things and retaining those that were good, which to him meant, in accord with the Scriptures. As we have also seen, he was at pains to remain within the evangelical tradition and he was more concerned with fundamental errors— the rejection of the ministry of the church by the Schwenckfelders, the ubiquity maintained by Jakob Andreae, the transubstantiation taught by Rome—than with secondary differences. But the Palatinate church, to this day, is a Reformed rather than a Lutheran church. In Ursinus's formulation of the doctrines of the Lord's Supper and double predestination it would have been Reformed, even if the Lutheran *Book of Concord* hadn't closed the door to reconciliation between the two branches of the Evangelical Reformation in Germany by its exclusion of the more Philippist teachings.[39]

No doubt it was not only the disputes and colloquies, the expositions and polemics of the first generation of reformers, that aided Ursinus in the formulation of his thought; it was even more the realization that conciliation with Rome was no longer possible after Trent. This realization allowed a more precise definition of doctrine to replace the search for compromise that had inspired the phraseology of the several editions of the Augsburg Confession. It is well known that such leading reformers as Calvin commonly favored such conciliation, and it is in this search for accommodation with others in the evangelical church that Ursinus was Philippist. In his Wittenberg letters to Crato, Ursinus repeatedly admires Melanchthon's views on methodology and language and his preference for an irenic solution of differences.[40] In dealing

37. Thus Sudhoff's *Theologisches Handbuch zur Auslegung des Heidelberger Katechismus* (Frankfurt: Hender Verlag, 1862).

38. On the defense against this: Sudhoff, *Handbuch*, passim, and Hinkle, see n. 22 above.

39. There is the ironic possibility that the writing of the *Book of Concord* was inspired by the Palatinate insistence on the harmony between their theology and that of Philippism: see the letter of Johann Casimir to August of Saxony, Dec. 19, 1571, in Kluckhohn, *Briefe*, 2:438.

40. E.g., to Crato, Oct. 3, 1556; also above, n. 20; and Burckhardt, "Zacharius Ursinus."

with Lutheran antagonists Melanchthon called upon his knowledge of Luther, who after all had approved Melanchthon's redactions of the Augsburg Confession.[41] Ursinus also recommended using Lutheran arguments in the polemics against Lutherans. As we have seen, he did so himself in 1564 and above all in his *Admonition* of 1581.

It is not the purpose of this essay to discuss the relationship between Philippism and Calvinism. But because most biographers of Ursinus deal with this relationship, mention must be made of their view that Melanchthon gradually moved towards Calvinism, without embracing it lock, stock, and barrel.[42] I have difficulty in accepting this thesis. Calvin, not having inherited the mantle of Luther's leadership and standing as he did outside the political realities of the German Reformation, was freer in searching for precise formulae than Melanchthon. The latter may have been nominally the leader after Luther's death, but in Flacius Illyricus, Justus Menius, and Johann Brenz, he had Lutheran spokesmen who could also claim familiarity with Luther and who had long been autonomous spokesmen for the Lutheran Reformation in their respective territories. Thus, Melanchthon, not merely because of his irenic disposition, but also because of his need for unity, could not easily abandon the language of compromise he had earlier developed between 1530 and 1555. Melanchthon also departed from Luther, and from Calvin as well, on the doctrine of the enslaved will, by adopting synergism, the view that after justification man could contribute to his salvation of his free will. Thus we may argue that on the Lord's Supper Melanchthon and Calvin both departed from Luther, with Calvin starting earlier and going further. On the matter of predestination, Melanchthon moved in the opposite direction from Calvin, who, if anything, embraced Luther's views more firmly in his own theology.

As we have seen, Ursinus differed from Melanchthon by retaining Luther's doctrine of the enslaved will and by using Calvinist formulations in the doctrines of predestination and the Lord's Supper, with, however, significant differences.

Although reserving for himself the right to "differ from Philip" in order to remain true to God's word—"if we base ourselves neither on Philip nor on the reputation of any other man . . . it does not mean that it differs from Philip but that it is in accord with God's word"—it is striking that his strongest writings are against those who were also opposed by Melanchthon.[43] In 1564,

41. The most famous instance, also used by the Heidelberg theologians, is Melanchthon's statement that Luther suggested that Melanchthon use the fathers on the Lord's Supper to clarify the doctrines. Gillet, 2:113ff., Klockhohn, *Friedrich der Fromme*, pp. 177–78; Sturm, p. 130. Sturm quotes a statement of Melanchthon's that would place the instance in 1539, much earlier than "just before Luther's death" as in Gillet. A series of citations from the fathers can be found in the *Commentary*, pp. 403–06, see also *Libellis Brevis de Coena Domini editus A Nivolao Selneccero . . . 1561 . . . adiectis . . . scholiis Zachariae Ursinii . . . 1565*, in *Urs. Opp.* 2:1457ff.

42. Most recently, Sturm, p. 73, passim.

43. Quoted by Sudhoff, *Olevian und Ursin*, p. 156, from Ursinus's defense of the catechism in 1564.

defending the Heidelberg Catechism against several attacks at once, he clearly singles out Flacius Illyricus, the man he once characterized in a letter to Crato (February 27, 1557) as "out to get Philip." The other, and most persistent, adversary was Jakob Andreae, whom he saw primarily as the defender of ubiquity, a doctrine also rejected by Melanchthon. Just as Ursinus refused twice the call from Bern, first out of loyalty to Frederick III in 1571 and then out of loyalty to his memory in 1577 it was no doubt loyalty to Melanchthon that motivated his ardor in the disputes with Andreae.

The biographers of Ursinus, anxious to establish his Reformed antecedents, have made much of his two stays in Zürich, first during his study trip of 1557–58 and again in 1560–61.[44] There he studied with Martyr and read Isaiah. When he left Breslau he reportedly told his uncle that he went to Zürich because now that Melanchthon was dead he did not want to return to Wittenberg. Even if we accept this hearsay evidence, it is likely that Wittenberg no longer appealed to Ursinus because without Melanchthon and his few friends such as Birkenhain and Ferinarius there, he felt alien. Wittenberg also was too much involved in the increasing polemics among Lutherans. Ursinus, as a senior graduate student or a junior faculty member, with strong connections to Crato and to his former fellow students, would inevitably have been drawn back into these polemics.

Ursinus was apparently not a frequent correspondent of Bullinger. In the period of the church discipline struggle in Heidelberg, he wrote Bullinger to ask him to exercise a moderating influence on Thomas Erastus. He referred to his admiration for Martyr, whose counsel, with that of Bullinger, he had sought and accepted when the opportunity to go to Heidelberg arose in 1561.[45] The reference could be read as a plea to Bullinger for help in a situation in which Ursinus found himself because he had accepted Martyr's counsel.

In any case, the recommendation to bring Ursinus to the Palatinate was made by Languet during the conference of Naumburg early in 1561.[46] There is no evidence that Ursinus was suggested by Bullinger or Martyr to substitute for Martyr, who had refused an earlier invitation. Unless Languet was already a Calvinist, crypto- or avowed (and there is no evidence that he was), we may assume that Languet recommended Ursinus, his acquaintance and fellow student of Melanchthon, as a courtesy only. It could be argued that Languet may have wanted to introduce an apparent Philippist into the Calvinist ranks of Heidelberg.[47]

44. Thus Good, "Catechism," pp. 242–55.

45. To Bullinger, Oct. 11, 1569; Mr. Ruetschli of Zürich, co-editor of the Heinrich Bullinger Correspondence, determined the number of letters received by Bullinger by place of origin. Of the 181 originating in Heidelberg, 27 were written by Ursinus, starting in Dec. 1564.

46. Sturm, p. 237. On the Naumburg Conference and its attempts to keep Frederick III in the Lutheran fold, see Hollweg, *Reichstag*, pp. 9ff.

47. See above n. 9, also my "Junius, Author of the *Vindiciae Contra Tyrannos,?*" *Tydschrift voor Geschiedenis* 84 (1971): 510–25.

For all their insistence on the importance of Ursinus's sojourn in Zürich, neither Lang nor Sturm find much direct evidence of Zürich theology in Ursinus's writings. When Ursinus quoted Zwingli, he cited those statements on the sacraments and the Lord's Supper that lent themselves most to a reconciling interpretation. Sudhoff also, in his handbook on the Heidelberg Catechism, sees in those statements only the seeds for later Reformed theology.[48] As Zwinglianism was the only movement censured by the Colloquy of Worms in 1557, it may have been a surprise to Ursinus that such a reconciling interpretation was possible.[49] We may assume that the Zürichers hastened to inform Melanchthon's pupil of the possibility.

Thus we are left with the portrait of Ursinus as a Reformed theologian whose early theology was formed in Philippist Wittenberg. The gradual formulation of that theology was first shaped in the polemics of Melanchthon's last years and later in Calvinist Heidelberg. But the final shape of his theology continued to take account of two general aims: the first, to distinguish most clearly between Reformed doctrines and "popish errors"; the second, to accommodate, as long as possible, but without surrendering the truth as he saw it, the various movements within the German Evangelical church.

---

48. To Birkenhain, Mar. 10, 1561; to Ferinarius, Apr. 12, 1561; Sturm, p. 194; Sudhoff, *Handbuch*, pp. 369ff.

49. On the Colloquy of Worms of 1557 and the condemnation of Zwingli, see Sturm, pp. 94ff.

9
PETER CANISIUS
1521–1597
JOHN PATRICK DONNELLY

LIFE   Peter Kanijs, or Canisius, was born at Nijmegen in 1521. Jakob Kanijs, Peter's father, was a man of culture who had attended the Universities of Paris and Orleans and had served as tutor to the sons of Duke René II of Lorraine. Later he proved an astute businessman and politician, serving nine terms as mayor of Nijmegen. As his eldest son, Peter received the best education available, first at the local Latin school, then at a nearby boarding establishment, and finally at the University of Cologne.

Cologne was a natural choice, even though the university had fallen on evil days, for the Rhine linked it to Nijmegen, and Jakob Kanijs had business connections there. Among staunch Catholics such as the Kanijs family, Cologne was renowned as the German Rome, filled with old churches and relics of the saints. Jakob entrusted his son to two outstanding priests, Andrew Herll and Nicholas van Esche, who introduced their fifteen-year-old charge to the Dutch and Rhenish spirituality of the late Middle Ages. Through van Esche, Canisius became friendly with Gerard Kalckbrenner and Johannes Lanspergius, the prior and subprior at the Charterhouse of St. Barbara, which was a shining exception to the usual deterioration of monasteries during that era. Lanspergius attained eminence as a mystic and as a controversial theologian. The Carthusian life attracted Canisius, especially after his best friend, Laurence Surius, entered the Charterhouse. Still Canisius hesitated, perhaps deterred by a prediction of a saintly Beguine that he was destined for a new order of priests. Surius later went on to edit the biographies of many of the saints. The friendship between Canisius and the Cologne Carthusians later broadened into a special bond of prayer between the Carthusians and the Jesuits.

At his father's request Canisius transferred to Louvain in 1539 to study law, but when Jakob then arranged a lucrative marriage for him, Peter countered by taking a private vow of perpetual chastity, returning to Cologne, and beginning theological studies. For centuries Cologne had been a center of scholasticism, famous for the lectures of Albert the Great, Thomas Aquinas, and Duns Scotus. Canisius esteemed the medieval scholastics throughout his life, but his own emphasis on Scripture and the Church Fathers suggests a preference for the humanist tradition in theology. He also learned Greek and Hebrew, languages much lauded by the humanists, but several fundamental drives of humanism never took deep root in his conservative temperament. He did not develop an interest in humane letters for their own sake, and although throughout his life he reread Cicero to sharpen his Latinity, style was for Canisius only a useful tool, never the expression of a distinctive ego.

In 1541 a Spanish Jesuit, Alvaro Alfonso, joined the college where Canisius was residing. Alfonso told Peter about the Society of Jesus and the work of Ignatius Loyola's earliest companion, Pierre Favre, at Mainz. Intrigued, Canisius took ship up the Rhine to learn more about the new order of priests. The meeting with Favre at Mainz ended his years of searching. "To my great good fortune I have found the man I was seeking—if he is a man and not an angel of the Lord. Never have I seen nor heard such a learned and profound theologian nor a man of such shining and exalted virtue . . . . I can hardly describe how the Spiritual Exercises transformed my soul and senses, enlightened my mind with new rays of heavenly grace and I feel infused with new strength . . . . I feel changed into a new man." Six months later Peter Canisius took his vows as the first German Jesuit.[1]

Shortly thereafter, he became the first Jesuit to publish a book. He is probably responsible for the German translation of the sermons of the Rhenish mystic Johann Tauler, which appeared at Cologne in 1543.[2] Three years later Canisius was ordained to the priesthood and began to publish the fruits of his patristic studies: two volumes of St. Cyril of Alexandria, including the *editio princeps* of Cyril's Genesis commentary. Since Erasmus had already published St. Cyril, the young student did not lack courage, but his edition is not remarkable for scholarship. More successful was his edition of St. Leo the Great that same year, which went on to be reprinted six times.

By this time Canisius had become the leader of nine young Jesuits studying at Cologne, but more important was his role in frustrating the efforts of Archbishop Hermann von Wied to Lutheranize his electorate. Had von Wied succeeded, the history of Germany could have been very different, since the majority of electors would have been Protestant. A Protestant emperor might have been the coup de grace to German Catholicism. Von Wied met

---

1. Otto Braunsberger, ed., *Beati Petri Canisii Societatis Iesu Epistulae et Acta* (Freiburg i. B.: Herder, 1896–1923), 1: 76–77. The Spiritual Exercises of St. Ignatius Loyola are a system of reflection and meditation, mainly on the life of Christ, designed for a thirty-day retreat under a skilled director. They aim at bringing a person's major decisions and way of life into line with God's will. The printed *Spiritual Exercises* contain rules and suggestions that the director adapts to individuals and their needs. Loyola considered Pierre Favre the best director among his early companions.

2. For the controverted authorship, see James Brodrick, *St. Peter Canisius, S.J., 1521–1597,* (New York: Sheed and Ward, 1935), pp. 38–40.

strong opposition from the university, the chapter of canons, the Jesuits, and the chancellor, Johann Gropper. When Charles V visited Cologne in 1545, the Catholic leaders chose Canisius to present their case against the archbishop. Later they sent Canisius to the emperor at Antwerp and at Geislingen. Charles was sympathetic but postponed action until his victory over the Lutherans at Mühlberg allowed him to depose von Wied.

Early in 1547 Cardinal Truchsess of Augsburg appointed Canisius as his theologian at the Council of Trent. Peter had hardly arrived at Trent when the council was transferred to Bologna. Canisius spoke only twice before the congregation of theologians, but he put his knowledge of German and Germany at the disposal of the other Jesuits at Bologna, Diego (Jacob) Laynez, Alfonso Salmeron, and Claude Lejay. He soon forged lasting friendships with each of them.

When the council was prorogued in June 1547, Loyola summoned Canisius to Rome where he entered a primitive form of the Jesuit tertianship, or final spiritual training. After making the Spiritual Exercises a second time,[3] he devoted several months to prayer, to service in the Roman hospitals, and to menial housework—scrubbing floors, washing dishes, and serving at table. At the end of this experience Loyola sent Canisius and nine others to start a college at Messina. The Sicilian venture was the first of three hundred colleges for lay students that the Jesuits established during Canisius's lifetime. At Messina he taught rhetoric and headed the division of humanities, and the experience gained there by trial and error stood him in good stead when he organized the first Jesuit colleges in Germany. Almost a year after landing in Sicily, he got new orders from Rome. The duke of Bavaria needed professors of theology at Ingolstadt, where the university had declined sharply after the death of Johann Eck in 1543. He was to join Lejay and Salmeron in restoring this citadel of Bavarian Catholicism.

From 1549 to 1580 Canisius worked in Germany as teacher, preacher, writer, Jesuit provincial, and adviser to the Catholic princes. His major bases of operations were Ingolstadt, Vienna, Augsburg, Innsbruck, and Munich, but his duties forced him to tramp the wretched roads of Europe more than any major religious figure of the era. In 1565 alone, when he served as unofficial nuncio to the empire, he logged five thousand miles. Seven times he went to Rome, but recurrent short trips, such as his sixty-one journeys between Dilligen and Augsburg and twenty-four climbs through the Alps from Augsburg to Innsbruck, probably entailed greater hardship.

Canisius was the first Jesuit to enter Poland when he came as theological adviser to the papal nuncio in 1558, first to Cracow and then to the Diet of Piotrków. The strength of Protestantism in Cracow and throughout the realm alarmed him. He found Polish Catholics xenophobic, backward, and filled with anti-Roman bias; the bishops and clergy seemed apathetic and

3. A Jesuit twice spends thirty days following the Spiritual Exercises of Ignatius Loyola, once as a novice and again as a tertian three years or so following his ordination to the priesthood.

avaricious. Typically, his reaction was not discouragement but a desire to labor and give his life for Catholicism in Poland.[4] Seven years later he helped send a group of Jesuits to Braniewo (Braunsberg), and they gradually developed into the flourishing Polish province of Jesuits. He was aided in this by Cardinal Stanislas Hosius, who had been urging on Canisius the establishment of the Society of Jesus in Poland as early as 1554 (see chapter 10). The correspondence between the Polish cardinal and the Dutch Jesuit witnesses to nearly thirty years of friendship and cooperation. Canisius gave valued advice when Hosius served as cardinal legate at the Council of Trent. For many years Canisius looked after the publication of Hosius's works in Germany, much of which was not routine. In the case of Hosius's *Solida Propugnatio* (Cologne, 1558) against Johann Brenz, Canisius divided the work into chapters and provided marginal summaries and an index. He encouraged Hosius late in life to take up his pen again and do battle for the Lord. For years Canisius supplied the cardinal with the latest books from German publishers; in turn Hosius sent him manuscripts from Rome for his controversial works.[5]

In 1580, when the Jesuit provincial, Paul Hoffaeus, sent him to supervise the founding of a Jesuit college at Fribourg in Switzerland, Canisius left Germany, never to return. Perhaps Hoffaeus was glad to get rid of the old man, for he had long opposed his absorption in controversial theology and objected to his strict opinions against taking interest on certain kinds of loans, but Hoffaeus also realized how much Canisius's prudence and reputation for holiness would advance the delicate negotiations with the Fribourg senate for the new college.[6] Fribourg, squeezed between Protestant Bern and the Vaud, needed a college to fortify its Catholicism and stop the drain of its youth to the Protestant academies of Bern, Basel, Lausanne, and Geneva. The initial funds for the college came, as so often, from the suppression of a monastery. Canisius took up the task of preacher at Fribourg and meanwhile tried to deal with monk-pensioners, with rents from the monastic lands, and even with the temporal jurisdiction of two villages. In 1582 the Jesuits opened their school in two rented houses, but it took three more years and generous help from the senate before work could begin on a permanent college.

Gradually Canisius had to cut back on his preaching, since his voice and his health generally were failing. In 1591 he began to use a cane to totter about. His growing inability to engage in the active apostolate galled him, as we see from the many references in his letters to the "decrepitude of old age."[7] He explained to a friend that "a useless old fellow like me has plenty of leisure," but he tried to contribute whatever he could. As long as he managed

---

4. Braunsberger, 2:318–63.

5. Braunsberger, 2:202f, 888; 3:490, 392f, 515f; 4:19f, 793f.

6. Brodrick, pp. 712–72; Burkhart Schneider, "Peter Canisius und Paul Hoffaeus," *Zeitschrift für katholische Theologie* 89 (1957): 304–30.

7. Braunsberger, 8:844.

to get about, he insisted on doing his share in washing the community dishes and sweeping the floors. Throughout his life he had devoted up to seven hours daily to prayer, but now he added quiet walks with his rosary. The citizens came to see his presence in Fribourg as a talisman, "the strongest defense and ornament of their republic."[8]

Writing was the one activity that his health permitted, and his productivity continued unabated. Although he kept revising his earlier works, he increasingly turned to composing devotional books. Canisius published the lives of several local Swiss saints, together with prayers that were attributed to them. As history these books are worthless, but history was incidental to his purposes. Thus his life of the holy *hausfrau* Ida was an exhortation to married couples, while his writings on the soldier-saints—such as that on St. Maurice, *A Mirror for Soldiers*—were intended for Swiss mercenaries. For the future emperor, Ferdinand II, Canisius composed a book of prayers. It is easy to dismiss such writings, but they found an eager audience. The great work of his last years was five large volumes of meditations and notes on the gospels for Sundays and feast days.[9]

THEOLOGY   Canisius is best known for his catechisms, which eventually appeared in five hundred editions in twenty-five languages. In Germany as in the rest of Europe before the Reformation, catechetical instruction for children had long centered on such traditional topics as the Creed, the Ten Commandments, and the Lord's Prayer. This material was often cast into verse for easier memorization and supplemented by explanations of the seven sacraments, the seven capital sins, the eight beatitudes, and similar material. Nevertheless, the pre-Reformation tradition had failed to capitalize on the invention of printing by placing effective catechisms in children's hands. Very early, Protestants began to fill this vacuum, culminating with Luther's large and small catechisms of 1529. Catholic catechisms were slow to appear, but by midcentury German Catholics could choose between the catechisms of Georg Witzel, Johann Gropper,

8. Braunsberger, 8:677, 883.

9. For a discussion of the literature on Canisius, see Engelbert M. Baxbaum, *Petrus Canisius und die kirchliche Erneuerung des Herzogtums Bayern, 1549–1556* (Rome: Institutum historicum S.I., 1973), pp. 1–11. Canisius's published works include three catechisms, three polemical works in theology, nine books of piety, eight volumes of sermons and sermon notes, and five books on the lives of the saints. Friedrich Streicher has produced a critical edition of the catechisms: *S. Petri Canisii Doctoris Ecclesiae Catechismi Latini et Germanici; I, Catechismi Latini; II, Catechismi Germanici,* (Munich: Officina Silesiana; Rome: Universitas Gregoriana, 1933, 1936). Other major works are: *Commentarii de Verbi Dei Corruptelis; I. Iohannis Baptistae Historia; II. De Maria Virgine Incomparabili* (Paris, 1584); *Notae in Evangelicas Lectiones* (Fribourg, 1591, 1593); *Meditationes seu Notae in Evangelicas Lectiones,* vol. 1, (Freiburg i. B.: Herder, 1939); vols. 2 and 3 (Munich: Officina Silesiana, 1955, 1961). For a listing of Canisius editions, see Carlos Sommervogel, *Bibliothèque de la Compagnie de Jésus* (Paris: Picard, 1891) 2:617–88.

Pedro de Soto, Michael Helding, and others, but none of these could rival that of Luther.[10]

Ferdinand of Austria had long desired a compendium of Catholic theology aimed at priests and educated laymen; Canisius, Lejay, and Laynez had all tried their hand at this project without much success. Early in 1553 Canisius turned instead to a large catechism, which so delighted Ferdinand that he promised it would be the only catechism allowed in Austria. The first edition, *Summa Doctrinae Christianae*, appeared anonymously at Vienna in 1555 and went through twenty printings in the first four years. Ferdinand and his advisers made the capital suggestion that Canisius provide marginal references to Scripture, the Church Fathers, and the ecumenical councils so that teachers and students could see the evidence that backed the statements of the *Summa*. Later Canisius helped Peter Buys (or Busaeus), a fellow Jesuit from Nijmegen, to compile the *Opus Catechisticum*, whose four volumes and 2,500 pages reprint the text of the *Summa* together with the passages referred to in its margins.[11] The first edition of the *Summa* has 213 questions and covers 69 pages in the Streicher critical edition; after the Council of Trent Canisius nearly doubled the length of the catechism by expanding his answers, by adding 9 new questions, and by reprinting almost verbatim the Tridentine decrees on original sin and justification. Marginal references to Scripture rose from eleven hundred to two thousand, while patristic citations jumped from four hundred to twelve hundred. Canisius seldom referred to scholastic theology since he preferred to base his vocabulary and teaching on Scripture and the fathers.

In 1556 a Latin grammar appeared at Ingolstadt that contained in an appendix the first edition of Canisius's *Catechismus minimus*. It occupies only seven pages in Streicher's edition. Editions in Latin and German quickly followed, often containing prayers, hymns, and instructions on confession and communion. The most popular of the Canisius series of catechisms was the *minor*, or *Parvus Catechismus Catholicorum*, of 1559, which was intended for adolescents and contained three innovations not found in its larger or smaller companions. It was often illustrated; especially lavish was the Plantin edition of 1589 with 102 engravings by Peter van der Borcht. Secondly, the *minor* often contains a calendar of the church year with elaborate references to readings for each day. Finally, it includes an appendix of thirty-seven scriptural quotations for students to quote against heretics; these quotations do not argue against any specific teaching but simply stress the value of tradition and the authority of the church. Only the *minor* and the *minimus* were designed for memorization. One reason for the success of the Canisius cate-

10. Jean-Claude Dhotel, *Les Origines du catéchisme moderne* (Paris: Editions Montaigne, 1967), pp. 15–98.

11. *Catechismi*, 1:38*–46*, 67*–70*; Braunsberger, 1:411–13; Brodrick, pp. 173–79; 221–24.

chisms was that they increased in length and sophistication as the child grew, while remaining familiar in wording, doctrine, and format. [12]

Most sixteenth-century catechisms, including those of Luther, Calvin, and the Council of Trent, have four major parts dealing with the Apostles' Creed, the Ten Commandments, the Lord's Prayer, and the sacraments, although the order of presentation varies. In contrast, Canisius divides Christian doctrine into two parts, "wisdom" and "justice." Under wisdom he deals with faith (the Apostles' Creed), hope (The Lord's Prayer and the Hail Mary), charity (The Ten Commandments and the precepts of the church), and the sacraments. The second part, devoted to justice, is shorter but more distinctive. Justice consists in fleeing evil and doing good. Canisius describes four categories of sin that the Christian must flee. In explaining how the Christian does good he takes up the works of mercy, the cardinal virtues, the gifts and fruits of the Holy Spirit, the beatitudes, and the evangelical counsels. He closes by explaining the four last things: death, judgment, hell, and heaven. Giving students information about Catholic doctrine was important, but Canisius's real goal was leading them to prayerfulness, to the frequent use of the sacraments, and to moral living based on intelligent religious conviction. The *justitia* of Canisius, chiefly derived from Augustine and Gregory the Great, is not an isolated philosophical virtue but includes theological justification and the whole of Christian living.

In one sense the catechisms of Canisius are among the least polemical of the Reformation era; they never mention Luther, Calvin, or any Protestant by name, and they seldom advert to Protestant doctrine, but simply present the arguments for the Catholic positions on disputed points. In their lack of direct reference to Protestant teaching they contrast with many Catholic catechisms such as those of Edmond Auger, the famous French Jesuit. Gradually even the French Jesuits came to prefer Canisius's catechisms to those of Auger, both because their section on justice and practical piety had no parallel in Auger and because they did not even bring up the alternative explanations of the Protestants. [13]

In another sense the catechisms of Canisius are profoundly anti-Protestant. Their heavy stress on good works was designed to oppose Luther's emphasis on faith. The division into two parts, one devoted to Christian wisdom and the other devoted to justice and devout living, clearly cuts against

---

12. Within Canisius's lifetime there were eighty-two printings of the *Summa* (twenty in the empire) and 132 Latin printings of the *Minor* (fifty-eight in the empire), plus four of the *Minimus*. There were thirteen printings each in German of the *Minor* and the *Minimus*. Stricher, *Catechismi*, (1:96*–168*; 2:16*–17*), lists the Latin and German editions, but there were many other vernacular translations, for example ten of the *Summa* and thirteen of the *Minor* in French: Dhotel, pp. 80, 81. For photo-reprints of early English translations, see *English Recusant Literature*, vols. 2, 32, 35; (Menston, Yorkshire: Scolar Press, 1968, 1970, 1971).

13. Dhotel, pp. 77–80.

Luther's link between faith and justification. In defending traditional Catholic faith and practice, Canisius shows little of the spirit of compromise found in Erasmians such as Georg Witzel. Canisius begins his tract on the sacraments in the *Summa* with a defense of the solemn rituals with which the Catholic Church surrounded the sacraments. He tries to build up a scriptural and patristic defense for the five sacraments that most Protestants rejected. Thus he sees the laying on of hands in the Acts of the Apostles as evidence for confirmation. He argues for transubstantiation but devotes more space to defending communion under one kind wherever custom and church authorities have sanctioned it. Because baptism caused little controversy between Catholics and mainstream Protestants, he treats it very briefly, giving it only a third of the space he devotes to holy orders. Clearly the needs of controversy produced an imbalance in treating the various points of doctrine; central truths on which there was general agreement get short shrift, while disputed questions suffer the elephantiasis so common in Reformation polemics. After explaining the Ten Commandments Canisius takes up the precepts of the church, which he prefaces with a long defense of church authority. The visible church is the city placed on a mountain, the pillar and foundation of truth that God fosters, preserves, defends, and vindicates. Anyone who rejects her doctrines or denies the authority of her ministers, particularly of the popes, is not a member of the church. Christians need the teaching of the church to recognize the Scriptures and to distinguish their true meaning from the false interpretations of heretics.

The controversies of the Reformation even intrude into the second part of the Canisius catechisms, which treats justice. In contrast to Luther, who defines sin as a transgression of God's law, Canisius builds on a Catholic theology of infused grace and defines mortal sin as a free act that destroys the spiritual life and brings death to the soul. Among the evangelical counsels he singles out for detailed treatment poverty, chastity, and obedience, which form the three vows of the monastic life.

The chapter on justice devotes a section to three traditional good works—fasting, prayer, and alms. Although Canisius begins by citing St. Augustine's threefold division of fasting into avoidance of sin, moderation in food and drink, and specific fasts commanded by church authorities, he concentrates on defending ecclesiastical fasts from Protestant attacks. His treatment of prayer contains little echo of his own training in the *devotio moderna* and the Spiritual Exercises; it heaps up commendations and examples of prayer from the Bible, but there is no hint of mysticism, little on inward union with God, nor much practical instruction on how to pray. His catechisms failed to prepare Catholics for the spread of systematic meditation, which was central to Counter-Reformation renewal. To almsgiving Canisius links the traditional seven spiritual and seven corporal works of mercy. He stresses that help for the needy must be generous, spontaneous, and universal, undertaken for the pure love of God rather than from human vanity, but the social dimension of charity is neglected. He devotes his ingenuity to discovering scriptural quotations urging charity rather than to suggesting concrete applications in a sixteenth-century context. His focus remains the spiritual profit of the giver rather than the help given the needy.[14]

Through most of his life German Catholics felt themselves on the defensive and suffered from an inferiority complex. To overcome this feeling of inferiority St. Peter encouraged Catholic controversialists, even though the effect of their polemics was more to hearten waverers than to win converts. He constantly hectored friends to enter the fray with new books. He was always ready to contribute a preface, correct proofs, or shoulder negotiations with printers. He felt that Erasmus, despite his erudition, had done a disservice to the church because his edition of St. Jerome attacked the monastic life that the hermit of Bethlehem had extolled. Accordingly Canisius prepared a selection of Jerome's letters and added a preface defending the religious life against his fellow Dutchman.[15] Selling in competition with the bulky, expensive edition of Erasmus, his handy octavo selection went through forty printings. During the late sixteenth century the exploitation of the Church Fathers grew in the polemical literature, and Canisius made himself a specialist on them.

Canisius was not a creative theologian, nor did he enjoy controversial theology, but at the command of Pius V he undertook to reply to the *Magdeburg Centuries*, the massive church history arranged by centuries that Flacius Illyricus and his associates at Magdeburg had produced (see chapters 1 and 2 above). The task increasingly absorbed his time from 1567 to 1577. He quickly recognized that to refute the centuriators, passage by passage, was beyond his powers. Still less could he have produced an alternative interpretation of Christian history such as Cardinal Baronius did in the *Annales* at the end of the century. Canisius therefore decided to concentrate his effort on the first century and devote a volume each to John the Baptist, Mary, and St. Peter. Each volume would be at once a work of piety, a theological essay, and a refutation of the centuriators by showing how they mishandled the three biblical figures. The first fruit of his labor was *Iohannis Baptistae Historia Evangelica* (1571), which expanded the scattered New Testament statements about the Baptist to 796 pages; each chapter begins with the scriptural verse, appends the comments of the centuriators, then gives the lengthy *censura* of Canisius. Protestant exegetes generally reacted against the patristic interpretation of St. John as the precursor of monasticism by toning down the strangeness of his lifestyle. Thus the camel's hair worn by the Baptist becomes sturdy peasant garb or even a stylish woven garment. For Martin Bucer, the Baptist, when he retires to the desert, should not be compared to a hermit but to somebody who moves from the Rhineland to a backward part of Lorraine. Zwingli and Calvin allegorize the desert to stand for the ruined spiritual

14. *Catechismi*, 1:169–80.
15. Braunsberger, 3:274–85.

condition of the Jewish people. Canisius counters that "the outstanding continence, abstinence and general austerity of life pertains to the ornament and fullness" of the Baptist's sanctity. His treatment of the Baptist's diet of honey and locusts widens into a case for Lenten fasting and abstinence. The recovery of the body of the Baptist by his disciples becomes a defense of relics. More important are sections on celibacy, the nature of true repentance, the role of good works in Christian sanctification, and vocation to the ministry. Canisius added a long preface that ranges over many areas of doctrine and many Protestant theologians. Anticipating Bossuet's *Variations*, he contrasts Catholic unity with Protestant diversity. Among others, he attacks the Antitrinitarianism of Michael Servetus, Bernardino Ochino, and Laelius Socinus, and even finds Luther lukewarm in the defense of the Nicene Creed. He enumerates and mocks the many Protestant theories of the Eucharist. Rather idiosyncratic views such as the Brenz-Andreae doctrine of the ubiquity of Christ's body (see chapter 3 above) and Calvin's treatment of Christ's descent into hell (a blasphemy as evil as anything in Mohammed or Arius) are skillfully used to blacken all Protestant teaching.[16]

Canisius published *De Maria Virgine Incomparabili* in 1577 to continue his attack on the centuriators; again, many other Protestants come under fire—Luther, Melanchthon, Calvin, and Brenz are cited over four hundred times each. Nevertheless, devotion overshadows polemics, for this enormous book is really a summary of the whole of Christian thought about the Virgin. The revised edition of 1583 contains four thousand references to Scripture and ten thousand to patristic and scholastic authors. These statistics suggest Canisius's strengths and weaknesses as a writer and theologian. His reading was very wide, but he lacked originality and critical acumen. He tried to convince readers by inundating them with quotations and citations drawn from earlier authorities. Canisius never got his projected volume on St. Peter the Apostle beyond preliminary notes. Friends at Rome urged him to continue, but the Jesuit provincial, Paul Hoffaeus, bitterly opposed the project. Canisius had become a perfectionist, constantly revising his manuscripts, constantly ransacking libraries and pestering others for new quotations. Hoffaeus felt that Canisius should stick to short devotional books in German, practical books for ordinary people. Canisius yielded. In the course of his life he published a dozen books of prayers and pious readings. Hoffaeus was probably right; Canisius was at his best as a director of souls and a devotional writer, and German Catholicism needed zealous pastors more than speculative theologians. Indeed, throughout Europe the Catholic Reformation did not rest on savants but on men of action, for it was basically a reform of piety rather than of ideas.

---

16. For Calvin, Christ's descent into hell implied that Christ underwent the internal torments of the damned in his soul. *Institutes*, 2:16.

ROLE IN THE
CHURCH
When the central period of Canisius's life began, with his return from Italy in 1549, it was obvious that the Interim had failed to pave the way for religious union in Germany. The princes, preachers, and people of north and central Germany were so unshakably committed to the Augsburg Confession that even Charles V at the zenith of his power could not uproot thirty years of Protestant growth. The region for Catholic reform during the lifetime of Canisius remained restricted to areas under Catholic princes, especially to Austria and Bavaria. Even in these areas Lutheranism was widespread among the common people and the lower nobility. Most Catholics were apathetic, so that without the support of the emperors and the dukes of Bavaria, the efforts of Canisius and the other Catholic reformers would have availed little in preserving these lands for the old church. Although Canisius lacked the qualities of a courtier, he soon became a confidential adviser to these princes because they respected his holiness and sincerity. His advice looked to one goal, the good of the church. The Catholic princes aimed at several conflicting goals, so that they often disregarded his advice, but in spite of disagreements Canisius and the Catholic princes retained their mutual respect.

Jesuit education in Germany began with the arrival of Canisius, Lejay, and Salmeron at Ingolstadt in 1549. During the next two decades the establishment of Jesuit colleges and universities was Canisius's most important work. The origins of these colleges varied. Sometimes the Jesuits established a separate college at an older university, as at Ingolstadt; sometimes they assumed control of an earlier foundation, as at the University of Dilligen; sometimes they started new schools from the ground up, as at Würzburg and Fribourg. Canisius played a major role in establishing the Jesuit schools at Ingolstadt, Vienna, Prague, Munich, Dilligen, Mainz, Innsbruck, Hall, Würzburg, Speyer, Regensburg, Augsburg and Fribourg. He played a less direct role in the foundation of eight others. Of these, Munich, Mainz, Dilligen, Vienna, and Würzburg averaged about nine hundred students each by the time of his death. All were fortresses of the Catholic Reformation and seedbeds for a new breed of priests. During the thirty central years of Canisius's apostolate, the first handful of German Jesuits grew to eleven hundred, most of them engaged in education.[17]

The colleges were usually established only after painful negotiations and often had strings attached. At Ingolstadt the Jesuits had to supply two professors of theology for the university and were pledged to serve the duke of Bavaria "in matters of religion wherever and in whatever way they can whenever he so requests them."[18] All too often the patron tried to endow the new colleges at the expense of a third party. A favorite device was to offer the

17. Berhard Duhr, *Geschichte der Jesuiten in den Länder deutscher Zunge in XVI, Jahrhundert* (Freiburg i. B.: Herder, 1907) 1:66–91, passim.

18. Brodrick, p. 268.

Jesuits the building and income of a decayed monastery or convent, either forcing the remaining monks or friars to move to another house of their order, or simply moving the Jesuits in as unwelcome guests. Again and again Canisius fought this sort of project, not always successfully.

Canisius realized that the students of his colleges were the key to the future of Catholicism in the empire. A pioneer of Jesuit educational practice and theory, he was convinced that young boys were pliant and that despite the ravages of original sin they could be guided to good habits. University students should be forced to live in supervised hostels, but the rigors of a Collège de Montaigu—the famous Paris college attended by Calvin and Ignatius of Loyola—would only drive students away. Regulations against dancing and fencing should not be enacted because they could not be enforced. Canisius insisted that the school buildings be kept clean, well heated, and in good repair. Few details escaped him: doors should be padded to close without noise. There should be a plentiful supply of balls and game equipment for the younger lads. Although corporal punishment was not altogether abolished, masters were to imitate Christ the Perfect Teacher in courtesy and gentleness toward their students. The study of Aristotle dom-inated the Jesuit curriculum, but the school libraries, always a special concern of Canisius, contained a surprising range of books. Training in piety invar-iably went hand in hand with academic subjects.

In June 1556 Loyola established the Jesuit province of upper Germany (Bohemia, Austria, and Bavaria) and appointed Canisius as its first provincial. Although the usual term of office was three years, he remained provincial, with short interruptions, until 1569. These were pioneer years with few customs and traditions to guide the Jesuits. Especially at the beginning many of the Jesuits were foreigners who were rushed into action before completing the long spiritual and intellectual training that later became a Jesuit hall-mark. The Jesuit lifestyle was then a novelty, and the early Jesuits had a charisma that attracted men of talent, energy, and holiness. These same qualities attracted eccentrics, however. Later the long training would sift out those unsuited to Jesuit life, but in the pioneer days too many of them got out into ministry and some even became superiors. [19] Beyond doubt, fellow Jesuits laid the heaviest crosses on the shoulders of Canisius, so that when he retired as provincial at forty-eight he was an old man, but by the same token these trials developed and displayed his sterling charity.

Canisius was a practical man. He judged that the three key men in every Jesuit house were the superior, the preacher, and the cook. In deciding to locate the Jesuit novitiate at Prague rather than at Vienna, he gave three specific advantages: Prague was politically more secure, enjoyed better

19. Each Jesuit community is headed by a superior responsible for the work and well-being, physical and spiritual, of the members who in turn owe him obedience. The superior owes obedience to the provincial and the provincial to the superior general, who from the time of Ignatius Loyola to the present has lived in Rome.

weather, and brewed better beer.[20] Bad beer meant sick Jesuits. An extra-ordinary number of Jesuits under Canisius had health problems, particularly tuberculosis, but not all the ailments were physical. The razor-tongued Father Jean Couvillon was an able Ingolstadt theologian but was given to neurotic guilt feelings, hallucinations, and temper tantrums, which alter-nated with periods of depression. He would skip community meals, then order special foods served in his room. Because his sickness was attributed to the bad beer of Ingolstadt (ironically only a few leagues north of Munich), Canisius called Couvillon to Regensburg and made him his own secretary. Couvillon never really recovered, but Peter's kindness helped him do much good work. At Vienna the problem was the superior, the Basque Juan Vitoria. Like Loyola he was a dreamer of great schemes for the glory of God, but he lacked common sense. A man of great personal austerity, he could not appreciate why his subjects were unhappy when he sold off most of the community's furniture in order to decorate the church. He insisted that everything at Vienna be done Italian style, even to the way the eggs were cooked. By 1561 three of his subjects could take no more and left the Jesuits. Canisius rushed to the spot and did his best to restore the situation with kindness all around. Vitoria's faults came from excessive zeal, but what could be said for the novice who served as cook for Canisius and absconded with two hundred crowns intended for the distribution to the poor? Or the Jesuit court preacher at Innsbruck who converted to Lutheranism? More bizarre was the young Englishman Edward Thorn who entered the Jesuits for adventure and a free education, while remaining a convinced Protestant; all went well until the young Jesuits studying at Dilligen were asked to make the Tridentine Confession of Faith. Here Thorn baulked and decamped to Protestant territory. These episodes are only samples of the trials that Canisius un-derwent as provincial.

Most German priests and bishops watched the spread of Protestantism with apathy and discouragement. The shortcomings of the Catholic clergy in carrying out their pastoral duties filled Canisius with anguish and fired his zeal. Nothing was more fundamental than their failure to preach. Despite his duties as teacher, writer, and superior, Peter found time to become one of the most effective preachers of the age. A stolid Dutchman who lacked flair and magnetism, he compensated by hard work and total sincerity. As a young professor of rhetoric Canisius had mastered ancient oratorical theory, but when he larded his early speeches with rhetorical flourishes, he found that he lost his audience. His mature preaching was simple, direct, and designed to move his listeners to holy living. Canisius was official preacher for seven years at Augsburg, five years at Innsbruck, and eight years at Fribourg. During these years he averaged two sermons a week, sometimes speaking for two hours or longer. Sometimes he preached almost daily. Some twelve thousand

20. Braunsberger, 3:190.

pages of sermon notes survive and witness to his careful preparation, with the main points written out in full and the margins aswarm with directions. It was these that he drew together at the end of his life into five volumes of notes on the gospel readings for Sundays and feast days. Two volumes appeared before his death, but three were not published until the twentieth century. These are not sermons so much as notes, prayers, and suggestions to help parish priests prepare their own sermons.

When Canisius was appointed cathedral preacher at Augsburg in 1559, Catholicism was nearly dead in that commercial heart of the empire. Only eight hundred Catholics made their Easter duty the year Canisius arrived, and his first sermon drew only fifty, but as his reputation spread his audience grew. During his first year he was responsible for nine hundred Augsburgers returning to the Catholic sacraments, and the whole tone of Catholic devotional life improved. Although his sermons at Augsburg were mainly explanations of doctrine, they also took up the problem of city poverty with great frankness. Both as preacher and adviser Canisius did not hesitate to present his own convictions, however unpleasing to his audience and patrons, even when more popular positions were within the limits of Catholic orthodoxy. He took a very conservative stand on usury, although the Fuggers were personal friends and generous supporters of the Jesuits.[21] Likewise, he argued against granting the chalice to the laity when this was a pet project of Emperor Ferdinand.

It would be pleasant to report that Canisius foreshadowed the ecumenical spirit in his dealings with Protestants, but he was a man of his acrimonious times. He accepted the provisions of the Peace of Augsburg that allowed princes and free cities to impose either Catholicism or Lutheranism, not because the Peace was an ideal but because it was the best settlement that political circumstances allowed. Constantly he urged Catholic princes to exercise their full rights under the Peace, even as the Lutheran princes were doing. Heresy was for Canisius a deadly plague, but he often esteemed individual Lutherans as men of sincerity and virtue. "They have gone astray . . . without contention, willfulness or obstinacy. Most Germans are by nature simple, homely folk. Born and bred in Lutheranism, they receive with docility what they are taught in schools, churches and heretical books, and that is why they have gone astray."[22] The distinction between formal, obstinate heresy and the material, guiltless heresy of the common folk was an important contribution in an age when most theologians assumed that false belief flowed from willful blindness. Only slowly did Rome come to accept this obvious distinction.

21. The Fuggers, the leading German banking family, resided in Augsburg. Canisius was particularly close to George and Anton Fugger and was responsible for the conversion of Ursula and Sybil Fugger. See Brodrick, pp. 435–37, 592–96.

22. Braunsberger, 8:131.

Canisius argued that the conversion of Lutherans in Catholic territories depended on driving out their religious leaders and replacing them with zealous priests from the new Catholic colleges and seminaries. Coercion against the common people, Canisius warned Rome, was neither wise nor feasible. Germany was not Italy or Spain. He finally persuaded the curia to ease regulations governing the conversion of Protestants in Germany. Canisius advised his fellow Jesuits to imitate the courtesy of Christ, who would not quench the smoking flax, in their dealings with Protestants. On the other hand he urged stronger action toward the German Catholic princes: Lutheran ministers should be expelled, publishing strictly regulated, and heretical books combed out of Catholic schools. Teachers and graduates at Catholic universities should be made to swear the *Professio Fidei Tridentinae*.[23]

Emperor Ferdinand made Canisius one of the six Catholic spokesmen at the Colloquy of Worms in 1557. The leading Lutheran spokesmen were Melanchthon, Johann Brenz, and Erhardt Schnepf. Canisius had little hope that this theological summit meeting would have any more success in finding a *via media* than had earlier imperially sponsored colloquies. His pessimism was shared by Melanchthon, whose opening speech repudiated the decrees of Trent and pledged loyalty to the *Confessio Augustana*. The most important speech of Canisius went straight to the crucial weakness of the colloquies: the inability of Catholics and Protestants to agree on the criteria of religious truth. He argued that Scripture was insufficient since it did not prevent division among Protestants or even among Lutherans. His speech gave an opening to Schnepf, a leading follower of Flacius Illyricus, who demanded a condemnation of Zwinglians, Majorists, and all who deviated from the *Augustana*. To Brenz and Melanchthon, who wanted to present a united Protestant front, this demand was deeply embarrassing. Melanchthon countered with efforts to purge the Flacians. For all practical purposes the split between Lutherans finished the colloquy, but before it broke up Melanchthon accused Canisius to his face of idolatry and blasphemy. Canisius remained calm and polite, but later in a letter to the new Jesuit general, Laynez, Canisius vented his exasperation at the Protestant leaders and rejoiced that the open discord in the Lutheran camp might induce the Catholic princes to abandon sterile colloquies and support a reopening of the Council of Trent.[24]

St. Peter Canisius,[25] the most important shaper of Catholicism in southern Germany during the late sixteenth century, combined the inwardness of the *devotio moderna* with an energetic apostolate in the service of the hierarchical church characteristic of the early Jesuits. His writings, especially his catechisms, gave meaning and direction to generations of German Cath-

23. Braunsberger, 1:44; 4:229, 509; 5:361; 6:582–83; 8:130.
24. Braunsberger, 2:175–77; Brodrick, pp. 385–421.
25. Canisius was beatified by Pius IX in 1864. Pius XI canonized him and declared him a Doctor of the Roman Catholic Church in 1925. His canonization process was encouraged by the Jesuits.

olics, while the twenty Jesuit colleges that he helped to found trained the priests, princes, and lay leaders who enabled German Catholicism to gain the religious and political initiative in the early seventeenth century and to continue as a rich cultural and spiritual tradition throughout the baroque era.

10
STANISLAS hOSIUS
1504–1579
GEORGE HUNTSTON WILLIAMS

LIFE   Stanislas Hosius (in Polish, Stanisław Hozjusz) embodied and implemented the first phase of the Counter-Reformation and hence was aptly called the savior of Catholicism in the Polish-Lithuanian Commonwealth, which at the time of Hosius's birth was the largest state in Europe. During Period III of the Council of Trent, he served as legate and, in the last three sessions, the legatine president. With the publication of his principal theological work, *Confessio Catholicae fidei Christiana* in 1553, he launched himself upon a pan-European career as diplomat, nuncio, and theologian that would end with his being considered one of the four most dangerous threats to Protestantism and a prospect for election to the Holy See. After his death, he became a recurrent candidate for beatification and eventual canonization. [1]

Hosius was born in Cracow in 1504, son of the devout Anna, of unknown ethnic origin, and Ulrich, a German immigrant who was a skilled artisan. That their son was named after the episcopal martyr of Cracow would suggest deep identification with the Polish religious past of the city. The family left, however, while Stanislas was a boy and settled in Vilna, capital of the Grand Duchy of Lithuania, which was constitutionally a major division of the Commonwealth of the Two Peoples. [2] There Ulrich became the curator of the royal castle, its walls and moats. Stanislas was educated by private tutors in

1. The first life of Hosius was that by his secretary Stanisław Reszka (Rescius), printed in the *Opera omnia* of Hosius, 2 vols. (Cologne, 1584). There is a modern edition of the *Vita*, ed. Józef Smoczyński (Pelplin, 1937). The major modern biography is by Anton Eichhorn, *Der ermländische Bischof und Kardinal Stanislaus Hosius*, 2 vols. (Mainz: Kirchheim, 1854–55). A popular biography, fully abreast of Hosian scholarship to date and by a major authority, is that of Józef Umiński, *Kardynał Stanisław Hozjusz, Biskup Warmijski*, 2nd ed. (Opole: Nakład Św. Krzyża, 1948). Not a biography but an important synthetic reflection on the life and thought of Hosius is that of Joseph Lortz, *Kardinal Stanislaus Hosius: Gedenkschrift* (Braunsberg:Herder, 1931).

2. In 1396 Queen Jadwiga of Anjou, sister and successor of Louis the Hungarian, who had ruled as king of both Hungary and Poland (1370–82), married Grand Duke Ladislas Jagiełło (1386–1434), the founder of the Jagellonian dynasty of the united Poles and Lithuanians, whose rule extended far beyond Kiev.

Latin, German, and Polish and early showed his proclivity toward omnivorous reading. Stanislas was impressed by the learning and discipline of the Dominicans, but his father prevented him from joining the order because he had different expectations for Stanislas's future.

Hosius matriculated August 29, 1519, at the Jagellonian University in Cracow and received his degree of bachelor of arts, partly on the basis of his advanced achievements on entry in December 1520, having studied under the English Erasmian, Leonard Coxe. He became a protegé of two successive bishops of Cracow, John Konarski (d. 1525) and Peter Tomicki (d. 1535), the latter also vice chancellor of the crown.[3] From 1523 to 1529 Hosius was active in the Erasmian circle[4] in Cracow that included John Deciusz, Alexander Trzecieski, and a later opponent, Andrew Frycz Modrzewski. In 1525, under the pen name of Stanislaus Cracovianus, he wrote a collection of Latin verses against Martin Luther. He read the Church Fathers, particularly Augustine, extended his knowledge of Aristotle and Cicero, and deepened his mastery of Greek to the point that in 1528 he had translated the homily of John Chrysostom as *Comparatio Regiae potestatis . . . cum Monacho*. That Hosius might have a source of income, Tomicki gave him, while he was still unordained, several benefices in Vilna, Troki, Wieluń, and Wiślica in 1527 and 1528.

In May 1530 he was sent by Tomicki with a stipend to pursue his interests in Italy. During one of his four years there he studied in Padua, where he had as classmates the future cardinal Reginald Pole and the future cardinal Otto Truchsess von Waldburg, and as professors, Hugo Buoncampagni (later to become Pope Gregory XIII, under whom Hosius would spend his last days in Rome) and Lazzaro Bonamico. It was from Bologna that Hosius, having studied Greek and Latin classics further, received his doctorate in both canon and civil law in June 1534. On his return to Tomicki's palace, Hosius had planned to call on Erasmus, who was at the time in Freiburg, but he was robbed on the way and had to return by the most direct route. Although his first biographer regarded the robbery as providential, and although in time Hosius ceased being an active Erasmian, he would never repudiate Erasmus. Indeed, it may be argued that the Erasmian influence continued not only in

3. The officialdom of the Polish-Lithuanian Commonwealth during the life of Hosius cannot be dealt with here. It must suffice to note that in the commonwealth, as in most other countries of the period, the main administrative—as distinguished from martial—officers were clerics, usually bishops, and often bishops of Cracow. Under the king the two highest civil functionaries were the crown chancellor, or grand chancellor of the crown, and the vice chancellor. Although in theory the first official dealt with internal affairs, the second with external, in practice their functions overlapped; and for stretches of time the king had only a vice chancellor to perform both functions.

4. I have suggested the degree to which Tomicki and the young Hosius were Erasmian in my "Erasmianism in Poland, 1518–1604," *The Polish Review*, 22 (1977): 3–50, esp. n. 74. In a memorable letter, perhaps drafted by Hosius, surely written by him as Tomicki's secretary, Tomicki urged Erasmus to accept the proffered cardinalate as a clear sign to the church no less than to the Protestants that he shared the same ideal of scriptural, patristic, and moral reform with Rome.

his Latin style, but also in his interest in political peace, in his dislike of the
contemporary Orthodox church, and in his great confidence in education as a
means of reform.

Hosius arrived in Cracow in September 1534 and became secretary to
Tomicki in the latter's capacity as vice chancellor. When Tomicki died in
1535, Hosius immediately wrote his biography, setting forth therein all that
was best in the statesman-churchman-humanist and projecting thus in-
directly something of his own ideal. By 1538 Hosius had been raised to the
rank of royal secretary and had received from King Sigismund I ("the Old")
benefices in Ermland (Polish: Warmia), Cracow, Sandomierz, Goląb, and
Radłów. Although still an Erasmian reformer intellectually, Hosius was
nevertheless primarily engaged in the service of the commonwealth. Insofar
as he was a churchman, he was an unordained—and rather substantial—
pluralist, although it must be added that he visited some of his benefices
and sought also to provide worthy vicars for them where necessary.

In 1544, after withdrawing from his secular duties for a season of
contemplation and inner preparation, Hosius was ordained to the priesthood.
In the same year he was elevated to grand secretary in the crown chancery. In
1545 in the provincial synod he first stood up as a priest in opposition to the
conditions that permitted the further spread of Protestantism—notably, at
this moment, Lutheranism. In 1547 at the synod in Łęczyca he vigorously
pressed the primate and the king to protest moving the Council of Trent to
Bologna, a move that would give the council a more Italianate character
than it already had in Trent, a city which was constitutionally, though not
linguistically, within the Roman Empire of the German Nation.

In February 1549, King Sigismund II Augustus (1548–72) appointed
Hosius bishop of Chełmno (German, Culm) and used him almost immediately (March 1548–March 1550) as ambassador to the Hapsburg courts in
Prague, Vienna, and in the Netherlands, the latter which had been integrated
by Charles V in 1548 into one jurisdiction as part of the Burgundian Circle
within the empire. The Polish king and his ambassador were concerned with
securing Hapsburg support or neutrality with respect to Ducal Prussia's
constant attempt to become independent of the Polish crown. In the summer
of 1550 Hosius visited his new see, where he found that the Prussian estates
opposed him because he was Polish. Hosius held his ground on this and other
issues and on November 25, 1550, could take satisfaction in his diplomacy at
the Hapsburg courts and with Duke Albert Hohenzollern himself, for the
duke renewed his oath of allegiance to the crown in Cracow with members of
the Ducal Prussian dietine attending the ceremony.

As bishop, Hosius participated in the joint synod of the provinces of
Gniezno and Lwów at Piotrków in 1551, at which he was commissioned by
the assembled episcopate to write what would become his most important
work, *Confessio Catholicae fidei Christiana*, which was completed in four days
and enthusiastically approved. It was first printed in Cracow in 1553. There

would be seventeen editions of the confession (Dillingen, Mainz, Antwerp, Paris, Lyons, Vienna, Ingolstadt) before Hosius became a legate for Period III of the Council of Trent, and in all some thirty editions in several languages were printed in his lifetime. Because of his royal chancery and diplomatic experience and his compelling defense of the Catholic faith, Hosius was designated a delegate to Period II of the Council of Trent (May 1, 1551–April 28, 1552), but domestic difficulties prevented him from attending. That role lay in the future.

In January 1551, Hosius was moved to the see of Ermland, a prince-bishopric almost completely surrounded by Ducal Prussia. He set about reforming his diocese in the spirit of the Council of Trent to date (Periods I–II, Sessions 1–16) and engaged in controversy with the town of Graudenz (Polish: Grudziądz), which had become largely Lutheran, as a result of the municipal *acta* of 1556. In the following year he wrote his second most important dogmatic work, a refutation of the *Confessio Wirtembergica* (1551) which Duke Christopher of Württemberg (d. 1568) had commissioned Johannes Brenz (d. 1570) to compose for presentation to the Council of Trent, Period II, a confession based on that of Augsburg. The Württemberg Confession was also conceived as a refutation of the papal theologian Peter Soto. The refutatory work of Hosius was entitled *Verae christianae catholicaeque doctrinae solida pugnatio* (1557).[5]

In the following year Hosius wrote two works. *De expresso Dei verbo libellus* (1558) was directed against Peter Paul Vergerio (d. 1564), the former bishop of Capodistria and papal nuncio for Germany, now a Lutheran theologian plying between Duke Christopher's court in Württemberg and the courts in Ducal Prussia and the Grand Duchy of Lithuania, all in the interest of Lutheranizing the whole of the commonwealth. The other work was directed primarily against his former Erasmian friend, now social and political reformer, Andrew Frycz Modrzewski (Modrevius, d. 1572) and notably against his *De Republica emendanda* (1549). Despite the fact that two-thirds of the population of the commonwealth, being Orthodox, pre-served such practices as clerical marriage, the liturgy in a language once close to the vernacular (Old Slavonic), and the chalice for the laity, Hosius was in no mind to concede these usages. They were the outward signs not only of the major new Protestant groupings but more dangerously of the older Czech Brethren, who were numerous in Great Poland right up to the borders of Royal and Ducal Prussia (especially after 1547) and hence to his own diocese. Aware of the new and the old Protestants, the Utraquists[6] and the Czech Brethren in their original homeland of Bohemia, groups that had been a fifteenth-century threat to the unity of the papal church, Hosius attacked

---

5. This work is commonly referred to as *Confutatio Prolegomenonorum Brentii.*

6. So named because, following John Hus, they demanded communion under both (*utraque*) kinds, i.e., bread and wine.

these practices, defended by the nominally Catholic Modrzewski, in *Dialogus de eo, nam calicem laico, et uxores sacerdotius permitti, et divina officis vulgari lingua peragi fas sit* (Dillingen, 1558). Hosius went further than dialogue; he prevented the use of the Cracow edition of Modrzewski's *De Republica* of 1551.

In 1558, the year of the publication of his two polemical books, Hosius was summoned by Pope Paul IV to Rome, whence he was dispatched to serve as nuncio in Vienna to help prepare for the council that the more concessive part of Catholic Christendom wished to consider *II Trent* and the other part wished to consider a conservative continuation of the first two periods and hence as *Trent, Period III*. Emperor Ferdinand I (1556–64) in Vienna had been the elected king of Bohemia and Hungary since 1526, but at the time of Hosius's nunciature Ferdinand's son Maximilian already had responsibilities as prospective king in Prague and in Pressburg (Hungarian: Pozsony) as well as being imperial successor to his father. It was with Maximilian that Hosius had much to do, for the emperor-to-be (1564–76) was well disposed toward making concessions to the Lutherans and to the various Hussites. In 1559 Hosius wrote his *Dialogus de Calice*, dealing again with lay communion in two kinds, an issue that had occupied him in part in the book against Modrzewski a year earlier.

While in Vienna Hosius was approached by the Jesuit Peter Canisius, (chapter 9 above) of Augsburg. Already in 1560, a year after the publication of the first volume of the *Magdeburg Centuries* (see chapters 1 and 2), Canisius had sensed the grave danger in the projected series. He besought the nuncio to encourage the pope and the curia to organize a scholarly refutation (which eventually appeared as the *Annales ecclesiastici* of Cardinal Caesar Baronius), but in the meantime he requested Hosius to communicate a sense of urgency also to the bishop of Augsburg, Otto Truchsess (d. 1573), who had been a classmate of Hosius in Italy.[7]

In January 1561 Hosius participated in the provincial synod of Gniezno in Warsaw and was there designated as a delegate to the Council of Trent, along with Bishop Jacob Uchański of Chełm (destined to the primate, 1562–81), and Bishop Valentine Herburt of Przemyśl. The king named his own representatives. Then in February 1561 Hosius became cardinal bishop of Warmia.

After the appointments of Cardinal Ercole Gonzaga of Mantua and Cardinal Jerome Seripando, general of the Augustinian Friars, as legates of the forthcoming council, and some vacillation in the curia, Cardinal Hosius was named the third papal legate *a latere* in his specialty as theologian. Given the problems he knew he would face at Trent, Hosius tried to convert Maximilian

---

7. The press founded in Dillingen by Bishop Truchsess did print the first but inadequate refutation, Konrad Braun, *Adversus novam Historiam ecclesiasticam* (1565). Hosius raised the question of something much more substantial in a letter to Cardinal Gugliemo Sirleto. See Ronald Diener, "The Magdeburg Centuries: A Biographical and Bibliothecal Study," Harvard Th.D. diss., Cambridge, 1978.

in Bohemia and his sister, Queen Catherine, third consort of Sigismund II Augustus, from their determined support of the chalice to the laity, which they argued on the basis of Matt. 26:27, "Drink of it, all of you."

With characteristic modesty Hosius approached Trent, with the determination to enter the city unnoticed, without the usual fanfare. He had hoped, in fact, to arrive in the early morning of the Feast of the Assumption, August 15, and to this end he quartered himself and his retinue for several days in the monastery of St. Michael's not far above the conciliar city. However, for a combination of reasons he did not arrive until August 20, 1561. The opening of the council was long delayed. Finally, in solemn procession on January 18, 1562, the five cardinal legates along with Cardinal Bishop Luigi Madruzzo of Trent entered the cathedral to be seated as corporate presidents with Cardinal Gonzaga in the center, Cardinal Seripando to his right, Cardinal Hosius to his left, with the futher places taken by Louis Simonetta and Madruzzo.[8]

In March 1563, legates Gonzaga and then Seripando died, making Hosius the legate to preside over the three remaining sessions from March 17, 1563, to the close of the council on December 4, 1563. (The sessions and their results are discussed in the last two sections of this chapter.)

Leaving Trent on December 11, 1563, Hosius faced difficulties in getting the decrees of "his" council ratified by his own countrymen. Although the Venetian republic had accepted the Tridentine decrees almost at once, in Spain under Philip II and in the Netherlands they were accepted in 1564 only insofar as they did not contravene existing privileges; in the empire in 1566 they were accepted with respect to dogma but without the approval of Maximilian II; in France in 1615 they were accepted only by the hierarchy but not by the King.

Five obstacles lay in the way of Hosius and the new legate and nuncio who followed him into Poland, Cardinal John Francis Commendone. (1) Primate Jacob Uchański (d. 1581) desired a national synod to consider reform in the light of the Tridentine decrees. (2) King Sigismund II, in the Diet of 1562, had freed the tribunals and other organs of state from the responsibility of implementing ecclesiastical decisions. (3) The king had recoiled from the attempts of the Holy See to convert his arch-enemy Tsar Ivan IV ("the Terrible") to Catholicism and involve him in sending delegates to the Council

---

8. The basic documents of the three periods of the Council of Trent were edited by Jodocus Le Plat, *Monumentorum ad historiam Concilii Tridentini spectantium amplissima collectio*, 7 vols. (Louvain, 1781–87). A modern critical edition is still in progress under the auspices of the Görres-Gesellschaft under the general heading, *Concilium Tridentinum* in three series: *Diarorum, actorum et epistolarum nova collectio*, with various volume editors (Freiburg i.B., 1901–). For the decrees alone, see Joseph Alberigo et al., *Conciliorum Oecumenicorum Decreta* (Basel, etc., 1962), pp. 698–775. George Grabka gives a useful overview in "Cardinal Hosius at Trent," *Theological Studies*, 7 (1946): 558–76; Henry Damien Wojtyska, *Cardinal Hosius: Legate to the Council of Trent* (Rome: Institute of Historical Studies, 1967) gives a fully documented account and assessment with a valuable bibliography that covers all aspects of the life and thought of Hosius.

of Trent. (4) The king had been hoping to divorce Catherine Hapsburg, whom first Hosius and now Commendone strongly supported. (5) With so many Protestant—and Orthodox—gentry and magnates within his realm, the king was on the point of being alienated from Catholicism, looking to Elizabethan England as a possible model for what king and primate might accomplish together.

Given this confluence of forces, it is remarkable that Hosius and Commendone achieved so much so fast. At the Diet of Parczów in 1564 the king solemnly accepted from the hands of Commendone the decrees of the council. They were confirmed by the diet, despite the effort of Uchański to postpone the action. The same diet, reversing its recent action opposing temporal implementation of ecclesiastical decisions, also went so far as to expel all *foreign* heretics. The decrees had still to be approved by the Catholic hierarchy of the commonwealth, meeting in synod. In the meantime, Hosius urged bishops to hold local synods in order that the decrees might be adopted in as many dioceses as possible. For Warmia itself the synodal adoption took place in Heilsberg in August 1565. In the same year Hosius founded a diocesan seminary in the most strongly Lutheran town of his diocese, Braunsberg.

To this same town, also in 1565, Hosius called the Jesuits to found their first college in the commonwealth. Since 1542 Hosius had come to admire the Jesuits because they were learned like the Dominicans (whom he had long respected) and in addition took the special fourth vow of loyalty to the Pope. Hosius had become personally acquainted with Jesuits Peter Soto, Alfonso Salmeron, and Peter Canisius; the Jesuit college in Vienna had been his second home during his nunciature there; and at Trent Salmeron and Canisius lodged in his house. In fact, Canisius was given credit for praying and comforting Hosius back to life during a serious illness the cardinal suffered at Trent. The single most important order for recatholicization was surely the Society of Jesus, and in the commonwealth one of the most influential Polish Jesuits was Peter Skarga (see chapter 11).

The year 1565 was notable in two other respects. Calvinist Elector Frederick III of the Palatinate had taken the lead in trying to bring together a united Swiss-Palatine Confession. In this context a collective work had been produced to which Hosius, now much better acquainted with Reformed thought than before, responded in his third most important theological work, directed at the Heidelberg and Zurich pastors, *Judicium et censura de judicio et censura ministrorum Tygurinorum et Heidelbergensium de dogmate contra adorandam Trinitatem in Polonia nuper sparso* (Cologne, 1565). This work was published in Polish the following year. Against the Reformed of Switzerland and the Palatinate, Hosius argued accusingly that whereas against the papal church the Reformed and the Lutherans had used exclusively Scripture, in opposing the Unitarians in Poland the same Reformed theologians had resorted to the tradition of the Fathers and the ecumenical councils to ground their trinitarian theology and their Christology. Hosius appealed to Protestants, including "the most consistent among them," the Unitarians, to return to the unity of the Church, to board the Bark of Peter, and to avoid the flood that would surely overwhelm a religiously disrupted society, as had happened in France. Although charged with fanaticism, Hosius was in this work, as in others, filled with love and concern for what he regarded as perilously lost sheep whose disparate confessional loyalties also endangered the commonwealth.

Upon the death of Pius IV, who had conceded to postpone what the council under Hosius's presidency had decreed, namely the chalice for the laity in the Empire and Hungary, Hosius was privately pushed forward as a most appropriate successor, but he refused even to attend the conclave in Rome lest he draw further attention to himself.[9]

The new pope, Pius V, wishing perhaps to keep the unpredictable primate Uchański in check, named Hosius *legatus a latere* on December 11, 1566, to preside over the national council convened in that very month. The council might have implemented, under Uchański, Queen Catherine's stubborn desire to have communion in both kinds, as Pope Pius IV had permitted in her brother Maximilian's realms. Uchański was at least able to postpone the acceptance of the decrees of Trent, and it would not be until the Synod of Piotrków in 1577 that Hosius would belatedly and from afar see "his" work at Trent confirmed commonwealth-wide by all the bishops in his native land.

From 1566 to 1568/69, Hosius was active in trying to make Ducal Prussia a more integral part of the commonwealth and for reasons of state was willing to tolerate Lutheranism there. At the same time, physically weakened though he had become, he attended the diet in Lublin in 1568–69, at which he opposed the Union of Lublin of 1569 because it would involve the Catholic crown in closer relations with vast numbers of Byelorussian and Ukrainian subjects by ceding the southern third of the Grand Duchy well beyond Kiev to direct administration by the crown. This union would inevitably facilitate colonization by the Polish gentry (*szlachta*) in the extensive region, leading to the greater intermingling of Catholics with Orthodox and with their married priests who practiced communion in two kinds for the laity, in a nearly vernacular liturgy. But Hosius's efforts were in vain. Before returning to Warmia, he reiterated his strong conviction that divisive Protestantism would be furthered by the constitutionally closer union of Lithuania and Poland and that Catholicism would thereby be weakened because of the cession of so much of lower Lithuania, almost wholly Orthodox in population, to direct royal Polish jurisdiction.

Opposed by his cathedral chapter, by Primate Uchański, by Sigismund II (for having prevented the divorce of Catherine), and even by the new nuncio

---

9. Józef Umiński, "Kandydatura Hozjusza na Stolicę Apostolską," *Przegląd Powszechny*, 191 (1931): 258–83.

Vincent dal Portico, Hosius chose to leave Warmia on August 20, 1569. He went to Rome, nominally to serve as permanent Polish ambassador to the Holy See and also to deal with the king's claims to his inheritance from Queen Bona Sforza (d. 1557). In Warmia, Martin Kromer, as auxiliary bishop, largely determined affairs thereafter, although Hosius never lost his concern for his diocese and his native land, as his letters amply attest. For example, he supported the election of Henry of Valois as successor to the heirless last Jagellonian in 1573, while seeking to weaken or repudiate the Confederation of 1573 and the Henrician Articles, which gave constitutional status to the *pax dissidentium de religione* and the royal oath to uphold that peace. The Articles were extraordinary at this stage of Poland's constitutional history, since they accorded legal equality to all Protestants, including Unitarians, alongside Catholics, as groups "dissenting from one another concerning religion."

After the brief reign of Henry, who literally became a fugitive in order to become Henry III of France, the election diet chose Stephen Bathory (1576–86), whom Hosius opposed because Bathory had as prince of Transylvania upheld the rights of the four licit faiths, even though he himself was a Catholic. In 1576, however, Hosius reconciled himself to Bathory and indeed cooperated with him in building a royal college in Cracow to prepare those destined to study in Rome. In Rome, Hosius began a hospice for visiting Poles. In 1572 Hosius was made a member of the Roman congregation for German or Imperial affairs, and in 1573, he was named *Poenitentiarius major*. Hosius died August 8, 1579, in a Roman suburb and was buried in his titular church, Santa Maria, in Trastevere.

THEOLOGY   Hosius was strongly papal in his theology, almost instinctively deferring to the infallible magisterium of the pope. Only in a few small ways did Hosius show theological cunning in making helpful distinctions and offering useful clarifications, but he was formidably learned and was indeed regarded by Peter Paul Vergerio as one of the four most dangerous theologians in the Catholic camp. Because of his constant reading of Scripture, the Fathers, the councils, and the writings of his adversaries, Hosius changed his positions over a lifetime of synodal and conciliar debate, letter-writing, and publication. He was flexibly responsive in discussion, but was also a man whose temperament and credulity made him somewhat vacillating toward higher authorities.

Hosius regarded the Council of Trent as primarily directed toward regaining the Lutherans for Catholic unity; only at the very end did he see the great hazard of the Reformed. Despite the profession of Orthodoxy over two-thirds of his commonwealth, Hosius seldom glanced in the direction of contemporary Orthodoxy in his preoccupation with the reunification of Western Christendom. He brought to Trent a Catholic theology that was primarily counter-Lutheran, and for that reason he remained to the end pro-German in his expectations. A host of evidence—that most of his writings were directed toward or against Lutherans; that he labored hard for a Lutheran delegation at Trent; that after the council he was named to the congregation for German affairs; that for a few months he swore temporal allegiance to Maximilian II, because he was in doubt about the duly elected Polish king; that he made much greater use of the German language than of Polish (using the latter only for correspondence with the less educated and in sermons preached in ethnic Polish territory); and, going further back, that he was of pure or half German ancestry—all these facts make clear that Hosius was a theological spokesman of Central Europe far more than of Poland-Lithuania. At the same time, he was the primary first-generational spokesman and implementer of the Counter-Reformation in his native land.

The principal detectable Polish influence in his theology is in the extraordinary importance given the pope, an attitude characteristic of many a Polish prelate in a country that included a high proportion of married, native-rite Orthodox priests. Poland also faced at close distance the Moslem-controlled ecumenical patriarch in Istanbul and the new Tsardom of Moscow (1547), whose metropolitan, a decade after Hosius's death, would become also a patriarch (1589). Unlike the Iberian and French prelates at the council, the Poles felt a special need for the pope not only as a symbol but also as the administrative and magistral embodiment of the principle of catholicity. If there was another distinctively Polish trait in Hosius's theology and praxis, it was his preference for education over coercion, and surely his preference for exile and suppression over the Iberian *auto de fé*.

In characterizing the theology of Hosius, from revelation to eschatology, besides calling it strongly papal in the sense of the pre-eminence of the papal magisterium and universal jurisdiction, one could aptly call it eucharistic. [10] Convinced that Luther had undermined the sacrificial character of the Mass in *The Babylonian Captivity* (1520), hence dissolving the priesthood into that of all believers and an undifferentiated ministry of the word celebrating only two sacraments, Hosius dwelt longest on the issue of the Mass, the more so as it was linked to the sacrament of ordination. Cardinal (Thomas de Vio) Cajetan of the Order of Preachers yielded to the Protestant view to such an extent that he maintained in *Tractatus de Missae Sacrificio* (1531) that the Last Supper was for him only a spiritual oblation and not a sacrifice like that on Calvary. Hosius—in his *Confessio* (1551, etc.), in his *Confutatio Prolegomenon Brentii* (1557), and in related works and letters connected with his legatine role at Trent—tended to use three words imprecisely: *sacrificium, oblatio,* and *immolatio*. A reader of his prelegatine thought could therefore sometimes find in his works the unclear juxtaposition of (1) the Supper-Mass and the Crucifixion, the one unbloody, sacramental, and mystical, the other, bloody,

10. See below, n. 16.

visible; or, (2) two sacrifices in the sense of two oblations or, (3) only one oblation, but two different sacrifices differing in mode; or, (4) two immolations (modes of sacrifice) and hence two sacrifices; or, (5) (as one of the first to so assert it) the sacramental immolation of Christ in the Supper-Mass before and after the Crucifixion.

Hosius based one of his arguments for the sacrificial character of the Mass—speaking generically thus of all his slightly variant formulations—on the application of Ps. 109 (110):4 to Christ as Priest for eternity "according to the order of Melchizedek" (Heb. 5:6). He held that just as the mysterious priest-king offered bread and wine (Gen. 14:18), so did Christ offer a sacrifice of himself at the Last Supper under the same species as Melchizedek. Hence Christ also repeatedly makes such a sacrifice in the Mass, the merits of the bloody sacrifice on Calvary being imparted to the faithful in the Host by that same Offerer, to whose mystical Body, as to the Head, they are united (first in baptism and confirmation, though he did not emphasize these sacraments). Hosius advanced another argument: in the Paschal Feast the lamb was first immolated and only then, of course, given to be eaten. Accordingly, at the Last Supper, which was the first Mass, Christ, the redemptive Lamb who takes away the sins of the world, in calling the bread and wine his Body and Blood, must have in this primordial action, anticipatory of actual death, immolated himself before the Crucifixion.

Besides using many generally known passages of Scripture and the Fathers, Hosius made special use of the *Ennarationes in Psalmum 109* (110) concerning Melchizedek, of the obscure Greek Oecumenius of the sixth century, and of the apocryphal *Constitutiones Clementinae*, which for this express reason he asked to be withdrawn from the Index!

As for allowing communion to the laity in both kinds, Hosius regarded this as almost wholly an issue of discipline. If he could have been convinced that conceding this point would win back any Lutherans or Utraquists in the Kingdom of Bohemia and elsewhere, including Czech Brethren in his native Poland, he would have been willing to make the concession, as would also Pope Pius IV. But in the end he was convinced that far from being a matter of piety on the part of the heretics—on whose behalf the Catholic petitioners, prelatial and political, sought the concession—it was essentially a pretext and that a disciplinary concession once made would simply serve as an excuse for further departure from the unity of the Latin church.

Bound up with the Mass and Last Supper was, for Hosius, the institution of the priesthood. He held that, though indeed there had been communion in both kinds during Christian antiquity, the Last Supper had been the occasion for the institution of the priesthood when the Apostles, representing the first priests, received both the Body and Blood under the species of bread and wine. When in the Council of Trent the seeming contradiction of two passages related to episcopacy were adduced, Hosius made the subtle distinction that at the Last Supper and first Mass (Luke 22:19) Christ gave the Apostles as priests the power *super corpus suum verum* and at Pentecost (John 20:22) he gave the Apostles as bishops the power *super corpus suum mysticum.*

We have seen that as a papalist, and even before his participation in the council, Hosius opposed the view held most strongly by most of the Iberians and Gallicans (but also by many more Italians than he would have expected): namely, that bishops are not only superior to priests but also derive their authority and perhaps even their jurisdiction directly by apostolic succession from Christ and not mediately from the pope. Hosius could distinguish between a theoretical immediate authority from Christ and the very practical and well implemented mediate authority from the pope. However, in his pre-Tridentine and Tridentine activity he was always at pains to safeguard the primacy of the pope in imparting both episcopal order and jurisdiction, and he helped prevent the zealous episcopalists (the *zelanti*) from pushing through a doctrine of episcopacy that would have disconnected it from an integral papalism.

Hosius dealt similarly with the burning question of episcopal reform, namely, the widespread problem of pluralism, which could have been elevated to the realm of reformation of doctrine. What the most ardent critics of pluralism desired was a *doctrine* of the divine right of residency of a bishop. The desirability of a functioning residency was by Hosius, however, kept to the level of discipline. Reform and exceptions were expressly allowed in the final formulation, even though in the process of conciliar debate Hosius had become so conscience-stricken by his own enjoyment of the proceeds of many Polish benefices, large and small, where he had not himself discharged the appropriate service, that he sought to send, from his rented house in Trent, some substantial reparations in Poland.

With regard to the Church in Council,[11] Hosius regarded the duly convened Ecumenical Council as coordinate in authority with Scripture, tradition, and the papacy. By "duly convened," he meant papally approved, for he was aware that emperors, not popes, had convened the decisive dogmatic councils of antiquity. As for the councils of his own time, he decisively opposed Luther's conception of a national council that was "free," in effect, of the pope, making doctrinal decisions. He held expressly that the Church and hence an ecumenical council must formulate doctrine, as distinguished from local reform and the local implementation of the decrees of an ecumenical council, "Faith is not Polish, not Lithuanian, not German," declared Hosius (*Confessio,* 1551), directing himself on this point against Luther's *Concilium Nationis Germanicae* [*To the Christian nobility of the German nation,* 1520] and also against Modrzewski. Modrzewski had proposed sending lay delegates to the Council of Trent, Period II (*Ad Regem . . . de legatis*

---

11. For the whole of his doctrine of the Church, see Lucien Bernacki, *La doctrine de l'Eglise chez le Cardinal Hosius* (Paris: Librairie Lecoffre, 1936); Gregory Maria Grabka, *Cardinalis Hosii doctrina de corpore Christe mystico* (Washington: Catholic University of America, 1945).

ad Concilium mittendis, 1547) and presented the idea of a national reforming council for the Polish Commonwealth (*De Republica emendanda*, 1551). Hosius saw to it that this extraordinary work of Modrzewski on the reformation of church, state, and society was forbidden circulation in the churches, rectories, and schools of the commonwealth. Yet Hosius, while inextricably involved in his ambassadorial Polish and eventually his nunciatory roles in Hapsburg politics and in his pre-Tridentine utterances and activities, readily recognized the pope's obligation to satisfy the emperor and the kings of Christendom as to the calling of a council, as his letters of 1547 to Paul III and Sigismund I the Old attest. At Trent, however, he became increasingly papalist on this score. [12] And in 1562 he edited and presumably wrote the long preface to Cardinal Reginald Pole's *De concilio* as an antidote to Heinrich Bullinger's *De conciliis*, which had come to his attention in 1561 while in Vienna on papal and conciliar business. Yet Hosius would never go so far as Albert Pighius, who held that an ecumenical council partook of the infallibility of the pope. He argued rather for the council's infallibility in matters of doctrine by virtue of the invocation of the Holy Spirit, the magisterium of the prelates, and the participation or approval by the pope. For this view he cited Epistle II of Pope Gregory I ("the Great").

As for the central missions of the Church, salvation and (in the terms of the age) justification, [13] Hosius, thinking as always about the revolution in doctrine wrought by Luther, marked out a middle course between that of Reginald Pole and Jerome Seripando over against the traditional, pre-Reformation view in which "justification" and "sanctification" had been virtually synonymous. In the *Confessio* and elsewhere, Hosius based justification on the virtue of charity, that is, the desire to do good deeds, an urge infused by grace. He was himself a man of nearly saintly gentleness and good will in all his personal relations, and when his home at the council became a bastion to which all repaired who favored his position, even his firmest opponents would never fault him for anything but "sweetness" and "credulity."

Yet for all his gentleness of deportment and the frailty of voice and frame that perhaps enhanced the impression of saintliness, [14] Hosius was uncharacteristically Polish and not on this point Catholic in his identification of heresy with schism, a view that automatically made two-thirds of the king of Poland's subjects not merely Orthodox schismatics but veritable heretics. Charged with the task of at least inviting the Orthodox to attend the council, he had no heart for it. At the very least their presence would have meant conciliar acknowledgment as valid for them practices he fervently opposed: marriage for clergy, the chalice for laymen, and liturgy in the vernacular.

12. Józef Smoczyński, "Ogólny ustrój Kościoła i prymat jurydykcyjny u Hozjusza," *Miesięcznik Diecezji Chełmińskiej* 3 (1933): 228–46.

13. Zygmunt Skowroński, *Stanisława Hozjusza nauka o usprawiedliwieniu* (Warsaw, 1937).

14. Józef Umiński, *Opinie o cnotach, swiątobliwości i zasługach Stanisława Hozjusza* ((Lwów: Ossolineum, 1932).

ROLE IN THE   In his multinational and multiethnic Polish-Lithuanian
CHURCH   Commonwealth, Hosius counseled and practiced a combination of rigorous re-Catholicization and internal Catholic reform, both in his diocese and in the commonwealth.
To a degree, he even encouraged some Polish radicals, like the early unitarian-
izing and often antipedobaptist Polish Brethren, as a way of weakening the
Reformed church. His eventual goal, however, was clearly stated: "One
king, one religion." If, however, the king should choose to tolerate Lutherans
and Calvinists, then he should also tolerate the Unitarians, who surely had as
much right to exist as the others, since they were in any case the inevitable
consequence of the Protestant revolt from Rome. On partly religious, partly
political grounds he also used the principle of *cuius regio, eius religio* to oppose
the Union of Lublin of 1569, which extended Crown lands and Polish
aristocratic hegemony over much of the land destined to emerge as modern
Ukraine, because for Hosius this prospect meant too much political recognition for Orthodox magnates—and possibly even Orthodox bishops in the
Senate and Orthodox gentry in the House of Deputies. But more for reasons of
state than religion, Hosius, from the beginning of his career as bishop, was
willing to make religious concessions to Lutheran Ducal Prussia, in return for
integrating it closer into the commonwealth instead of its remaining a nearly
autonomous fief of the crown, with no participation in the affairs of the diet of
the commonwealth. At the same time, as prince-bishop of Warmia, with
much of the population of the towns and even the villages Germanized and Lutheranized, he used force in driving out the Lutheran citizens of Braunsberg,
where he established the first Jesuit seminary and collegium in Poland. He
acted similarly in Elbing. He vigorously supported the election of Henry of
Valois in 1573, while opposing the *pax dissidentium de religione* (see above, p.
165). In his theoretical writings on heresy and coercion in religion he drew
heavily on Augustine.[15] But though he was responsible for inciting the
students of Cracow to the eventual destruction of the Calvinist church there,
he preferred, by temperament and conviction, to establish religious unity in
his own land more by education than by massive coercion. He bestirred
himself, therefore, to expand the activities of the Jesuits to win back defectors
from the Roman church and in Orthodox lands to win the Orthodox over to
Latin Christianity by educating the youth of the Byelorussian and Ukrainian
nobility on the one hand and by extending the work of various preaching and
eleemosynary orders in all directions within the commonwealth on the other.

Outside Poland, Hosius is best known for his role at the Council of
Trent. As Period III of the council opened, the Spaniards were particularly
insistent that the council should concern itself with the reform of the papal
church, while Hosius and the Imperials (the bishops and abbots of the

15. Francis Zdrowski, *The Concept of Heresy according to Cardinal Hosius* (Washington: Catholic
University of America, 1947).

Empire) considered the main purpose of the council to be to win back the Lutherans by getting them to Trent with initial concessions regarding discipline. The Imperials, as early as February 15, 1562, demanded that the council not refer to itself as "continuous" with that of Period II, that it postpone matters of doctrine and institutional reform until the arrival of the Protestants, who should be provided with safe-conducts, and that the Augsburg Confession not be condemned to the Index. In one spirit the emperor, the queen of Poland, the duke of Bavaria, many of the French bishops, and the Venetians called for the chalice for the laity, while the duke of Bavaria and the Venetians went further in calling also for clerical marriage.

The Imperials introduced into the discussions the *Libellus reformationis*. In fifteen articles composed at Ferdinand's order, it demanded not only such radical points as the chalice for the laity, but also the diminution of the power of the pope, severe reform of the curia, abolition of exemptions, and liturgical reform including the Mass in the national language. Although the emperor withdrew the *Libellus*, he and many others still insisted on the chalice for laymen, citing the words of Jesus in John 6:54: "Amen, amen, I say to you unless ye eat the flesh of the Son of Man and drink his blood, ye shall not have life in you." Some fathers argued that this passage meant spiritual communion in the blood of Christ, which was of course the intention for laymen. Others argued that the passage in fact justified only the established Latin usage of communion in both kinds for priests and bishops as successors of the Apostles. Hosius held to the spiritual interpretation; but when John 6:54 was joined with Matt. 26:27 about giving the cup, in which Jesus said, "Drink of it, all of you," Hosius felt obliged to enter the debate to save his position. When on July 14, Hosius received the news that his suffragan at Warmia, Martin Kromer, had attended the festival in the cathedral of Prague in honor of John Hus, he decided that because of its disciplinary and unitary significance he must hold the line on the chalice, convinced that it was a secondary issue to the Bohemian and Lutheran heretics and that conceding to it would fail to return them to the unity of the Church. Hosius's view prevailed.

To some extent, though it was not articulated, we may surmise that the conception of Hosius of the sacrificial character of the Mass was bound up with his conservative position on whether laymen should receive the wine-blood, the clearer in suggesting sacrifice of the two species. [16] When the problem of the oblation of the Mass had been decided in favor of Hosius's sacrificial view, the problem of the lay chalice again came up. On this issue, Hosius, as head of the Oblationists, had already psychologically prevailed over the Cajetanists (Hosius's term). On both issues the council followed him on his central doctrinal concern and his psychological-pastoral preference: the asseveration

16. Stanislaus Frankl, "Doctrina Hosii de sacrificio Missae cum decreto Tridentino comparata," *Collectanea Theologica*, 16 (1935): 281–339; Jan Bochenek, *Stanisława Hozjusza nauka o Eucharystii* (Warsaw, 1936).

of the sacrificial character of the Mass and the reservation of the cup to the celebrant clergy.

The French phase of Period III of the council extended from November 1562 to December 1563. The dominant figure among the French was Cardinal Charles de Guise. In France the Colloquy of Poissy had taken place in 1561, and the first of eight wars of religion had broken out between Huguenots and Catholics in March 1562. The presence of the French at Trent made Hosius more vividly aware than before of the danger of Reformed Christianity. In his own country, save for nearly independent Ducal Prussia and to a lesser extent Royal Prussia, the bulk of Protestants in the commonwealth were like the Huguenots in France, under the protection of powerful aristocratic patrons. He became aware, too, of their catholic tendency to hold together across territorial and national boundaries.

In the debate over episcopacy in connection with the canons of anathema, as distinguished from the preliminary exposition of the Catholic doctrine, the French joined the Spaniards in insisting again on the *jure divino* character of episcopacy, reviving the phraseology acceptable to Julius III in Period II, to read thus: "Si quis dixerit episcopos, *jure divino institutos*, non esse, etc." For the ardent papalists the insertion of the phrase "instituted by divine right" imperiled the authority of pope vis-à-vis national bishops. At this point Hosius sought to make a distinction different from that of the Jesuit superior general and papal theologian, Jacob Laynez. Laynez distinguished between the *potestas ordinis* of a bishop received by divine right through a call and through the traditional consecration and the *potestas jurisdictionis*, deriving from the pope. But as much concerned as was Philip II of Spain for the *jus divinum* of episcopal residence and at the same time for the formal declaration of the council in Period III as continuous with the previous two periods, by July 18, 1563, he instructed his prelates to desist from their insistence on either point. Some zelanti, however, still insisted that the bishop derived his power of jurisdiction over his people by virtue of his consecration. Cardinal de Guise proposed on December 1, 1562, that canon 7 should read more specifically "instituted by Christ" but that an entire new canon 8 should then spell out the primacy of the pope. At this conjuncture Hosius agreed with the Spaniards on this compromise, but the extreme episcopalists were not satisfied. In the end, however, the phrasing of canon 7 was toned down to a statement of the superiority of bishop over priest, while Hosius was firm that canon 8 should clearly assert that bishops assume their functions by authority of the Roman pontiff.

After the deaths of the two original Italian cardinal-legates, Hosius presided, as ranking legate among a partly new group of five legates, over the last three sessions of the Council of Trent: Session XXIII, which dealt with orders and seminaries; Session XXIV, which dealt with matrimony; and Session XXV, which dealt with purgatory, the invocation of saints, the veneration of relics and images, and indulgences. Hosius showed special interest in the establishment of diocesan seminaries everywhere. He surely had special influence also on several major, immediately post-Tridentine achievements such as *The Revised Index,* the Tridentine Confession of Faith, and the Roman Catechism, all in 1564. Throughout Period III of his legatine authority, Hosius was called the *Arbiter Concilii.* Peter Sforza Pallavicino summed up the collective impression of the fathers, saying that Hosius guided the council with his learning, sanctified it by his piety, and sanctioned it by his authority.[17] He was a quiet but effectual leader in his personal as well as his legatine efforts to negotiate with the Spaniards, the imperial representatives, and the French in order to weld the nine sessions under his co-legatine authority into a Period III of the Council of Trent rather than permitting them to be considered a second Council of Trent. Consequently, the work of the three periods cumulatively had the epochal significance that it did. Yet, in the definitive edition of the proceedings of the council—which documented aspects of debate that never became embodied in the final doctrines, canons, and reforms of the bull of promulgation *(Benedictus Deus)* of January 30, 1564—references to Hosius and to his activities are much less prominent than one would expect. Thus, in retrospect we must scale down characterizations of him as "the second Augustine," "the pillar of the Church," "the hammer of heretics," "the Polish Patriarch," "the new Bessarion," "the Polish God" (all from Stanislas Reszka, Hosius's secretary and first biographer). But it is not off the mark to say that he was, indeed, "the savior of Catholicism in Poland" (quoting Ludwig von Pastor) and "the death of Luther" (quoting Franz Hipler). Hosius was a spokesman of Catholicism for both Eastern and Central Europe, almost as much a German in his stance as he was a Pole. Surely through his *Confessio* of 1551 and through his legatine authority at Trent, Hosius did as much as anyone to allow the three periods to be construed as a single Council of Trent. He was a protector of the church, doing as much as anyone to safeguard papal primacy, the dependence of the episcopate on the pope in canonical terms, the sacrificial character of the Mass, the celibacy of the clergy.[18] His voice prevailed in the postponement of a decision on the chalice to the laity and in all the other conservative or counter-reformatory features of Tridentine Catholicism. When many western national hierarchies and Catholic rulers—like the duke of Bavaria, the doge of Venice, the emperor, the Polish queen, many distinguished theologians, and on some points (like the chalice), the pope himself—would have made more concessions to what they superficially understood to be the demands of the Protestants, Hosius, to his credit, knew the Protestants too well—preeminently the Lutherans, but toward the end also the Reformed. He realized that concessions of the kinds clamored for by zelanti and learned theologians alike would not have sufficed to bring back the theologians who advised the Protestant princes. Thus his instincts and

17. *Istoria del Concilio di Trente,* 2 vols. (Rome, 1656), vol. 2, XV, vi, 3.
18. Franciszek Zaworski, *Doctrina Cardinalis Stanislai Hosii de coelibatu ecclesiastico* (Rome, 1957).

insights were probably correct in tightening the structure of the church for the missions and the wars of religion that were to come. If he was not original as the theologian-legate of Trent, he was theologically and psychologically the most astute, for all his mildness, keeping in good shape and renewing where necessary the smallest battlements of the papal fortress, just as his father had faithfully safeguarded the royal castle at Vilna.

11
PETER SKARGA
1536–1618
GEORGE HUNTSTON WILLIAMS

LIFE

Peter Skarga[1] was for his contemporaries the very embodiment and implementation of the spirit of the Counter-Reformation. To this day any Pole, in the homeland or abroad, whether appreciatively or critically, would think of the Jesuit preacher, polemicist, popular hagiographer, and historian as the most imposing ecclesiastical figure in the history of the Polish-Lithuanian Royal Commonwealth. From the rise of Erasmian humanism and Protestantism in around 1525 when Lutheranized Ducal Prussia became a fief of the Polish crown in a ceremony of vassalage in Cracow until the final disappearance of the Royal Republic in the series of three partitions that wholly dissolved it in 1795, Skarga or his memory long dominated the thought of Catholics in the commonwealth. Yet this eminent figure was wholly derivative in his theology; in his theory of the state and of religious warfare; in his models for good works for the urban poor; and in his belated defense of the peasants, who were oppressed alike by the crown, the nobles, and the church, secular and monastic. But in two respects he was distinctive in his concerns, activities, and writings. First, few other Counter-Reformation court preachers served a ruler whose subjects were of so many religious beliefs: Jews, Moslems, Greek Orthodox, Armenians, Czech Brethren, Lutherans, Mennonites, Calvinists, and Unitarians. Second, Skarga may have been unique among Catholic leaders of his age in professing to be a prophet to his people. In his many sermons, the Old Testament prophets as critics of society are prominent. Today one can scarcely distinguish some of his sermons of sociopolitical import from sermons of his Puritan or Presbyterian contemporaries in England and Scotland, except by the identity of the "idolators," "blasphemers," and "potential traitors." It is difficult to communicate a suf-

1. There is no life of Skarga in English. The most recent life in Polish is that of Tadeusz Tazbir, *Piotr Skarga* (Warsaw: Książka i Wiedza, 1962), a scientific-popular account, illustrated, but with no bibliography. The fullest account in a Western language is that of l'Abbé Auguste Berga, *Pierre Skarga* (Paris: Société française d'imprimerie 1916), an excellent, appreciative, but critical account, fully based on Polish sources, though suffering in printing from many errors in the Polish.

ficiently vibrant impression of the vitality and fierceness, and yet charity and reasonableness, of this diminutive arbiter of Poland's destiny. Nor can one easily convey the resonance, cadence, and resourcefulness of his language in polemic and preachment—a style and vocabulary that divested as much as possible of the enormous influence of Latin, significantly shaped the Polish language as it is used to this day.

Peter Skarga was born in 1536, in Grójec in Mazovia, the most solidly Catholic region of the commonwealth, son of a member of the lower *szlachta* ("gentry"). The *szlachta* lived by a myth that they constituted a fraternal order (comprising perhaps ten percent of the population) of theoretical equals, derived from an ancient stock distinguished ethnically from the peasantry and townspeople. The latter were mostly Jews, Germans, or peasants turned artisans. Because the *szlachta* felt that they were not merely a class but also almost a race set apart (Sarmatianism),[2] there was a double sanction for the harshness with which even the most humble *szlachta* could sometimes treat the peasants on their estates. When in addition to a sense of a difference in class and race there was a difference in religious confession, the ingredients were present for unusually bitter relations between the *szlachta* and the ordinary people of village or town. Thus Skarga attributed the social inequities of the Commonwealth to the selfishness of the *szlachta* in general and of the Protestants in particular.

That he should eventually come to use the language of the peasants almost exclusively, rather than Latin, and that he should in the end be conspicuously identified with the cause first of the urban poor and then of the peasants, are no doubt related to his origins. He was born in a region where the *szlachta* were not only the most solidly Catholic but also the most numerous proportionately (thirty percent of the population). There, many a *szlachcic* was probably similar in appearance and bearing to an English yeoman turned squire, working, perhaps with his wife, alongside their few dependents and children. Thus it was perhaps the most important thing about his life that Skarga was born to a *szlachcic* in a house that a farmer today in the People's Republic of Poland would consider scarcely adequate.

Skarga attended the parish school in Grójec. At nineteen he became the director of the parish school of St. John's in Warsaw, where later he would preach his influential sermons at the opening and closing of the diet. St. John's was at the time the seat of an archdeanery; only centuries later was it elevated to the rank of cathedral of the capital. But it was in that Gothic church that the solemnities connected with the royal election or the opening of the diet took place. In 1611, during the course of Skarga's lifetime, the administrative capital was moved definitively from Cracow to Warsaw. It is noteworthy that in the very year that Skarga became director of St. John's

---

2. They professed to derive from Sarmatians or Scythians who were accorded the rights of freemen by Alexander the Great, while at the same time they modeled their institutions, e.g., the very term *Senate*, upon those of Royal-Republican (not Imperial) Rome.

parish school, Nuncio Luigi Lippomino was suggesting to King Sigismund II Augustus (1548–72) that he execute "eight or ten of the most important heretics" to put a stop to the spread of Protestantism in Poland, while at the same time Lippomino was devoting himself to setting up a permanent nunciature.

From 1557 to 1562 Skarga came under the patronage of the palatine of Lublin, Andrew Tęczyński, and in 1558 matriculated at the conservative Jagellonian University, where he received only the bachelor of arts degree rather than the master of arts degree, which was the normal termination of studies in Cracow at the time. Skarga became tutor of the son of the palatine, and together the Cracow alumnus and the youth went to Vienna in 1560. On the death of his Lublin patron, Skarga enjoyed the episcopal patronage (1562–64) of Jacob Uchański of Kujawy, who later became primate of the Catholic Church in Poland. Skarga found him altogether too lenient toward Protestants, a kind of vacillating Polish Erasmian Gallican who was willing to consider communion in two kinds and a married clergy. In 1563, while still in lower orders, Skarga was made a canon; and, in 1565, chancellor of the collegial church.

But by 1564 he had already decided to become a priest and was ordained in Lwów, which had the distinction of possessing Latin-rite, Armenian-rite, and Byzantine-rite archiepiscopal or metropolitical cathedrals. As priest of the cathedral parish, Skarga immediately won acclaim for the zeal of his sermons, for his visitations of the sick and the imprisoned, and for his polemics against heresy.

When in 1565 the Jesuit order was introduced to Poland by Bishop Hosius of Warmia (see chapter 10), Skarga decided that he wished to join it. Although he was prompted in 1566 to accept an invitation to become tutor to John Christopher Tarnowski, son of Hetman John Tarnowski in Gorliczyń, he carried out his deeper intentions, from 1569 to 1571 in the Jesuit novitiate in Rome.

On returning home, Skarga was appointed professor at the second Jesuit college of the commonwealth, at Pulusk (the first was at Braunsberg in Warmia). He converted members of the Lithuanian Radziwiłł (Radvila) family who had been leading Calvinist protectors, and one of these converts became bishop of Vilna. As a consequence, in 1573 Skarga was appointed vice-rector of a new Jesuit college in Vilna, the capital of the grand duchy. From this base he established or enlarged Jesuit colleges in Livonia in both Estonian-German Dorpat and Latvian-German Riga; in Byelorussian Polock and Nieświeżå, both in the Grand Duchy of Lithuania; and in Lublin in Little Poland. In 1580 Skarga became the first rector of the Jesuit college in Vilna, which was raised to the near university rank of academy, where he served until 1584.

While in Vilna Skarga was openly vilified by Calvinists and the Orthodox, especially as he occasionally hinted at the use of coercion in restraining them from the exercise of their constitutionally guaranteed religious freedom. He translated from the Latin of the English Jesuit Edmund Campion (martyred in 1581) *Decem rationes* [Ten Proofs], a defense of the Roman Catholic position against Protestant coercion, (Vilna, 1584).[3] He continued to take an especial interest in the Jesuits in England and Scotland and later persuaded Chancellor John Zamoyski to write to King James, urging as much toleration of Catholics in his kingdoms as the Polish king, Stephen Báthory (1576–86), in his.

In the midst of these duties Skarga rendered into vivid Polish a selection from the eight-volume *Sanctorum priscorum patrum vitae* (1551–60) of Aloysius Lippomani. To Lippomani's selection Skarga added biographies of several recently sainted martyrs, *Lives of the Saints of the Old and the New Testament* (Vilna, 1579).[4] Perhaps more than any other work, this collection frequently printed and enlarged, fixed in the minds of the Polish devout a conception of heroic saintliness. At the same time, it greatly influenced the evolution of the converging language of *szlachcic* and serf.

In 1584 Skarga moved to Cracow where, until 1587, he had as his base the Church of St. Barbara. In his very first year there he established the Brotherhood of Mercy *(Bractwo Miłosierdzia)* and engaged again in the eleemosynary activity that characterized his ministry in St. John's in Warsaw. Soon thereafter he established a second religious order, the Brotherhood of St. Lazarus of Bethany and the St. Nicholas Chest *(Skrzynka Świętego Mikołaja)* to protect girls in the city from prostitution. In 1588 he founded the Bank for the Devout Poor *(Bank Pobożności)*, which charged little or no interest to the poor, to enable those too proud to beg to get back on their feet. All four of these institutions, associated with his Church of St. Barbara, were based upon Roman models like the Mons Pietatis, which he had come to know when he was studying in Rome. They won for him a place in the hearts of the downtrodden and forgotten in Cracow and far beyond. In 1588 Skarga printed a number of collected sermons given before the Brotherhood, including also one by the papal legate translated from the Latin, that of the later Pope Clement VIII, *The Readings of the Brotherhood of Mercy in Cracow in St. Barbara's.*[5]

3. Its Polish title, *Dziesięć wywodow*. All of Skarga's Polish titles are given in English in the text and in their archaic spelling in the footnotes.

We are fortunate in having a guide to all the imprints of Skarga into the early twentieth century, arranged first according to collected works, then by individual works in a systematic way: polemical, with subdivisions; apologetic, with subdivisions, etc. and with many illustrations of the title pages of first editions, some of which are exceedingly rare, like the one before us. This work is that of Konstanty Otwinowski, S.J., *Dzieła X. Piotra Skargi T. J.: Spis Bibliograficzny* (Cracow: Akademia Umiejętności, 1916).

4. *Żywoty Świetych*: also Cracow, 1585, 1592, 1598, 1601, 1603, 1610, 1615—to mention only the imprints during Skarga's lifetime.

5. These and the rules of the several other organizations are printed in modern Polish by Stanisław F. Michalski-Iwieński, ed., in Piotr Skarga, *Pisma wszystkie*, 5 vols. (Warsaw: Ultima Thule, 1923–30), 4: 1–207.

The elected successor of Stephen Báthory was King Sigismund III Vasa (reigned 1587–1632), who was the son of John III Vasa of Sweden and Catharine Jagello (sister of Sigismund II Augustus). The year after his accession Sigismund called Skarga from St. Barbara's to be court preacher, while another Jesuit became the royal adviser. Skarga would serve in that capacity from 1588 to 1612.

In this commanding position Skarga gained a hearing throughout the land. As one who believed that the magnates were pulling the country apart, oppressing their peasants, and also greatly weakening the central government, Skarga began to evolve his prophetic political ideas. He accompanied Sigismund *via* Vilna to Reval to rejoin his father John III in Finland. In Vilna, Skarga took note of the fact that all copies of his *On the Unity of the Church of God under One Pastor* (Vilna, 1577) had been bought up and burned in and around the city except for one worn copy.

While he was preparing the second edition of *On Unity* (1590), a major series of interconfessional outbreaks had taken place, prompting him to write his *Warning to the Evangelicals* [Calvinists] *and Jointly to All Non-Catholics*.[6] It was published anonymously because there was widespread criticism of Jesuits at this moment, even among Catholics.

The background leading up to this book was an outbreak after Ascension Day vespers on May 23, 1591. It was an ancient custom to make vivid Christ's ascension over the devil by representing the latter in an effigy, which was carried out of the church after vespers to be cast into the water ("the deeps") to signify Christ's final victory. The procession of schoolboys took it into their heads to pass by the house of the Brog family in St. John's Square, a residence which served as the place of worship for the Calvinists of Cracow. A great crowd of loiterers joined in, while the Calvinists, who had been alerted, came armed, and killed two of the mob and wounded some two hundred. Enraged by such extreme and random violence, the Catholics took their revenge by burning the Brog house to the ground. Not satisfied, the rioters also destroyed the meeting place of the Polish Brethren.[7] No doubt encouraged by what had happened in Cracow with impunity, Catholics in Vilna burned the Calvinist church on June 9 and 10.

Skarga's *Warning* opens with uncommon moderation:

6. *Upominanie do Ewanyelikow y do wszystkich społem nie Kátholikow* (Cracow: 1592; Poznań, 1592; Cracow, 1600 and 1610).

7. The minister of the Minor Church was Albert Kościeński; at its location the Church of St. Thomas now stands. Berga, in *Skarga*, (p. 229) says that the place of the Unitarians was destroyed on June 28; but the "Nieznana Kronika Arjańska," [unknown chronicle], ed. Kazimierz Dobrowolski, *Reformacja w Polsce*, 4 (1926), pp. 167f. indicates that disaster to both the Major and Minor Church edifices occurred in the same riot. The dates are given as May 25–27. The "Unknown Chronicle" also says that schoolboys proceeded to the cemetary, dug up and destroyed the bodies and remains of Protestants and also destroyed the eleemosynary establishment of Jan Przypkowski, elder of the Minor Church.

I invoke the Spirit of love and Christian bounty and declare, before Him
who knows everything even before it happens, that I would not wish to
say anything in hatred nor to stir up antipathy. The Rejecting all anger and
bitterness of heart, and with the conviction that God inspires, I am
speaking in Polish for the good of Poles, as brother to brethren, as
kinsman to kinsman, as neighbor to neighbor. It is true that heresy is
bad, but the persons are good; that the errors are bad, but the characters
are worthy of praise; that apostacy is bad, but that blood to us is precious;
that the sins are bad, but that frailty deserves [only] that it be deplored.
My very dear brethren, ye evangelical brethren, have supplied Catholics
with a clear motivation to destroy the [two] chapels of Cracow—a
motivation grave and invincible for the more susceptible among them.[8]

Clearly Skarga regrets the violence in Cracow and the destruction of two
edifices, but then he goes on with strong feeling to remind Protestants that
the landlords among them have seized several thousand Catholic parish
churches, assigning traditional revenues to the upkeep of Protestant ministerial families and schools. He renounces the use of force to regain these
edifices and acknowledges freely that Protestantism has spread swiftly because
of the personal misconduct of Catholic priests. He warns the Protestants that
their confederations at Chmielnik on July 25 and September 22, 1591, and at
Radom on February 22, 1592, are of no avail and urges Poles to abandon the
German or French "stepmother" (Lutheranism, Calvinism) and return to
their loving Polish mother. He reminds Catholic readers of the danger of
contamination from too close contact with the heretics. He also informs them
that the entire hierarchy of the commonwealth has in 1577 gone on record as
unswervingly opposed to the Confederation of Warsaw of 1573, which
contained the Protestant condition of imposing religious freedom (*Pax
dissidentium de religione*) in return for joining in the vote for Henry of Valois
(1573–74) (see chapter 10 above). Then he urges the faithful to follow the
renewed leadership of the church in restoring confessional unity to the
commonwealth.

When the Lutheran king John died in Sweden in 1592, the Catholic
Sigismund, as his oldest son, proceeded to Uppsala in the company of Nuncio Germanico Malaspina to be crowned Swedish king (1593–1598/1600).
Sigismund stayed in Stockholm from August 1593 to September 1594 to
consolidate his rule there, leaving behind in Cracow his court preacher, who
had asked to be excused on the ground of fatigue.

---

8. This opening is from the French translation of Berga, in *Skarga*, p. 231. Berga himself
apparently had before him only a modern Polish summary of the contents of the uncommon *Warning*. What
is quoted above is presumably exactly what Skarga said, as the nearly four page summary of the remainder of
the book in smaller font is itself a summary of the book by an unnamed author who was not basically
favorable to Skarga. Alas, for want of the original the unidentified summary must also be used.

Skarga employed his relative leisure in a Jesuit houseselecting from his many sermons given between 1563 and 1593 ninety-eight, which were published in *Sermons for Sundays and Feast Days* (Cracow, 1595).[9] Many others were to follow in print, and yet others to be composed and preached. The sermons in the collection are arranged according to the liturgical year and are difficult to date precisely, except for occasional references contemporary to the occasion of the delivery. They have been characterized as a whole as homilies in the process of becoming modern sermons. They begin with the text of the gospel for the day, which is clarified and then made the basis for a twofold presentation ending in a prayer.

Passing by his collection of *Sermons for Special Occasions* of 1600,[10] we take up his sermons delivered on the day after the Nativity of Mary, (September 9, 1601) in Vilna to King Sigismund in armor, at the head of his cavalry, as Sigismund was about to set out to resist the invasion of Livonia (a Polish fief after the wars of Stephen Báthory and the Treaty of Jam Zapolski, 1582). The invader was Sigismund's uncle Charles IX, who contested the claim of the Polish king to the throne of Lutheran Sweden since Sigismund, of course, was intensely Catholic.

In his sermon Skarga commended the king, citing biblical precedents for putting himself and the nation in jeopardy by heading the army instead of placing immediate military operations in the hands of his Hetman. A Lutheran hearing this sermon, horrified by some of its implications, transcribed it and translated it from Polish into German, and Dr. Daniel Cramer (who was perhaps the original auditor) published it in Leipzig in 1602, as *Von der Hauptfrage An Haeretico sit Fides servanda: . . . eine erschreckliche, blutdürstige Jesuiter Predigt.* Although the question Skarga set himself to deal with was the personal hazard to the king, the shocked Lutheran was right in renaming it "Whether faith is to be kept with a heretic"; for, in fact, Skarga does suggest that the greater danger is not the hazard to the king at the head of his army but rather the danger in the presence of large numbers of heretical (Lutheran and Calvinist, even some Unitarian) officers and footmen in his army, who would plausibly have some sympathy with the invading Protestants. Accordingly, counting on their doing their duty as Poles against the common foe, as Catholic and Protestant knights and footmen face the Protestant Swedes, after victory is won the king can tolerate a measure of confessional warfare among the exhausted fighters in the chronic confusion of any battlefield! But there is in the translation the implicit counsel not to keep faith with heretical Polish fellow-fighters after the worst is over. Skarga knew he had to reply to the accusation of bloodthirstiness and the counsel of treachery within the fraternity of the religion-divided *szlachta*, and by presenting his

---

9. *Kazania a niedziele y święta całego roku* (Cracow, 1595, 1597, 1602, 1609, 1618).

10. *Kazania Przygodne* (Cracow, 1600), which was printed together with sermons on the seven sacraments up front.

original Polish text he was able to charge Cramer with printing a tendentious translation. He answered Cramer fully in *Sermon on Setting out for War* (Cracow, 1602, 1610) with a clarification of the immediate situation, the sermon itself in Polish, the testimony of a number of distinguished signatories testifying that this version is what they had indeed heard at Vilna, and Cramer's animadversions. [11]

In 1603 Skarga printed in a one-volume Polish abridgment the early parts of the twelve-volume *Annales ecclesiastici* (1588–1607) of Cardinal Caesar Baronius (d. 1607).

In 1604 Skarga directly took on the Polish Brethren, whom he had particularly singled out in earlier writings on heresy, in a work entitled *The Humiliation of the Arians and a Summons of Them to Expiation and to the Christian Faith*, [12] a work that was Skarga's reaction to a certain Racovian Confession in thirty-eight articles. [13] After the publication of the Racovian Catechism in Polish at Raków in 1605 (see chapter 12 below), one of its coauthors, Pastor Jerome Moskorzowski (who would later prepare a Latin version of it dedicated to James of Scotland and England), was made the named object of Skarga's polemic entitled *A Renewed Humiliation* (Raków, 1608). In the meantime Skarga renewed his opposition to the constitutional argument for the existence of noncomformity in *Discourse Concerning the Confederation* [of Warsaw]. [14] In two other works he vigorously defended the Jesuit order.

In 1609 he published four sermons based on Acts 17 entitled *Areopagus*, that he had preached before the king in Vilna when he was en route to fight the Muscovites, which dealt with natural theology and goodness among pagans. Taking as his text Paul's speech on Mars Hill, Skarga compared Polish tribunals unfavorably with the administration of justice by pagans, even when unenlightened by revelation. In 1610 he published his second very large collection of *Occasional Sermons*, the sequel to his published sermons for

11. The whole is printed in *Pisma wszystkie, Wśiadane na Woynę, Kazánie,* 3:14–39.

12. *Zawstydzenie Arianow y wzywanie ich do pokuty y wiary chrześciańskiey* (Cracow, 1604).

13. *Konfessya Rakowska.* This was not identified by Tadeusz Pasierbiński, *Hieronim z Moskorzowa Moskorzowski* (Cracow: J. Mianowski, 1931), who deals with the debate between Skarga and the Unitarians. It is quite possible that the Synod of Raków of 1602, at which Faustus Socinus was present (see chapter 12, below) drew up this *Konfessja.* All that we known of the contents of the synod, preserved in a unique manuscript, went up in flames in Warsaw in 1944. During eighteen sessions of which Delio Cantimori and Elizabeth Feist have preserved a partial transcript, it would appear at this juncture that, when the old *Catechesis* of George Schomann of 1574 seemed no longer representative, a new *Konfessja,* preparatory to the Racovian Catechism in Polish of 1605, was produced. See their *Per la Stori degli Eretici Italiani del Secolo XVI in Europa* (Rome: Reale Accademia, 1937), pp. 258–75. It may have been very similar in form to the forty-two articles of the *Unterrichtung* of Christopher Ostorodt (Raków, 1604), which came out of the Colloquium in Raków in 1601 and the synod there of 1602. A part of the *Unterrichtung* and the titles of all articles are translated in my *Polish Brethren, 1601–1685,* Harvard Theological Studies, 33 (1978) pp. 149–68; see also my translation of Hieronim Moskorzowski's *XIV Articles* (1607), ibid., pp. 197–204.

14. *Wtore zawstydzenie przeciw U{rodzonemu} P. Jaroszowi Moskorzowskiemu* (Cracow, 1607 (two printings), 1610, 1615).

Sundays and Feast Days and largely selected at the same time. In 1610 Skarga also republished a number of his works, some revised, some simply reprinted. In 1610 he returned to the Orthodox in his *On the Threnodies and Lamentations of Theophilus Orthologus.* [15]

In 1611 he printed two *Invitations*: one, *To Penitence*, a summary of his sermons to the diet; the other, *To the Saving Faith*, directed to Protestants. Skarga's last published work was his *Sermon on the Victory over the Muscovites* [at Smolensk, June 13, 1611] *and Thanks to the Lord God*, a sermon he delivered in Vilna. He was too frail to accompany the king this time any further into battle. [16]

Skarga asked the king to relieve him of his court duties. After a long delay, the king consented. Skarga went to peaceful Sandomir in 1612, where he preached the last three sermons of his life. Then he had a sudden impulse to return to Cracow and to the College of St. Peter, which he had founded. He spent all his time in his room, reposing in his bed, wearied and sick, but always alert, reading Scripture, praying, and meditating, always hoping that he could write one last work on virtues. He died in his sleep September 27, 1612.

THEOLOGY   It was in Vilna, the capital of the Grand Duchy, of Lithuania in the midst of numerous Calvinist churches that had
been long sponsored by a branch of the Radziwiłł family,
in essentially Byzantine-rite territory, where there were in addition to Calvinists and the Orthodox some seventy other sects, that Skarga published his *Pro sacratissima Eucharistia contra haeresim Zuinglianam* (Vilna, 1576; Cracow, 1610). [17] It is directed against a lost work on the subject by the local Calvinist Andrew Wolan (ca. 1530–1610), royal secretary and outspoken defender of the rights of the peasants. Skarga's refutation of Wolan, in three parts, begins with the Tridentine asseveration of Transubstantiation, somewhat illogically goes on to the Real Presence (of which Transubstantiation is only the most highly developed doctrinal expression), and then argues the many dangers of partaking of the sacrament unworthily. Surely Skarga could not be expected to be original, only cogent, in an argument so long under dispute among Protestants themselves and so clearly formulated at the Council of Trent. But it is of interest that he became himself aware of the illogicality of his three-part arrangement of *Eucharistia* and sent to Wolan a

15. *Na Threny y lament {Melecius Smotrycki}* (Cracow, 1610).

16. *Ná Moskiewskie zwyćięstwo* (Cracow, 1611).

17. Translated by Edward J. Dworaczyk from the modernized Polish translation of Jan Tarnowicz as *The Eucharist* (Milwaukee:Bruce, 1939). The work is divided into only two parts in seventy continuously numbered chapters, the last of which is on the need for frequent communion. As for Wolan, see Andrezej Węgierski, *Libri quattuor Slavoniae Reformatae* (Amsterdam, 1679), p. 45.

version that began, in fact, with the Real Presence before taking up Transubstantiation as its consistent explanation.

While directing a college in the Lithuanian capital, a town filled with Protestants, Skarga was also surrounded in Vilna by Orthodox prelates, priests, and monks. As early as 1574 he had in manuscript a document that would be published in altered form three times, the first in Vilna in 1577, entitled *On the Unity of the Church of God under the One Pastor* [the Pope].[18] In general, the Jesuits were not in favor of the revival of the principles of the Union of the Council of Florence but preferred, rather, to reach the aristocratic families of Lithuanians, Byelorussians, and Ukrainians by way of educating the sons and heirs and inducing them to convert directly to Latin-rite Catholicism. On strategy Skarga differed from many of his fellow Jesuits. He dedicated *On Unity* to the Orthodox prince Basil Constantine Ostrozhskyi, Castellan of Kiev, Exarch of the Patriarch of Constantinople for Orthodoxy in the commonwealth, and patron of a thousand churches of the Orthodox diocese of Łuck-Ostróg, who could equip an army of two thousand mounted *szlachta* and from fifteen to twenty thousand footsoldiers.[19] Skarga had made the acquaintance of Ostrozhskyi when the latter attended funeral services for John Christopher Tarnowski, his brother-in-law and the former tutee of Skarga, who preached funeral sermons for him at both Gorliczyń and at Tarnów.

Because of the extreme rarity of the original *On Unity*, one must depend upon the testimony of others about its contents. One writer says that Skarga was satisfied with the Florentine formula as the basis of Union,[20] another says that he insisted in the first edition on extreme, though not complete, Latinization,[21] while another, devoting himself wholly to the Union of 1595–96 and to Skarga's role therein, says that on the main issues Skarga insisted only on the procession of the Holy Spirit from the Father and the Son *(Filioque)*, on the acknowledgment of the pope as sovereign and supreme over the One Church above all nations, and on the independence of the truly universal Church from any lord, king, tsar, sultan, or emperor in matters

18. The title of the first edition is *O iedności Koscoła Bożego pod iednym Pasterzem*. The only edition of *O iedności* in North America is that of Cracow, 1885, based upon the Vilna edition of 1738, which represents Skarga's version of 1590 with his *Obrona synodi Brzeskiego* as part 4.

19. The rivers in Volhynia flowing north to the Prypeć, Łuck on the Styr Ostróg on the Horyń, are today deep into the Soviet Ukraine south of Pinsk. Throughout the chapter the geographical names, except for the biggest cities and rivers are given in the then lingua franca of the Commonwealth: Polish. Constantine, who derived his name from the second town mentioned, is also known as Ostrogski or Ostrowski.

Constantine would have worked for ecumenical unity if all the Greek patriarchs would have joined with the pope. For more on Constantine and his eventual support of an Orthodox-Protestant federation against the Catholics in the commonwealth, see my "Protestants in the Ukraine," *Harvard Ukrainian Studies*, II, in two installments: no. 1 (Mar. 1978), pp. 5ff, and no. 2 (June 1978), pp. 17ff.

20. Berga, *Skarga*, pp. 195ff.

21. Tazbir, *Skarga*, pp. 80ff.

spiritual. According to Skarga the refusal of the Orthodox church to give obeisance to the pope, recognized as *primus* in the universal Church by innumerable Greek Fathers, means that it must do obeisance to the sultan instead and to Orthodox princes or, in Muscovy, to the tsar.[22] As for differences of a lower level of significance, Skarga argues only that clerical celibacy has pastoral advantages because the priest is not involved in family, garden, and domestic-economic affairs; that the use of Old Slavonic in the liturgy, far from bringing the worshipers closer to God, excludes both priests and laymen from participation in the culture and science of a Latin, a living ancient language that must indeed be learned but, when mastered, enables anyone to speak or correspond universally, be it with an Indian or with a Pole. The first edition said that no Slavic language could be raised to the level of theological precision: "Only Latin and Greek in which the holy faith spread throughout the world and took root."

On Unity may well be Skarga's most important single work, which, considerably revised, he republished in 1590. (It is to this version that further references are made.) In it the Orthodox, who were impressed by the charity and knowledge of the preacher of unity, found themselves quickly disabused of at least some of the worst charges against Roman Catholics and Jesuits. The second edition of the book is divided into three parts, in each of which Skarga seeks to make as much use as possible of the Greek Fathers to support his claim that there can be only one Holy Catholic Church of which the pope is supreme pastor and Christ's vicar. He raises the question of whether salvation is possible in separation from the pope, whom Kiev had acknowledged in the thirteenth century. He gains good will among the Orthodox by showing the plague common to them both in Vilna and its environs, the fission of Protestant sects in bewildering confusion. This fission occurs precisely, he argues, because the Protestants of the Latin West have abandoned the authority of the pope, with the consequence that they really have many gods—Zwinglian, Saxon, Calvinist, Anabaptist, Arian, and so forth. He insists that this fissiparous Protestantism has gone wild in spurious fecundity because it is unable to recognize that the Christ and his vicar are one, just as the soul and the body are one. The pope derives his authority from Peter, but the Protestants say Peter was never even in Rome, only Paul. Surely the Orthodox will agree this argument is carrying antipapalism to the limit. He is even humorous about this, agreeing that the evidence is traditional but recalling a certain foreigner who left Rome on a rainy day, returned a year later on a rainy day, and then concluded that in Rome it rains every day.

In the second part of *On Unity* he insists on the union of the Orthodox with the Holy See, having distinguished between the *heresies* of the various

---

22. Józef Tretiak, *Piotr Skarga w dziejach i lituraturze Unii Brzeskiej* (Cracow: Akademia Umiejętności, 1912), pp. 53–74. The abrasive quotation from the edition of 1577, *O iednosći*, is based upon an extract therefrom in Mychajlo Voznajk, *Geschichte der ukrainischen Literatur*, vol. 16, *bis 18. Jahrhundert* (Giessen: Wilhelm Schmitz, 1975), p. 41.

Protestants and the mere *schism* of the Orthodox. This schism has a fourfold explanation: (1) the ambition of the patriarchs of Constantinople; (2) the frequent lapses into heresy of the Constantinopolitan patriarchs from the very beginning; (3) the tyranny of the emperor and now the sultan and the tsar respectively over the patriarchs in Constantinople and in Moscow and the uncanonical interference of each in the spiritual life of the Orthodox church; and (4) the resentment of the eastern emperor and his patriarch against the pope in the creation of the Western Empire under Charlemagne and later Otto, as if there could be two Holy Universal Churches but not two empires! Skarga then deals with some eight accusations of the Orthodox church against the Latin church, of which only one is really at issue: the *Filoque*. All the other differences, he states, are surely tolerable; the Greeks need not accept seven of the eight as their own usage or belief.

The third part of *On Unity* is "On admonitions and the reprimand of the Ruthenian peoples for standing with the Greeks when they should be uniting with the Holy Church and the Roman See." The subtitle says "Russian" instead of "Ruthenian," but Skarga and his contemporaries meant by "Russian" the Orthodox of Ruthenia,[23] long a part of the crown; of Volhynia, Poldolia, of the palatinates of Bracław and Kiev, and of all "Byelorussian" territory south and east of *ethnic* Lithuania. He did not mean the Muscovites. But returning again to Athanasius, Basil of Caesarea, John Chrysostom, Gregory of Nazianzus and their recognition of the Apostolic See, he says that if the Ruthenians would but accept the sovereignty of the pope and his decrees, the lesser matters would be tolerable on either side. Skarga argues that if the Orthodox would rejoin the One Holy Catholic Church and be saved, perhaps the Muscovites (the Great Russians, for whose salvation the Orthodox subjects of the Polish king would naturally be especially concerned) would in due course follow suit!

Skarga's idea would presently come to fruition in modified form.

In 1582, Skarga returned to the problem of the Eucharist, publishing his *Artes duodecim Sacramentariorum seu Zuinglio-calvinistarum* (Vilna, 1572),[24] in which, against the local Calvinists, Skarga assumes the stance of Martin Luther in holding that the eucharistic theology of Zwinglians and Calvinists is identical and that both, with the Anabaptists and Unitarians, are "Sacramentarians," and that none of these groups have any sense of the Real Presence. He followed this up with a translation into Polish and adaptation of his earlier work against Wolan, *The Seven Pillars on which the Catholic Doctrine of the Most Holy Sacrament of the Altar Stands* (Vilna, 1582).[25]

---

23. Red Russia with Lwów its chief city could in a more limited sense be called Ruthenia; but the term Ruthenia was seldom if ever in this period used for Orthodox nonethnic Lithuania, i.e. for the Byelorussians.

24. Republished in Cracow, 1610.

25. Reprinted in Cracow under the same title: *Siedm Filarow, na ktorych stoi katholicka nauka o przenaświętszym Sakramencie Ołtarza* (1610).

Alarmed by the new power of the Metropolitan of Moscow—who had been raised to the dignity of patriarch by the tsar in 1589—to attract the restive Byzantine-rite two-thirds of the population of the commonwealth, who were often under Polish lords, Skarga reprinted in Cracow a second edition of his *On Unity*, which he now entitled *Concerning the Government and the Unity of the Church of God* (Cracow, 1590), which this time he directed, not to Prince Ostrozhskyi, but to King Sigismund Vasa.[26] In adapting the book to new circumstances, he recognized that he had been too abrasive on the three points of clerical marriage, the benumbing effect of Old Slavonic in the liturgy, and the control of the clergy by the temporal order, and he decided to be more tactful. In the face of the new dangers he greatly strengthened the first of the three parts from thirteen to nineteen chapters, drawing heavily upon the work of Cardinal Bellarmine, S.J., without due acknowledgment (which was not a necessity in that era). He emphasizes that the best government is monarchy and that for the community of salvation the only form appropriate is monarchy, that of the pope, whose church has not only the traditional marks of Catholicity—unity, continuity, universality, and apostolicity (these he had mentioned already in the first edition)—but also spiritual fecundity in missions, dogmatic formulations, and miracles, and the very name "Catholic."[27]

Although in 1597 Skarga wrote a defense of *The {Uniate} Synod of Breześć*,[28] the year stood out as that of the most famous of all his writings, *Sermons to the Diet*.[29] It is now known that although Skarga as court preacher opened and closed the diet with a sermon in St. John's Church in Warsaw, he would not have delivered all eight sermons in the single year 1597. In fact, fully conversant with the sermon genre, he used it as a pattern for eight tracts for the times with, no doubt, valid reminiscences of what he had once or even many times said in one diet sermon or another. They might in this respect be compared to Cicero's legal orations, meant to be read rather than heard in their definitive form.

Before even mentioning their main themes, I must point out at once that in one of them Skarga actually called himself a prophet: "And I also, your weak and unworthy prophet, I alert you to the iniquities, the injustices, the

26. *O rządzie y iedności kościoła Bożego.*

27. Berga admirably summarizes the changes in the second edition and shows in parallel columns the close dependence of Skarga on Bellarmine, in *Skarga*, pp. 223–30.

28. *Synod Brzeski* (Cracow, 2 printings, 1597); translation by Bishop Adam Potiy into Byelorussian (Vilna, 1597). See also n. 23 above.

29. *Kazania Sejmowe* (Cracow, 1597, 1600, 1610); modern critical edition with 106-page introduction by Janusz Tazbir, 3rd, amplified ed. (Cracow: Ossolineum, 1972); French translation with important notes, ed. l'abbé Auguste Berga, *Les sermons politiques, Sermons de Diète, 1597* (Paris: Société d'imprimerie, 1916). Berga assumed that in some form these sermons were actually delivered. This has long been assumed, as by Jan Matejko in his famous huge historic canvas, "Skarga" (1864). See my *Polish Brethren* for a reproduction thereof (plate F), with perhaps the fullest explanation in English of the characters crowded into the dramatic scene.

calumnies, and the perfidies by which this Kingdom and its inhabitants are infected."[30] This statement should be compared by way of confirmation with the opening words of his *Warning*, wherein Skarga said that he was in this instance, also, directly inspired by God. Throughout the *Sermons to the Diet* he readily takes upon himself the mantle and the distinctive manner of the prophets, like Isaiah, Ezekiel, Jonah in crucial moments in their careers, and pronounces their words as though he were indeed called by God as a prophet in the critical sense of the word. Although Skarga by conviction was a proponent of royal absolutism, he was not a proponent of an unconstitutional arbitrary monarch who would not heed his senators in diet assembled or his chosen court preacher!

The pretext for the political sermonic tracts was that the Lithuanian senators and deputies had, by their opposition, caused the premature closing of the diet. The issue was in large measure the effort of the Orthodox bishops, fully supported by Prince Constantine Ostrozhskyi, to have their complaints against the union fully aired. The principal business of the diet—with Nuncio Enrico Cardinal Gaetano present to press the papal-Hapsburg cause—was to decide whether to form a common Christian front against Sultan Mohammed III (1595–1603).

Out of what Skarga called the "six major maladies of the Commonwealth," he made eight sermonic tracts, the first being an introduction. He identified these maladies as (1) the want of love and the prevalence of class greed in the commonwealth; (2) interior discords and divisions; (3) the grave hazard to true religion, caused by the introduction and constitutional sanction of pestilential heresy (a problem so grave that it made up the material for two sermons); (4) the weakening of the central government and the royal power by the magnates; (5) the many unjust laws and inequities in application of laws; and (6) the crimes and public sins that cry to heaven for retribution. As the sermons changed somewhat in content in two further editions of the collection in the author's lifetime and as one was to be later withdrawn from the collection, we shall at first characterize the whole of the first edition of 1597 without too close attention to the individual sermons and mention at a later point the significance of at least two of the more important changes in later reprintings.

Aware of the unusual attachment of the *szlachta* to liberty (that is, liberty for their class), Skarga distinguished four kinds of liberty, three of which he considered good: the freedom of the Christian from Satan; the civil liberty to elect a king; and the "golden freedom" of every Pole to serve a constitutional king—not a tyrant like the tsar or the sultan. The "bad freedom" is really license in the guise of confederations, of princely pride in utter autonomy, of forbidden assemblies (in contrast to confederations, which had a certain

---

30. Sermon 8; Janusz Tazbir, ed., *Kazanie Sejmowe*, p. 177 and n.; Berga, ed., *Les Sermons Politiques*, p. 176.

constitutional validity by precedent). He considered that forbidden assemblies would surely lead to tyranny. Similarly there are four laws, but *all* of
these have their proper place: natural law written on the tablets of the heart;
revealed law; ecclesiastical law; and royal-constitutional law. Skarga exhorts
his readers (whom he calls "auditors") to obey all these laws and to beware of
that diabolic freedom. Ever since his sojourn in the novitiate in Rome (where
he served as Vatican penitentiary for pilgrims from all Slavic lands) he had had
a special fear of the Ottoman Turks, and in a famous passage he had them in
mind as the rod of God's anger and the staff of his indignation for the
chastisement of the commonwealth, if it should fail to mend its ways swiftly.
As he did not specifically name the foe, many later generations of Poles found
in this sermon a remarkable, prophetic warning of invasion from Sweden, of
the eventual partition among Prussia, Austria, and Russia, or even of the
more recent adversaries in partition, then domination and then worse than
decimation:

> In the midst of your discord there shall come a neighboring enemy and,
> taking advantage of your disunity, he shall say: "Their hearts are
> divided, now they will perish." And he will not let slip away so
> propitious an opportunity to destroy you and exercise his tyranny. Such
> is that which awaits him who wishes you ill and he will say [cf. Psalm 35
> (34): 25]: "Aha, aha, we are going to devour them. Their foot has slipped
> and they cannot escape us." And this disunity will bring unto you
> slavery that will bury your liberties and turn them into mockery; and it
> will come to pass what the prophet [cf. Isaiah 24:2] said: "As with the
> serf, so with his master; as with the servant girl, so with her mistress; as
> with the people, so with the priest; as with the poor, so with the rich; as
> with the buyer, so with the seller."[31] The fiefs and the great prin-
> cipalities which are now united under the Crown, cohering thus as a
> single body of the nation, they will detach from it and separate them
> from it as a consequence of your discords, while at the present, with
> harmony, the force of your arms can be immense and formidable to your
> enemies. The palatinates will abandon you as an orchard after the fruit
> has been picked and the harvest shed is abandoned to be blown down by
> the slightest wind. You will become like the abandoned widow, you
> who govern other peoples; and you will become for your enemies an
> object of ridicule and derision.
>
> Your language, the language of this Kingdom, the only one that
> remains free among the Slavic realms, you will lose and with it your na-
> tion. And even the scattered remnants of this people, so ancient and so
> travelled everywhere in the world, you will lose and, as it has happened
> to others, you will be absorbed by an alien people who hate you.

31. Skarga has slightly altered the order of the groupings; in Isaiah the priests and people, for
example, come first.

You will not only be ruled by a King not of your blood and your election, but shall also be without your country and your Kingdom: aimless vagabonds, destitute and despised wherever ye go; pushed and kicked and jostled ye shall be where once ye commanded respect.

[Cf. Deut. 28:47f.]: "Your enemies ye will serve as hewers of wood and drawers of water, while ye yourselves go naked and suffer hunger and thirst; and upon your necks they will place iron yokes of great weight and unspeakable humiliation because ye will not have served the Lord your God in joy and contentment of heart when ye had abundance," because as a consequence of that abundance ye will have disrespected criminally the King, the priest, and the others in authority under the cover of an infernal liberty, not willing either "to bear the easy yoke of Christ" [Matt. 11:30] or to practice obedience [to the Church].[32]

Skarga thus forewarned the nation in prophetic fashion and with scriptural allusions that he could presuppose to be readily recognizable by his auditors. In another sermon (the eight), Skarga distinguishes three kinds of divine threats: warnings like those of a parent, which may not be implemented if those who are warned change their ways; threats that, though meant for the present, are, because of God's ways, only brought to bear on a succeeding generation; and threats that are absolutely irreversible for the present or future because God has hardened the hearts of the proud. Presumably there is something of all three kinds of threat in the foregoing moving oracle.

Because among all the dangers to the Commonwealth Skarga thought heresy the worst menace, he devoted the fourth and fifth sermons to it. In these sermons and elsewhere Skarga mentions the Polish Jews only in passing and with no particular feeling, since their status, religious and political, was uncontested so long as they did not proselytize. His whole concern is for those who have accepted Christ but deformed him and his teaching concerning the temporal order and salvation through the Holy Catholic Church. Skarga, as is often the case, was ill informed about his enemies. He charges the Lutherans and the Calvinists, for example, with believing that the king or magistrate has authority only if he is in a state of grace. But this position was only true of the neo–Donatist Hussites and their successors in Poland, the Czech Brethren. However, the charge seemed all the more plausible to Skarga for the reason that these three groups were fully federated throughout the Commonwealth since the Consensus of Sandomir of 1570. Then he referes to "Anabaptist" Antitrinitarians who, as pacifists, imperil the commonwealth, recognizing as their only king "him crowned of thorns." Actually, the Polish Brethren, though against aggressive war in the Erasmian tradition, were divided on the issues of exercising magistracy themselves and bearing arms.

---

32. Sermon 3; Janusz Tazbir ed., pp. 66f.; Berga, ed., pp. 92f. These are presumably the words Skarga is uttering as he is captured vividly on the canvas of Matejko. See n. 20 above.

They scarcely ever, unless someone particularly wished it, allowed rebaptism; but they did practice believers' baptism by immersion for their offspring. In any case, for Skarga the only true, saving religion with respect to heaven, and the only cementing religion for the state, is Catholicism, because monarchy is the best of governments and the Catholic church is hierarchically monarchial.

From there, we come logically to the sixth sermon, on royal monarchy. We have already adduced his distinction between three "good liberties" and one "bad liberty" and the four kinds of laws. This is an appropriate place to remark that this sixth sermon aroused especially strong opposition. In fact, Poland was to experience a civil war *(rakosz)* led by Nicholas Zebrzydowski (1604–06) on the specific issue of King Sigismund's attempt to exercise absolutist powers like his peers in other realms. In the third edition of *Sermons of the Diet* (Cracow, 1610) Skarga would see fit to leave this sermon out of the collection. Of further interest is the fact that the extended excoriation of the inexpressible callousness and cruelty of the lords, magnates, and prelates against the serfs would be added to the formerly seventh, now sixth sermon, where Skarga, founder of so many urban eleemosynary services for the disadvantaged, belatedly lifts up the cause of the serfs as brothers in Christ with the lords.

ROLE IN THE CHURCH   More than any other figure in this book, Skarga was of such a generation and temperament and especially in such a place to be the shaper of two traditions in the Catholic Church: the tradition of Catholic Polish nationalism and the tradition of the Slavic Uniates.

The political and ethnic outlines of the cultural achievement of the Polish-Lithuanian Commonwealth can be seen to this day in the Soviet Socialist Republic of Lithuania with its capital Vilnius, Byelorussia with its capital Minsk, and the Ukraine with its capital Kiev. What is today's Ukraine—resulting from the Union of Lublin of 1569, whereby the grand duchy ceded directly to the crown its territory south of the Pripet River and southeast far beyond Kiev—was during most of the last fifty years of Skarga's life a vast area opened up to further expansion of Polish lords and their institutions, including the Latin church. It was a Byzantine-rite territory of which, in the age of Skarga, the *then* Ukraine was only one of several palatinates. But the religious achievement of these Byzantine-rite territories has all but disappeared, except for the several millions of Uniate Ukrainians of the diaspora in Canada, the United States, and elsewhere, who are still loyal to the Union of Brześć-Litewski of 1595–96. Space does not permit delineation of the active role of the Byzantine-rite prelates and princes themselves in the union nor of the fierce opposition of some Orthodox lords, priests, lay brotherhoods, and peasants to the union. But we have seen how Jesuit Skarga departed from the general policy of his own order and indeed how he passed through three stages within himself in successive editions of *On Unity*, adopting a progressively more benign attitude toward the distinctive features of the Byelorussian and especially of the Ukrainian Greek Catholic faithful in Union with Rome.

The synods and concordat of Brześć-Litewski, which comsummated the Union, meant that the Metropolitan of Kiev and two of the once-Orthodox bishops in the Commonwealth were made senators in the diet, along with both Uniate and Orthodox princes. Several snyods of the Orthodox were on the point of becoming Uniate in Brześć: December 2, 1594 with seven bishops present; June 12, 1595 with nine present. Two bishops, Adam Potiy (Pociej) of Wolodymyr and Cyril Turlecki of Pinsk-Turlów, were delegated by the second synod to go to Rome by way of Cracow to confirm the Union. While they sojourned in Cracow, Skarga besought the king to extend to them generous traveling expenses and, on his own, on October 19, 1595, Skarga wrote to Claudius Aquaviva, the Jesuit superior in Rome, asking him to support the Union actively.[33] In the letter Skarga communicates a sense of the great danger of the visit of Patriarch Jeremiah II of Constantinople to Great Russia, because his presence in the East would attract the numerous Byzantine-rite subjects of the Polish king, the peasants and Cossacks among them being often bitter and prone to unrest and sedition. He says further that Prince Ostrozhskyi is also opposing Union, since it does not include all of the Eastern patriarchs at once; and that there is talk of a common front of Protestants and holdout Orthodox. He urges the superior general to be especially hospitable to the delegation and not to insist on all the terms of the Union of Florence of 1439.[34]

Despite Ostrozhskyi's misgivings, the Union was officially proclaimed in Rome on December 23, 1595; the two "Ruthenian" bishops, Potiy and Turlecki, promised the pope to hold yet a third synod at Brześć to proclaim the union. The synod was opened October 6, 1596, and Skarga was named by the king to be one of the Latin-rite representatives there. He made a speech there, which is now lost. Skarga tried to convince his friend Ostrozhskyi to participate in the partial Union, but the prince refused and carried several bishops back with him into Orthodoxy.[35]

Despite the still controversial Union, much of the commonwealth had nevertheless become papal, the greatest geographical expansion of the

33. It is published by Jan Syganski, S.J., *Listy ks. Piotra Skargi T.J. z lat 1566–1610* (Cracow: Wydawnictwo Towarzystwa Jezusowego, 1912), no. 124, pp. 259–61.

34. In a letter the previous month Skarga asked the superior to relieve him of his position at court to give himself time to prepare for death. The revelations of his inner and outer life embodied in the rich correspondence of 147 letters has been turned into *Działność Ks. Piotra Skargi* (Cracow: Wydawnictwo Towarzystwa Jezusowego, 1912) by the editor of the letters.

35. Potij, who had been castellan of Brześć, on being widowed, had been urged by Ostrozhskyi to become a monk, whereupon he appointed him bishop of the city he owned. Potij would become the third Uniate metropolitan of Kiev.

Counter-Reformation in Europe. The Union in turn weakened the Protestants relative to the population now under the pope. The Uniates as Catholics no longer needed the Confederation of Warsaw as a protection of their rights, although, to be sure, before the Confederation of 1573 the legal status of the Orthodox had never been challenged. Yet the *Pax dissidentium* of the confederation had come to be construed as the constitutional basis of the freedom of the Orthodox. Now suddenly a large contingent of the Byzantine-rite population, except for the Orthodox holdouts, could no longer be counted upon by the Protestants to be especially concerned with the *Pax* or with the coronation oath required of each elected king to uphold the *Pax*. Now with the formerly Orthodox Uniates at his side, Skarga could proceed with the developing of the second tradition: loyalty to the pope as the basis of "Polish" nationalism.

In this new situation of enhanced ecclesiastical, if not liturgical, unity in the commonwealth, Skarga published in succession *The Legal Prosecution of the Confederation* (Cracow, 1595) and an enlarged version of it and answer to Protestant criticism, *Legal Prosecution with respect to the Confederation with Correction and Refutation of the* [unidentified] *Adversary* (Cracow, 1596).[36] The term *proces* (translated "legal prosecution") in both Polish titles comes from a new provision in the *Pacta conventa* of 1587 (which had led to the election and coronation of Sigismund III with Protestant support) that the King-elect not only uphold by oath the *Pax dissidentium de religione* as an ongoing part of the Warsaw Confederation stipulation for kingship in Poland in perpetuity but also that the king henceforth promise to engage actively in legal proceedings against violators of this *Pax*, that is, engage in a vigilant royal *Processus Confoederationis*, in the new specialized sense of "legal prosecution" or "procedure." The immediate occasion leading to the insertion of the provision was an attack—on the eve of the election of Sigismund Vasa—on the family house of Brog and the Calvinist meeting place in Cracow (the attack that had prompted Skarga's *Warning* had happened a few years earlier, in 1591). Skarga adroitly turns the phrase into the sense of a "prosecution" of the very idea of the original Confederation with its *Pax dissidentium* of 1573, not to say its most recent amplification of 1587.

The enlarged version is divided into five parts: (1) Whence came the liberty of the Protestants to take over as many as three thousand churches for their own use? Surely the bad conduct of some priests does not give the lord the right to make a replacement, only the bishop. (2) Who is to be regarded as a heretic? Surely whoever introduces new doctrines, whoever intrudes ministers into the places of priests without a divine call, whoever appropriates church property, and whoever revives ancient heresies. (3) What are the damages to state and society, no less than to religion, of this liberty, which even Theodore Beza, whom he cites, repudiates? He responds that there are

---

36. *Proces Konfoederaciey; Proces na Konfoederacia z popráwa y odpráwa przeciwnika.*

three purposes in social organization expressed in the state: (1) to assure
social peace, a goal even among the social animals; (2) to make citizens
honorable and virtuous, a goal common to the pagan and the Christian state;
and (3) if the state is Christian, to aid citizens or subjects in achieving eternal
salvation by supporting and causing them to embrace the true, saving
religion. He points out that the Puritans of England, for example, do not even
believe in the immortality of the soul (an extraordinary misrepresentation).
Although it is true that Christian mortalism and an eventual resurrection of
the righteous only were held by John Milton, how could Skarga have known
that at his time of writing? The full formulation of Christian mortalism could
have been more appropriately ascribed to the majority of his Polish Socinian
foes (see chapter 12 below).

In the fourth part, concerning the punishment of heretics and false
prophets, Skarga is inconclusive. He says that as many as three thousand
Catholic churches have been preempted by Protestant landlords for heretical
use—and this by force. Yet he does not bring himself to champion force in
return, holding only that to inscribe religious toleration of heresy in the
constitution of the Republic (the *Pax dissidentium*) is intolerable for even the
most reasonable Catholic. In sum, toleration is at best a provisional necessity
because of the large number of heretics. But one does not feel that Skarga
himself would ever go so far as the papal nuncio's suggestion of 1555 that the
most important heretics be executed. In the fifth part Skarga seeks to demonstrate that, far from preventing civil war and confessional fratricide, the
confederation has in fact greatly complicated the situation in the commonwealth and will so weaken it that there will be bloodshed.

To the end, Skarga only endured tolerance as a political necessity,
believing that ideally, Protestants and Orthodox should return to the Church
of Peter. In his untiring apostolate, Skarga was the greatest of Poland's
Roman Catholic churchmen in the century of Renaissance, Reformation, and
Counter-Reformation. He was a distinctively *Polish* Jesuit and Catholic, in
that for all his devotion to the universal Church, he was concerned for that
universality as it would keep his beloved multi-ethnic nation a strong and
righteous part of a larger Catholic Christendom; a Jesuit who was as determined as any of his brethren in the order to uphold royal absolutism and to
suppress heresies and schism, but he never resorted to covert machinations
and sought to win by reason rather than by coercion and surely not by
bloodshed. Like his brethren, Skarga sought to reconvert the rich and
powerful, but he also became increasingly courageous in his prophetic rebuke
of the misuse of baronial and princely and even royal power and increasingly
specific in his defense of the urban poor and, at length, of the exploited and
often cruelly mistreated peasants.

12
FAUSTUS SOCINUS
1539–1604
ZBIGNIEW OGONOWSKI
(Translated by Zofia Grzybowska)

LIFE

Faustus Socinus (in Italian, Fausto Sozzini) was born on December 5, 1539, in Tuscany in the city of Siena. He came from an affluent family related to eminent Italian families that included popes Pius II, Pius III, and Paul V. As a young man, he was not particularly studious, and the education he acquired in his early years was mainly literary.

He left Italy for the first time in 1561 for Lyon, where he was a merchant. At that time he became interested in radical religious concepts encountered among his friends and close relatives, particularly his uncle, Laelius, one of the prominent Italian heretics. After Laelius's death in 1562 Faustus went to Switzerland, and shortly afterwards he wrote *Explicatio primae partis primi capitis Evangelii Joannis* [Commentary on the first chapter of St. John's gospel].

In 1563 Socinus returned to Italy, first to Siena and later to Florence, where he joined the court of Grand Duke Cosimo I of Tuscany as secretary to Paul Orsini, a court dignitary and relative of the grand duke. For twelve years he lived the life of a ducal courtier. During that period now and again Socinus composed poems on not only politics and morals, but love poems as well. At the same time, however, he maintained close connections with heterodox Italian emigrants in Switzerland, Poland, and Transylvania. As time passed, Socinus began to think that he was wasting his best years and considered retiring from court life to devote himself to the studies that had attracted him in his youth. The death of Cosimo I prompted his decision. Though urged by Cosimo's successor, Francis II, to stay at court, Socinus left Italy in 1574.

His first stop was Basel, which at that time was a point of convergence for religious heterodoxy. There, in an atmosphere of free discussion, Socinus wrote two important tracts which, though long unpublished, were circulated in manuscript copies. The first of these, the product of two years' work and finally completed in 1578, was the tract *De Jesu Christo Servatore* [On Jesus Christ the Savior], printed no earlier than 1594 in Poland in Cracow. This is the most original of his works and contains the core of his doctrines.

The second tract, written in Basel in 1578, was *De Statu primi hominis ante lapsum* . . . [On the condition of the first man before his fall]. It was finally printed in 1610 in Raków.

In the fall of 1578 Socinus traveled to Kolozsvar in Transylvania (today Cluj, in Romania), on the way visiting Cracow for the first time. In June 1579 he was again in Cracow. He never left Poland again, spending the last twenty-four years of his life in that country.

In 1580, in Cracow, Socinus wrote a fourth important tract, which completed the construction of his religious doctrine, entitled *De Sacrae Scripturae Auctoritate* [On the authority of the Holy Scriptures].

In Cracow Socinus felt at home. There was a sizable Italian colony, and in addition there was the Antitrinitarian church whose members, called Arians in Poland, preferred the name "Polish Brethren." Socinus maintained close connections with the Arians, took part in their meetings and discussions, attended their synods, and expressed the wish to join their church. He refused, however, to undergo a second baptism through immersion, since he believed that baptism may be required only for converts to Christianity from a different religion. Since this view was in conflict with the view of the leaders of the church, Socinus was never officially made a regular member. However, his relations with the leadership of the church remained friendly, and he willingly performed missions assigned to him, for example, defending the Church of the Polish Brethren in several polemical tracts directed against its enemies.

In March 1583 Socinus left Cracow to settle in Pawlikowice (southeast of Cracow) on the property of Christopher Morsztyn, a well-to-do nobleman and longtime supporter of the Polish Brethren. In 1583 Socinus married his host's daughter Elizabeth, who the next year bore their only daughter, Agnes.

The year 1587 was not happy for Socinus. The death of his wife in September dealt him a hard blow and he fell seriously ill. The same year brought the news of the death of Francis II, the grand duke of Tuscany. Once ducal protection ceased, Socinus's family properties were considered to be owned by a dangerous heretic and were confiscated, and the flow of his income from Italy also ceased. At the same time, however, the death of Francis II made it possible for Socinus to come into the open. A long time before, he had promised the duke that he would not publish under his own name any book opposed to Catholic doctrines, but now he felt free from this obligation.

In the mean time Socinus's authority among the Polish Brethren increased. He acquired a following, particularly among the young, and his influence grew.

In this period he decided to consolidate his theological opinions in one work. This plan was realized in 1592 in *Praelectiones theologicae* [Theological lectures], a work consisting of twenty-seven chapters. In all probability, these were the lectures that Socinus delivered to the theologians and leaders of the Polish Brethren in Cracow, to which he had returned from Pawlikowice in 1588.

1596 is considered to be the year in which Socinus assumed de facto leadership in the Church of the Polish Brethren. In this year his staunchest opponents disappeared and Rationalist Unitarianism finally triumphed in the Church of the Polish Brethren.

From the middle of the sixteenth until the third decade of the seventeenth century, Poland was the most tolerant country in Europe, called *haereticorum azylum et refugium* (the asylum and refuge of heretics). Even though the established and privileged religion remained Catholicism, various Protestant sects (Lutheran, Calvinist, Czech Brethren) and the Orthodox church (in the eastern parts of the commonwealth) enjoyed full freedom. Full tolerance was also extended to small communities of Moslems. Although Antitrinitarianism was generally hated by Catholics and Protestants alike, the Polish Brethren were also free to practice their religion. Transylvania and Poland were the only countries in the Christian world where Antitrinitarianism was tolerated. Towards the end of the sixteenth century, however, the situation in Poland worsened due to the constant propaganda of the Catholic clergy in general and the influence of Jesuit schools in particular, and religious fanaticism began to grow. Attacks on Protestant, and particularly Arian, churches began and were not always suppressed with sufficient energy by the authorities. The majority of participants in those disorders were students.

Socinus was subjected to one of those attacks on April 30, 1598, when a group of students from the University of Cracow invaded his lodgings while he was sick in bed. Shouting insults, the assailants dragged him barefooted and half-clothed to the city hall where a bonfire consumed his books, papers, and correspondence. He himself was threatened with death in the flames unless he revoked his doctrines. When he refused to comply, the mob dragged him towards the Vistula River, perhaps to drown him. Only the intervention of Marthin Wadowita, a university professor who happened to be there, saved him from the hands of his oppressors. Fearing that he might be attacked again, Socinus left Cracow.

He settled in Luslawice, near Tarnow, an important center of the Polish Brethren, which was to become his last permanent residence. After 1600 he would visit Raków, the capital of Antitrinitarianism, and there on several occasions he presided over synods and theological conferences. In 1604 he died in Luslawice at the age of sixty-five.

THEOLOGY   The bulk of Socinus's work—at least three-quarters of his literary production—was written in Poland and is closely tied to the history of the Church of the Polish Brethren. While these later works of Socinus contributed nothing basic to his doctrines, which were formulated in Switzerland and partly even earlier in Italy, Socinus's Polish writings are a valuable source of detailed information about his religious ideas.

When he arrived in Poland his doctrines had a good deal in common with the doctrines of the Polish Brethren, doctrines such as the negation of the Holy Trinity, the negation of the preexistence of Jesus, the conviction that the moral commands of the Gospel—including those in the Sermon on the Mount—must be practiced, and so forth. At the same time, there were essential differences between his doctrines and the contemporary Unitarian views of the Polish Brethren. Socinus contrasted the anthropological pessimism shared by Arian theologians, which bore a Lutheran-Calvinist stamp, with his own humanistic optimism, which is reflected in the idea that man is able naturally to develop the will to follow Christ and thus achieve salvation. Mystic tendencies, such as the conviction that to know religious truth required supernatural assistance and illumination by the Holy Spirit, he contrasted to his belief that man's natural reason is completely adequate to interpret Holy Scriptures correctly.

It is clear, in historical perspective, that the differences separating the two doctrines were more substantial than their similarities. It seems, however, that neither Socinus nor the theologians of the Polish Brethren were fully aware of the extent of their differences, at least at the time. The uniting factor that both doctrines had in common was Antitrinitarianism with a Unitarian tendency, a position that contrasted sharply with the belief shared by the rest of the Christian world. It is from this point that we shall begin the discussion of the theological doctrine of Socinus.

Antitrinitarianism and Christology

The first chapter of St. John had a singular importance for Christian doctrine: it was a foundation for the doctrine on the Trinity, providing the partisans of trinitarian teaching with their principal arguments.

The first of Socinus's tracts, written in 1562, *Explicatio primae partis primi capitis Evangelii Joannis*,[1] attempts to give an interpretation of the evangelist's words that differed from the traditional one by negating the dogma of the Holy Trinity. The opening words of St. John's Gospel are familiar to Christians: "In the beginning was the Word, and the Word was with God, and the Word was God. The same was in the beginning with God. All things were made by Him . . ." (John 1:1–3). Trinitarians interpreted this passage, in accordance with the established traditional understanding, as follows: In the beginning, that is, before time, before anything was created, there was the Word *(Logos)*, that is, the second person of the Trinity, the Son of God, coexistent with God the Father (the Word was God). At a certain defined time

---

1. *Bibliotheca Fratrum Polonorum, Opera Socini Irenopoli post annum* 1656 (in fact, Amsterdam, 1668) vol. 1, pp. 75 ff. (Hereafter cited as BFP, *Op. Soc.*) On the first edition of the *Explicatio*, see Lech Szczucki, *Ze studjów nad socynianizmen. Nieznane wydanie "Explicatio" Fausta Socyna* [From studies on Socinianism: an unknown edition of "Explicatio" of Faustus Socinus] in *Rocznik Biblioteki Narodowej* 4 (1968): 155–65.

the Word (that is, the Son of God) became man (Word became flesh), the historical Jesus Christ, while not ceasing to be God.

According to Socinus, this understanding is contrary to reason and conflicts with other scriptural passages. His own interpretation is as follows: "Beginning" must be understood not as eternity, but as the beginning of Jesus' evangelical teachings. It is contrary to reason to believe that an undefined Word *(Logos)* existed before time. This latter view was accepted under the influence of Platonic philosophy, while the Gospel contains clear and simple ideas. It is impossible to accept the literal meaning of the expressions of the evangelists, since they frequently resorted to metaphoric and hyperbolic expressions. So the "Word" means Jesus indeed, the historical man, the Son of Mary, who was crucified but not the eternal *Logos*. By calling him "Word," John meant that Jesus was proclaiming the word of God, that is, God's will. It is equally nonsensical, according to Socinus, to accept the literal meaning of the expression, "and the Word was God." We frequently find that the word "God" is used in the Scriptures metaphorically and hyperbolically, that is, in an exaggerated sense, in order to stress the rank and the meaning of the person so called. And thus Scripture calls angels, rulers, and judges "gods." That is how the word "god" ought to be understood in John's Gospel. St. John calls the Word, who is Jesus Christ, "God," not in the sense that he is equal to the true God, which is contrary to reason, but in order to stress the dignity of Christ, who was given by God the mission to build the "new world" since "all things were made by Him." Jesus is not therefore the God of Israel. He is a man who, although foreseen in God's plans before time, was born at a given time.

Equally untrue, Socinus believes, is the view regarding Christ's atonement for our sins. This question, which Socinus left untouched in his first tract, received extensive attention in later writings. Socinus argued that the dogma of atonement and satisfaction is contrary to reason and a sense of justice. The true role of Christ was to demonstrate to people how to be saved. Jesus affirmed his teachings by dying on the cross, to prove that no sacrifice, including death and suffering, should deter people from fulfilling God's commands. Finally, the resurrection affirmed the truth of Jesus' teachings. The resurrection therefore, and not the death and martyrdom of Jesus, is of central importance; it verified his words and is a testimony that what he did and said is irrefutable truth. It gives us a final assurance that just as he was resurrected, we also, if we are obedient to him, shall be raised from the dead. In this sense Christ may and should be called Savior. After his resurrection by God, Christ was given full power over the world and people. In this sense Christ may, and should, be called God.

Nevertheless, the Scriptures call Christ the Son of God. How is this to be understood? It is true that Jesus was born of the Virgin Mary by the power of the Holy Spirit, but this fact is not the reason why Jesus is called the Son of

God. His condition as the Son of God is the result of the "likeness" (*similitudo*) between the Father and Son, a likeness which consists of three factors:[2]

1. Knowledge: Jesus knows human hearts and minds. None of the prophets or angels had that knowledge.
2. Immortality: Jesus was the first and the only man who rose from the dead to live eternally. The Scriptures mention Enoch and Elijah, but they were not resurrected from the dead; and it is doubtful whether they were made immortal.
3. Power: Jesus has power over human minds and bodies. He also commands good and bad spirits and judges men, rewarding them according to their merits with eternal life or punishing them according to their sins.

Jesus' power is not unlimited, however. It extends only to all that is connected with the Church, and only to those people who are in the Church. The expression "Christ's Church" must be understood broadly. Members of the Church are not only those who obey him, and not only those who profess him, but include also those having any knowledge of him whatsoever, even those who hate him, because if they hate him they know of him. Similarly, the knowledge of Christ is not present to the hearts of people outside his Church.

It remains only to mention that the expression "Holy Spirit" does not denote, according to Socinus, the third person of the one God.[3] The Holy Spirit is not a person. This expression signifies the power of God and the "effectiveness of God's actions" (*Virtus atque efficacia Dei*); in particular, this power, when called the Holy Spirit, sanctifies people.

The Doctrine of Justification According to Socinus

The Doctrine of justification taught by the theologians of the Reformation was an expression of profound anthropological pessimism, particularly in its Calvinist form. Its main points are: first, that man, tainted with original sin, is incapable of any act, however insignificant, which would have a justifying value in the eyes of God; and second, that salvation is possible only because Christ, through His death on the cross, atoned for human sins. To be saved, men must have strong and ardent faith in the redeeming role of Christ's martyrdom. Faith, however, is not a personal merit of the man who believes, but is an unmerited gift of God, dependent on God's grace. Hence, the formula: *non propter fidem, sed sola fide*. God extends his grace to those, and only to those, whom he selected arbitrarily. Free will is fiction. Without the grace of God we are irrevocably doomed. Only the elect receive the grace of God, by no merit of their own.

2. *Epitome Colloquii Racoviae habiti anno 1601*, ed. Lech Szczucki and Janusz Tazbir (Warsaw: Biblioteka Pisarzy Reformacyjnych no. 5, 1966), pp. 35–39.
3. *Epitome Colloquii*, p. 42.

Socinus's conception of justification was altogether different. In the first place, Socinus understood original sin differently.[4] There is no original sin, as it is described by traditional theology, Catholic or Protestant. Adam's transgression burdened Adam alone. There is no reason to believe that the sin of one man destroyed in all men the ability to follow justice. If that ability is not perfect in people, this imperfection is not because of Adam's sin, but because of an ingrained habit of wrong actions. Free will survived Adam's fall. Moreover, the mere idea that man is deprived of free will is absurd. Without free will there is no religion, because religion is nothing else but an effort to obey God.[5]

Equally absurd, and even blasphemous, according to Socinus, is the theory of predestination, according to which God destines some to the glory of eternal life, while destining others to eternal condemnation.

Here, however, Socinus poses the following question: Is it possible to assert that there is free human will if one admits the view that God, from the beginning of time, knew all human deeds and thoughts? And furthermore, that he knew how each man would act in each concrete case, even before that man came into this world? Indeed, such a divine foreknowledge is incompatible with the principle of human free will. Therefore it must be admitted that God has no such foreknowledge! We shall return to this extremely interesting point in Socinus's doctrine again.

While differing so strongly from Protestant theology by accepting the doctrine of free will, Socinus explained the concept of justification as if he shared some points in common with the doctrine of the Reformation. But these similarities, as we shall see, were actually quite superficial.

First, our justification by God is not the result of the sanctity of our life and of our innocence; it would not be so, even if we were completely innocent and saintly, which we never are. Socinus expressed this idea in formulae borrowed from scholastic theology: the sanctity of our life, he says, is not a "cause which would move God to justify us" *(causa impulsiva)*, neither is it an "efficient cause" *(causa efficiens)* of our salvation.[6] It is not so, because even before time, God, of his own will, decided to save people on condition that they believe in Christ. Second, faith in Christ is an unmerited gift of God, because no one given the opportunity to believe in Christ deserves that gift.[7] (These two points in Socinus's conception, taken out of the context of his entire doctrine, might suggest that he stands nearer the Reformation than he really does. However, further understanding of his premises and conclusions refute such a supposition.) Third, belief in Christ is given not to people

4. Ibid., pp. 51–53.

5. "Decretum enim [Dei] necessarium tollit omne *liberum arbitrium. Quo sublato omnis etiam religio,* quae nihil aliud est quam conatus oboediendi, *concedat necesse est*" [emphasis added, Z.O.], *Epitome Colloquii,* p. 55.

6. *Tractatus de Justificatione,* in BFP, *Op. Soc.* 1:603a.

7. Ibid., p. 602b.

arbitrarily selected, but to *all* people to whom the Gospel is taught.[8] Fourth, faith, which justifies us, consists not only in the conviction that the words of Christ are true. Such "faith" *(assensus, persuasio)* may be possessed by the wicked and by those disobedient to God. Justifying faith consists in "confidence" *(fiducia, confidencia)* that God will fulfill the promise of eternal life made through Jesus.[9] But such a faith necessarily involves obedience to God's commands. Obedience is not the result of faith, but its "substance and form." Briefly stated, Socinus believed that the "faith which justifies us is obedience to God."[10] Fifth, faith that Christ's promises will be fulfilled, that is to say, that faith which justifies us, arises in us as a result of our free will. The decision to believe is ours.[11] How does this faith arise?

There is a constant struggle in us between reason and inclination; reason counsels us to follow justice, even to our own disadvantage, while inclination leads us to whatever is most advantageous. It depends therefore on our free will whether we act justly and refrain from wickedness—even if it is to our disadvantage—or whether we do what is to our immediate profit, even though we understand that we should not act that way. He who decides to follow the counsel of reason, even to his disadvantage, is easily led to believe that God, who rewards the just and punishes wrongdoers, exists. He who follows his own inclinations, cannot reach this conviction, or can do so only with great difficulty, because such a conviction is inconvenient for his designs.[12] Briefly, the cause and the foundation of faith is man's desire and tendency to do what is right and to avoid what is unjust.

The grace that God gives to people is the teachings of Christ, which contain, in addition to strict moral commandments, the promise of the reward most desired by people, namely, an eternal life of happiness.

The entire process of the emergence of faith was explained by Socinus in a naturalistic manner, without resort to supernatural assistance even in the form of an indirect divine impulse. An intervention of that sort, in Socinus's opinion, would destroy all human merit and would make salvation dependent on the Creator's whim. This supernatural assistance appears, nevertheless, at a

8. *De Jesu Christi Servatore*, pt. 4, in BFP, *Op. Soc.*, 2:240a. Cf. *Tractatus de Justificatione*: "Deus *omnes*, quibus Christi Evangelium annuntiatur, salvos facere vult . . ., si modo eidem Evangelio credant atque obediant; ut autem credere atque abedire possint, *omnibus* generatim concedit" [emphasis added, Z.O.], in BFP, *Op. Soc.*, 1:603b.

9. *Tractatus de Justificatione*, BFP, *Op. Soc.*, 1:671a, 623a.

10. Ibid., p. 610b: ". . . quae fides, obedientiam praeceptorum Dei, non quidem ut effectum suum, sed ut suam substantiam et formam continet atque complectitur. . . . Fidem, hanc scilicet, qua justificamur, Dei obedientiam esse." Cf. *De Jesu Christi Servatore*, in BFP, *Op. Soc.*, 2:234a: "Ex quo factum est, ut Christo, sive Christi verbis credere, idem significet, atque illi obedire . . . , Christo autem, sive ejus verbis non credere, idem sit, atque illi non obedire."

11. *De Jesu Christi Servatore*, BFP, *Op. Soc.*, 2:240b–41.

12. "Brevis discursus de causa, ob quam creditur aut non creditur Evangelio . . ." BFP, *Op. Soc.*, 2:455–57.

certain stage. According to Socinus's conception, supernatural assistance does not reduce in any degree the personal responsibility of man.

The commandments of the New Testament that call for the imitation of Christ, are both just and consonant with reason, but their fulfillment requires such a degree of heroism, such self-denial, that they seem to overreach the natural capacities of man. In order to fulfill them, conviction or hope that obedience shall earn the desired reward of eternal life are not enough. To persist in the endeavor and resist all temptations, certitude in needed that this reward exists. This certitude God creates in our hearts "by the power of his Spirit" (*virtute Spiritus sui*). This grace is granted to those, and those only, who, made aware of the reward, not only accept that it is true, but also prepare to reject wickedness and to be wholly obedient to the Gospel's commandments, and then persist in their pious purpose.[13]

Negation of Divine Foreknowledge

The problem of "divine foreknowledge" (*praescientia* or *praenotitia divina*) was discussed by Socinus in detail in *Praelectiones theologicae* while refuting the doctrine of predestination.[14]

The thesis that God from all eternity has a sure and unerring knowledge of "future contingencies" (*futura contingentia*)—that is, of those things that could happen but may not (obviously of future acts of the human will)—has been supported, according to Socinus, by three arguments: (1) that the notion of divine nature immanently contains the notion of this unerring foreknowledge, so that it would be impious to think of God otherwise; (2) that it is scarcely probable that things are different, although they could be different, if that were God's will; (3) that it is supported fully by the Scriptures. We shall not discuss here the third argument. We shall present only how Socinus deals with the first two.

Partisans of divine foreknowledge claim that free will is incompatible with divine prescience. It follows that God is unable to grant free will to man. This opinion is both impious and contrary to what they themselves say, that the first man had free will before his fall (here Socinus refers to Calvin's *Institutiones*, lib. I, cap. XV, 8). However, having put this argument aside, Socinus then considers what reasons the adversaries could present in support of the first argument, and finds two:

1. That for God everything that exists is present, because he himself is beyond time and exists in eternity, where nothing is earlier or later. This reasoning cannot, however, be accepted, since time, whatever theologians may say, always has a past and future. Time did not begin with the creation of

13. Ibid., p. 456b.

14. BFP, *Op. Soc.* 1:544b–50a. I have reported Socinus's views on this topic in my book *Socynianizm a Oświecenie. Studia nad myśla filozoficzno-religijna arian w Polsce XVII wieku* [*Socinianism and enlightenment: studies on the philosophical-religious ideas of Arians in Poland in the seventeenth century*] (Warsaw: Państwowe Wydawnictwo Naukowe, 1966), pp. 270–73 and n. 10.

the world. Only the measuring of time began with the creation of the sun and stars. Therefore even for God, past, present, and future exist. Consequently, God knows things past, present, and future as such.

It must be observed incidentally that Socinus refers to the notion of *absolute time*, as did Gassendi later in the seventeenth century and Newton after him. Whether these notions of absolute time are really identical cannot be answered with certainty. The matter requires further investigation.

2. It can be said that God is omniscient, and that if he should not know something, he would not be omniscient. But even this argument is not convincing. God really knows everything, but only those things that are "capable of being known" *(quae scibilia sunt)*. Future contingencies are not in this category.

To disprove the second argument, the question must be put differently. Partisans of divine foreknowledge claim that divine foreknowledge is incompatible with free will. We claim the same, adds Socinus, and we stand fast by it. The question arises, which is more probable: That God refused free will to man to preserve divine foreknowledge, or that he granted free will and renounced foreknowledge? If we accept that there is no free will in man, there results the absurd situation that God is the cause of human sins. There is nothing absurd, however, in maintaining that not all is known to God by unerring knowledge. Indeed, is it essential for God to have this foreknowledge? Is it not enough that God, by his unlimited power, wisdom, and knowledge, governs and directs everything, so that God will always direct whatever man does to his glory? Conversely, acceptance of the thesis of foreknowledge makes God a passive witness of all events *(Deus otiosus)*, removing him from constant care of the people, and the immediate direction of the affairs of the world.

Essential Truths; Anthropomorphic Conception of God
To the extent that Socinus stresses obedience to the moral commandments of the Gospel, he somewhat devalues religious dogma and religious knowledge. This devaluation is not absolute, because without some knowledge of religion there is no belief in Christ, and belief, however it may be understood, is a condition of salvation. This devaluation takes two forms: first, Socinus is convinced that only belief in a small number of religious dogmas, the so-called "essential truths," is required for salvation; secondly, he is convinced that erroneous religious views do not prevent salvation. Only acts contrary to the Gospel's ethics make salvation impossible. Essential truths are, generally, those without which faith in Christ and the fulfillment of his promises are impossible. [15] These truths are clear and commonly understandable. Even views totally erroneous and noxious, such as belief in the Trinity and in predestination, do not rule out salvation, though they may make it difficult.

15. *Epitome Colloquii*, p. 16.

These notions were presented with clarity and proper argumentation by Socinus in theological seminars held towards the end of his life in Raków in the years 1601–02.[16] It is also worth noting that in these same Raków lectures, Socinus formulated his views regarding hell.[17] He was of the opinion that expressions such as "punishments of hell," "eternal condemnation," and "eternal suffering" are metaphors that Jesus intentionally used in order to adapt his doctrine to the mode of thinking of those whom he taught. It must be accepted, therefore, that not all shall rise on the day of the last judgment. The thesis that the impious shall be left to their fate, that is, eternal death, nonexistence;—and the obedient and just shall be called to eternal glory, may be attacked, Socinus said, on the following grounds: (1) Justice requires that the wicked should be punished. (2) People knowing that they will not suffer after death shall persist in their sins.

The first of these arguments Socinus answered as follows: If it seems unjust that the wicked should not be punished, it would be even more unjust—and this would be the greatest injustice—if God, who made man mortal, should then make him immortal in order to make him suffer. It is more acceptable that the impious shall rise on the day of judgment, see the glory of God, and then die forever. The latter view, however, seemed to Socinus less likely than the previous one, that is, that their fate is simply nonexistence.

The second argument Socinus dealt with as follows: They are in error who think that people may be forced to reform and repent by the threat of hell. It is possible that such a threat would be a deterrent if punishments were visible and could be tested visually. He who will not reform because of a reward as magnificent as eternal life offers little hope of being restrained by the fear of punishment. He who will not believe in a reward will not believe in a punishment.

Rationalism and Agnosticism

If there is divine revelation, human minds not only may grasp it and interpret it independently, but it is essential that they should, since otherwise revelation would be unnecessary.[18] To be understandable, revelation must be given in a form and expressed in categories accessible to the human mind. Revelation must follow the principles of reason. If a religious doctrine contains teachings contrary to reason, this doctrine is untrue in those points contrary to reason. Such untrue views and teachings must be absolutely rejected, even if partisans of them invoke the greatest authorities. To Socinus, there is on earth no greater authority for a man than his own reason.

16. Ibid., p. 16, p. 63.
17. "De statu mortuorum usque ad diem ultimum," in *Epitome Colloquii*, pp. 88–102.
18. BFP, *Op. Soc.*, 1:343a.

Although Socinus stressed that revelation must be interpreted by human reason, he claimed that reason on its own is unable to know God and things divine. There is no natural religion. Entire nations have no idea of the existence of God. Here Socinus referred to the recent discovery of primitive peoples in Brazil. The only source of the knowledge of God is divine revelation. He who is not reached by divine revelation is unable to have a premonition of God's existence.[19]

The question then arises, how do we know that Scripture, which allegedly contains the words of God, was divinely inspired? Or how do we know that the word, which is reputedly divine, really comes from God? Catholicism appeals primarily to the testimony of the Church, whose authority is a guarantee of the authenticity of God's word. This is the position that was first expressed by St. Augustine: *Ego Evangelio non crederem nisi me commoveret auctoritas Ecclesiae* ("I would not believe in the Gospel, if it were not for the authority of the Church"). Protestantism points to the "internal testimony of the Holy Spirit" *(testimonium Spiritus Sancti internum)*. Socinus, who rejected both the authority of the Church and the supernatural inspiration of the Holy Spirit, sought what might be called today a naturalistic solution to the question of authority.

Socinus distinguishes the following: (1) There are people who, though dubious of the authority of Scripture, agree that Christian religion is true; (2) there are also those who reject this opinion and either doubt that it is the true religion, or simply think it false. The second variant includes, according to Socinus, two classes of peoples: those who think that there is, or that there may exist, a true religion, and those who think that there is no true religion at all.

As regards the first variation, Socinus thinks that it is easy to prove the authenticity of revelation. It is enough to refer to his philosophical and historical argument given in *De Sacrae Scripturae Auctoritate*. For non–Christians who believe that there is a true religion, Socinus suggests a comparison of Christianity with other religions, which should prove its superiority and excellence. For convinced atheists, Socinus counsels the use of rational arguments but concludes that there are no arguments that would prove, *without doubt*, that God exists and that Christianity is a true religion. "It is certain," he wrote in *De Sacrae Scripturae Auctoritate,* "that whoever considers religion as a human invention and ridicules it, thinking that it is vain to expect God's reward for just deeds and punishment for wicked deeds, will also ridicule miracles reducing them to natural causes."[20]

---

19. *De Sacrae Scripturae Auctoritate*, BFP, *Op. Soc.*, 1:273b; *Praelectiones theologicae*, in ibid., pp. 537–539b. Socinus's views on natural religion and differences in this question between Socinus and later Socinianism, beginning with Crell, are treated in detail in chap. 2 of my book *Socynianizm a Oświecnie Socinianism and Enlightenment*, "Socinus and Crell, Divergencies on Their Views of Natural Religion," pp. 78–104.

20. *De Sacrae Scripturae Auctoritate*, BFP, *Op. Soc.*, 1:279b–280a.

What, therefore, is the reason why some believe in God and revelation while others do not, if rational arguments are not decisive? Christian churches explain it by means of God's grace. Socinus rejected this explanation. Acknowledgment of God's existence and of the true nature of Christian religion depends, in the last resort, on a moral position: By the wisest ordinance of God, truths of religion are not self-evident, so a possibility of choice between virtue and wickedness exists in man. The reward of immortality promised by the Gospels is so great and desirable that there is no one who would not do even more than required by Christ's commands, should it be certain that the promises of Christ are true. Because reward is not so certain, wicked people, or those who do not love virtue for itself, prefer not to believe in its reality and possibility. Those who love virtue easily believe in God. The fact that religious truths are not indisputable makes it possible to distinguish between the wicked and just.[21]

ROLE IN THE CHURCH   Socinus's doctrine became, in the beginning of the seventeenth century, the official doctrine of the Church of the Polish Brethren, whose followers came to be called Socinians.

In the generation that followed Socinus, however, Socinianism underwent certain modifications. More stress was put on the rational elements in the doctrine, and it was emphasized that Socinianism is a "rational religion" (*religio rationalis*). The view of Socinus that there is no natural religion was abandoned, because it was thought that this thesis devalued the role and function of reason. From the end of the second decade of the seventeenth century, Socinians were proclaiming the opposite view.

Later, as attacks on Socinianism increased in Poland as well as in Western Europe, and as both Catholic and Protestant branded Socinianism the most dangerous of heresies, Socinian theologians began to modify other aspects of the doctrine, probably to make it less shocking and more acceptable to Christian opinion. In the second half of the seventeenth century the view on Jesus and the Atonement of the Socinians was given a more moderate form.

In 1658 the diet of the Commonwealth of Poland passed a resolution prohibiting Antitrinitarianism under penalty of death. The Polish Brethren were given the choice either to convert to some other Christian denomination that was accepted in the country or to leave Poland in three years' time. The resolution seems today an act of religious fanaticism, as it certainly was. It should be considered however, in the light of the general conditions then prevailing in Europe. Catholic Poland was still officially tolerant toward other

---

21. This question is treated in detail in my book *Socinianism and Enlightenment*, chap. 1, "Criteria of the Truth of Christianity according to Faustus Socinus," pp. 15–77.

Protestant churches after this resolution, although their development was in fact restricted. A mere ten years earlier, in 1648, the English parliament had passed an ordinance penalizing Antitrinitarian confession by death (the Draconic Ordinance). Finally, eighteen years later in 1685, when the Edict of Nantes was revoked in France, the Huguenots became subject to brutal repression which caused their mass exodus from France.

At any rate, the 1658 resolution brought an end to the Antitrinitarian church in Poland. The majority of Polish Brethren accepted Catholicism; a minority chose emigration. The main body of emigrants went to Transylvania, where the Antitrinitarian church continued to function officially. The intellectual elite went west to settle in Holland, where the Polish Brethren found support and assistance among sympathizers, mostly Remonstrants. There they continued their publishing activities, the main result of which was the publication in Amsterdam (1665–68) of a monumental work in several folio volumes: *Bibliotheca Fratrum Polonorum quos Unitarios vocant . . .* [The library of the Polish Brothers, who are called Unitarians]. The *Bibliotheca* included writings of some leading theoreticians and theologians of the Socinian movement, beginning with the complete works of Socinus.

The vigorous propaganda effort conducted by the Polish Brethren and their sympathizers in Western Europe during the seventeenth century, which continued even after their exile from Poland, had some effect, especially in Holland and Great Britian. In addition, the harsh anti–Socinian edicts and the numerous theological tracts branding this doctrine as the most pernicious of the heresies excited curiosity and interest about the sect.

Socinianism, once expelled from Poland, was never reborn as a church, and its doctrines were nowhere accepted in their entirety. However, many of the ideas that it proclaimed were accepted by sympathizers among independent theologians of liberal tendencies—ideas such as the following: the view that religion should follow the principles of reason; the Unitarian conceptions of God; the irenic idea linked to the doctrine of essential truth; the view that salvation is possible in all Christian churches on condition of fulfillment of the moral commandments of the Gospel; and finally the principle of religious tolerance, to which Socinus's successors, beginning with Crell, devoted a good deal of attention.[22]

These and similar ideas were shared by thinkers in other religious centers, but orthodox theologians erroneously attributed the main source of all these ideas to Socinianism. Hence, at the end of the seventeenth and in the course of the eighteenth century, they branded as Socinianism all religious opinions that gravitated toward liberal and rationalistic opinions. On the other hand, the charge of Socinianism, which was so compromising to ortho-

22. The Socinians' attitude to toleration is discussed in my book *Z zagadnień tolerancji w Polsce XVII wieku* [Problems of toleration in Poland in seventeenth century], Warsaw: Państwowe Wydawnictwo Naukowe, 1958, Part 2: "Tolerance and Religion."

dox theologians, had a positive connotation to the ideologists of the Enlightenment. In the milieu of the Enlightenment it was strongly stressed, often with exaggeration, that Socinian doctrine had embraced concepts of great worth for the rationalist and humanistic tradition. Therefore, almost all leading representatives of the intellectual movement who consciously and frankly proclaimed themselves to be transmitters of that tradition considered Socinianism to be the forerunner of the Enlightenment.

CONTRIBUTORS

RONALD E. DIENER, Th.D., Harvard University, is executive director of Ohionet and editor of *Ohionetwork*. He has served as the director of the Center for Reformation Research in St. Louis, Kentucky.

JOHN PATRICK DONNELLY, S.J., who received his doctorate from the University of Wisconsin at Madison, is associate professor in the Department of History at Marquette University. His publications include *Reform and Renewal* and *Calvinism and Scholasticism in Vermigli's Doctrine of Man and Grace*.

OLIVIER FATIO, Th.D., University of Geneva, is currently dean of the theological faculty and professor of church history at the University of Geneva. Among his books are *Méthode et théologie: Lambert Daneau et les débuts de la scholastique réformée* and *"Nihil pulchrius ordine," Lambert Daneau aux Pays-Bas*.

ROBERT M. KINGDON, Ph.D., Columbia University, is director of the Institute for Research in the Humanities and professor of history at the University of Wisconsin at Madison. His most recent publication is *The Political Thought of Peter Martyr Vermigli: Selected Texts and Commentary*.

ROBERT KOLB, Ph.D., University of Wisconsin at Madison, is assistant professor in the departments of Religion and History at Concordia College, St. Paul. He has written *Andreae and the Formula of Concord, Six Sermons on the Way to Lutheran Unity* and *Nikolaus von Amsdorf (1483–1565), Popular Polemics in the Preservation of Luther's Legacy*.

FRED KRAMER is professor emeritus at Concordia Theological Seminary. He recently published a two-volume translation of Martin Chemnitz's *Examination of the Council of Trent*.

ZBIGNIEW OGONOWSKI, Ph.D., Warsaw University, is professor and chairman of the Department of History of Modern Philosophy and Social Thought at the Polish Academy of Sciences in Warsaw. He has recently published studies on the thought of John Locke and the philosophy and social thought of seventeenth-century Poland.

OLIVER K. OLSON, Th.D., Hamburg University, is a research fellow at the Herzog-August Library, Wolfenbüttel, and visiting associate professor of theology at Marquette University.

211

JILL RAITT, Ph.D., Divinity School of the University of Chicago, is associate professor of historical theology at the Divinity School of Duke University. She is the author of *The Eucharistic Theology of Theodore Beza: The Development of the Reformed Tradition*.

DERK VISSER, Ph.D., Bryn Mawr College, is professor of history at Ursinus College. His publications include "Reality and Rhetoric in Abelard's *Story of My Calamities*" and "Hubert Languet, Crypto Calvinism and the *Vindiciae Contra Tyrannos*."

ROBERT C. WALTON, Ph.D., Yale University, is professor of theology and director of the Seminar für neue Kirchen- und Theologiegeschichte at Westfälische Wilhelms-Universität in Münster. Among his works are "Bullinger und die Autorität der Heiligen Schrift" in *Festschrift für Kurt Aland* and "Europäische Kirchengeschichte aus amerikanischer Sicht."

GEORGE HUNTSTON WILLIAMS, Ph.D., Union Theological Seminary, is Hollis Professor of Divinity Emeritus at the Divinity School of Harvard University. His most recent publications include *The Mind of John Paul II Wojtyla: The Origins of His Thought and Action, The Polish Brethren, 1601–1685,* and *American Universalism.*

INDEX

Aargau, 69
Accident, accidental, 9, 118
Adiaphora, Adiaphorists, 4, 22, 28, 63, 65
Agnosticism, 205–07
Agricola, 27
Alba, duke of, 10
Albert Hohenzollern, duke, 159
Albert the Great, 142
Albrecht, duke (of Prussia), 40, 41, 42
Alfonso, Alvara, 142
Alloeosis, 79
Anabaptism, Anabaptists, 24, 28, 56, 65, 85, 93, 186
Andrada, Jacob Payva, 45, 46
Andreae, Jakob, 31, 50, 53–68, 93, 95n38, 108, 136, 150; catechetical tracts, 55–56, 62, 64–65; "Confession and Brief Explanation of Certain Disputed Articles," 63–64; disputation with Ursinus re ubiquity, 121, 138; "Epitome" of *Formula of Concord*, 66–67; *Six Christian Sermons on the Divisions Which Have Continued to Surface . . . .*, 64–65; "Swabian Concord," 65, 66
Anhalt, Wolfgang von, 21
Anthropological pessimism, 198, 200
Antinomianism, 28
Antitrinitarianism, Antitrinitarians, 28, 65, 150, 190, 197, 198–200, 208. *See also* Polish Brethren
Antwerp, 10, 143
Apostles' Creed, 110
Apostolic succession, 73, 82, 168
Aquaviva, Claudius, 192
Aquinas, Thomas, St., 74, 115, 142; *Summa Theologica*, 116
Arians. *See* Antitrinitarians
Arians, Polish. *See* Polish Brethren
Aristotle, 11, 13, 27, 116, 118, 152, 158; *Nicomachean Ethics*, 114; *Physics*, 114; *Politics*, 114
Aristotelianism, Ciceronian, 112

Arius, 150
Arminius, Arminianism, 87, 110
Arnold, Gottfried: *Unparteyische Kirchen- und Ketzer-Historie*, 35
Athanasius, 74, 186
Atonement (dogma), 199, 200, 207
Augsburg, 154; Peace of *(1555)*, 8, 36, 55, 103, 154. *See also* Diet of Augsburg
Augsburg Confession *(Confessio Augustana)*, 8, 21, 26, 44, 50, 51, 68, 136, 137, 151, 155, 171; its *Apologia*, 42, 122; *Variata* edition, 8, 127, 128
Augsburg Interim, 3, 21, 22, 36, 54
August, Elector of Saxony, 11, 25, 53, 56, 57, 66, 67, 68, 125n16, 133n31
Augustine, St., 45, 74, 75, 78, 108, 111, 131, 147, 148, 158, 170, 206; *De haeresibus ad Quodvultdeum*, 106, 115; *Enchiridion*, 114–15
Authority, 26; of church and clergy, 148, 168–69, 172; of civil officials, 4; crisis of, in Protestantism, 16; in doctrine, 9; of kings, 101; of pope, 82, 168; of Scripture, 16, 206–07

Baptism, 45, 46, 58, 78, 80, 83, 97–98, 148, 191, 196
Baronius, Caesar, 13, 35; *Annales ecclesiastici*, 149, 161, 182
Barthold, Laurentius, 39
Basel, 195
Basil of Caesarea, 186
Báthory, Stephen, king, 165, 178, 179, 181
Bavaria, 143, 151
Bellarmine, Robert, cardinal, 35, 46, 110, 187
"Bergic Book," 67
Bern, 91, 92, 144
Bernard of Clairvaux, 48
Beza, Theodore (Dieudonné de Besze; Theodorus Beza Vezelii), 5n18, 58, 59, 60, 83, 86, 89–104, 126n20, 193; *Abraham sacrifiant*, 91, 100–01; *Alphabetum graecum*, 91; *Annotationes,*

213

Beza, Theodore (*continued*)
91, 100, 101, 114; *Confession de la foi chrestienne*, 91, 94, 128; *Confessio Christianae*, 85; and Daneau, 107, 108, 110, 111, 113, 115, 116; *Du droit des Magistrats sur leurs subiets*, 101; "In Obitu Joannis Dampetri," 90n3; *Poemata*, 90; *Quaestionum et Responsionum Christianorum libellus*, 94, 97; *Summa totius christianismi*, 116; *Tabula praedestinationis*, 91; translation of New Testament into Latin, 91, 101; translation of Psalms, 101
Bible, 16, 40, 70, 74, 84, 206–07; New Testament, 4, 10, 32, 47, 61, 76, 83, 85, 95–96, 131, 148, 171, 190, 198–99; Old Testament, 91, 167, 189n31, 190; Vulgate, 45. *See also* Scripture
Bible de Genève, 100
Biblical fideism, 7n32, 11–12, 16
Bibliotheca Fratrum Polonorum quos Unitarios vocant . . ., 208
Birkenhain, Abel, 123n9, 126n20, 138
Bishop(s), 36n17, 37
Bolsec, Jerome, 91
Book of Concord, 26, 36, 126, 136
Boquin, Peter, 134
Bossuet: *Variations*, 150
Bourges, 105; university of, 89–90
Braun, Joseph, 6
Braun, Konrad: *Adversus novam Historiam ecclesiasticam*, 161n7
Braunsberg (town), 163, 170, 177
Braunschweig, 25–26, 42–43, 44, 63
Braunschweig-Wolfenbüttel (duchy), 43
Bremgarten, 69, 71, 72
Brenz, Johann, 55, 56, 57, 58, 59, 62, 79, 93, 95n38, 137, 144, 150, 155; Bullinger's struggle against, 72; *Confessio Wirtembergica*, 160; two natures of Christ, 60, 61, 87
Breslau, 122, 124, 125
Brethren of the Common Life, 69, 74
Brück, Christian, 9–10, 23
Bullinger, Heinrich, 69–87, 91n19, 93n30, 104, 124, 138; *About the Shameless Wickedness of the Anabaptists*, 85; *Catechesis pro adultioribus scripta*, 85; *Commentaries on the Pauline Epistles*, 85; *Concerning the Appointment and Function of Bishops . . .*, 85–86; *Concerning the Authority of Scripture*, 85; *Concerning the Prophet's Office*, 85; *De conciliis*, 169; *De origine erroris in Divorum ac simulacrorum cultu*, 90; *De Testamento*, 80; *Decades*, 74, 85, 86; *Der alte Glaub*, 80; *History of the Reformation*, 85; *The Origins of the Ana-*baptists, 85; *Summa Christlicher Religion*, 85; *Treatise on Christian Marriage*, 71, 85; *Zürich Letters*, 86
Buoncampagni, Hugo (later Gregory XIII), 158
Büsser, Fritz, 85

Caesarius, Johannes, 112
Cajetan, cardinal (Thomas de Vio): *Tractatus de Missae Sacrificio*, 166
Cajetanists, 171
Calvin, 5n18, 58, 83, 84, 89n1, 92, 101, 102, 109, 116, 124, 127, 137, 147, 152; on baptism, 97–98; catechism of, 136; on Christ, 95, 150; and Daneau, 106, 111, 114, 115, 116; designated Beza his successor, 87, 92; eucharistic theology of, 186; favored conciliation, 136; indebtedness to Luther, 128; *Institutes of the Christian Religion (Institutiones)*, 85, 94, 135, 203; on John the Baptist, 149–50; on justification, 96; library of, 93; on predestination, 91, 99
Calvinism, Calvinists, 57, 58, 61, 92, 104, 108, 111, 137, 175, 177, 190; in Cracow, 170, 179–80, 193; Geneva international center of, 87; Crypto-Calvinism, 22n4; Crypto-Calvinist party, 68, 111, 123n9
Campion, Edmund, 178
Canisius (Kanijs), Peter, 28, 141–56, 161, 163; *Catechismus minimus*, 146; *De Maria Virgine Incomparabili*, 150; *Iohannis Baptistae Historia Evangelica*, 149–50; *A Mirror for Soldiers*, 145; *Opus Catechisticum*, 146; *Parvus Catechismus Catholicorum*, 146; *Summa Doctrinae Christianae*, 146, 148; works, 142, 145–46, 149–50, 154, 155–56
Canon, 77
Carolinum, 86
Carthusians, 141
Cartwright, Thomas, 86, 87
Casimir, Johann (son of Frederick III), 58, 103, 125, 126
Cassiodorus, Flavius M. A.: *Historia Tripartita*, 45
Castellio, Sebastian, 91, 124
Catechetics, 32, 38
Catechism(s), 55, 56, 145–48; Calvin, 136; Canisius, 145, 146–48, 155–56; Heidelberg, 63, 124, 127, 128, 129–31, 134–36, 138, 139; Luther, 26; Major and Minor (Ursinus), 127–28; Moibanus, 122; Racovian, 182; Roman (*1564*), 173

Catherine Hapsburg, consort of Sigismund II
    Augustus, 162, 163, 164
Catherine de Medici, 92
Catholic Church. *See* Roman Catholic Church
Causes (instruments), principle of, 94, 96–97,
    98, 100
Chalcedon, 47. *See also* Christ: of Chalcedonian
    formula
Chandieu, Antoine de, 107, 111; *Confirmation de
    la discipline ecclesiastique . . .* , 117–18
Charity, 147, 169
Charles V, 3, 16, 20, 54, 143, 151, 159
Charles IX, 181
Charles Emmanuel of Savoy, 102
Chemnitz, Martin, 26, 31, 39–51, 63, 65, 93,
    95, 96, 108; and Andreae, 57; *De duabus naturis
    in Christo*, 47; *Examen Concilii Tridentini*, 44–
    46, 50; *Harmonia Evangelistarum*, 44; *Loci
    theologici*, 44; work on *Formula of Concord*, 66–
    67
Christ: Ascension, 60, 96; of Chalcedonian
    formula, 75; first of Elect, 99; powers as God-
    man, 95–96; preexistence of, 198, 199; pre-
    figurations of, 80; as Priest for eternity, 167;
    as Son of God, 199–200; teachings of, 202; two
    natures of, 12, 22n4, 27, 30, 47–48, 58,
    60–61, 63, 68, 72, 79, 80, 93, 95–96. *See
    also* Ubiquity (doctine), Ubiquitarians
Christianity, 135, 147. *See also* Church, the
Christology, 12, 60–61, 63, 65, 66, 67, 74, 93,
    95, 96, 164; Antitrinitarianism and, 198–200
Christonomy, 15
Christoph, duke, 54–55, 56, 57, 62, 63
Christopher, duke (of Württemberg), 160
Chrysostom, John, St., 45, 158, 186
Church, the, 55, 68, 127, 132–33, 148, 169,
    200; authority of, 82–83; primitive, 73–74;
    universal, 194
Church discipline, 36–37, 55, 73, 86, 99–100,
    109, 134, 167, 169; Daneau's contribution
    to, 117–18; struggle re, 126, 133–34, 138.
    See also Disciplinists
Church Fathers, 70, 73–74, 77, 111, 114–15,
    119, 129, 142, 158, 167; Chemnitz's study of,
    40, 41, 43, 45, 47–48
Church government, 16, 62
Church history, 33, 34, 45. See also *Magdeburg
    Centuries*
Church militant, 81–82
Church of England, 86–87
Church reform, 77, 168, 170
Church-state relations, 3–6, 9, 16, 36–37, 68,

    75, 81, 85–86, 118, 119, 133n31, 134;
    Chemnitz on, 42–43; in Geneva, 93, 101–102;
    in Leiden, 109–10, 119
Church triumphant 79, 82
Church visible and invisible, 81–83, 132–33,
    148
Chytraeus, David, 24, 27, 31, 50, 57, 65, 66
Cicero, 27, 142, 158
Cipelli, Giambattista (Baptista Egnatius), 1
Circumcision, 80
Clergy, 77–78, 82, 85–86; Catholic, 153, 180;
    celibacy of, 150, 185
Codex Bezae, 100, 103
Coligny, Gaspard de, 92, 99
*Colloquies: Lutheran/Roman Catholic (Worms,
    1557)*, 8, 9, 56, 124, 139, 155; Lutheran/
    Reformed (Marburg, *1529*), 71, (Maulbronn,
    1564), 63, 121, 126, 129n26, (Montbéliard,
    1586), 58, 59, 93; Roman Catholic/Reformed
    (Bern, *1528*), 71; (Poissy, *1561*), 57, 92,
    172; Inter-Lutheran (Altenburg, *1568–69*),
    25, (Weimar Disputation), 23–24, 29n11
Cologna, 141–42; university of, 70, 141
Commendone, John Francis, cardinal, 162–63
Commonwealth of the Two Peoples, 157
Communicatio idiomatum (communication of
    attributes), 47–48, 63, 72
Communion, lay, 8, 148, 161, 162, 164, 167,
    171–72, 173
Communion of saints, 132
Concordianist movement, 67
Condemnation, 130–31. *See also* Excommunica-
    tion
Confederation of Warsaw of *1573*, 165, 180,
    193, 194
Confessions: of Andreae, 60–61, 63–64;
    common, for German Lutherans, 60, 62; doc-
    trine as, 12; of Faith, French, 93; First Hel-
    vetic, 72; Hosius's *Confessio Catholicae fidei
    Christiana*, 159–60; Lutheran (*Formula of Con-
    cord*), 50; Magdeburg, 1550: *Instruction and
    Warning*, 4; Racovian, 182; Second Helvetic,
    72, 73, 77, 86, 104; Swiss-Palatine, 163; of
    the Theologians and Ministers of Heidelberg,
    128; Tridentine, 173; of Wigand, 26–27, 33;
    Württemberg, 60–61, 160. *See also* Augsburg
    Confession
Confirmation, 46, 148
Confutationsbuch (Book of Confutation, 1559), 8,
    23n6, 25
Consensus of Sandomir, 190
Consistories, 36–37

Constitutiones Clementinae, 167
Consubstantiation, 126n20
Conversion, 49, 62–63, 170, 184
Council of Trent, 3, 56, 72, 136, 144, 146, 155,
    159, 167–69; catechisms of, 147; Canisius
    theologian at, 143; Chemnitz's *Examen* on, 44–
    46, 50; Period II, 160, 161, 168–69, 171;
    Period III, 157, 160, 161, 164, 165–66, 170–
    73; ratification of decrees of, 162–63, 164
Counter-Reformation, 87, 148, 157, 166, 175,
    193
Couvillon, Jean, 153
Covenant, 74, 75, 76, 79–80
Cracovianus, Stanislaus (pseud.). *See* Hosius,
    Stanislas
Cracow, 158–59, 165, 178, 196; Calvinism in,
    170, 179–80, 193
Cramer, Daniel, 181, 182
Crato, Johann, 122, 123, 125, 134, 136, 138
Creeds, 26, 73, 75, 150; Nicene, 150; Niceno-
    Constantinopolitan, 75. *See also* Confessions
Crell, Fortunas, 206n19, 208
Curaeus, Joachim: *Exegesis perspicua,* 22n4
Cyprian, 74, 107
Cyril of Alexandria St., 142
Czech Brethren, 160, 167, 175, 190

Damascene, John, 47; *The Orthodox Faith,* 116
Damnation, 49, 134
Daneau, Lambert (Lambertus Danaeus), 58, 103,
    105–19; autobiography, 106; commentary
    on Augustine's *De haeresibus ad Quodvultdeum,*
    106; *Compendium sacrae theologiae,* 110, 117;
    De Jurisdictione omnium judicum dialogus, 105;
    Elenchi haereticorum, 108, 112; *Ethice christiana,*
    108, 111, 114, 117; *In Ev. secundum Matthaeum
    commentarii brevissimi,* 114; *In Petri Lombardi
    librum primum sententiarum commentarius,* 115;
    In prophetas minores commentarii, 114; *In tres
    Joannis et unicam Judae Epistolam,* 114; *Methodus
    tractandae scripturae,* 108, 113; *Nihil pulchrius
    ordine,* 117; *Orationis Dominicae Explicatio,* 114;
    Physica Christiana, 108, 114; *Politice christiana,*
    111, 114; *Priorem Epistolam ad Timotheum com-
    mentarius,* 114; *Quaestionum in Ev. secundum
    Marcum liber unus,* 114; *Les Sorciers,* 108; trans-
    lations by, 107n9; *Transubstantiation,* 113;
    *Vetustissimarum primi mundi antiquitatum libri
    III,* 111
Deacons, 94, 118
d'Etaples, Lefèvre (Faber Stapulensis), 70, 74,
    89

Dialectic, 105, 106, 112–14, 116. *See also*
    Method
Diener, Ronald E., 19–38
Diet of Augsburg, *(1566),* 24, 86, 103–04
Diet of Parczow, 163
Dilligen, university of, 151
Dilthey, Wilhelm, 15
Disciplinists, 133
Divine foreknowledge, 201, 203–04
Doctrine, 9, 75; pure, 12; and reason, 205
Donnelly, John Patrick, 141–56
Draconic Ordinance, 208
du Bourg, Anne, 105, 106
Duns Scotus, John 74n5, 142

Eber, Paul, 56, 63
Ecclesiastica historia. See *Magdeburg Centuries*
Ecclesiastical Ordinances of Geneva, 118
Eck, Johann, 143
Ecumenical Councils, 73, 168, 169
Ecumenism, 136, 190
Edict of Beaulieu, 107
Education: as conversion, 170, 184. *See also*
    Jesuits, colleges of
Edward VI, king of England, 81
Elders, 99, 118
Elect, the; Election, 49, 51, 61, 65, 82, 97–99,
    122n3, 129, 200; in Andreae, 59–60; in
    Bullinger, 82, 84; sacraments and, 78, 98;
    in Daneau, 116; in Ursinus, 122, 132–33,
    134. *See also* Predestination
Elizabeth I, queen of England, 86, 103
Embden, Levin von, 21, 22n5, 23, 24
England, 14, 86–87, 93, 100, 103, 163, 178;
    Antitrinitarians penalized in, 208
Episcopacy (doctrine), 100, 168, 173; *jure divino*
    character of, 172; residency of, 168, 172
Erasmians, 148, 158, 159
Erasmus, Desiderius, 1, 70, 74, 87, 114, 142,
    149, 158n4; *Annotations,* 86; Hosius and, 158–
    59; *Paraphrases of the New Testament,* 86
Erastianism, Erastians, 87, 133n31
Erastus, Thomas, 73, 87, 133, 138
Eucharist, 131, 150, 186; theology of, 22, 27,
    91n19, 150, 183, 186. *See also* Communion,
    lay; Lord's Supper
Eusebius of Caesarea, 35
Eutychianism, 61
Evangelical church, 53, 54–56, 127, 128, 129,
    136
Evangelical Reformation in Germany, 136
Evangelienbuch, 10

Excommunication, 83, 118, 133–34; right of, 72

Faber, Basilius, 34
Faith, 51, 55, 76, 79, 97–98, 129, 147, 200, 201–03; dialectic and, 112; historical, 97; justification through, 59, 128, 129, 134; and sacraments, 132; universality of, 168
Fall, the, 84, 94, 201, 203
Fanaticism, religious, 197, 207
Farel, William, 91n19, 60
Fatio, Olivier, 105–19
Favre, Pierre, 142
Ferdinand I, emperor, 8, 56, 154, 155, 161, 171
Ferdinand II, emperor, 145
Ferdinand of Austria, 146
Ferinarius, Johann, 123, 138
Ficino, Marsilio, 73
Flacian circle, 4, 5, 7–8, 9. See also Gnesio-Lutherans
Flacius Illyricus, Matthias, 1–17, 25n8, 62–63, 65, 67, 128, 137, 138, 155; biographies of, 1, 17, 29; Book of Confutation, 8; Catalogus testium veritatis, 1, 14, 33–34; Clavis Scripturae, 10, 11, 15; conflict with Wigand, 29–30; De Praetorum Libertate, 9n38; De vocabulo fidei, 2–3; edited church-historical documents, 15; edited Magdeburg Centuries, 14, 33, 149; Glossa compendaria, 10; and Gnesio-Lutheranism, 23n6; Liber de veris et falsis adiaphoris, 5; On the Materials and Limits of the Sciences and the Errors of Philosophy in Divine Matters, 11; sin as substance of man, 9, 13, 24, 28, 29–30n11; in Weimar Disputation, 23–24; works, 3, 5, 10–11, 13–15
Flinsbach, Cunman, 60
Formula Consensus of 1675, 77
Formula of Concord, 13, 25n8, 43, 48, 49, 50–51, 57, 58, 65, 66–67, 92, 93, 104
Fortresse of Fathers (Puritan manifesto), 5
Foxe, John: Book of Martyrs, 14
France: Confession of Faith, 93; at Council of Trent (Period III), 172–73; Edict of Nantes, 208; Lutheran influence in, 57; ratification of decrees of Council of Trent, 162; Reformed Churches in, 91, 106, 107
Francis II of Tuscany, grand duke, 195, 196
Frankfurt on the Oder, university of, 39–40
"Frankfurt Recess," 8, 56, 127
Frederick III, elector, 63, 86, 125, 126, 134, 138, 163
Free will. See Will, freedom of

Fribourg, 144, 151
Fugger family, 154

Gaetano, Enrico, cardinal, 188
Gallus, Nicolaus, 4, 10, 21n3
Geldsetzer, Lutz, 17
Geneva, 87, 106–07, 108–09; Academy at, 92, 102–03, 107; church-state relations in, 93, 101–02; Ecclesiastical Ordinances of, 118
Gerhard, John, 44, 46, 51
Gerlach, Stefan, 108
German Reformed Church: corpus doctrinae of, 128–29, 136
Germany, 103; Catholicism in, 142–43; Evangelical areas of, 53, 54; federalism in, 25; Lutheranism in, 50, 51, 63–64; princes, 8–9, 103, 104, 154, 155; Protestantism in, 7, 36, 142–43, 151, 153–54, 155; religious unity in, 151
Gerson, Jean, 73, 74
Gnesio-Lutherans, 4, 23, 24–25, 29, 55, 56, 62, 66, 67, 123; and Andreae, 57, 65; differences with Philippists, 25, 64, 65; and ecclesiastical control, 68
God, 75–76, 94, 116; absolute sovereignty of, 75; anthropomorphic conception of, 204–05; relation with man, 80, 84
Gonzaga, Ercole, cardinal, 161, 162
Good works, 28, 63, 128, 147, 148–49, 150, 175
Göppingen, 54, 55, 91n19
Göppingen, university of, 33n14
Gospel, 11, 32, 78, 129, 130, 198; comfort of, 59, 61. See also Bible; Scripture
Government, 7, 72, 127, 187, 188–89. See also Church-state relations
Goulart, Simon, 107
Grace, 49, 70, 84, 95, 98, 169, 200, 202; and human will, 96; infused, 148, sacraments and, 79–80
Gregory I (the Great). See Popes
Gregory of Nazianzus, 186
Gropper, Johann, 143, 145
Grynaeus, Johann Jakob, 111, 116
Grzybowska, Zofia, 195–209
Guise, Charles de, 172
Guise family, 57, 103
Gwalter, Rudolf, 86, 110

Hagen, Bartholomaeus, 60
Hamburg, 7–8
Harmony of Confessions (Harmonia confessionum

Harmony of Confessions (continued)
  fidei), 104, 107
Harnack, Adolf von, 33n15
Hausammann, Susi, 74
Heidelberg, 123, 125–26
Heidelberg Catechism, 63, 124, 127, 128, 129–31, 134–36, 138, 139
Heinrich, Julius (son of Duke Julius), 43, 63
Helding, Michael, bishop, 5, 6, 8, 21, 27, 146
Heliand, 10
Hell, 205
Helmstadt, university of, 31
Hemmingsen, Niels, 111, 114
Henetus, Theodor (pseud.). *See* Flacius Illyricus, Matthias
Henrician Articles, 165
Henry IV, 93
Henry VIII, king of England, 85, 86
Henry of Valois, later Henry III of France, 165, 170, 180
Herburt, Valentine, bishop, 161
Heresy, heretics, 23n6, 112, 118, 154, 167, 170, 177, 181–82, 188, 193, 195; as danger to Polish-Lithuanian Commonwealth, 190; Flacius's sin as substance, 9, 13, 24, 28; punishment of, 194; and schism, 169, 185–86; Socinism, 207, 208
Hermeneutics, 15–16, 74, 114
Hesshus, Tilemann, 24, 25, 30n11, 65, 126n20; controversy with Wigand, 26, 29, 30–31, 37
Hoffaeus, Paul, 144, 150
Holy Communion. *See* Communion, lay; Lord's Supper
Holy Spirit, 74, 75–77, 78, 83, 84, 130, 206; in Beza, 95, 96–97, 100; in sacraments, 78–79; in Socinus, 200
Hosius, Stanislas (Stanislaw Hozjusz), 157–74, 177; biographies of, 157n1, 173; *Confessio Catholicae fidei Christiana,* 157, 159–60, 166, 169, 173; *Confutatio Prolegomenon Brentii,* 166; *De expresso Dei verbo libellus,* 160; *Dialogus de Calice,* 161; *Dialogus de eo . . . ,* 161; *Judicium et censura de judicio . . . ,* 163–64, *Solida Propugnatio,* 144; *Verae christianae catholicaeque doctrina solida pugnatio,* 160; works, 158, 160–61, 163–64, 166
Hotman, François, 105, 107
Huguenot Psalter, 101
Huguenots, 99, 101, 103, 172, 208
Human nature, 117. *See also* Man
Humanism, 70, 142, 175, 198
Hungary, 164; Reformed Church of, 86

Hus, John; Hussites, 8, 160n6, 161, 171, 190
Hyperius, Andreas, 111; *De Theologo,* 113; *Topica theologica,* 112
Hypocrites, 92, 131, 132–33
Hypostatic union, 47, 95, 11. *See also* Christ, two natures of

Immortality (reward of), 202, 203, 205, 207
Inclination, 202
Index of Forbidden Books, 167, 171; Revised, 173
Infallibility, 169
Ingolstadt, university of, 143, 151
Interim. *See* Augsburg Interim
Irenaeus, St., 45
Irenaeus, Christopher, 31n12, 74

Jagello, Catharine, 179
Jagello, Ladislao, grand duke, 157n2
Jagellonian, last, 165. *See also* Sigismund II Augustus
Jagellonian University, 158, 177
James, king of England and Scotland, 178
Jena, 32, 38; university of, 7, 21, 23, 24–25
Jerome, St., 45, 149
Jesuits, 28, 44, 61, 141, 163, 179; Canisius, 142–56; colleges of, 143, 151–52, 156, 163, 170, 177, 184, 197
Jesus. *See* Christ
Jewel, John, bishop, 86
Jews, 175, 190
Johann Albert, duke of Mecklenburg, 24
Johann Friedrich I, 9, 25
Johann Friedrich II, duke, 7, 8–9, 10, 23, 25, 62
Johann Wilhelm, duke, 23, 25, 64, 66
John III Vasa, 179, 180
John the Baptist, 149–50
Judex, Matthaeus, 22, 23, 24, 31n12, 32, 34–35
Julius, duke (of Braunschweig-Lüneburg), 26, 31
Julius, duke (of Braunschweig-Wolfenbüttel), 43, 57, 63, 64, 65
Justice, 147, 148–49, 199, 201, 202, 205
Justification, 12, 41, 55, 63, 116, 137; in Andreae, 59; in Beza, 95, 96, 98; in Bullinger, 74; by faith, 128, 129, 134; forensic, 12, 59; in Hosius, 169; in Osiander, 41, 42; and sanctification, 98–99; in Socinus, 200–03

Kalckbrenner, Gerard, 141
Kappel War, Second, 71–72
Kawerau, Gustav, 17

Kickel, Walter: *Vernunft und Offenbarung bei Theodor Beza*, 104
Kings, authority of, 101
Knox, John: *Monstrous Regiment of Women*, 103
Kolb, Robert, 53–68
Königsberg, 38, 42; university of, 26, 40, 41
Körner, Christoph, 66
Kramer, Fred, 39–51
Kromer, Martin, 165, 171

Lactantius, 74
Lang, A., 127, 128, 139
Languet, Hubert, 123, 125n16, 138
Lanspergius, Johannes, 141
Last Supper, 166–68
Latin rite, 5–6, 184–85
Lausanne, 92; Academy, 91
Lauterwar, Christian (pseud.). *See* Flacius Illyricus, Matthias
Law(s), 3, 12, 28; canon, 115; ceremonial, 80; ecclesiastical, 82–83, 189; four kinds of, 189, 191; judicial, 81; letter and spirit of, 77; in Luther, 11; moral, 81, 202, 203, 204–05; natural, 74; third use of, 28, 67
Laynez, Diego (Jacob), 143, 146, 155, 172
Leiden, university of, 103, 108, 109
Lejay, Claude, 143, 146, 151
Leo the Great, St., 142
Libellus reformationis, 171
Liberty, 188–89, 191
Lippomani, Aloysius: *Sanctorum priscorum patrum vitae*, 178
Lithuania, 157, 160, 164, 191. *See also* Polish-Lithuanian Commonwealth
Liturgy, 5–6, 16, 171, 187
Loci communes, 11, 32n13, 33, 40, 44, 70, 74
Loci dogmatici, 32, 33
Lombard, Peter, 70; *Sentences*, 108, 115
Lord's Supper (doctrine), 45, 58, 63, 65, 74, 83, 123, 126n20, 137; in Beza, 97; in Bullinger, 72, 80, 83; controversy re, 91, 92, 93; Holy Spirit and, 78; Lutheran doctrine re, 130; in Reformed teaching, 46–47; in Ursinus, 129–32, 136, 137, 139. *See also* Communion, lay; Eucharist; Real Presence
Low Countries, 103, 110
Loyola, Ignatius, St., 142, 152
Lübeck, 7–8
Lublin, palatine of, 177
Ludwig, duke, 64, 66
Ludwig, elector, 58, 126
Lüneburg, 7–8

Luppetino, Fra Baldo, 1–2, 10
Luther, 2, 4, 19, 20, 39, 40, 42, 44, 50, 58, 59, 62, 68, 70, 77, 92, 101, 135, 137, 158, 169, 173, 186; approved of armed resistance, 4–5; *The Babylonian Captivity*, 166; biblical fideism of, 7n32, 11–12, 16; Calvin's indebtedness to, 128; catechisms, 26, 145, 146, 147; on Christ's human nature, 61; Coburg letters of, 15; *Concilium Nationis Germanicae*, 168; criticized by Canisius, 150; death of, 20; defense of teaching of, 45; definition of sin, 148; doctrine, 8, 9; Flacius vowed to establish theological legacy of, 11–12, 17; letter and spirit in, 11; *On the Bondage of the Will*, 13; on predestination, 49; *sola fide* doctrine, 96, 148; works of, influenced Bullinger, 74; and Zwingli, 71
Lutheranism, 4–5, 7–8, 23n6, 36, 53, 73, 93, 137, 142–43, 151, 190; Aristotle in, 11; Christ's nature in, 95–96; controversy and disunity in, 7, 13, 44, 49, 50–51, 55, 56, 57, 58, 64, 91, 92; doctrine re Lord's Supper, 22n4, 48; evangelical, 57, 127, 129; in Germany, 50, 51, 63–64; impact of Chemnitz on, 50–51; orthodoxy of, 35, 62; in Polish-Lithuanian Commonwealth, 159, 160, 161, 164, 165, 167, 170, 173; predestination in, 48–49; and Reformed churches, 46–47; sacraments in, 130; theology in, 11–13; ubiquity in, 79; unity in, 62, 63, 64–68; in Venice, 1–2
Luykx, Boniface, 6

Madruzzo, Luigi, cardinal, 162
Magdeburg, 21–23, 32, 38, 39; Gnesio-Lutheran resistance in, 4–5, 7, 13, 21
Magdeburg Centuries (Ecclesiastica historica), 14, 33–35, 149–50, 161; Wigand's work on, 22–23, 24, 28–29, 33–35
Magistracy, magistrates, 72, 73, 81, 134, 190; in Geneva, 102; in Leiden, 109, 119
Major, Georg; Majorists, 12, 23, 28, 155
Man: role in salvation, 137, 198, 203; sin as substance of, 9, 13, 24, 28, 29–30n11
Manes; Manicheans, 13, 24, 28
Marguerite of Navarre, 89
Marian exile, 5n18, 86
Marot (translator of Psalms), 91, 101
Marriage, 83, 100
Marsilio of Padua, 85–86
Martyr, Peter, 116, 125, 138
Mary, mother of Jesus, 149, 150

Mass, the, 6, 24, 54, 70, 166–68, 171–72, 173.
    See also Liturgy
Maulbronn. *See* Colloquies
"Maulbronn Formula," 66
Maximilian II, emperor, 104, 161–62, 164, 166
Mazovia, 176
Mecklenburg (duchy), 24, 32, 37
Meilan articles of *1531*, 72
Melanchthon, Philip, 3, 20, 23, 25n8, 27, 56,
    68, 86, 111, 112, 116; attacked by Canisius,
    150; and Chemnitz, 40, 41, 42; at Colloquy of
    Worms, 155; and Daneau, 113, 114; doctrine
    departed from Calvin and Luther, 137; and
    Flacius, 3–4, 6, 7, 9, 12, 15, 17; forensic
    justification, 12, 59; influence on Bullinger,
    70, 74; as leader of Adiaphorists, 22; *Loci
    communes*, 11, 32n13, 33, 40, 44, 70, 74;
    Lord's Supper, 126n20; philosophical
    humanism of, 7n32; Ursinus's loyalty to,
    122–23, 124, 128, 138. *See also* Philippism,
    Philippists
Menius, Justus, 137
Mercersberg Movement, 127n22
Messina, 143
Method, methodology: in Wigand, 31–35; in
    Flacius Illyricus, 11, 14–15; in Chemnitz, 45;
    in Bullinger, 73; in Daneau, 105, 106, 112–
    14, 115, 116, 117; in Ursinus, 123n8, 124,
    131, 136
Milton, John, 194
Ministry, 75, 99–100, 118, 129, 136, 150; of
    the keys, 133n31
Mirković, Mijo, 1, 17
Missa Illyrica, 6
Modrzewski, Andrew Frycz, 158, 168–69; *De
    Republica emendanda*, 160–61
Moibanus, Ambrosius, 122
Monarchy, 187, 191
Monasteries, 141, 144, 152
Moral conduct, 117, 147
Moral discipline, 127
Morality Ordinance of 1531, 72
Morely, Jean, 118
Moritz, elector, of Saxony, 6, 7, 17, 25
Mörlin, Joachim, 41, 42
Mortalism, Christian, 194
Moses, 77
Moslems, 166, 175, 197
Musaeus, Simon, 23n7, 24
Musculus, Andreas, 31, 66
Mystical body, 76

Necessity (doctrine), 27
Netherlands, the, 159, 162
Nicholas of Lyra, 115

Obedience (to God), 202, 204–05
Oblationists, 171
Ochino, Bernardino, 150
Oecumenius: *Ennarationes in Psalmum 109*, 167
Ogonowski, Zbigniew, 195–209
Olevianus, Caspar, 126, 127n22
Olson, Oliver K., 1–17
Oporinus, Johann, 22, 23n7, 32
Orange, churches of, 93
Ordination, 70, 78, 100, 166
Orthodox, the, 164, 169, 177, 194
Orthodox church. *See* Polish-Lithuanian Royal
    Commonwealth, Orthodox practice in
Orthodoxy, 35, 57, 62, 68, 73, 76, 111, 208–
    09; doctrine, 77
Osiander, Andreas; Osiandrism, 12, 23, 41, 42,
    55, 59
Osiander, Lucas, 53, 108
Ostrozhskyi, Basil Constantine, 184, 187, 188,
    192
Ottheinrich, elector Palatine, 56

Pacta conventa of *1587*, 193
Palatinate, the, 58, 63, 86, 136, 163
Palatinate-Neuburg, 55
Palatinate Reformed Church, 132, 133
Pallavicino, Peter Sforza, 173
Pappus, Johann, 58
Pareus, David, 129, 134
Paris, 56, 89
Passover, 80
Pastors, 100, 102, 118
Paul, St., 4, 32, 59, 76, 77, 112, 132, 185
Pauli, Simon, 24, 31
Pax dissidentium de religione, 165, 170, 180, 193,
    194
Peace of Amboise, 92
Peasants, 175, 176, 179, 191, 194
Permission (doctrine), 128
Peter, St., 149, 150, 185
Peucer, Caspar, 66, 68, 125n16
Philip II (Spain), 162, 172
Philippism, Philippists, 7, 9, 12, 22n4, 56, 65,
    123; Andreae's alienation from, 57, 61, 63,
    67; Crypto-Calvinism, 22n4; Crypto-Calvinist
    party, 68, 111, 123n9; and church-state re-
    lations, 68; and Gnesio-Lutheranism, 25, 64,

65; and real presence doctrine, 66; Ursinus and, 123, 124–25

Philosophy, 11–12, 32

Piety (concept), 74

Pighius, Albert, 169

Poland, 196; Catholicism in, 142–43, 197; civil war in, 191; nationalism in, 191, 193; prohibited Antitrinitarianism, 207–08; Protestantism in, 143; Reformed Church of, 86; religious tolerance in, 197

Pole, Reginald, 158; *De concilio*, 169

Polish Brethren, 170, 179, 182, 190–91, 196, 198; expelled from Poland, 207–08; Socinus leader of, 197

Polish-Lithuanian Royal Commonwealth, 175, 180, 191–93; Catholicism in, 157, 158n3, 164, 170; dangers to, 188–90; Orthodox practice in, 160–61, 164, 165, 166, 169, 170, 184–86, 187, 191–92, 193; Protestantism in, 159, 160, 164, 165, 170, 172, 173, 176, 180, 193; social inequities in, 176

Pomeranus, Dr. (John Bugenhagen), 2

Pope (office), 82, 165, 166, 168, 171, 187; authority of, 148, 172, 185; and Ecumenical Councils, 169; primacy of, 168, 173; sovereignty of, 185, 186

Popes: Clement VIII, 178; Gregory (the Great), 73, 147, 169; Julius III, 172; Paul III, 169; Paul IV, 161; Paul V, 195; Pius II, 195; Pius III, 195; Pius IV, 164; Pius V, 149, 164; Pius IX, 155n25; Pius XI, 155n25

Power: absolute and ministerial, 82; of the keys, 78

Praetorius, Gottschalk, 34

Prague, 63, 159

Prayer, 75, 148

Preaching, 76, 77, 78, 97, 118; failure of Catholic clergy in, 153

Predestination, 58, 74, 82, 91, 137; in Beza, 91, 99, 104; as doctrine of comfort, 48–49, 99, 133; double, 72–73, 75, 84, 128, 133, 136; in Lutheranism, 48–49, 58, 60; in Socinus, 201, 203; supralapsarian, 99; in Ursinus, 128, 129, 132, 133, 136, 137. *See also* Elect, the; Election

Presbyterianism, Presbyterians, 87, 93

Priesthood, 167–68. *See also* Clergy; Ministry

Professio Fidei Tridentinae, 155

"Prophesying, the," 71, 86

Prophets, prophecy, 72, 77; false, 194; Skarga as, 175, 187–88

Protestant academies, 144

Protestantism, 87, 194; and authenticity of Scripture, 206; crisis of authority in, 16; diversity in, 150, 185; divisions in, 8–9, 46–47, 155; in Germany, 7, 36, 142–43, 151, 153–54, 155; Hosius's threat to, 157; legal existence within Holy Roman Empire, 17; in Poland, 197; in Polish-Lithuanian Commonwealth, 159, 160, 164, 165, 170, 172, 173, 175, 180, 193; refuted by Canisius, 147–48; relation with Rome, 8, 92, 124, 136, 155; in Swiss Confederacy, 86; Zwinglian, 72. *See also* Lutheranism

Prussia, Ducal, 159, 160, 164, 170, 172, 175

Puritanism, 113, 194

Radziwiłł (Radvila) family, 177, 183

Raitt, Jill, 89–104, 105–19

Raków, 197. *See also* Synods

Rationalism, 205–07

Real Presence (doctrine), 22n4, 44, 46–47, 48, 60–61, 70, 186; in Andreae, 61, 62; in Beza, 97; controversy re, 63, 66, 95; in Skarga, 183–84; in Ursinus, 128, 129, 130–32, 136, 137. *See also* Eucharist; Lord's Supper

Reason, 198, 208; in Socinus, 199, 202, 205

Redemption, 96; universal 49. *See also* Justification; Salvation

Reformation, 3, 7, 8, 12, 13–15, 85; Catholic, 151; episcopal duties in, 37n17; Flacius's role in saving, 16–17; French, 90

Reformed academies, 111, 115

Reformed Church, German, 128–29, 136

Reformed Church of the Rhineland Palatinate, 73

Reformed Protestantism, 44, 58, 75, 86, 163–64, 170, 172, 173; differed from Lutheran teaching, 46–47, 91; eucharist in, 22n4; as evangelical, 129; in Germany, 103–04, 128–29, 136; in Low Countries, 110; catholicity of, 73–74

Regeneration, 12. *See also* Justification; Sanctification

Reissing, Franciscus Leopoldus de, 50

Religion, 79; coercion in, 94–95, 170, 177–78, 194; and free will, 201; freedom of, 178, 180, 201; heterodoxy in, 195; natural, 206, 207

Religious unity, 3, 164, 165–66, 193

Religious warfare, 175, 181–82. *See also* Resistance, right of

Remonstrants, 208

Reprobation, 116, 131, 133–34

Resistance, right of, 5, 17, 101
Resurrection, 199
Revelation, 76, 112, 205–06. *See also* Scripture
Roman Catholic Church, 56, 57, 78, 84, 85, 93, 148; attacks on Lutheranism, 44; and authenticity of Scripture, 206; catechisms, 145–46; in Europe, 173; German, 54, 55, 149, 151–56; impact of Chemnitz's *Examen* on, 46, 50; monarchial, 191; in Poland, 142–43, 197; in Polish-Lithuanian Commonwealth, 157, 158n3, 164, 170, 175, 180, 191–93; reconciliation of Protestants with, 8, 92, 124, 136, 155; refutations of *Magdeburg Centuries* by, 35; Skarga shaper of traditions in, 191; Ukrainian Greek Catholics and, 192; unity of, 150, 185; wars with Huguenots, 172
Rostock, 37, 38; university of, 24, 31, 35
Rulers, Christian. *See* Magistracy; Kings
Ruthenians, 186

Sacramentarians, 22, 23, 24, 28, 129, 186
Sacraments, 45–46, 75, 78–81, 83, 97, 128, 129, 148; composite definition of, 130; and faith, 132; and letter and spirit of law, 77; Reformed doctrine of, 98–100
St. Bartholomew's Day Massacre, 101, 105, 107
Saint-Pourçain, Durand de, 115
Salmeron, Alfonso, 143, 151, 163
Salvard, Jean François, 104, 107
Salvation, 70, 74, 75, 133, 169, 200, 201–02, 208; by faith, 79; good works and, 28; human will in, 7, 59; man's role in, 137, 198, 203
Samland, 30, 32, 37
Sanctification, 95, 98–99, 116
Sarmartianism, 176
Satan (Devil), 82, 84
Satisfaction (dogma), 199
Saxony, 8, 20, 25, 63, 67–68
Schism, 169, 185–86
Schisma Prutencia, 31
Schlüsselburg, Conrad, 26, 29, 31
Schmalkald Articles, 42
Schmalkald League, 4, 5n18, 20
Schmalkald War, 4, 40, 54, 55; term, 20n2
Schnepf, Erhardt, 54, 155
Scholasticism, Scholastics, 35, 74, 111, 115, 142, 146
Schwenckfeld, Kaspar; Schwenckfelders, 12, 23, 56, 65, 136
Scripture, 75, 77, 113, 168; authenticity of, 206–07; Daneau's plan to base all knowledge on, 111, 117; interpretation of, 100, 148;

and religious unity, 155; self-authenticating, 76
Selnecker, Nikolaus, 31, 57, 63, 66–67, 108
Seripando, Jerome, cardinal, 161, 162, 169
Servetus, Michael; Servetians, 28, 72, 150
Siebenburgen, 86
Sigismund I (The Old), king, 159, 169
Sigismund II Augustus, king, 159, 162, 164, 177, 179, 193
Sigismund III Vasa, king, 179, 180, 181, 187, 191
Simonetta, Louis, 162
Sin, Sinners, 72, 83, 94–95, 118, 147; defined, 148; effect of, 9; forgiveness of, 61; God as cause of, 204; as man's substance, 9, 13, 24, 28, 29–30n11; original, 13n48, 65, 67, 117, 200, 201
Skarga, Peter, 163, 175–94; *Artes duodecim Sacramentariorum seu Zwinglio-calvinistarum*, 186; *Areopagus*, 182; biographies of, 175n1; *Concerning the Government and the Unity of the Church of God*, 187; *Discourse Concerning the Confederation*, 182; *The Humiliation of the Arians . . .*, 182; *Invitations: To Penitence; To the Saving Faith*, 183; *The Legal Prosecution of the Confederation*, 193; *Legal Prosecution with Respect to the Confederation . . .*, 193–94; *Lives of the Saints . . .*, 178; *Occasional Sermons*, 182–83; *On the Threnodies and Lamentations of Theophilus Orthologus*, 183; *On the Unity of the Church of God under One Pastor*, 179, 184–86, 192; *Pro sacratissima Eucharistica contra haeresim Zuinglianam*, 183–84; *The Readings of the Brotherhood of Mercy . . .*, 178; *A Renewed Humiliation*, 182; *Sermon on Setting Out for War*, 182; *Sermon on the Victory over the Muscovites*, 183; *Sermons for Special Occasions*, 181; *Sermons for Sundays and Feast Days*, 181, 182–83; *Sermons to the Diet*, 187–91; *The Seven Pillars on Which the Catholic Doctrine of the Most Holy Sacrament . . .*, 186; *Thanks to the Lord God*, 183; *The{Uniate}Synod of Brześć*, 187; *Warning to the Evangelicals and Jointly to All Non-Catholics*, 179–80, 188; works, 178, 181–83
Slavic Uniates, 191–93
Socianism, 206n19, 207–09
Society of Jesus. *See* Jesuits
Socinus, Faustus (Fausto Sozzini), 195–209; *De Jesu Christo Servatore*, 195; *De Sacrae Scripturae Auctoritate*, 196, 206; *De Statu primi hominis ante lapsum . . .*, 196; *Explicatio primae partis primi capitis Evangelli Joannis*, 195, 198;

Praelectiones theologicae, 196, 203
Socinus, Laelius, 150, 195
Sola gratia, (doctrine), 49, 51, 96
Soto, Peter (Pedro), 146, 160, 163
Sovereignty, 101
Spain, 162
Spangenberg, Cyriacus, 30n*11*, 67
Spangenberg, Johann, 20–21
Spiritual Exercises, 142, 143, 148
Staphylus, Friedrich, 56
Stapulensis, Faber. *See* Lefèvre d'Etaples
State, the, 175, 194. *See also* Church-state
    relations
Strassburg, 58, 62
Strassburg, Concord, 60
Strigel, Viktorin, 9, 13, 23–24, 62–63
Sturm, Erdmann K., 123, 139
Sturm, Johann, 58, 112, 124
Sudhoff, Karl, 121, 127n*22*, 134, 139
Superintendents, 36n*17*, 37, 42n6
"Swabian Concord," "Swabian-Saxon Concord,"
    65, 66
Swiss Confederacy, 71, 72, 75, 80, 86
Swiss-Palatine Confession. *See* Confessions
Swiss Reformed churches, 73
Switzerland, 72, 163
Synergism, 137
Synods: of Brześć-Litewski, 192; of Drodrecht,
    119; of Dort, 87; of La Rochelle, 107; of Mid-
    delburg, 109, 119; of Piotrków, 164; of
    Raków, 182; of Zerbst, 68

Taborite party, 8
Tarnoswki, John Christopher, 177, 184
Tauler, Johannes, 142
Tertullian, 73, 74, 82, 106
Theological method, 31–33, 34, 35
Theology: of Andreae, 58–62; of Beza, 94–100;
    of Bullinger, 73–84; of Canisius, 145–50; of
    Chemnitz, 40–41, 43–49; of Daneau, 110–17;
    dialectic and, 113; differs from philosophy,
    11–12, 32; education in, 70–71, 115; of
    Flacius; 11–16; of Hosius, 165–69; Lutheran,
    32; Reformed, 63, 73–74, 75, 129, 136; of
    Skarga, 183–91; of Socinus, 195–96, 197–
    207; of Ursinus, 126–35, 139; of Wigand,
    26–36, 37
Thorn, Edward, 153
Thuringia, 23n6, 24, 25, 32, 36–37
Tolerance, 194, 197, 207–08
Tomicki, Peter, 158, 159
"Torgau Book," 66–67

Tradition, 168; oral, 77
Transubstantiation (doctrine), 70, 126n*20*, 136,
    148, 183–84
Transylvania, 197, 208
Treaty of Jam Zapolski, 181
Trinity (doctrine), 74, 75–76, 94, 198–200
Truce of Passau, 54
Truchsess, Otto, cardinal (bishop of Augsburg),
    143, 158, 161
Truths, essential, 204–05, 208
Tübingen, 56, 123, 124; university of, 54, 57
Twesten, August, 2

Ubiquity (doctrine), Ubiquitarians, 5, 61, 72,
    79, 87, 93, 95, 108, 115, 121, 126n*20*, 128,
    129, 136, 138, 150
Uchański, Jacob (Primate), 161, 162, 163, 164;
    patron of Skarga, 177
Ukraine, 191
Ukrainian Greek Catholics in Union with Rome,
    192
Ulrich, duke of Mecklenburg, 24
Ulrich, duke of Württemberg, 53–54
Union of Brześć-Litewski, 191, 192–93
Union of Florence, 192
Union of Lublin, 164, 170, 191
Union of the Council of Florence, 184
Unitarians, 93, 163, 164, 165, 170, 175, 186,
    198; Rationalist, 197
Unites States: Lutheran Church in, 51
Unity. *See* Religious unity
Ursinus, Zacharius, 121–39; *Admonition, Anto-
    pokrisis*, 126n*20*; biographies, 121, 124–25,
    127n*22*, 137, 138; catechisms, 127–28;
    Commentary on the Heidelberg Catechism, 124,
    125n*15*, 129, 134–35; correspondence, 121,
    122, 123n9, 126n*20*, 134, 136, 138; *Defense*
    of the Heidelberg Catechism, 128; *Inaugural
    Oration*, 124; *Theses*, 124–25; works, 126,
    128–29, 137–38
Utility (argument of), 27
Utraquists, 160, 167

Valentia, Gregory de, 58
Valla, Lorenzo, 39, 73
Venice, 1–2
Vergerio, Peter Paul, 1, 160, 165
Vermigli, Peter Martyr, 86, 111
Vienna, 159
Vilna, 157, 177, 179, 183
Viret, Pierre, 91, 92, 111
Visser, Derk, 121–39

Vitoria, Juan, 153
Vlačić (or Francovic), Matija. *See* Flacius Illyricus, Matthias

Waldburg, Otto Truchsess von. *See* Truchsess, Otto
Walton, Robert C., 69–87
Waremund, Johannes (pseud.). *See* Flacius Illyricus, Matthias
Warmin, 165, 170, 177
Wars of Religion, 92, 101, 106, 172, 174
Weber, Hans Emil: *Reformation, Orthodoxie und Rationalismus*, 36
Weimar Disputation, 23
Wied, Hermann von, archbishop, 142–43
Wigand, Johann, 10, 19–38, 65; autobiography, 27–28; *Christliche Erinnerung von der Theologen in Meissen von Abendmal . . .* , 22n4; in conflict with Flacius, 29–30; *De Anabaptismo*, 29; *De Adiaphorismo*, 29; *De Maiorismo*, 29; *De Manichaeismo*, 29; *De Manichaeismo renovato*, 30n11; *De Osiandrismo*, 29; *De Sacramentarismo*, 29; *De Schwenckfeldianismo*, 29; *De Seruetianismo seu de Antitrinitarijs*, 29; *De Stancarismo*, 29; *De Synergismo*, 29; *Liber de Antinomia*, 28; *Refutatio*, 21; *Syntagma*, 27, 32–33; works, 27, 28, 29; works on natural history, 26, 35
Wilhelm, landgrave of Hesse, 63, 64

Will, 7, 8, 62–63, 96, 128, 137; freedom of, 9, 63, 65, 94–95, 200, 201, 202, 203–04
William of Orange, 109, 117
Williams, George H., 157–74, 175–94
Wismar, 32, 37, 38
Wittenberg, 39, 40; university of, 2, 3, 7, 20, 25, 33, 40, 41, 42, 54
Wittenberg Concord, 72
Wittenbergers, 56, 63, 64, 65
Witzel, Georg, 145, 148
Wolan, Andrew, 183, 186
Wolmar, Melchior, 89–90
Word, the, 12, 76, 117; Jesus Christ as, 198–99; letter and Spirit of, 76–77; written record of, 77. *See also* Scripture
Worms, 56. *See also* Colloquies
Württemberg, 54, 63; Confession of, 160; duke of, 7; prince of, 65–66

Zanchi, Jerome, 59, 60, 108, 111, 116
Zastrizill, Count de, 93
Zebrzydowski, Nicholas, 191
Zerbst. *See* Synods
Zürich, 71, 72, 81, 138–39; center for theological education, 86; economic changes in, 69–70; freedom to preach in, 72
Zwingli, Huldreich; Zwinglianism, 60, 65, 70, 83, 86, 139, 149–50, 155; and Bullinger, 71, 72, 73, 74–75, 76, 77, 79, 81, 85; eucharistic theology of, 186; *Ratio Fidei*, 80